Children of Laughter and the Re-Creation of Humanity

Children of Laughter and the Re-Creation of Humanity

The Theological Vision and Logic of
Paul's Letter to the Galatians

Samuel J. Tedder

FOREWORD BY
John M. G. Barclay

CASCADE *Books* · Eugene, Oregon

CHILDREN OF LAUGHTER AND THE RE-CREATION OF HUMANITY
The Theological Vision and Logic of Paul's Letter to the Galatians

Copyright © 2020 Samuel J. Tedder. All rights reserved. Except for brief quotations in critical publications or reviews, no part of this book may be reproduced in any manner without prior written permission from the publisher. Write: Permissions, Wipf and Stock Publishers, 199 W. 8th Ave., Suite 3, Eugene, OR 97401.

Cascade Books
An Imprint of Wipf and Stock Publishers
199 W. 8th Ave., Suite 3
Eugene, OR 97401

www.wipfandstock.com

PAPERBACK ISBN: 978-1-7252-5263-9
HARDCOVER ISBN: 978-1-7252-5264-6
EBOOK ISBN: 978-1-7252-5265-3

Cataloguing-in-Publication data:

Names: Tedder, Samuel J., author. | Barclay, John M. G., foreword.

Title: Children of laughter and the re-creation of humanity : the theological vision and logic of Paul's letter to the Galatians / by Samuel J. Tedder ; foreword by John M. G. Barclay.

Description: Eugene, OR: Cascade Books, 2020 | Includes bibliographical references.

Identifiers: ISBN 978-1-7252-5263-9 (paperback) | ISBN 978-1-7252-5264-6 (hardcover) | ISBN 978-1-7252-5265-3 (ebook)

Subjects: LCSH: Paul, the Apostle, Saint. | Bible. Galatians—Criticism, interpretation, etc.

Classification: BS2685.52 T43 2020 (print) | BS2685.52 (ebook)

Manufactured in the U.S.A.   07/01/20

I dedicate this book to my family. My beautiful wife Helena and our four precious children Evita, Jonathan, Amanda, and Linda have all lived through the birth pains and joys involved in researching and writing this book. Together we share the passion to serve God's new creation purposes in this world.

"For through the law I died to the law, so that I might live to God. I have been crucified with Christ; and it is no longer I who live, but Christ lives in me. The life I now live in the body, I live depending on the Son of God who loved me and gave himself for me. I do not set aside God's grace, for if right-relatedness comes by the law, Christ died in vain."

(Apostle Paul, Galatians 2:19–21. All Scripture translations are the author's own.)

Contents

Tables and Figures | x
Foreword by John M. G. Barclay | xi
Preface | xiii
Acknowledgments | xv
Abbreviations | xvii

Chapter 1: Introduction | 1
   Review of Six Perspectives on the Theological Vision
      and Logic of Galatians   2
      Martin Luther   2
      The New Perspective on Paul   5
      The Radical New Perspective on Paul   12
      J. Louis Martyn and the Apocalyptic Perspective   16
      Daniel Boyarin and Paul's Allegorical Mode   19
      John M. G. Barclay and the Incongruity of Grace   20
   Key Questions for This Book   26
   The Argument and Approach of This Book   29
   Construction of the Book: a Guide for the Reader   33

Chapter 2: Galatians 4:21—5:1 as the Vantage Point | 35
   The Function of Galatians 4:21—5:1 in the Letter   35
      Galatians 4:21—5:1 as a Culmination Point   36
      Galatians 4:21—5:1 as a Pivotal Passage   44
   Structural Analysis of Galatians 4:21—5:1   47

Chapter 3: The Theological Potential in the Abraham Narrative | 55

The Method 55
The Big Picture 59
The Births of Ishmael and Isaac 61
    The Birth of Ishmael 62
    The Birth of Isaac 64
    Ishmael Is Excluded 68
    The Climax: Abraham's Faith and the Near Sacrifice of Isaac 69
Abraham and the Promise of Blessing that Extends to All the Nations 72
Circumcision and the Identity of the People of God 81
Conclusions 86

Chapter 4: The Theological Potential in Isaiah's Vision of Restoration | 89

The Method 89
The Vision of Restoration in the Immediate Context of Isaiah 54:1 95
Intratextual Thematic Analysis of the Vision of Restoration in Isaiah 101
    The Structure of the Book of Isaiah 102
    Barren Woman Giving Birth 103
    A Tale of Two Cities 108
    The Spirit and Fruitfulness 113
    The Servant and Generating the Community of Servants 116
    The Identity of the Many Children and the Nations' Inclusion 123
Conclusions 132

Chapter 5: Paul's Allegorical Practice in Galatians 4:21—5:1 | 134

Context for Paul's Allegorical Practice 134
    The Relationship between Text and Allegorical Interpretation 135
    The Sociocultural Function of Allegory 138
Philo's Allegorical Practice 140
Paul's Allegorical Practice and Intertextuality 148
The Broader Horizon of Meaning in the Abraham Narrative 154
The Broader Horizon of Meaning in the Exile-Restoration Paradigm in Isaiah 159

Chapter 6: Configuring The Theological Vision and Logic of Galatians from the Vantage Point of 4:21—5:1 | 165

Method for an Intertextual Reading of Galatians 4:21—5:1   165
Vision of Restoration and the Alienation-Restoration Paradigm   168
    The Jerusalem above   168
    The New Creation   169
    The Kingdom of God   171
    Inheritance and Inaugurated Restoration   172
    Present Jerusalem, Jerusalem Above, and the Alienation-Restoration Paradigm   177
Children of Promise according to the Pattern of Isaac   179
    The Pattern of Isaac's Birth and the Abrahamic-Isaianic Promise   179
    Promise of Restoration and Generation by the Spirit   185
    Integrating the Gentiles into the Recalibrated Story of Israel   189
Hagar and the Covenant from Sinai that Leads to Slavery   195
The Role of Christ as the Isaianic Servant in the Covenant of Promise   200
Paul's Labor Pains and the Formation of New Creation Communities   207
Synthesis   215
    Sequential Reading of Galatians 4:21—5:1   215
    Configuration of the Theological Vision and Logic of Galatians   218

Chapter 7: Conclusions | 222

Appendix | 233
Bibliography | 235

Tables and Figures

Table 1. Development of Themes in Galatians 2:16—4:7 | 40

Figure 1. The "Intertextual Fields" in Rabbinic Midrash and in Paul's Allegoresis | 153

Figure 2. Schematic Presentation of the Generation of the "Children of Promise" | 184

Foreword

PAUL'S LETTER TO THE Galatians is, and always has been, central to the understanding of Paul's theology, precisely because it is so heated: when the temperature (and the stakes) are this high, the essential features of the good news rise to the surface. Samuel Tedder's fresh analysis of the vision and logic of Paul's gospel in Galatians is thus extremely welcome, and he makes a unique contribution to its interpretation in at least three respects:

First, Tedder takes the allegory about Abraham's two sons (Galatians 4:21—5:1) as his vantage point for viewing the whole letter. This is a part of the letter that exegetes regularly shy away from, or pass over with embarrassment: what is Paul doing using "allegory," and why does he go over the Abraham story once again? Is this passage merely "playful," or a decorative addition to an argument already made? Far from it, shows Tedder. With a fine analysis of what Paul means by "allegory," and by careful examination of the way Paul handles the scriptural texts and extends their interpretative field, he shows that this passage is not just structurally pivotal in the letter to the Galatians, but the point where the central themes of the letter come together in a uniquely revealing way. In other words, he succeeds brilliantly in putting this passage back on the map, and directing attention to it as *central* to the interpretation of the whole letter.

Secondly, following the clues evident in this allegory, Tedder demonstrates the significance for Paul of *both* the Abraham narrative *and* the Isaianic prophecies, as the *combined* scriptural matrix of Paul's theology. It is as if Paul's discourse throughout the letter sits on top of these two scriptural tectonic plates, but the allegory-passage is where these plates most directly meet, pushing that remarkable paragraph (Gal 4:21—5:1) up above the surface of the text. Tedder rightly emphasizes that Paul's theology is always *hermeneutical*, reflecting and recalibrating his scriptural heritage. In two notable chapters in this book, he explores the theological potential in these two bodies of Scripture, using literary tools to explore their dynamics. As he rightly emphasizes, Genesis and Isaiah could be read in a variety of ways, but he here offers a sophisticated reading of their "meaning potential" when viewed with Pauline interests. This is an unusual but very fertile way of treating the relationship between Paul and his scriptural resources, and could provide a template for others to imitate. It differs from a "narrative" reading of Paul's relationship to the scriptural story (illustrated by theses of a "continuing exile"), but it is equally serious about the ways Paul's thought is shaped by the patterns, themes, and dynamics of his scriptural base.

Thirdly, by examining the theology of the "present Jerusalem" and the "Jerusalem above" (Paul's "tale of two cities"), Tedder expertly highlights Paul's emphasis on the divine generative agency that brings Isaac to birth, gives fertility to the barren Jerusalem, and establishes the "new creation." Tedder's title brings out well the sheer impossibility of God's action from a human perspective (hence the laughter), and Paul's amazement at the powerful innovations created by the Christ-event and the gift of the Spirit. Much as we find this difficult to handle within the intellectual limits of the post-Enlightenment West, Paul's whole theology is predicated on making God the subject of action-verbs—God as the powerful, re-creative agent who changes human reality. Tedder rightly brings us face-to-face with that central facet of Paul's thought, and thereby renders Galatians a rich resource for those many millions, throughout the world, who find this understanding of God to resonate with their experience.

These three interwoven elements establish this book as a major contribution to our understanding of Galatians. Tedder's treatment of Galatians displays all the virtues of scholarship: he gives the closest attention to the details of the text, expertly weaves his way through the thickets of scholarly disagreement, and forges his own distinctive path. The result is a fine, cutting-edge contribution to scholarship on Paul—but also more than that, a rich resource for the contemporary reading of a letter that continues to provoke and inspire its readers to a unique degree.

John M. G. Barclay

Lightfoot Professor of Divinity
Durham University, England

Preface

THIS BOOK IS A revised version of my PhD thesis that I wrote to Durham University during 2013–2017. I set my work to a scholarly context in the introduction; here I want to offer a more personal note on the motivations and questions that have driven this project.

A passion for the subject matter and an inquisitive disposition have been the wellspring for researching and writing this book. I became passionate about the Bible in my teen years, and have ever since been drawn especially to reading Paul's letters. In reading Paul, I have wanted to capture deeper and clearer his conception of the gospel. Justification by faith has been the dominant mode to articulate the gospel in the Finnish Pentecostal movement to which I belong, and which has been shaped by the context of the Lutheran state church in Finland. I was not quite satisfied with the forensic/judicial emphasis that it brought to the gospel (I now know that Luther has more dimensions). There was something more dynamic and life changing in the presentation and experience of the gospel that I sensed with Paul. This initial sense has been expanded and refined with my research, and this book expresses it with the deep-rooted theme of new creation that I now believe best captures Paul's conception of the gospel.

Questions about Paul's hermeneutic have also been the driving force to research Paul. These questions rose initially from the disorienting realization that the way I understood Paul reading his Scriptures did not quite follow the hermeneutical rules that were commonly taught (the text can only mean what it meant in its initial context). I found a fruitful way to engage my questions in Richard Hays's *Echoes of Scripture in the Letters of Paul* as well as with Rikk Watts in a class on the New Testament use of the Old at Regent College. There I did my first analysis of Paul's hermeneutic in Gal 4:21—5:1. I focused then only on the role of the Abraham narrative in it, and did not arrive at a fully satisfactory grasp of Paul's allegorical interpretation. This left a spark for further investigation that took me to

Durham to do PhD research on Paul's hermeneutic. I am forever grateful to my supervisor John Barclay for encouraging me to take my research further, and use my analysis of Paul's hermeneutic to get to his theology. This direction led to an ambitious project to configure Paul's theological vision and logic in his letter to the Galatians from the vantage point of an intertextual reading of Gal 4:21—5:1.

I feel privileged to have been able to dedicate so much time to follow my passion in pursuit of a better grasp of Paul's hermeneutic and his conception of the gospel. My hope is that this book will enrich others as they dig deeper into Paul's thought, and in doing so, learn more about what changed his world and continues to bring about new creation in ours.

Acknowledgments

I WOULD LIKE TO thank my PhD supervisor and friend Professor John Barclay for believing in me and my project from its inception to its publication as a book, and for honoring it by writing a foreword. His constant encouragement, incisive guidance, and mature wisdom gave me a perfect space to grow as a scholar and have passion in my research. I am also grateful for the stimulating discussions, and the critical yet always constructive eye of my secondary supervisor Jan Dochhorn. The evaluations and recommendations of my examiners N. T. Wright and Dorothea Bertschmann also helped to strengthen my work, for which I am grateful. I thank the Northern Bridge Doctoral Training Partnership (AHRC) for the generous financial support and professional training that I received during my PhD work in Durham.

The wider academic community in Durham and my fellows at 50 North Bailey Post Graduate Study Center (Tavis Bohlinger, Robert Haynes, Jerry Lofquist, David Merrill, Hallur Mortensen, and Ruth Perrin) contributed to a rich and stimulating research experience. Thank you for your friendship. I am grateful for King's Church Durham, and for Dr. Mark Bonnington for showing that scholarship and vibrant spirituality can be combined.

I have had several opportunities at Nordic New Testament Conferences in Aarhus (2015) and Reykjavik (2018) to share my work and interact with my Nordic, and other, colleagues (especially René Falkenberg, Paula Fredriksen, Marianne Bjelland Kartzow, Katja Kujanpää, Jacob Mortensen, Mark Nanos, Lauri Thurén, and Magnus Zetterholm), which has also helped to refine my thoughts on Paul and deepen my understanding of other perspectives. I am grateful to Sami Yli-Karjanmaa who gave expert instruction in my revision phase that sharpened my analysis of Philo's allegorical method. I wish to thank also my colleagues and students at The Theological School of Finland (Suomen Teologinen Opisto) for a wonderful environment to grow together with questions and passion for God, his Word, and his work in this world.

The foundations for my journey of learning were laid at home. I am grateful to my father Chris who modeled and taught me the love of truth—to inquire with an open mind, and to have humility to search together for better understanding. I thank my mother Lea for instilling in me a warm love for humanity. Thank you mom and dad for your support and love.

It has been a great joy to work on publishing my book with the wonderful people at Cascade Books. Thank you Calvin, Chris, Savanah, Stephanie, and Zechariah! I regard everything that made the writing of this book possible as a gift from God. To him I owe my deepest gratitude.

Abbreviations

Bibliographic and General:

AB	Anchor Bible
BBR	*Bulletin for Biblical Research*
BCE	Before common era
BDF	Blass, Friedrich, and Albert Debrunner. *A Greek Grammar of the New Testament and Other Early Christian Literature*. Translated and revised by Robert W. Funk. Chicago: University of Chicago Press, 1961.
BHT	Beiträge zur historischen Theologie
BTB	*Biblical Theology Bulletin*
BThSt	Biblisch-Theologische Studien
BZAW	Beihefte zur Zeitschrift für die alttestamentliche Wissenschaft
BZNW	Beihefte zur Zeitschrift für die neutestamentliche Wissenschaft
CE	Common era
EvT	*Evangelische Theologie*
FRLANT	Forschungen zur Religion und Literatur des Alten und Neuen Testaments
HNT	Handbuch zum Neuen Testament
HTKNT	Herders Theologischer Kommentar zum Neuen Testament
ICC	International Critical Commentary
JBL	*Journal of Biblical Literature*
JETS	*Journal of the Evangelical Theological Society*
JSNT	*Journal for the Study of the New Testament*
JSNTSup	Journal for the Study of the New Testament: Supplement Series
JSOT	*Journal for the Study of the Old Testament*

JSOTSup	Journal for the Study of the Old Testament: Supplement Series
JTI	*Journal of Theological Interpretation*
JTS	*Journal of Theological Studies*
LNTS	Library of New Testament Studies
LXX	Septuagint, Greek Old Testament
MT	Masoretic text
NIGTC	New International Greek Testament Commentary
NovTSup	Supplements to Novum Testamentum
NT	New Testament
NTOA	Novum Testamentum et Orbis Antiquus
NTS	*New Testament Studies*
OT	Old Testament
PACS	Philo of Alexandria Commentary Series
SBL	Society of Biblical Literature
SBLDS	Society of Biblical Literature Dissertation Series
SBLSymS	Society of Biblical Literature Symposium Series
SNTS	Society for New Testament Studies
SNTSMS	Society for New Testament Studies Monograph Series
SPhilo	*Studia Philonica*
THKNT	Theologischer Handkommentar zum Neuen Testament
VT	*Vetus Testamentum*
VTSup	Supplements to Vetus Testamentum
WBC	Word Biblical Commentary
WTJ	*Westminster Theological Journal*
WUNT	Wissenschaftliche Untersuchungen zum Neuen Testament
ZNW	*Zeitschrift für die neutestamentliche Wissenschaft*

Ancient sources

Abr.	Philo, *De Abrahamo* (*On the Life of Abraham*)
Cher.	Philo, *De cherubim* (*On the Cherubim*)
Det.	Philo, *Quod deterius potiori insidari soleat* (*That the Worse Attacks the Better*)
Her.	Philo, *Quis rerum divinarum eres sit* (*Who Is the Heir of Divine Things?*)

Leg.	Philo, *Legum allegoriae* (*Allegorical Interpretation*)
Migr.	Philo, *De migratione Abrahami* (*On the Migration of Abraham*)
Mos.	Philo, *De vita Mosis* (*On the Life of Moses*)
Opif.	Philo, *De opificio mundi* (*On the Creation of the World*)
Praem.	Philo, *De praemiis et poenis* (*On Rewards and Punishments*)
Prob.	Philo, *Quod omnis probus liber sit* (*That Every Good Person Is Free*)
Somn.	Philo, *De somniis* (*On Dreams*)
Spec.	Philo, *De specialibus legibus* (*On the Special Laws*)
CD	Qumran, Cairo Geniza copy of the Damascus Document
1QH	Qumran, Hodayot (Thanksgiving Hymns)
1QS	Qumran, Rule of the Community
1QSb	Qumran, Rule of the Blessings
4Q285	Qumran, Sefer Hamilhamah
4QpIsa[a]	Qumran, Commentary on Isaiah
Jub.	Jubilees
Sib. Or.	Sibylline Oracles

Old Testament

Gen	Genesis
Exod	Exodus
Lev	Leviticus
Deut	Deuteronomy
Josh	Joshua
Judg	Judges
1 Sam	1 Samuel
2 Kgs	2 Kings
1 Chr	1 Chronicles
Job	Job
Ps	Psalm
Isa	Isaiah
Jer	Jeremiah
Dan	Daniel
Mic	Micah
Mal	Malachi

New Testament

Matt	Matthew
Acts	Acts
Rom	Romans
1–2 Cor	1–2 Corinthians
Gal	Galatians
Phil	Philippians
Eph	Ephesians
1 Thess	1 Thessalonians

1

Introduction

"No one will ever say the last word on this Epistle."[1]

PAUL'S LETTERS ARE THE first documents that link us with the first-century Jesus movement, and his letter to the Galatians is one of the earliest writings that deal with the impact of the message about Jesus—the gospel—reaching beyond the Jewish world.[2] Galatians is therefore a foundational document for the movement that became known as Christianity. It was written in the mid first century CE—only about 20 years after the events of the crucifixion and resurrection of Jesus (the Christ-event) that, together with the subsequent experience of the Spirit, form the core of Paul's gospel message—to the groups of believers Paul had earlier established in the Roman province of Galatia.[3] In the letter, we are presented with Paul's passionate re-proclamation of the "truth of the gospel" and its implications for all humanity in the context of a challenge by a "distorted gospel" that compels non-Jewish/Gentile believers to be circumcised (males) and adopt the observance of the Mosaic Law (Gal 1:1–9; 3:1–5; 5:2–12; 6:11–18).

The letter's passionate personal tone, condensed argumentation, and creative use of Israel's Scriptures continue to generate various configurations of its message. Since the Reformation, a traditional Lutheran reading has dominated the scholarly scene until the emergence of the *New Perspective*

---

1. Bligh, *Galatians*, i.

2. For a general chronological account of Paul's life and letter writing, see Riesner, "Pauline Chronology," 9–29; and his larger work, *Die Frühzeit des Apostels Paulus*.

3. Riesner argues for the South Galatia (Roman province) position, interestingly finding correspondence between the geographical direction in Paul's mission and Isa 66:18–21, and claims that Galatians was written before the apostolic council in Jerusalem ("Pauline Chronology," 20–23). For a traditional argument for the South Galatia hypothesis, see Longenecker, *Galatians*, lxi–lxxii. For a new angle in support of the South Galatia view that looks at the role the table of nations in Gen 11 plays in Paul's mission, see Scott, *Paul and the Nations*.

on Paul in the 1970s and 1980s. Yet neither has the new completely eclipsed the traditional reading, nor has the development of more new perspectives ceased. This book joins in the ongoing discussion about the configuration of Paul's theological vision and logic in Galatians by claiming that an unparalleled vantage point for the task is found in Gal 4:21—5:1 where key aspects of Paul's hermeneutic are made visible, the development of important themes is brought together, and the move is prepared towards the final section of the letter that exhorts the Galatians to live in accordance with the "truth of the gospel." I use the terms vision and logic to focus my inquiry on Paul's understanding of what the gospel is set to perform (vision), and how it is configured in relation to Scripture, the Jew-Gentile divide, and the Mosaic Law in the new situation brought about by the Christ-event (logic).

In this introductory chapter, I first review six configurations of Paul's theological vision and logic that have been chosen because they offer perspectives that shape my approach and raise important questions with which I interact in this book. After the review, I articulate the key questions this book addresses, and chart my approach and argument, both of which will be developed fully with each step of the book.

Review of Six Perspectives on the Theological Vision and Logic of Galatians

To focus my review, I tease out an answer from each of the following six perspectives to the core question of the letter: Why does Paul resist the requirement for Gentile circumcision? In anticipation of my own approach, I also note what role Gal 4:21—5:1 has in the different configurations.[4]

Martin Luther

The letter's antithetical presentation of the law and gospel, and its passionate tone provided Luther with a focal point to express his central Reformation teaching. My review is based on Luther's 1535 commentary that represents his fully developed Reformation perspective.[5]

---

4. I recognize that not all commentators include 5:1 in the passage, and hence I use throughout this book with each scholar that I discuss the delineation that they have made. I discuss my reasons for including 5:1 later in my structural analysis of the passage.

5. The 1535 commentary is based on a series of lectures on the letter in Wittenberg in 1531 that were recorded and compiled into a commentary in 1535, which Luther authorized (editor's preface in Luther, *Galatians*, 1–2).

Luther helpfully outlines his understanding of the argument of Galatians in the *Introduction* that he himself wrote to the commentary: "St. Paul goeth about to establish the doctrine of faith, grace, forgiveness of sins, or Christian righteousness, to the end that we may have a perfect knowledge and difference between Christian righteousness and all other righteousness."[6] The key for Luther is to distinguish Christian righteousness as *passive* righteousness, in which the human receives the benefits of Christ by faith in contrast to all other forms of righteousness that are *active,* i.e., have to do with works.[7] Thus, Luther configures the theology of Galatians around the theme of righteousness by faith in opposition to the "works of the law."[8] Luther was aware of the option of taking the "works of the law" as referring only to certain aspects of the Jewish Law (the ceremonial Law), and yet he rejected that view (represented by Jerome and Erasmus),[9] insisting the question is about the whole Law, including the Ten Commandments, as well as any set of laws/traditions that were taken as necessary for righteousness before God: "[t]ake thou the work of the law therefore generally for that which is contrary to grace. Whatsoever is not of grace, is the law, whether it be judicial, ceremonial, or the Ten Commandments."[10] For Luther, the central concern is that no works are brought by any means into the mechanism of justification, which is solely by the grace of God.

Luther reads Galatians with generalizations (any law and any works) that have a focus on applying the text to his Reformation context. But underlying this is Luther's construction of the specific occasion of the letter. Paul's original battle was against "the other gospel" that held that it is not enough to believe in Christ or to be baptized, but that one must also be circumcised "after the manner of Moses" to be saved—"Christ began the building, Moses must finish it."[11] Furthermore, Luther recognizes that the specific focus of the letter is on opposing the requirement of circumcision of male Gentile believers, and yet having the implication that circumcision should not be regarded as necessary for righteousness even for the Jews: "Paul then did not reject circumcision as a damnable thing, neither did he

---

6. Luther, *Galatians*, 21.
7. Luther, *Galatians*, 22.
8. I spell *law* with the uppercase when it is a reference to the Mosaic *Law*, and otherwise with the lowercase.
9. Wengert, "Martin Luther on Gal 3:6–14," 92–96.
10. Luther, *Galatians*, 128; commenting on Gal 2:16.
11. Luther, *Galatians*, 63.

by word or deed enforce the Jews to forsake it.... But he rejected circumcision as a thing not necessary to righteousness...."[12]

Luther's understanding of Paul's logic in resisting the requirement of circumcision becomes clear with his comments on Gal 5:2 (if you let yourselves be circumcised, Christ will be of no benefit to you), where he highlights that the problem is adding something to *faith in Christ* to be saved.[13] By faith, Luther means trust placed in Christ in contrast to confidence in works to bring righteousness.[14] Thus, the problem with circumcision arises when it is the object of trust to gain merit with God (whether by the Gentile or by the Jew). This is contrary to the gospel, because it makes the work of Christ of no value—living as if Christ had not come.[15]

Despite the strong antithesis between Christ and law, or faith and works, Luther is able to retain a place for the law in Paul's gospel. For Luther, there is a wrong and a right way to do the law. The wrong way is to do the law to be justified by it.[16] The right way is first to believe, and then by faith perform the law.[17] In Luther's illustration about the right place for works, we get an example of his view on justification that is also about participation, or union with Christ,[18] that enables the right doing of the law:

> *In him we are by faith, and he in us.* This bridegroom must be alone with the bride in his secret chamber, all the servants and family being put apart. But *afterwards*, when he openeth the door and cometh forth, then let the servants and handmaids return, to fulfil their ministry. There let charity do her office, and let good works be done.[19]

When Luther comes to Gal 4:21–31, he takes it as an illustration of the argument Paul has already made in the letter.[20] Luther is attracted by Paul's antithetical construction of the passage to once again "set forth plainly the

---

12. Luther, *Galatians*, 94–95.
13. Luther, *Galatians*, 447.
14. Luther, *Galatians*, 448, also 22, 24.
15. Luther, *Galatians*, 448, 454. Luther clarifies this point in his comment on Gal 2:21 claiming that, if the law is needed for salvation, then Christ loses his role as the savior (146–47). Luther directed stronger criticism on the church's practices for gaining merit than on his perception of the self-righteousness of the Jews, because the church is guilty of it even when knowing the Messiah (17).
16. Luther, *Galatians*, 249.
17. Luther, *Galatians*, 247.
18. This aspect in Luther's theology has been highlighted in Mannermaa and Stjerna, *Christ Present in Faith*.
19. Luther, *Galatians*, 142; emphasis added.
20. Luther, *Galatians*, 417.

difference between the law and the Gospel."[21] Thus, the two women and the two covenants (4:23–25) become an expression of the antithesis between the law and the gospel, and between the Old and the New Testaments/ covenants.[22] Also, the two Jerusalems (4:25–26; the present and the above) come to represent the people of the law and the people of the gospel—the church.[23] Although Luther applies the legalistic character of the present Jerusalem to any group that relies on the law for righteousness, and most pointedly to the "papists," it is Luther's antithetical construction between the synagogue and the church[24]—between Judaism and Christianity as representatives of legalism and grace—that created a legacy, which later scholarship has sought to modify or distance itself from.[25]

The New Perspective on Paul

The Lutheran bishop and biblical scholar Krister Stendahl began to chart in the 1960s and 1970s the shift in the reading of Paul's letters that would later become known as the *New Perspective on Paul* (NPP). Stendahl argued that Paul's formulation of "justification by faith" must be understood firmly in the context of his Gentile mission, and that it has to do specifically with the Jew-Gentile relationship:

> a doctrine of justification was hammered out by Paul for the very specific and limited purpose of defending the rights of Gentile converts to be full and genuine heirs to the promises of God to Israel.... We think that Paul spoke about justification by faith, using the Jewish-Gentile situation as an instance, as an example. But Paul was chiefly concerned about the relation between Jews and Gentiles—and in the development of *this* concern he used as one of his arguments the idea of justification by faith.[26]

---

21. Luther, *Galatians*, 425.
22. Luther, *Galatians*, 425.
23. Luther, *Galatians*, 420.
24. Luther, *Galatians*, 423.
25. This legacy is reflected, e.g., in Betz's commentary on Galatians: "[on 4:30] ... if God has given the inheritance to the Gentile Christians ..., the Jews are excluded from it, and the Christians constitute the 'Israel of God' (6:16).... According to Galatians, Judaism is excluded from salvation altogether, so that the Galatians have to choose between Paul and Judaism" (*Galatians*, 250–51).
26. Stendahl, "Paul Among Jews and Gentiles," 2–3; emphasis original.

Stendahl also challenged Luther's focus on the conscience. He claimed that Paul did not share Luther's struggle with his own conscience (Paul had a "robust conscience"),[27] nor did Paul preach justification by faith to consciences plagued by guilt: "Paul's thoughts about justification were triggered by the issues of divisions and identities in a pluralistic and torn world, not primarily by the inner tensions of individual souls and consciences. His searching eyes focused on the unity and the God-willed diversity of humankind, yes, of the whole creation."[28] Thus, rather than focusing Paul's gospel on the individual's relationship with God, Stendahl perceived a more horizontal (social) dimension in it—the gospel is about the unity of humanity, and especially the bridging of the Jew-Gentile divide.

The moves charted by Stendahl were elevated to a new pitch after the work of E. P. Sanders that undercut the construal of Judaism as a religion of works-righteousness, which was the foil for Luther's reading of Galatians. Sanders argues in his *Paul and Palestinian Judaism* that, rather than being legalistic, the pattern of religion in Judaism is best described by *covenantal nomism* that emphasizes the priority of grace as the basis for obedience to the Law.[29]

Coming to Paul, Sanders perceives that Paul agrees generally with Judaism on grace and works: "in Paul, as in Jewish literature, good deeds are the *condition* of remaining 'in', but they do not *earn* salvation."[30] However, Sanders maintains that in other ways Paul's pattern of religion is essentially different from that of Palestinian Judaism: Paul uses righteousness as a transfer term, whereas in Judaism it is about maintenance of status among the elect;[31] repentance, which is essential to the pattern of *covenantal nomism*, is not part of Paul's scheme;[32] sin is primarily a power to be freed from rather than transgression;[33] and being among the saved is about participating *in Christ* for Paul, rather than being a member *in Israel*.[34] Consequently, Sanders finds it striking that, for Paul, "everyone—whether Jew or Gentile—must *transfer* from the group of those who are perishing to the group of those

---

27. See Stendahl's famous essay: "The Apostle Paul and the Introspective Conscience of the West."
28. Stendahl, "Paul Among Jews and Gentiles," 40.
29. Sanders, *Paul and Palestinian Judaism*, 421–22.
30. Sanders, *Paul and Palestinian Judaism*, 517; emphasis original.
31. Sanders, *Paul and Palestinian Judaism*, 544.
32. Sanders, *Paul and Palestinian Judaism*, 546.
33. Sanders, *Paul and Palestinian Judaism*, 546–47.
34. Sanders, *Paul and Palestinian Judaism*, 547.

who are being saved."[35] The logic in this runs from solution to plight: "for Paul, the conviction of a universal solution preceded the conviction of a universal plight."[36] Sanders's insistence on the solution—Christ—determining the shape of Paul's view about the plight is reflected also in his overall emphasis on the Christ-event as generating the shape of Paul's theology: "Paul appears as one who bases the explanation of his gospel, his theology, on the meaning of the death and resurrection of Jesus, not as one who fitted the death and resurrection into a pre-existing scheme, where they take the place of other motifs with similar functions."[37]

Where Sanders highlights the discontinuity between Paul's conception of the gospel and the matrix of Palestinian Judaism, the further development of the NPP has emphasized continuity between Paul and his Jewish matrix, especially the Scriptures of Israel. This is most characteristic in the work of N. T. Wright, but before I review his configuration of Galatians, I present the key moves that James Dunn has made that also underlie Wright's reading.

Dunn is commonly attributed with coining the actual phrase *The New Perspective on Paul* that was the title of his Manson Memorial Lecture in 1982, and the subsequent reprint in 1983.[38] Appreciating the work of Sanders in undercutting the construal of Judaism as a religion of works-righteousness, Dunn, however, develops the NPP differently from Sanders.[39] In his 1983 paper, Dunn focuses the NPP on Gal 2:16 with a new definition for the "works of the Law." He notes that the statement on justification in Gal 2:16 follows immediately the debates at Jerusalem and Antioch that focused on two issues: circumcision (Jerusalem) and food laws / ritual purity (Antioch).[40] Thus, Paul's denial of justification by "works of the Law" is to be understood in relation to these specific issues.[41] The works of the Law in Galatians are then, according to Dunn, about particular observances: circumcision, food/purity laws, and observance of special days (4:10).[42] The Jews themselves, and the Greco-Roman observers, regarded these as characteristic and distinct Jewish practices that separated the Jews from other

---

35. Sanders, *Paul and Palestinian Judaism*, 547–48; emphasis original.
36. Sanders, *Paul and Palestinian Judaism*, 474.
37. Sanders, *Paul and Palestinian Judaism*, 555–56.
38. Dunn, "New Perspective," 95–122. However, see Wright (*Paul and His Recent Interpreters*, 64–87) and Zetterholm (*Approaches to Paul*, 118) for discussion on the genesis of the NPP, and how the same expression and similar views were used earlier by Wright.
39. Dunn, "New Perspective," 102, 109. Also Dunn, *Theology*, 143.
40. Dunn, "New Perspective," 107.
41. Dunn, "New Perspective," 107.
42. Dunn, "New Perspective," 107, 115.

peoples.⁴³ Thus, Dunn identifies circumcision as the prime *identity marker* of membership in the covenant people, and the food laws and observance of special days (Sabbath) as expressions of covenant loyalty.⁴⁴ Dunn also defines the "works of the Law" as *badges*—observances that covenant people do to distinguish themselves as such.⁴⁵ Consequently, Dunn argues that Paul's resistance to Gentile circumcision is not about opposing works-righteousness with justification by faith in relation to gaining merit with God, but about circumcision—"works of the Law"—and faith in Christ being two mutually exclusive alternatives for *defining the people of God*.⁴⁶ Dunn understands that Paul constructs faith in Jesus Christ as the new identity marker of the people of God that renders the previous markers—circumcision included—superfluous, in contrast to Peter and the Jewish believers at Antioch who regarded them as complementary.⁴⁷

Dunn's reading of Gal 5:1–6 in his later commentary deepens the explanation. He identifies freedom as the *leitmotif* of the letter, which means freedom for the Gentiles from having to submit to distinctly Jewish practices.⁴⁸ Since circumcision had become the mark of the Jew as distinct from the Gentile, it had become a means of ideological and national imperialism.⁴⁹ Thus, the problem with circumcision—"coming under the Law"—is that it means adopting the total Jewish way of life, that is, complete assimilation and absorption of any distinct Gentile identity.⁵⁰ This is contrary to Paul's gospel, in which identity is rooted in Christ independent of circumcision.⁵¹

Wright agrees with Dunn that Paul's opposition to the imposition of the "works of the Law" on the Gentiles is about a false conception of what should define the new people of God. However, Wright's emphasis is more

43. Dunn, "New Perspective," 107–8.
44. Dunn, "New Perspective," 108–9; also Dunn, *Commentary*, 136–37.
45. Dunn, "New Perspective," 110.
46. Dunn, "New Perspective," 112–13. At this point Dunn perceives that Paul breaks from the other Jewish Christian understanding, which held that faith in Jesus as Messiah was just a narrower definition of covenantal nomism.
47. Dunn, "New Perspective," 112–13; also Dunn, *Commentary*, 138. In Dunn's later work, circumcision is not categorized as superfluous, but only as relativized by the cross; it is totally proper in the Jewish mission, but not in the mission to the Gentiles (*Theology*, 31–32).
48. Dunn, *Commentary*, 260–63. The "yoke of slavery" denotes for Dunn the obligations and privileges of the Jew, but even more a metaphor of the defeated people in war being brought under subjection to the other. This confirms for Dunn that Paul is taking issue with the nationalistic overtones of Jewish insistence on the law (262–63).
49. Dunn, *Commentary*, 265.
50. Dunn, *Commentary*, 266–67.
51. Dunn, *Commentary*, 265.

on the role of the positive vision for the unity of the reconstituted people of God (worldwide family of Abraham) rather than the negative aspect of the Torah creating a "trap of nationalism":

> The thought which drives Paul into this paragraph [Gal 3:10–14], then, has to do with the question of what happens to the promises to Abraham, granted the plight of the Jews which is brought about by the Torah. This is more than simply the plight of the sinner convicted by a holy law; more, too, than the plight of Israel caught in the trap of nationalism. The thought is as follows: God promised Abraham a worldwide family, characterized by faith. The promises were entrusted to Israel, the people whose life was lived ὑπὸ νόμον [under Law]. The Torah, however, held out over this people, the agents of promise, the curse which in fact had come true, and was still being proved true, in the events of the exile and its strange continuance right up to Paul's day and beyond. How could the promises, the blessings promised to Abraham, now reach their intended destination?[52]

The above quotation exemplifies also the most distinctive feature in Wright's reading of Galatians: his emphasis on narrative.[53] Paul inhabited a shared Jewish narrative world, and, Wright argues, Paul's particular retelling of Israel's story that has come to its climax in Jesus underlies his theological vision and logic in Galatians.[54] Wright's understanding of the shape of Paul's retelling of Israel's story can be summarized in the following manner:

a. It has a *covenantal frame* that is shaped by the primacy of the Abrahamic promise of a single worldwide family of God and by the giving of the Torah, which is at the same time "blocking" the promise, but also creating the conditions for the promise to be fulfilled, as it focuses the sin of the world on Israel where it can be dealt with.

b. The plight of Israel is the curse of the Law in her *ongoing exile*, and the solution is the covenant renewal/restoration, in which the Gentiles have a share.

---

52. Wright, *The Climax of the Covenant*, 142.
53. Wright acknowledges the importance of the work of Hays (*Faith of Jesus Christ*) in the new appreciation of narrative in Paul. For a discussion on the role of narrative in Wright's overall construction of Paul's theology, see White, "N. T. Wright's Narrative Approach," 181–204; see also Wright's response to White in the Epilogue to the same volume, 731–35.
54. Wright, "Gospel and Theology," 89.

c. The climax of the story is in the solution that is brought about by Jesus as Israel's representative—*the Messiah*—who deals with the curse of the Law in his death, and inaugurates the restoration in his resurrection.[55]

In Wright's more recent work, he develops further the exile-restoration scheme that stands at the center of his construction of Paul's retelling of Israel's story, especially in terms of how the "strange continuance" of the exile was conceived in Paul's Jewish world. First, Wright argues that there are two central biblical texts (Deut 27–30 and Dan 9) that stand out in Jewish reflections on the exile-restoration scheme. The text from Deuteronomy charts "a *single historical sequence*,"[56] and "functioned in the second-Temple period as a prophecy about the bad times to come (specifically, the extended exile) and of the covenant renewal that would ultimately come about."[57] The idea of an *extended exile* is derived from the book of Daniel that extends Jeremiah's prediction of seventy years of exile to seventy times seven years (Dan 9:2, 24–27).[58] By doing this, Wright perceives that Daniel is "positioning himself and his people within the continuous narrative promised by Moses . . . ."[59] But this positioning did not end with Daniel, Wright argues, as many different Jewish groups "were anxiously trying to work out when Daniel's 'seventy weeks' would be over," and "they were reading their own situation, again and again, within the single flow of national narrative which they found in Deuteronomy 27–30."[60] Although Wright recognizes that there were different ways in which many Jews, Paul included, located themselves in the narrative as being in a state of an extended exile, e.g., as a "geographical reality" (some diaspora Jews), or being the "advance guard of the 'real return from exile'" (the Qumran community), the common denominator is that there was a "*theological* awareness of being at a particular stage within the overall continuing narrative."[61] Thus, the key aspect in Wright's construction of the exile-restoration scheme in Paul's retelling of Israel story is the state of an *ongoing/extended* exile within a *continuous* narrative.[62]

---

55. Wright, *The Climax of the Covenant*, 137–56.

56. Wright, *Christian Origins and the Question of God. [Vol. 4]: Paul and the Faithfulness of God*, 143; later abbreviated as *PFG*.

57. Wright, *PFG*, 118.

58. Wright, *PFG*, 142.

59. Wright, *PFG*, 143.

60. Wright, *PFG*, 145–46; see also 162.

61. Wright, *PFG*, 140; emphasis original.

62. Wright, *PFG*, 140; emphasis original.

Wright's focus on reading Galatians with a mind tuned to Paul's retelling of the story of Israel is concomitant with his understanding that Paul's primary theological matrix is Israel's Scriptures:[63]

> But at the heart of it all—not as an occasional added extra, but as the living force within the whole thing—there lies Paul's fresh reading of Israel's scriptures as the unfinished narrative of creation and covenant which, attaining its *telos* in the Messiah, now reaches out, still as Israel's story, to embrace the whole world, as Israel's story always aimed to do. The types and patterns fit within this larger framework. The playful allegories and poetic reworkings give it further, sometimes paradoxical, embodiment. But the story remains the story.[64]

For Wright, Paul's "playful allegory" in Gal 4:21—5:1 does not determine the shape of Paul's retelling of Israel's story in Galatians, but rather continues to express what has already been established in the main argument of the letter.[65] Accordingly, Wright perceives that the allegorical retelling of the story of Abraham's two sons continues to address the issue of "the actual 'inheritance' of Abraham's family" or "the public demarcation of Abraham's family."[66] To be clear, Wright insists that Gal 4:21—5:1 is not about disinheriting Judaism—setting up the opposition between Judaism and Christianity—as it is rather about "two very different visions of the essentially Jewish belief that the Messiah has come and that what matters is the formation of Messiah-communities."[67]

The central aspect in Paul's vision and logic in Galatians is, for Wright, Israel's story that climaxes in the Messiah as a fulfillment of Jewish eschatological hopes. He perceives that this eschatological aspect is present in Paul's quotation of Isa 54:1 in Gal 4:27, which is connected to the notion of restoration after exile.[68] With this, Wright spells out the centrality of eschatology in his configuration: "[a]nd the point of locating all this [the ecclesiology of the single community] within 'eschatology' should now be clear. *This is not a debate about 'types of religion.' It is a matter of eschatology.*"[69] The radical implications that Paul draws from his eschatological convictions are

---

63. Here, Wright acknowledges the impact of the ground-breaking work of Hays, *Echoes of Scripture*.

64. Wright, "Israel's Scriptures," 552.

65. Wright, *PFG*, 1133.

66. Wright, *PFG*, 1134.

67. Wright, *PFG*, 1135.

68. Wright, *PFG*, 1137–38.

69. Wright, *PFG*, 1138; emphasis original.

reflected in the contrasts he sets between the "two covenants" (Abrahamic vs. Mosaic) and the two Jerusalems (4:22–26) that reiterate the point that Paul has been making about the invalidity of applying the Law of Moses in the new era of the Messiah.[70]

Wright's emphasis on configuring Paul's message by his Jewish matrix and Israel's Scriptures underscores Paul as a Jew who is engaged in an intra-Jewish debate about the implications, when Israel's story is reconfigured by its fulfillment in Jesus the Messiah: "he [Paul] claimed to be speaking as a true Jew, criticizing—as did many who made similar claims—those who embraced other construals of Judaism, on the basis that Israel's God had now acted climactically and decisively in Jesus, the Messiah."[71] Thus, Wright locates Paul firmly *within* the context of first-century Judaism. Ironically, the proponents of the *Radical New Perspective on Paul* have adopted *Paul within Judaism* as a title to highlight their distinction from both Luther and the NPP.

The Radical New Perspective on Paul

The Radical New Perspective on Paul (RNPP) is a title that has been used to describe a reading that radicalizes aspects of the NPP.[72] Some proponents of the RNPP, however, would rather use the title *Paul within Judaism* to emphasize their insistence on locating Paul *within* Judaism as opposed to readings that place Paul in opposition to Judaism (Luther: grace vs. law; faith vs. works), or infer that Paul thought that something was wrong with Judaism (NPP: ethnocentricity).[73] I find it problematic that the options for understanding Paul *within* Judaism would be restricted only to how the RNPP proponents envision it. Hence, I use the more apt title *Radical New Perspective on Paul*.

The RNPP portrays Paul as a Torah observant Jew, a Pharisee—before and after his encounter with the risen Jesus[74]—whose only issue with the Law is its wrong application to the Gentiles, and not with the Law in relation to the Jews.[75] The RNPP radicalization of the Jew-Gentile distinction is also re-

---

70. Wright, *PFG*, 1139–40.

71. Wright, "Letter to the Galatians," 196–97.

72. Zetterholm, *Approaches to Paul*, 127–63. Also Eisenbaum, *Paul Was Not a Christian*, 65–66.

73. Nanos and Zetterholm, *Paul Within Judaism*, 1–11. Also Thiessen, *Paul and the Gentile Problem*, 11.

74. Eisenbaum, *Paul Was Not a Christian*, 132–49.

75. Eisenbaum, *Paul Was Not a Christian*, 62.

flected in the claim that Paul's vision is driven by a view of an eschatological restoration, in which the nations come to join Israel's monotheistic worship while remaining distinct from Israel and the Jews.[76] Eisenbaum expresses the eschatological logic in Paul's resistance to Gentile circumcision thus: "it is necessary that Gentiles remain Gentiles on the Day of the Lord, when the God of Israel is shown to be the one God of the world."[77]

The starting point in the RNPP reading of Paul's letters is to take to one extreme Stendahl's move to locate the context of Paul's theology squarely in his Gentile mission by insisting that Paul must be read as *addressing* (practically) *exclusively* the non-Jews, and that the *content* is also about the Gentiles and does not concern the Jews.[78] Matthew Thiessen's *Paul and the Gentile Problem* is an example of a reading of Galatians that begins here:

> These claims [including Gal 2] to having divine authority to preach to gentiles suggest that he [Paul] wrote primarily, perhaps even exclusively, for gentiles-in-Christ. Therefore, when Paul quotes Jewish scriptures or comments on the Jewish law, he does so in relation to his mission to non-Jews. . . . at virtually every point modern readers need to interpret Paul's letters in light of this intended gentile audience.[79]

Thus, together with 1 Cor 7:19, Gal 5:6 and 6:15, the hermeneutical key in Thiessen's configuration is to separate the Law that has been given to the Jews from the commandments given to the Gentiles: "[Paul] argues that Jews should keep the laws that God has laid upon them, while gentiles should be satisfied with the laws that God has laid upon them, not coveting those laws that God has given to Jews alone."[80]

Thiessen develops the logic that underlies this distinction further. He argues that Paul underwent a change in his view on the solution to the Gentile problem. Paul was involved in his earlier life in Judaism (Gal 1:13–14) in a proselytizing Gentile "mission" that aimed to make Gentiles

---

76. Fredriksen, "Judaizing the Nations," 241–44; 249–50. Also Eisenbaum, *Paul Was Not a Christian*, 96–98. One area of variance within the RNPP appears in the identity of the Gentiles vis-à-vis Israel, e.g., Johnson Hodge: adopted into the Abrahamic family by baptism into Christ, the seed of Abraham (*If Sons, Then Heirs*, 4); Nanos: incorporated into a newly created people of God (*Irony of Galatians*, 99–100).

77. Eisenbaum, *Paul Was Not a Christian*, 171.

78. Johnson Hodge concedes that Paul can write about the Jews, but maintains that the real concern has to do with the Gentiles: "Paul is clear that he is the apostle to the gentiles (Rom 11:13) and that he is writing *to* gentiles, even if he writes *about* Jews at times" (*If Sons, Then Heirs*, 11; emphasis original).

79. Thiessen, *Paul and the Gentile Problem*, 11.

80. Thiessen, *Paul and the Gentile Problem*, 10.

into Jews by circumcision (Gal 5:11).[81] But after the revelation of Christ, Paul had come to realize that the Gentile problem was deeper still, and that circumcision could not provide the needed solution.[82] The deeper problem was the lack of genealogical connection with Abraham. Circumcision could not remedy this, because the only right fulfillment of the "whole law" of circumcision (Gal 5:3) is to perform it on the eighth day from birth,[83] which is predicated on being born to the right lineage: "[t]he descendants of Abraham through Isaac and Jacob practiced infant circumcision, demonstrating that they alone were and are the rightful heirs of God's promises to Abraham."[84] Thiessen's argument rests on the premise that Paul read Genesis 17 in line with the Jewish tradition (especially Jubilees) that emphasizes the eighth day requirement (Gen 17:14 LXX) as the *only* valid practice of circumcision.[85] Thus, to require circumcision from the Gentiles is, for Thiessen's Paul, trying to apply a remedy that could not solve the Gentile problem of not being born to the Abrahamic lineage.

In charting Paul's newfound solution to the Gentile problem, Thiessen focuses on Gal 4:21–31, which continues the emphasis on Abrahamic "sonship" in Paul's vision and logic in Galatians. Thiessen understands that Paul uses the figure of Ishmael "to call into question his opponents' claim that if the Galatians undergo circumcision they would become covenantal heirs."[86] Isaac, in contrast, is used to configure the manner in which Gentiles are made sons of Abraham: "[t]he birth of Isaac is, from first to last, the result of divine action and prerogative, or, as Paul would say, through divine promise (δι' ἐπαγγελίας, Gal 4:23) and according to the pneuma (κατὰ πνεῦμα, 4:29)."[87] Thus, Thiessen perceives that the contrast between Ishmael and Isaac focuses the logic in Paul's resistance to Gentile circumcision in the following manner: "[c]ircumcision and adoption of the Jewish law are a

---

81. This view depends partly on Thiessen's understanding of Paul's earlier life in *ioudaismos* to mean "his former inclination to promote judaizing behaviour" (*Paul and the Gentile Problem*, 40).

82. Thiessen, *Paul and the Gentile Problem*, 41.

83. For Thiessen's reading of keeping/not keeping the "whole Law" in Gal 5:3 and 6:13, see *Paul and the Gentile Problem*, 91–96.

84. Thiessen, *Paul and the Gentile Problem*, 80.

85. Thiessen, *Paul and the Gentile Problem*, 77–82. Thiessen's premise is a continuation of his earlier work *Contesting Conversion*. I engage his reading of Gen 17 in ch. 3 under the heading: Circumcision and the Identity of the People of God.

86. Thiessen, *Paul and the Gentile Problem*, 88.

87. Thiessen, *Paul and the Gentile Problem*, 89.

dead end for gentiles because God did not intend for the Jewish law to make gentiles into sons of Abraham."[88]

The emphasis on the *pneuma* as the means to connect the Gentiles to the Abrahamic lineage leads to Thiessen's novel argument about how "God would rewrite gentile genealogy in order to make them Abraham's sons and seed."[89] For Thiessen, Paul's gospel insists that "gentiles must somehow become genealogically descended from Abraham,"[90] because only in that way would they participate in the Abrahamic promises that deal with the problems of morality and mortality.[91] Hence, Thiessen builds an elaborate case for the centrality of Abrahamic sonship in the argument of Galatians.[92] As Thiessen probes after how Paul thought the gospel was pre-proclaimed to Abraham (Gal 3:8), he notes that Paul connects the Abrahamic promise of blessing to all the nations with the reception of the *pneuma* (3:1–5, 14), and argues that the *pneuma* must be found within the Abrahamic promise.[93] He locates it in Gen 15:5 in the promise that Abraham will have descendants like the stars.[94] Using a wide variety of Second Temple Jewish, early Christian, and rabbinic sources, Thiessen suggests that the promise of the stars does not refer only to the quantity, but also to the *quality* of the descendants.[95] According to Thiessen, stars were understood as angelic beings, and thus as pneumatic in many Jewish and Christian texts.[96] Hence, the pre-proclamation of the gospel to Abraham is in the promise of pneumatic descendants, and the promise comes true to the Gentiles by the singular Abrahamic seed Christ (Gal 3:16):[97] "by being pneumatically placed in Christ, who is Abraham's seed and who at one time existed in Abraham, gentiles become Abrahamic seed and find themselves to be in Abraham."[98] This is not merely a spiritual connection but a real genealogical one, since, according to Thiessen, *pneuma* is understood by Paul in some (Stoic) sense materially: "[i]n receiving the *pneuma*, then,

88. Thiessen, *Paul and the Gentile Problem*, 105.

89. Thiessen, *Paul and the Gentile Problem*, 100. I do not translate *pneuma* here simply as spirit, since Thiessen's use of the term *pneuma* is distinct.

90. Thiessen, *Paul and the Gentile Problem*, 105. Thiessen develops further the argument of Johnson Hodge, *If Sons, Then Heirs*.

91. Thiessen, *Paul and the Gentile Problem*, 148–54.

92. Thiessen, *Paul and the Gentile Problem*, 106–8.

93. Thiessen, *Paul and the Gentile Problem*, 129–32.

94. Thiessen, *Paul and the Gentile Problem*, 132–35.

95. Thiessen, *Paul and the Gentile Problem*, 135–40.

96. Thiessen, *Paul and the Gentile Problem*, 140–47.

97. Thiessen, *Paul and the Gentile Problem*, 111–28.

98. Thiessen, *Paul and the Gentile Problem*, 127.

the gentiles undergo a material transformation—again, to use a modern analogy, they undergo gene therapy—which addresses their genealogical deficiencies as gentiles."[99] Thus, Thiessen's configuration of Paul's theology in Galatians emphasizes the role of the Abraham narrative in it, although heavily mediated by other ancient sources.

In the above sections, I have presented the main contours of the NPP and the RNPP that have challenged the traditional Lutheran reading of Galatians and emphasized the necessity to locate Paul more firmly within his Jewish matrix, and thus to construct his theological vision and logic with reference to the potential that the Scriptures of Israel offered him. I now present briefly two other perspectives that raise important questions about the shape of Paul's gospel (Martyn: apocalyptic) and his hermeneutic (Boyarin: allegory) before I review the recent work of John Barclay that challenges some of the assumptions in the post-Sanders era, and provides a new paradigm for discussing Paul's theology.

J. Louis Martyn and the Apocalyptic Perspective

The perspective of J. Louis Martyn is a parallel development to the NPP that follows the impulses from the work of Karl Barth (emphasis on the vertical act of God from above) and Ernst Käsemann (apocalyptic; cosmic scope of salvation).[100] A guiding principle in Martyn's approach is that, rather than asking about the underlying matrix in Paul's thought, the means to probe Paul's intentions in the letter is to inquire *how the first recipients understood it*.[101] Hence, to capture the message of Galatians, Martyn sets up a reading scene, in which he takes "a seat in one of the Galatian congregations" with one ear tuned to Paul and the other to the opposing voice of the "Teachers."[102] Martyn defines the "Teachers" as Jewish Christian missionaries, and thus the debate is internal to the church, and the polemic in the letter is not about Christianity against Judaism, but about the tension between two different Christian understandings of the Gentile mission.[103] This construction is vital in Martyn's reading of Gal 4:21—5:1. He argues that Paul's use of the language of "begetting" and "giving birth," with the contrasting expressions: "by the power of the flesh" and "by the power of the

---

99. Thiessen, *Paul and the Gentile Problem*, 117.

100. See analysis by Barclay, *Paul and the Gift*, 130–50; and Wright, *Paul and His Recent Interpreters*, 135–86.

101. Martyn, *Galatians*, 42.

102. Martyn, *Galatians*, 42.

103. Martyn, *Theological Issues*, 77–84.

promise/the Spirit," refers to the way "Paul speaks of two different ways in which churches are being begotten among the Gentiles at the present time, and thus of two different Gentile missions."[104]

More importantly, Martyn defines the polemic of the letter in terms of God's apocalyptic act in Christ against religion.[105] By this move, he generalizes the issue away from the particularities of the Jewish Law to the general characteristics of religion, which he defines in terms of differentiation of sacred and profane, means for humans to seek blessedness, and the superstitious attempt to know "god" and influence him.[106] Hence, according to Martyn, Paul thinks that demanding circumcision—taking the Law to the Gentiles—is to engage in a mission that is marked at its center by the impotence of religion.[107] Martyn avoids casting Judaism as such in this pejorative light of religion, as he further defines the issue to be about the counterfeit gospel of the Teachers, in whose Gentile mission the covenant understanding of the faith of Israel is not valid, because it is now about getting Gentiles into the covenant from outside of it.[108] In this context, the teachers' message about coming under the Law via circumcision to secure forgiveness falls under religion, which is about a circular exchange that places God in debt.[109]

In contrast to the counterfeit gospel of the teachers, Paul understands the gospel as God's *apocalyptic* act in Christ. This is the heart of Martyn's interpretation of Paul's theological logic. By apocalyptic, Martyn does not mean either revelation or the imminent expectation of the *parousia*, but God's invasion of the cosmos in Christ.[110] The key passage for this is Gal 6:14–15 (Martyn's translation): "As for me, God forbid that I should boast in anything except the cross of our Lord Jesus Christ, by which the cosmos has been crucified to me and I to the cosmos. For neither is circumcision anything nor is uncircumcision anything. What is something is new creation."[111] Martyn recognizes the radical nature in Paul's words that deny any significance both to circumcision and to non-circumcision.[112] Since the old cosmos (construal of reality) consisted of pairs of opposites, denying

---

104. Martyn, *Theological Issues*, 199. Also, the "two women" and the "two covenants" refer to the two missions (203).
105. Martyn, *Theological Issues*, 78.
106. Martyn, *Theological Issues*, 79.
107. Martyn, *Theological Issues*, 82.
108. Martyn, "Apocalyptic Gospel," 248.
109. Martyn, "Apocalyptic Gospel," 247–48.
110. Martyn, "Apocalyptic Antinomies," 411–14.
111. Martyn, *Galatians*, 10.
112. Martyn, "Apocalyptic Antinomies," 412–14.

real existence to this central pair (Gal 3:28 describes other pairs) is in essence the declaration of the death of the old cosmos.[113] This text also directs Martyn to view Christ's crucifixion as a cosmic event that brought about the death of the old cosmos and the birth of the new creation.[114] Hence, Martyn perceives that the body of the letter to the Galatians is a "sermon" centered around answering two key questions: "What time is it?" and "In what cosmos do we actually live?"[115] From this apocalyptic perspective, circumcision and the Law belong to the old cosmos, and hence, to insist on them would be to live in the world before Christ, and not in the real world brought about by his cross and resurrection.[116]

The cosmic scope and the apocalyptic character of the Christ-event are also crucial in Martyn's interpretation of Gal 2:15–21. Martyn rephrases justification as *rectification*, because he understands it to be about God making right what has gone wrong, rather than about forgiveness for breaking moral/religious norms.[117] The human dilemma is not primarily guilt, but being enslaved to powers beyond human control.[118] Correspondingly, salvation is not about repentance and forgiveness, but about deliverance from enslaving powers (death, curse, Law, etc.).[119] Hence, the act of salvation is apocalyptic—God invades the cosmos to deal with the malignant enslaving powers.[120] Consequently, faith is not, for Martyn, firstly the human act of believing, but rather denotes Christ's act—his faithful death.[121] For Martyn, the fundamental antinomy is not between two human actions—faith and works of the Law—but between divine and human action.[122] In this apocalyptic gospel, God is not responding to human faith by justification, but acts first in Christ to right what has gone wrong, and then by the proclamation of the gospel elicits the human response of faith/trust, which is in fact the fruit of the Spirit.[123] To add circumcision with salvific potency to the redemptive, apocalyptic act of God is to violate the gospel and to be separated from that act.[124]

113. Martyn, "Apocalyptic Antinomies," 413–14.
114. Martyn, *Galatians*, 278.
115. Martyn, *Galatians*, 23.
116. Martyn, *Galatians*, 573.
117. Martyn, *Galatians*, 250.
118. Martyn, *Galatians*, 308.
119. Martyn, *Galatians*, 272.
120. Martyn, *Theological Issues*, 82.
121. Martyn, *Galatians*, 271.
122. Martyn, *Galatians*, 271.
123. Martyn, "Apocalyptic Gospel," 250–52.
124. Martyn, *Galatians*, 471, 477.

Daniel Boyarin and Paul's Allegorical Mode

Daniel Boyarin's *A Radical Jew: Paul and the Politics of Identity* is a reading of Paul that is in tune with the focus on the social dimension of the Jew-Gentile relationship, but with a radically different interpretation. His cultural reading of Paul from a Jewish perspective is openly informed by the culture of the reader, and understands Paul as a Jewish cultural critic.[125] The starting point in Boyarin's configuration of Paul's theological vision and logic of Galatians is the passage in 3:27–29: "for as many of you as were baptized into Christ, have put on Christ. There is neither Jew nor Greek, neither slave nor free, neither male nor female. For all of you are one in Christ Jesus. Now, if you belong to Christ, then you are also Abraham's seed, heirs according to the promise."[126] Boyarin claims that Paul was a Hellenistic Jew who was motivated by a Hellenistic desire for the One, which produced in him the vision for a universal human essence beyond difference and hierarchy.[127] He argues that the unification of humanity is the coherent core in Paul's theology,[128] and that the letter to the Galatians is entirely devoted to the theme of the new creation of God's one people.[129] Hence, Paul's opposition to Gentile circumcision is due to the fact that circumcision is the most complete sign of the connection of the Law to the concrete body of Israel, and that the insistence on the literal—the physical—is a stubborn clinging to difference and resistance to the universal.[130] Furthermore, Boyarin perceives that Paul's vision for a non-differentiated, non-hierarchical humanity means that cultural specificities must be eradicated, whether or not the people in question were willing.[131]

Boyarin also argues that the impulse toward universalism motivated and enabled Paul's move towards allegory.[132] According to Boyarin, Paul (with Philo) belongs to the tradition of a platonic mode of thinking with

---

125. Boyarin, *Radical Jew*, 1–3.

126. Boyarin, *Radical Jew*, 6.

127. Boyarin, *Radical Jew*, 7. Boyarin recognizes that Hellenism alone did not influence Paul, and further clarifies that Paul's universalism was born out of the union of Hebraic monotheism and Greek desire for unity and univocity (106). Nevertheless, Boyarin claims that the Hellenistic influence is the key that provided the means for Paul to reinterpret the universalistic tendencies within biblical Israelite religion (52).

128. Boyarin, *Radical Jew*, 36.

129. Boyarin, *Radical Jew*, 106–7.

130. Boyarin, *Radical Jew*, 36–37, 69.

131. Boyarin, *Radical Jew*, 8. This perceived non-toleration of difference is what Boyarin most stringently opposes in Paul's cultural vision (8–10; 220–68).

132. Boyarin, *Radical Jew*, 8.

external and internal realities, although Paul's dualism does not radically devalue the body, and yet presupposes a hierarchy of spirit and body.[133] Galatians 4:21–31 is the key text that convinces Boyarin of the centrality of allegory in Paul's theology. He perceives that this passage is "the climax of the entire argument and preaching of the letter, in which all of its themes are brought together and shown to cohere."[134] It is here that Paul's theological vision for the erasure of difference is demonstrated, and where the method by which that is accomplished is found, namely allegory.[135] But, in Boyarin's construal, allegory is not merely the interpretative method, as it is also a revelation of the structure of reality, and hence becomes Paul's whole mode of doing theology.[136] Allegory reveals, for Boyarin's Paul, that the particular signifies the universal.[137] In the case of circumcision, the true meaning of circumcision is the allegorical one: "inscription in the spirit," "writing on the heart," which enables universal applicability.[138] Hence, the problem with the requirement that Gentiles must be circumcised in order to join the people of God is about an inadequate realization that "the physical observances that constitute the physical Israel as the people of God have been transmuted and fulfilled in the allegorical signification in the spirit, thereby constituting the faithful Gentiles as Israel in the spirit."[139] Thus, the logic in Paul's resistance towards Gentile circumcision is, according to Boyarin, also hermeneutical: the danger is to resort "back into the fleshly hermeneutic of literal interpretation of circumcision."[140]

John M. G. Barclay and the Incongruity of Grace

With John Barclay's recent work, we come to reassess some of the central issues that Sanders raised that led to the development of the NPP/RNPP. In *Paul and the Gift*, Barclay develops a new approach for the discussion of Paul's conception of grace in relation to Judaism. Part of the foundation for Barclay's configuration of grace in Paul's theology is to connect it to the category of gift, understood in its first-century context.[141] Another integral

133. Boyarin, *Radical Jew*, 14–15.
134. Boyarin, *Radical Jew*, 32.
135. Boyarin, *Radical Jew*, 22, 32.
136. Boyarin, *Radical Jew*, 32–36.
137. Boyarin, *Radical Jew*, 35.
138. Boyarin, *Radical Jew*, 91.
139. Boyarin, *Radical Jew*, 112–13.
140. Boyarin, *Radical Jew*, 34.
141. Barclay, *Paul and the Gift*, 11–65, 183–85.

part of Barclay's foundation is his discussion of the history of reception, i.e., the different ways Paul's conception of grace has been configured that continue to shape the way grace is understood.[142] Yet the decisive feature in Barclay's approach is the development of the analytical tool of the "six perfections of grace" that aid in discerning the particular way Paul, or any author, discusses grace/gift. The idea of "perfecting" a concept is about the "tendency to draw out a concept to its endpoint or extreme,"[143] which is to be expected especially when it is discussed in relation to God: "[s]ince God is *ens perfectissimum* ('the most perfect entity'), concepts used with reference to God are likely to appear in their most complete, extreme, or absolute form."[144] Furthermore, Barclay argues that grace/gift should not be viewed as a monolithic concept, but rather as a "multifaceted phenomenon" that creates the possibility for it to be perfected in multiple ways, of which Barclay identifies six:

1. *Superabundance* is about the "size, significance, or permanence of the gift."
2. *Singularity* refers to the attitude/motivation of the giver that is regarded exclusively as benevolent.
3. *Priority* focuses on the "timing of the gift," which is taken to be always prior to any actions of the recipient.
4. *Incongruity* refers to a type of a gift that is given "without regard to the worth of the recipient."
5. *Efficacy* describes a gift that "fully achieves what it was designed to do."
6. *Non-circularity* defines a one-way gift that "escapes reciprocity."[145]

These distinctions in conceptions of grace provide Barclay with the analytical tool to redress Sanders's comparison between the patterns of religion in Judaism and Paul.

Barclay notes that Sanders's emphasis on sequence in the pattern of *covenantal nomism* in Palestinian Judaism (distinguishing "getting in" from "staying in") naturally led to his emphasis on the *priority* of grace.[146] Yet Sanders's discussion about grace mixes in other "perfections" of grace without duly distinguishing them (especially between priority and

---

142. Barclay, *Paul and the Gift*, 4–5, 79–182.
143. Barclay, *Paul and the Gift*, 67.
144. Barclay, *Paul and the Gift*, 68.
145. Barclay, *Paul and the Gift*, 70–75.
146. Barclay, *Paul and the Gift*, 152–54.

incongruity), and thus results in "homogenization" of Second Temple texts that operate with different perfections of grace.[147] Barclay's alternative approach modifies Sanders's claim that "grace is everywhere in Judaism" by arguing that *grace is not everywhere the same*.[148] Barclay's own analysis of five representative Second Temple Jewish writings (The Wisdom of Solomon, Philo, The Qumran Hodayot, Pseudo-Philo, and 4 Ezra) highlights the diversity of the material with regard to their conception of grace: "our texts are irreducibly diverse; to characterize them all as products of a 'religion of grace' would hardly be illuminating."[149] Furthermore, Barclay observes that the question about the congruity or incongruity of grace—are God's gifts given without regard to the recipients' worth or not?—was a matter of ongoing debate within Judaism.[150] Consequently, Barclay challenges Sanders's conclusion that Paul is in essential agreement with Judaism on grace (priority), and instead emphasizes that Paul is a participant within the "ongoing Jewish dialogue in which the motif of grace was perfected in various ways," and thus Paul is "neither against Judaism nor in undifferentiated agreement with all his fellow Jews."[151]

Barclay's perspective on Galatians is thus also a reading that places Paul within Judaism, and yet differently than the NPP/RNPP. The main distinction comes with Barclay's emphasis on the centrality of the logic of grace as an incongruous gift in Paul. Barclay's new way to discuss grace moves beyond the NPP without resorting to the Lutheran discourse of grace vs. works. Instead, Barclay discusses grace in relation to concepts of worth and value that are also intrinsically social:

> Paul's theology in Galatians is significantly shaped by his conviction, and experience, of the Christ-gift, as the definitive act of divine beneficence, given *without regard to worth*. By its misfit with human criteria of value, including the 'righteousness' defined by the Torah, the Christ-event has recalibrated all systems of worth, creating communities that operate in ways significantly at odds with both Jewish and non-Jewish traditions of value. This incongruous gift has subverted previous measurements of symbolic capital, establishing its own criteria of value and honor that are no longer beholden to the authority of the Torah. The Christ-event *as gift* is thus the foundation of Paul's Gentile mission, in which Paul resists attempts to

---

147. Barclay, *Paul and the Gift*, 158.
148. Barclay, *Paul and the Gift*, 158.
149. Barclay, *Paul and the Gift*, 313.
150. Barclay, *Paul and the Gift*, 315–18.
151. Barclay, *Paul and the Gift*, 320–21.

reinstitute preconstituted hierarchies of ethnic or social worth, and forms alternative communities that take their bearings from this singular event.[152]

Barclay further explains the logic of the *incongruous gift* in Paul's resistance to the requirement of Gentile circumcision in his comments on Gal 5:2–6 that highlight the power of the unconditioned gift to relativize any other source of value or worth:

> to require circumcision of Gentile believers is to place the Christ-event within the parameters of worth defined by the Jewish tradition, and that would make the Christ-gift conditioned by something outside and before itself, in this case the values of Jewish ethnicity and Torah. . . . 'in Christ Jesus', Paul insists, 'neither circumcision is worth anything (τὶ ἰσχύει) nor uncircumcision' (5:6). The Greek τὶ ἰσχύει is derived from the world of finance, and means, 'is worth something'. Both conditions are denied differential value (neither is worth more than the other) because the gift was given in Christ without regard to either.[153]

Thus, the incongruent character of the Christ-gift subverts the role of the Torah as an ultimate authority.[154] Rather than the Torah, or any other preexisting value system, defining the norms for the new communities, Barclay highlights that the experience of the unconditioned Christ-gift generates a new social dynamic. In fact, Barclay underscores that the theological vision driving Paul's gospel is the formation of innovative communities: "the theology of Galatians drives towards *the formation of innovative communities*, which not only span the boundary dividing Gentiles and Jews, but practice a communal ethos significantly at odds with the contest-culture of the Mediterranean world."[155] Furthermore, in development from his earlier work *Obeying the Truth*,[156] Barclay now argues that the community expression of the Christ-gift, as described chiefly in Gal 5—6, is an essential *embodiment* of the gospel without which it simply loses its meaning: "Paul's 'good news' is composed of the announcement of an event, the death and resurrection of Jesus as the gift of God. But the meaning of that event, and

---

152. Barclay, *Paul and the Gift*, 350; emphasis original.
153. Barclay, *Paul and the Gift*, 392–93.
154. Barclay, *Paul and the Gift*, 385.
155. Barclay, *Paul and the Gift*, 443.
156. Barclay concluded in his earlier work that Paul's purpose in the parenetic section was to convince the Galatians of the moral sufficiency of his strategy in the face of the attraction of the Law (*Obeying the Truth*, 216–20).

its quality as unconditioned gift, is discovered only in its social embodiment, in social experience and practice."[157]

Barclay identifies that the "radical rationale" for Paul's "norm-breaking" Gentile mission stems initially from Paul's experience of his own calling (Gal 1:15-16): "Paul's 'calling in grace', unconditioned by his worth, undermined his previous confidence in the defining values of his former 'Judaism'. There is now for him no stable Jewish tradition whose boundaries might be enlarged to embrace outsiders. On the contrary, he announces an event that reformulates the identity of both Jew and non-Jew."[158] Yet the full formation of Paul's view on the incongruous Christ-gift and its implications was, according to Barclay, a combination of "Paul's experience, scriptural re-reading, reflection on the story of Christ, and extended interaction with 'un-judaized' believers."[159] However, Barclay emphasizes the *hermeneutical priority* of the Christ-event in Paul's re-reading of Israel's Scriptures in a way that distinguishes his approach from Wright's.[160] Where Wright emphasizes Paul's retelling of Israel's story as a continuous narrative within a covenantal frame, to be sure, from the perspective of the Christ-event as the climax of the covenant, Barclay downplays the role of the covenant or the existence of an underlying continuous narrative, in which Christ acts as the climax: "Wright's notion that Paul 'saw himself on a map, a grid, constructed . . . out of the controlling narratives of ancient Israel' hardly fits what we have found in Galatians . . . ."[161]

The influence of Martyn's approach can be perceived in Barclay's emphasis that Paul connects Christ only with the trajectory of promise, and even here without a sense of a linear development:

> [T]he Christ-event completes a narrative line projected by the divine promise, but not a narrative progression in human history. By a slanted reading of the promise of Abraham's 'seed', Paul finds reference not to multiple generations of Israelite history, but to a single seed, Christ (3:16), and only after and in Christ to a plurality (3:29). In between there is no development in the story of Israel, no progress or preparation for the future.[162] . . . there is no exodus, no entry into the land, no temple, no division of the

---

157. Barclay, *Paul and the Gift*, 440.
158. Barclay, *Paul and the Gift*, 361.
159. Barclay, *Paul and the Gift*, 361.
160. In highlighting the priority of the Christ-event in Paul's hermeneutic, Barclay also inverts Hays's *Echoes of Scripture in the Letters of Paul* to "echoes of the gospel in the Scriptures of Israel" (*Paul and the Gift*, 418).
161. Barclay, *Paul and the Gift*, 413; and discussion in 400–410.
162. Barclay, *Paul and the Gift*, 412.

kingdoms, no exile, and no return. All we have is an interval during which the heir waits for the time set by the Father (4:1–2).[163]

But Barclay does not simply follow Martyn's emphasis on the punctiliar character of the Christ-event (apocalyptic invasion) that is completely discontinuous with the story of Israel, as he makes a distinction between discontinuity on the human level—"[a]t the *human level*, the Christ-event is a matter of discontinuity and reversal"[164]—and continuity on the level of divine promise—"the narrative arc from the Abrahamic promise to Christ."[165]

Barclay perceives that the hermeneutical priority of the Christ-event that shapes Paul's sense of divine continuity and human discontinuity comes to its sharpest expression in Gal 4:21—5:1.[166] Hence, the births of Ishmael and Isaac become paradigms for how Paul conceives "salvation-history." Ishmael—born according to the flesh (4:23, 29)—represents what Paul rejects: an account of salvation that is located "on a standard historical map"; whereas Isaac—born by the promise and according to the Spirit (4:23, 29)—represents what Paul finds true about the Christ-event: an act of God to generate a people "contrary to all conditions of the possible," and thus it is not a standard historical phenomenon with a human cause-effect pattern.[167] Furthermore, Barclay perceives that Paul fills the central categories in the narrative of the births of Abraham's two sons with new meaning that is derived from the "Christ-centered narrative sketched earlier in the letter."[168] Thus, the category of *slavery* that describes both Hagar and the present Jerusalem is about slavery "under the authority of the Torah (4:21) or Sinai (4:24–25), which can be classified as 'slavery' only from the perspective of the culture-relativizing 'freedom' created by God's gift in Christ (2:4; 5:1)."[169] Also, the polarity between "flesh" and "Spirit" in the births of Ishmael and Isaac is "made visible only since the gift of the Spirit of Christ (3:2–5, 14; 4:6)."[170]

In summary, Barclay's configuration of the theological vision and logic in Paul's letter to the Galatians proceeds from Paul's perfecting of grace as

163. Barclay, *Paul and the Gift*, 413.
164. Barclay, *Paul and the Gift*, 412; emphasis original.
165. Barclay, *Paul and the Gift*, 414.
166. Barclay, *Paul and the Gift*, 415.
167. Barclay, *Paul and the Gift*, 414.
168. Barclay, *Paul and the Gift*, 416.
169. Barclay, *Paul and the Gift*, 416–17. Barclay makes clear that the categories of "slavery" under the Torah and "freedom" do not map on to the dichotomy of Judaism vs. (Gentile) Christianity, as they both encompass Jews and Gentiles (417n64).
170. Barclay, *Paul and the Gift*, 417.

an incongruous gift that shapes both his understanding of the past—his rereading of Israel's Scriptures—and his conviction about the present establishing of the new communities that need to embody the gospel.

Key Questions for This Book

The above review of six different perspectives to reading Galatians gives rise to the key questions that this book interacts with. They can be divided into three interconnected categories: structural, hermeneutical, and theological questions.

Structural questions. The different perspectives have placed more weight on different parts of the letter that in turn direct the reading of the whole. Dunn's development of the NPP places emphasis on the second chapter of the letter that orients the discussion towards its historical context that defines and narrows the discussion on Paul's opposition to Gentile circumcision. Wright's reading gravitates towards the central section of Gal 3–4 that locates Paul's vision and logic in Paul's retelling of Israel's story with a rereading of Israel's Scriptures. By contrast, the beginning and end chapters (1–2 and 5–6) seem to hold most weight in Barclay's reading that emphasizes the logic of the incongruent Christ-gift (language of grace/gift being especially prominent in Gal 1–2) and the vision of the formation of innovative communities (Gal 5–6). Martyn's apocalyptic reading takes its coordinates from the cosmic emergence of the new creation by the cross of Christ in Gal 6:14–15, and finds its vision in the programmatic proclamation of the dissolution of the polarities of the old cosmos in Gal 3:28. Likewise, Boyarin identifies a Hellenistic vision in Gal 3:27–29, but gives also much weight to Gal 4:21–31 where he finds the allegorical mode as the key to Paul's theological logic. For different reasons, Thiessen also highlights Gal 4:21–31 as a key passage that encapsulates Paul's emphasis on Abrahamic sonship. These different starting points for the various perspectives raise the question: Does Galatians contain within the flow of the argument a passage (or passages) that could be argued to offer the best vantage point to configure its theological vision and logic?

Hermeneutical questions. If one aspect must be singled out as the main reason for the plurality of perspectives, the conception of Paul's hermeneutic would rank rather high on the chart. Furthermore, how Paul's theological matrix is conceived results in the different constructions that emerge from it. Boyarin's emphasis on the Hellenistic matrix, and his conception of Paul's allegorical mode produce a picture of a universalistic Paul that takes aim at particularity. The NPP/RNPP emphasis on Paul's Jewish matrix generates readings of Paul's theology that are more firmly fitted within the conceptual world of Judaism, and yet with different configurations. Wright focuses on the role of Israel's Scriptures and on Paul's retelling of Israel's story from the perspective of its fulfillment that gives Paul's theology a narrative shape and a sense of continuity that has implications for both the Jews and Gentiles. The RNPP's insistence that Paul's hermeneutical key is the distinction between the Jew and Gentile results in a reading of Galatians where the problem with the Law has to do only with its application to the Gentiles. Thiessen's view on Paul's "hermeneutical conversion" places Paul into certain reading traditions that mediate a reconstructed view of the Gentile problem that emphasizes the necessary continuity with Abrahamic genealogy. Sanders and Martyn place all the weight on the Christ-event generating the shape of Paul's theology, which results in an emphasis on discontinuity. Barclay's modified version of this also emphasizes the hermeneutical priority of the Christ-event, and yet retains a connection with Israel's story that incorporates continuity in the divine trajectory of the promise, but is discontinuous on the level of human history. These different views on Paul's hermeneutic generate the following questions: What is the theological matrix for Paul's vision and logic? And more specifically: How do Israel's Scriptures function in Paul's theological matrix? How does the Christ-event and the experience of the Spirit impact Paul's reading of Scripture, and shape Paul's retelling of Israel's story?

As the NPP and RNPP have highlighted, the Jew-Gentile divide is a central feature in the letter to the Galatians. Yet it is not clear how this distinction functions for Paul. Is it, as the RNPP insists, a hard and fast divide that must not be transgressed in order to follow Paul's theological vision and logic? Or is there, as Barclay has pointed out, something about the Christ-event that relativizes the distinction for Paul? The conception of the Jew-Gentile distinction has also implications on how Paul's retelling of the story of Israel is understood in Galatians. This raises the additional question: How does Paul's retelling of Israel's story navigate the Jew-Gentile divide, i.e., how are the Jews and Gentiles located in it?

Theological questions. The different perspectives configure Paul's theological vision and logic in various ways. For Luther, the scope of the gospel is the individual's conscience, and the letter is about justification by faith that excludes any works, circumcision included, from the way to find favor with God. Wright perceives that community is central in Paul's vision that is about the one worldwide family of Abraham. The central logic here is found in the eschatological fulfillment of the story of Israel by the Messiah—the reconstitution of the people of God—that renders the Torah outdated. The RNPP shares the eschatological focus, and yet perceives the logic in the necessity to keep the Gentiles as distinct from the Jews. Thiessen develops this further with his emphasis on the inability of circumcision to remedy the Gentile problem that is about the lack of genealogical connection with Abraham. Martyn raises the vision to a cosmological scale, in which the logic of the letter is about perceiving the cosmic implications of the divine apocalyptic invasion. Boyarin's universal vs. particular dichotomy is at the heart of his construction. Barclay's configuration is centered on the Christ-event as an incongruous gift that generates new innovative communities. Hence, the two central questions in this research are: What is the vision that drives Paul's mission and proclamation of the gospel? What is the logic in Paul's gospel that resists Gentile circumcision?

In addition to these big theological questions there are other more specific issues that require attention in my configuration of Paul's theological vision and logic in Galatians. At the center of all the different perspectives is the question about Paul and the Law. Luther perceived the problem with the Law in general terms as the false object of trust in a legalistic attempt to gain merit with God. The NPP has emphasized a more specific problem in the Law's function to maintain the Jew-Gentile divide that was blocking (and preparing) the fulfillment of the Abrahamic promise of blessing to all the nations. For Wright, the Law is also the cursing agent that effects Israel's exile, which Christ bears on the cross to release the blessing of restoration in his resurrection. The RNPP perceives the problem with the Law only in its application to the Gentiles and not in its covenant-maintaining function with the Jews. Martyn is similarly careful to focus the problem on the wrong application of the Law to the Gentiles, in which context it functions in the mode of circular exchange that places it under the category of religion. In Boyarin's configuration, the Law insists on the particular Jewish identity, and is thus the enemy of universal unity of humanity. For Barclay, the Law is a norm that upholds systems of worth and value that are relativized by the incongruous gift of Christ. Hence, this book also addresses the question: How does the Law function in Paul's theological vision and logic? This can be expressed in terms of the tension between Paul's negative and positive perspectives on the Law: How can Paul connect the Law with slavery, on the one hand, and find a positive role, or fulfillment for it, on the other hand?

One of the aims of this book is to offer an *integrative reading* of Galatians that can incorporate and coordinate the various concepts/themes that Paul uses in the articulation of his theological vision and logic. The different perspectives illuminate the potential of the material for different configurations of the content and relationships between these. The Lutheran construal focuses on the concept of righteousness, whereas the NPP/RNPP places special emphasis on "sonship" and inclusion in the people of God.

Hence, I inquire how righteousness relates to the other related concepts. The concepts of blessing and curse, freedom and slavery, Spirit and flesh are also integrated into Paul's theological logic in various degrees and various ways. Luther coordinates them around his theme of the right kind of righteousness. For Wright, they gain their coherence in Paul's covenantal narrative. Barclay emphasizes their christological orientation and sociological dimension. Martyn highlights these as components in the way Paul distinguishes the old and new cosmos, and talks about God's act of salvation in opposition to religion. Boyarin perceives spirit and flesh as important hermeneutical categories, whereas they are for Thiessen the different media of genealogical connection with Abraham. The most plausible configuration of Paul's theological vision and logic should have the ability to incorporate and coordinate all the central concepts within its system without force, and without the need to omit "embarrassing" texts.

This book seeks to provide insights to all the questions in the above three categories, yet not with equal weight. The main contribution of my work is on the hermeneutical dimension that offers a unique perspective on the configuration of Paul's theological vision and logic, which in turn facilitates discussion about the other theological questions. Chapter 2 charts my approach to the structural questions; chapters 3 and 4 form the foundation for my analysis of Paul's hermeneutic in chapter 5, and also for the intertextual reading of Gal 4:21—5:1 in chapter 6 that offers the vantage point in this book to engage the theological questions that concern Galatians as a whole. The key questions will finally be addressed in a condensed and synthesized manner in the conclusions in chapter 7.

The Argument and Approach of This Book

The aim of this book is to configure Paul's theological vision and logic in his letter to the Galatians. I argue that the best vantage point for configuring the contours of Paul's presentation of the gospel in Galatians is the passage in 4:21—5:1 due to its strategic function in the letter, and because the passage reveals aspects of Paul's hermeneutic that lead to a clearer perception of his theological vision and logic.

This is an audacious claim, since the passage in question has often been sidelined due to the allegorical mode of Paul's engagement with Israel's Scriptures. Yet, as the above review indicates, some recent work has drawn the passage closer to the center of Paul's thought. Boyarin has turned the downplaying of Paul's allegory upside down, as he detects in Paul's allegory the heart of his mode for doing theology. I agree with Boyarin that Gal

4:21—5:1 is a central text, but I am unsatisfied with Boyarin's understanding of Paul's allegorical mode and with his consequent configuration of Paul's theology. Contrary to Boyarin, I argue in chapter 5 that Paul's allegorical mode is essentially intertextual. Thiessen has also given much weight to Gal 4:21—5:1 in his configuration of Paul's theological vision and logic in relation to the Abraham narrative and the theme of Abrahamic sonship. The deficiency in Thiessen's reading is the one-sided attention it gives to the Abraham narrative without recognizing how the quotation from Isa 54:1 in Gal 4:27 impacts the way Paul appropriates the theological potential in the narrative of the births of Abraham's two sons. I argue that an integral feature in Paul's hermeneutic is his reading of the Abraham narrative *together with* the Isaianic vision of restoration that shapes his vision of the gospel as being about the re-creation of humanity—Jew and Gentile included—and configures its logic by the paradigmatic birth of Isaac and the alienation-restoration paradigm that is encapsulated in the image of the barren woman giving birth to many children in Isa 54:1.

My approach for configuring Paul's theological vision and logic in Galatians navigates most closely between the perspectives of Wright and Barclay. Together with Wright, I affirm that Paul's primary theological matrix is Israel's Scriptures, and that Paul's conception of the gospel is to be understood in the context of Israel's story. My key interest is in the *hermeneutic* in, and the *shape* of, Paul's retelling of Israel's narrative, and how he incorporates the Gentiles into it. In particular, I analyze how the birth of Isaac and the exile/alienation-restoration paradigm in Isaiah function in Paul's theological vision and logic.[171] I argue that the vision of inaugurated restoration is central to Paul's conception of the Christ-event and the gift of the Spirit, but that this does not necessarily mean that he had a sense of a prior reality of an ongoing/extended exile. Rather, I argue that it is the reality of the inaugurated restoration that configures for Paul the realm of existence outside of it as being a form of alienation. In sum, I argue that Paul perceives the Christ-event and the gift of the Spirit as the fulfillment of the Isaianic promise of restoration (that is also the fulfillment of the Abrahamic promise of blessing to all the nations in their inclusion in the new-creation people of God), but that Israel's experience of exile, as interpreted theologically by Isaiah, acts more as a paradigm (rather than a prior ongoing stage) that Paul reapplies to describe the realm of existence outside of Christ.

Thus, I perceive, together with Wright, that eschatological fulfillment of the Abrahamic-Isaianic promise is an important part of Paul's vision and

---

171. See discussion in ch. 5 for my preference to use the language of alienation-restoration ratehr than exile-restoration.

logic. However, Donaldson has rightly pushed the discussion towards seeking a *deeper explanation* for *how* the vision of restoration provides a logic for Paul to resist Gentile circumcision, and for what happens to the Torah in the fulfillment of the hope of Israel.[172] It is not self-evident why the Gentiles could not be integrated into the one people of God via circumcision, or why the Torah could not function normatively in the new eschatological age of restoration based on a different re-appropriation of the scriptural tradition. To explore Paul's deeper reasoning, I capitalize on the insights of Barclay's work that has successfully resuscitated grace, and brought it to the center stage in Paul's logic. I perceive that Barclay's configuration of the logic of the incongruent grace is a very plausible explanation for Paul's resistance to the requirement of circumcision, and for the relativization of the Torah. However, Barclay's approach emphasizes the hermeneutical priority of the Christ-event to the extent that, at least in practice, it underplays the *formative* role of Scripture as the matrix from which Paul finds the resources to configure the meaning and implications of the Christ-event and the experience of the Spirit. I argue that Scripture, and especially the Abraham narrative and Isaiah's vision of restoration, contain the theological potential from which Paul can develop (and not only to reflect on) the conviction for the logic of incongruent grace together with his experience of the Christ-event. Hence, I combine in my approach Wright's emphasis on the role of Israel's Scriptures and Barclay's focus on the shape of Paul's gospel in my attempt to configure Paul's theological vision and logic in Galatians.

My approach is a literary analysis that employs a variety of literary methods, as they appear relevant for each step in the development of the argument in this book. In chapter 2, I execute *structural analyses* of the whole letter and of 4:21—5:1 that is focused on *content*. In chapter 3, I perform a *narrative analysis* to highlight the theological potential in the story of the births of Abraham's two sons. To draw out the theological potential in the Isaianic vision of restoration that is encapsulated by Isa 54:1 (in its immediate context), I devise and execute an *intratextual thematic analysis* of the book of Isaiah in chapter 4. Finally, based on my analysis in chapter 5 that demonstrates Paul's allegorical reading to be essentially intertextual, I undertake in chapter 6 an *intertextual* reading of Gal 4:21—5:1 that enables my configuration of Paul's theological vision and logic in the letter in conversation with the Scriptures of Israel.

With the integral role that intertextuality plays in my work, I echo the approach of Hays: "I approach the task of interpretation not by reconstructing the historical situation in the churches to which Paul wrote, not

---

172. Donaldson, "Paul within Judaism," 284–93.

by framing hypothetical accounts of the opponents against whom Paul was arguing, but by *reading the letters as literary texts shaped by complex intertextual relations with Scripture.*"[173] I develop my intertextual method further at the beginning of chapter 6, which includes establishing criteria to analyze the intertextual relations between Paul's text and the texts of Scripture he interacts with. I note here that my method is focused on *text production* rather than text reception.[174] Hence, my analysis of the intertextual relations and their theological import is not limited by what can be postulated about the ability of the recipients of Paul's letter to appreciate them.[175] Thus, I avoid the pitfall that Francis Watson observes in a minimalist approach, in which "Paul's own interpretative freedom combines with his audience's scriptural ignorance to ensure that the original context is erased."[176] Rather than taking a seat as a listener among the Galatian congregations (Martyn), I take the position of an *interpreter* whose task is to probe into *Paul's line of thought* in light of Paul's most likely matrix in order to capture the vision and logic that is *present in his text*. This kind of intertextual approach is not about reading between the lines,[177] but about following the lines in Paul's text that lead to the matrix of Scripture it draws from.

I limit the scope of my intertextual approach to scriptural texts, and do not apply Watson's enlarged approach that places Paul in a three-way

173. Hays, *Echoes of Scripture in the Letters of Paul*, xi; emphasis added.

174. For more on this distinction, see Huizenga, "Old Testament in the New," 29–30.

175. For a discussion on the role of the recipients in Paul's use of Scripture, see Stanley, *Arguing with Scripture*, 40–48; and Wagner, *Heralds of the Good News*, 18–19. I do not think we can be certain about the readers of the letter (are the "opponents" included?). Other factors impinge on the question about the recipients' ability: How have they been prepared to recognize the context of Scripture? Is Paul aiming at the lowest common denominator, or writing the letter to be explained and studied? (See Wright, *PFG*, 1452). I agree with Wischmeyer that it is conceivable that there were also believers of devout Jewish families among the Galatians, and that some of the Gentile believers could have been associated with the synagogue prior to Paul's coming. These would have made them already familiar with the Scriptures and contributed to the fact that Scripture could function as the shared basis for argumentation. Wischmeyer also argues that Septuagint-readings, Synagogue lectures, and, most importantly, Paul's own teaching ministry had trained the recipients to follow Paul's argumentation from Scripture ("Wie kommt Abraham?," 147–49).

176. Watson, *Paul and the Hermeneutics of Faith*, 495; later abbreviated as *PHF*.

177. Compare with Kahl's approach who postulates that the allusions to the Roman empire in Paul's letter are a semi-hidden transcript that "requires encoded forms of speech and reading 'between the lines,' on the part of his hearers and of his contemporary interpreters alike" (*Galatians Re-Imagined*, 252). The reading "between the lines" approach is one of the reasons I am not persuaded by her argument that Paul's problem with the law is not with the Jewish Law as such, but with how it is caught up in the Roman imperial "law."

intertextual conversation: Paul, Scripture, and other interpreters of Scripture.[178] The enlarged approach highlights the semantic potential of the text of Scripture that allows for different interpretations.[179] Also, Watson's approach satisfies the criticism directed at Hays's work that Paul should not be read only in direct relation to Scripture, but also in relation to interpreted Scripture.[180] While I recognize the value of the enlarged intertextual approach, I choose to focus in this book on a more limited "three-way conversation," in which Paul reads the Abraham narrative together with the book of Isaiah. Excluding other interpreters of Scripture from the conversation is a limitation in my approach, but it does guard me from the problem that I perceive in, e.g., Thiessen's work. Thiessen's heavy emphasis on other ancient sources informing the reading possibilities that we can imagine for Paul would, at best, increase the historical plausibility of the reading. But, rather than sharpening the reading of Paul, the lenses that Thiessen employs unnecessarily cloud Paul's logic. This, I argue, is especially the case in the complex argument about the pneumatic people based on a reading of Gen 15:5 in light of various ancient sources. My approach offers a more straightforward solution for the connection Paul makes between the Abrahamic promise and the gift of the Spirit by giving attention to Paul's actual hermeneutical practice in Gal 4:21—5:1 that is reflected also elsewhere in the letter (see chapter 6). Thus, although my approach may be limited (lacking the enlarged three-way conversation), it has a clear focus on Paul's own text and the texts with which Paul explicitly interacts. The power of this approach to offer a satisfying reading of Paul's theological vision and logic in Galatians is for the reader to decide.

Construction of the Book: A Guide for the Reader

To guide my reader, I offer here a summary of how this book is constructed:

> *Chapter 2* establishes the argument for holding Gal 4:21—5:1 as the best vantage point for configuring the theological vision and logic of the letter. It includes a structural analysis of the letter as a whole, as well as of 4:21—5:1. These form the foundation for the following analyses.
>
> *Chapters 3 and 4* explore the theological potential in the intertexts that Paul explicitly indicates in Gal 4:21—5:1. *Chapter 3* focuses on the theological potential in the Abraham narrative of the births of his two sons.

---

178. Watson, *PHF*, 1–5.
179. Watson, *PHF*, 3–4.
180. See, e.g., Evans, "Listening for Echoes of Interpreted Scripture," 47–51.

Chapter 4 focuses on the theological potential underlying Paul's quotation of Isa 54:1, as the themes that are embedded in it (within its immediate context) are analyzed in the context of the whole book of Isaiah.

Chapter 5 analyzes Paul's hermeneutic, i.e., allegorical practice in Gal 4:21—5:1, which then informs my approach to reading the letter to the Galatians in chapter 6.

Chapter 6 offers an intertextual reading of Gal 4:21—5:1 with discussions that demonstrate how the passage functions as a vantage point to focus Paul's theological vision and logic in the whole letter.

Chapter 7 draws the work together to discuss the key questions that were articulated in chapter 1 in light of the insights gained in chapters 2–6.

2

Galatians 4:21—5:1 as the Vantage Point

THE CHOICE OF GAL 4:21—5:1 as the vantage point for configuring the theological vision and logic of Galatians is based initially on two factors:

1. The passage has a strategic function in the letter as the culmination point for the preceding argument and as a bridge into what follows.
2. The passage coordinates and clarifies important themes for configuring Paul's vision and logic.

I substantiate the first claim here in chapter 2, and also begin to demonstrate the second that is filled out in chapter 6. In addition, I argue in chapter 5 that an analysis of Paul's actual allegorical practice in Gal 4:21—5:1 exposes key features of Paul's hermeneutic that are vital for configuring his theological vision and logic in the letter.

The Function of Galatians 4:21—5:1 in the Letter

I analyze here the role that Gal 4:21—5:1 has in the letter to the Galatians, and demonstrate why this makes it an unparalleled vantage point for focusing the message of the letter.

As my review of the different perspectives in chapter 1 indicated, many scholars do not perceive that Gal 4:21—5:1 contributes new substance to the overall argument. Luther thought that Paul could have ended the letter at 4:20, but then it occurs to him to come up with an allegory to paint the matter to the eyes, which he had already explained in words to the ears.[1] Dunn also thinks that 4:21-31 "could be regarded not so much as a further or independent argument, but as an illustration or additional documentation of the point already made."[2] A similar sentiment was also present in the ap-

---

1. Luther, *Galatians*, 414.
2. Dunn, *Galatians*, 243.

proaches of Wright and Barclay.³ On the one hand, this view recognizes that the passage has much in common with what has preceded it in the letter, but, on the other hand, in saying that it does not add anything of substance, it fails to perceive how 4:21—5:1 acts as the culmination point for the development of key themes in the letter, and is thus the place to reap the harvest for configuring Paul's theological vision and logic. Furthermore, the passage also prepares for what follows and offers a vantage point to configure the flow of the argument in the whole letter. To prepare for my analysis in chapter 6 that demonstrates the potential of the passage in these respects, I discuss here two statements about the function of 4:21—5:1 in the letter:

1. Gal 4:21—5:1 is the *culmination point* for the preceding argument.

2. Gal 4:21—5:1 is a *pivotal* passage between the more theological and more exhortative sections.⁴

My analysis of the function of 4:21—5:1 in the letter is focused on content and thematic development, rather than rhetorical or epistolary elements.⁵

Galatians 4:21—5:1 as a Culmination Point

The beginning and end of Gal 4:21—5:1 connect the passage with the central concern of the letter: the danger of the Galatians to submit to living "under the Law" (4:21) away from the "freedom" in Christ (5:1). This danger is expressed at the beginning of the letter in terms of the Galatians' turning to *another gospel* due to the pressure of the troublemakers who distort the *true gospel* (1:6–7). This outward pressure of a distorted gospel instigated also Paul's rebuke of Peter's hypocritical actions towards the Gentiles that compelled them to Judaize, i.e., to adopt the Jewish way of life according to the Mosaic Law (2:11–14).⁶ What was at stake, for Paul, was the proper

---

3. However, Wright can be seen to move towards the position espoused in this book: "the 'allegory' of Sarah and Hagar, in Galatians 4.21–5.1, can be seen both as the culmination of the long argument from the start of chapter 3 and also as setting up the terms for the concluding (and quite complex) exhortations" (*PFG*, 1133).

4. I hesitate to make rigid distinctions in Paul's thought between theology and ethics—indicative and imperative. See discussion by Rabens, "'Indicative and Imperative,'" 285–305; and Zimmermann, "'Implicit Ethics.'"

5. However, as de Boer recognizes, these two approaches can hardly be separated—what is said and how it is said are interrelated (*Galatians*, 15). Rhetorical and epistolary approaches are not part of my analysis here, but they offer important insights that could be pursued further.

6. On this understanding of "Judaize," see Barclay, *Obeying the Truth*, 36n1; also Novenson, "Paul's Former Occupation in *Ioudaismos*," 24–39, especially 30: "'Judaizing'

understanding of the new reality of Christ and its implications for the question of how anyone, Jew and Gentile alike,[7] can be established in a right relationship with God (*dikaioō*),[8] and what role the Law has in it (2:16–21). At this point in the letter, it is clear that its sharp tone results from the two trajectories that Paul perceives to be antithetical: the way of the true gospel that consists of *faith in Christ* (*pistis christou*),[9] and following the claims of a distorted gospel that demands *works of the Law* (*erga nomou*)[10] for being rightly related with God (1:6–9; 2:5, 16–21).

I argue in the following that the antithetical trajectories of the true and false gospels are developed throughout the letter with evolving themes that culminate in 4:21—5:1. The beginning of Gal 3 develops the antithetical relationship between Law and faith in Christ in terms of the *works of the Law* versus *"hearing of faith"* (*akoē pisteōs*) (3:2) that are also expressed with categories of *flesh* and *Spirit* (3:3).[11] The Galatians are expected to recognize

---

is not what Paul's opponents are doing; it is what the Galatian believers are contemplating doing."

7. Pace the RNPP insistence that Paul is only concerned about the Gentiles. E.g., Johnson Hodge's comments on Gal 2:16: "I read it as Paul staging a conversation with his colleagues (other Jewish teachers) about how gentiles might be made right with God: through the faithfulness of Christ and not through the works of the law.... Gentiles are 'sinners', in need of being made righteous, or being brought into a right relationship with God and being made moral. Jews, already God's people, know how to accomplish this" (*If Sons, Then Heirs*, 58). She seems to comment only on 2:16a, understanding *anthrōpos* as Gentile only, and neglects 2:16b.

8. I translate *dikaioō* and *dikaiosynē* in a rather open way (establish in a right relationship / right-relatedness) to indicate my understanding that these concepts are not end-point concepts for Paul, but rather concepts that are filled with content/meaning in the course of the development of his argument. My translations also indicate the relational focus that these concepts run into (e.g., children of God, heirs).

9. I understand *pistis christou* here with an objective genitive sense, or, as Barclay calls it, "genitive of quality" that refers "to the faith exercised by believers that signals their dependence on and reconstitution by Christ" (*Paul and the Gift*, 380). For discussion on *pistis christou*, see the essays by Dunn and Hays in Hays, *Faith of Jesus Christ*, 249–97; and the collected essays in Bird and Sprinkle, *Faith of Jesus Christ*. It seems that, since linguistic and grammatical arguments have not settled the question, it is the wider understanding of Paul's theology that influences the choice (see Barclay, *Paul and the Gift*, 381–84). I develop my understanding of the relationship between faith and Christ in ch. 6.

10. I understand *erga nomou* to refer to the general observance of the Law and not restricted to the specific practices highlighted by the Gentile mission (e.g., circumcision). Cf. Barclay, *Paul and the Gift*, 373–75.

11. I use here a very wooden translation "hearing of faith" to leave its meaning ambiguous. I discuss in ch. 6 the possibility of this expression alluding to LXX Isa 53:1 (cf. Rom 10:16–17), which would imply that it is about hearing the message about Christ that evokes faith.

that it was the "hearing of faith" that constituted their reception of the Spirit, and coming to live "under the Law" is tantamount to living according to flesh. Paul develops further the significance of the reception of the Spirit in evaluating the "works of the Law" versus "hearing of faith" dichotomy and grounds it with an appeal to the Abraham narrative (3:6–14).

Paul establishes first that Abraham found right-relatedness (*dikaiosynē*) with God by faith (3:6), and thus it follows that the children of Abraham also derive their identity from faith (*ek pisteōs*) (3:7). Furthermore, the Gentiles receive the promised *blessing* with Abraham on the mutually shared ground of faith (3:8–9). Thus, blessing is brought into the same conceptual field with *dikaiosynē*. In the dense argumentation in Gal 3:10–14, Paul first spells out the reality of life "under the Law": it produces *curse* despite its promise of life (3:10–12). What incurs the curse is not doing everything written in the Law (3:10). Hence, Paul again contrasts the "works of the Law" (doing the Law) with faith, now in relation to right-relatedness (*dikaiosynē*) and receiving blessing, in which the Law fails to produce both, but faith succeeds (3:11–12). Paul then defines the faith that produces blessing christologically: Christ redeemed "us," those under the curse of the Law, by becoming cursed himself (3:13), and thus made possible that the "blessing of Abraham" could reach the Gentiles so that "we" could receive the promised Spirit by faith (3:14). This is a very condensed argument that requires deciphering in terms of who are the "us" in 3:13 and the "we" in 3:14, and how the redemption from curse, blessing to the Gentiles, and the reception of the Spirit are connected (see chapter 6). At this point, I simply note that Paul's "truth of the gospel" presents faith in Christ as the means to receive right-relatedness with God, blessing, and the Spirit. In contrast, Paul perceives that the trajectory of the false gospel implies observance of the Law that does not bring right-relatedness and blessing, but rather a curse.

The development of the trajectory of the true gospel shifts in emphasis from faith to *promise* that is configured in terms of a *covenant* in Gal 3:15–18. The pre-proclamation of the gospel to Abraham about the blessing of the nations by faith (3:8) was construed in 3:14 in terms of the reception of the *promise* of the Spirit. In Gal 3:15–18, Paul first relates how the *promises* given to Abraham (the plural most likely refers to the repeated promise of blessing) were specified to his "seed," which Paul interprets to refer ultimately to Christ (3:16). Paul also understands that this (repeated) promise constitutes a *covenant*, and then, having appealed to human customs that do not allow reductions or additions to covenants (3:15),[12] he argues that the

12. Cf. Oakes: "Paul uses human analogy to explain God's actions. In particular, he discusses the characteristics of human covenants, probably mainly thinking of wills, as being fixed documents" (*Galatians*, 118–19). Paul himself quickly places the focus

covenant of promise, which was established by God, cannot be made void by the Law that was given later (3:17). Another shift also takes place at the end of this section that anticipates the direction of the argument; the concepts of right-relatedness and blessing are now replaced by the term *inheritance* (3:18). Again, Paul highlights the antithesis claiming that the inheritance cannot be by the Law, because it would no longer be of promise, by which God initially gave it to Abraham (3:18). Thus, Gal 3:15–18 signals a shift in the argument of the letter, in which Paul's proclamation of the truth of the gospel is focused on the covenant of promise and inheritance.

At this point Paul pauses to answer the question that arises from leaving the Law outside of the trajectory that leads to inheritance (3:19). Rather than relegating the Law completely to an antagonistic relationship with the promise, Paul explains that the limitation of the Law is in its inability to make alive (*zōopoieō*), and hence it was unable to produce right-relatedness (3:21). In other words, the problem with the Law is that it cannot bring deliverance from the universal problem of sin (*alla synekleisen hē grafē ta panta hypo hamartian*) (3:22a). Paul also explains that, besides the "soteriological" limitation, the Law is also constrained temporally—the Law acted as a custodian (*paidagōgos*) until the time of the revelation of faith/Christ (3:23–24). Now that Christ has come, the custodian is no longer needed (3:25), i.e., life "under the Law" is no longer appropriate in light of the new reality in Christ.

In what follows, Paul continues to develop the theme of inheritance in relation to being *children*. Paul claims that through faith in Christ all become "sons" of God (3:26; the masculine form "sons" is used of all believers—male and female alike—and indicates that their status is derivative of Jesus being the "Son" of God), and are made one by incorporation into Christ in baptism (3:27–28). This oneness in Christ restructures identity, as those in Christ are no longer defined in terms of Jew or Greek, slave or free, male or female (3:28). Believers in Christ are also regarded as Abraham's children, "seed," and *heirs* according to the promise (3:29).

In Gal 4:1–7, Paul reconfigures what has been said up to this point by using the ideas of being children and inheritance, and setting them in contrast to life "under the Law" and the concept of *slavery*. In 4:1 Paul refers to the social reality in which the potential heir's status is no different to the status of a slave as long as he is under-aged (*nēpios*); the heir is under the household managers until the appointed time set by the father (4:2). Using this social reality to illustrate his point, Paul states that similarly "we" were enslaved under the

---

on the scriptural "covenant of promise." Hence, this should be regarded as the primary matrix that is being illustrated by notions of human covenants.

elements of the cosmos (*stoicheia tou kosmou*)[13] until the fullness of time when the Father sent his Son to redeem those under the Law so that "we" would receive adoption as "sons" (*huiothesia*) (4:3–5). This process of redemption from slavery to "sonship" echoes the earlier argument of redemption from curse to blessing.[14] Again, "sonship" is configured in relation to the Spirit; because the "we" have been made "sons," they have been given the Spirit of God's Son that confirms their "sonship" with the cry, *Abba*, Father (4:6; cf. 3:14).[15] Paul then pits "sonship" against slavery in relation to inheritance: in this new reality of Christ and the Spirit—in the fullness of time—people are no longer slaves but "sons," and, as such, made heirs by an act of God (*dia theou*)[16] (4:7). In chapter 6, I return to these two central texts (3:10–14 and 4:3–7) to demonstrate how the reading of 4:21—5:1 sheds light on these condensed arguments, especially in relation to the story of Israel.

At this point, I summarize with Table 1 the flow of Paul's argument in terms of the development of the themes that Paul has used in building it.

Table 1. Development of Themes in Galatians 2:16—4:7

Gal 2:16–21		Gal 3:1–5		Gal 3:8–14		Gal 3:14–18	
Faith in Christ	Right-re-latedness	"Hearing of faith"	Spirit	Faith in Christ	Blessing / Spirit	Covenant of Promise	Inheritance
Works of the Law		Works of the Law	Flesh	Works of the Law	Curse	Law	

---

13. For a discussion on the meaning of the *stoicheia tou kosmou*, see Barclay, *Paul and the Gift*, 408–10; and Martyn, *Galatians*, 393–406. It seems that they refer to the four physical elements (earth, water, air, fire), but also to the way the "cosmos" is divided into pairs of opposites (Martyn).

14. For discussion on the relationship between 3:13–14 and 4:3–6, see Hays, *Faith of Jesus Christ*, 74–82.

15. Cf. Hays who understands that Paul is reasoning from the effect (Spirit) to the cause (adoption) with the purpose of convincing the Galatians that it is because of the reception of the Spirit that they can know that they are "sons" (cf. 3:2–5) (*Faith of Jesus Christ*, 99).

16. *Dia theou* is an unusual expression, and hence it is the likely original reading (supported by P[46], ℵ original hand, A, B, C original hand) that has received multiple scribal alterations.

	Gal 3:19–22		Gal 3:23–29		Gal 4:1–7	
	Faith in Christ	Promise	Faith in Christ	"Sons"/Heirs	"Sons"	Spirit/ Inheritance
	Law		"Under the Law"		Slaves	

In Gal 4:8–20, Paul picks up the tone of amazement and outrage at the Galatians' desire to "come under the Law" (cf. 1:6–9; 3:1–5). Paul reminds the Galatians of their former life when they did not know God, and were in slavery to things that are not by nature gods (4:8–9). But now that they know God, or better yet, are known by God (an interesting moment where Paul "corrects" himself to emphasize the orientation of the gospel in divine action rather than human), Paul is amazed at their desire to turn again to slavery, to turn towards the weak and worthless elements by adopting Jewish calendrical observances (4:9–10; cf. 4:21).[17] Paul is worried for the Galatians; he is worried that his labor has been in vain (4:11). Thus, Paul begins an appeal that recalls his initial ministry among the Galatians. He calls them to become as he is (4:12), remembering how he came among them (4:13–15). Paul is worried that the Galatians' zeal is being misdirected; the troublemakers—proponents of the "distorted gospel"—want to direct the Galatians' zeal away from Paul towards themselves (4:17). But this is not about party politics, it is about what each party represents. Paul is not only fighting to win the Galatians' zeal back to him; he is in labor pains so that *Christ* would be fully formed among them (4:18–19). He wants to be present with them and change the tone of his voice, because he is perplexed about their turn towards the troublemakers' "distorted gospel" (4:20).[18] As Betz remarks, Paul knows his "wish is at present not fulfillable and that the letter must suffice as a substitute."[19]

---

17. Pace Kahl who argues that the calendrical observances refer to the Roman festivals (*Galatians Re-Imagined*, 218–27).

18. I understand *allaxai tēn phōnēn mou* (4:20) to refer to a change in the tone, and not to indicate Paul's desire to move from the letter to oral communication (pace Betz, *Galatians*, 236). I also do not perceive that his desire is to change the tone to be more friendly and joyous (pace Martyn, *Galatians*, 426), since that is what he could have done, but does not do. Instead, I understand that this expression indicates the seriousness of the situation that calls for a sharp address that brings the Galatians to a place of decision. This is what he does in 4:21—5:1.

19. Betz, *Galatians*, 236. Aune defines a letter as "a substitute for oral communication" (*Literary Environment*, 158), and "a surrogate for the presence of a friend" (172; with reference to Thraede's study on friendly letters, *Grundzüge griechisch-römischer Brieftopik*).

But although he cannot be present, he can change the tone of his voice.[20] This is in fact what he does in 4:21—5:1, which thus represents what Paul wanted to do, if he were present with them.[21]

Gal 4:21—5:1 begins with an expression of Paul's perplexity that resembles the tone that he has had throughout the letter (cf. 1:6; 3:1–5; 4:8–9), but the tone changes within the flow of the passage. With the initial question, "tell me" (4:21), Paul invites the Galatians to a "dialogue" with him around the interpretation of Scripture that challenges the Galatians to follow Paul's hermeneutical practice (cf. 4:12 "become like me"). This is different from the tone in the rhetorical questions earlier. Furthermore, as Hansen has observed, Paul's tone also changes to deliver the force of his argument with the controlling imperatives of the letter that call the Galatians to a place of decision: the Galatians must do away with the draw to come under the Law (4:30), resist the "yoke of slavery," and stand firm in the "freedom" in Christ (5:1).[22] Paul is led to this change in tone in his labor pain; he is in pain because the Galatians are called to be a new community, the "Jerusalem above" people (language of labor in 4:19 and 4:27), that derives its identity from the act of God in Christ and the Spirit (5:1; 4:28-29) rather than from the observance of the Law (4:21; 5:1). Hence, Gal 4:21—5:1 expresses acutely Paul's deeply felt burden that is driving his letter writing.[23]

In Gal 4:8-20 Paul addressed the Galatians' situation more directly in the face of the challenge by the troublemakers and their "distorted gospel." From 4:21 onwards, Paul continues in this line, as he gathers together what he has said before, and applies it directly to the situation at hand. In this climactic moment, the weighty themes that have appeared earlier in the letter come together and follow the development that has taken place in the course of the argument: the shift in emphasis from faith to promise; blessing related to the Spirit; right-relatedness configured in terms of "sonship" and inheritance.[24]

The shift that began in 3:15–18 is reflected in 4:21—5:1, as the antithetical trajectories are configured not in terms of right-relatedness or blessing, but in relation to "sonship" and inheritance. The theme of

---

20. Although the imperfect form of the main verb—"I wish" (*ēthelon*)—that governs both of the infinitives (to be present, and to change the tone) makes it a wish that cannot be fulfilled, I suggest that Paul actually continues to partially fulfill the second part of his wish; it is the best he can do with the letter.

21. Cf. Oepke, *an die Galater*, 146–47. Also Mußner, *Der Galaterbrief*, 315–16.

22. Hansen, *Abraham in Galatians*, 145–50.

23. The other passages that seem as specially marked out to express the burden of the letter are 5:2–12 and 6:11–16.

24. Cf. Wolter, "Das Israelproblem," 9.

"sonship"—generating the children of God who are the heirs of the promise of Abraham (3:26—4:7)—is present in the theme of the births of Abraham's two sons (4:23-24, 28). But "sonship" is not only configured in relation to Abraham, since the Galatians are also to identify themselves as children of the mother "Jerusalem above" (4:26). The issue of inheritance (cf. 3:18, 29; 4:1-7) takes center stage in the climactic scriptural exhortation in 4:30. Also, the trajectory that leads to inheritance is focused on divine action in Christ (5:1) and the Spirit (4:29) rather than on faith. However, as faith is always presented in relation to Christ, so it is possible that faith is also implied in the call to stand firm in the freedom of Christ (5:1).[25]

The dominating themes of slavery and freedom, and the generation of "sons" in 4:21—5:1, follow the development that began in 3:23—4:10, in which inheritance is the result of realized "sonship," and the state of slavery is something that even the potential heir is subject to prior to the "fulness of time" (4:1-4).

The designation of the cities as "present Jerusalem" and "Jerusalem above" reflects the eschatological framework of the letter (1:4 present evil age; 6:15 new creation) and also the eschatological logic in 4:1-7 (appointed time, fullness of time). The antithesis between the Law and promise that has been configured in relation to time and covenant (cf. 3:10-25) is developed by the "allegorical" two covenants, in which Hagar/Ishmael represents the Sinai covenant—Law—that corresponds with the "present Jerusalem," whereas the "free woman" and the birth of Isaac represent the promise that corresponds with the "Jerusalem above" (4:21, 23, 24-28, 31).

The connection made in Gal 3:1-5 between flesh and the Law in contrast to life in the Spirit is also advanced in 4:21—5:1. Ishmael is born from flesh, and represents the reality of coming "under the Law" and slavery (4:23), whereas Isaac and the Galatians are generated by the Spirit (4:29) that correlates with freedom (4:31).

In summary, Gal 4:21—5:1 is the culminating passage for the argument that Paul has developed up to this point for three reasons:

1. Important themes that have appeared prior in the letter come together in 4:21—5:1.

2. Not only do prior themes come together in 4:21—5:1, but their development culminates here, and their relationships are coordinated, which facilitates a focused analysis of Paul's theological vision and logic.

25. The verb stand (*stēkō*) is closely tied to the theme of faith elsewhere in Paul: "stand (*stēkete*) in the faith" (1 Cor 16:13); "... we were comforted ... through your faith, for now we live, if you stand (*stekete*) in the Lord" (1 Thess 3:7-8).

3. Galatians 4:21—5:1 follows strategically the indication of Paul's burden for writing the letter (4:19-20), and thus, it acutely expresses Paul's defense of the truth of the gospel that the Galatians need to line up with.

In Gal 4:21—5:1, Paul has taken his argument to a "mountain top" that gives a vantage point to gaze more clearly at the path that has been trodden. Crucially, it is exactly a written work—Paul's letter—rather than oral communication when being physically present that enables this strategic role for 4:21—5:1. The recipients (and later interpreters) can "reread earlier sections of a document not completely understood or fully appreciated on the first reading."[26] I explore this potential in chapter 6 where I reread the message of the letter in light of 4:21—5:1. But 4:21—5:1 is not only a vantage point to gaze backwards, as it also prepares for what is ahead so that the argument can be followed to the end with a better sense of direction and purpose. It is to this pivotal quality of Gal 4:21—5:1 that I turn next.

Galatians 4:21—5:1 as a Pivotal Passage

The last verse of Gal 4:21—5:1 represents the pivotal role that the passage has in the flow of the letter: "the restatement of Christ's liberating activity and the two imperatives of 5:1 make it the climax of both the pericope and indeed of the letter, by summing up what precedes and introducing what follows."[27] On the one hand, the call to stand firm in freedom by resisting the "yoke of slavery" (5:1) applies the scriptural exhortation in 4:30 to the Galatians. Furthermore, it encapsulates the change in tone (4:20) that began with the imperative in 4:12 ("become like me," cf. 2:4-5), and was heightened with the stark contrasts drawn in 4:21-31 that direct the recipients of the letter to a place of decision. But, on the other hand, the choice set forth in 5:1 between freedom in Christ and the "yoke of slavery" paves the way for the following elaboration of the terms of the decision that Paul challenges the Galatians to make.

In Gal 5:2-4, Paul explains the "yoke of slavery" in terms of circumcision and the obligation to keep the whole Law (5:2-3). Submitting to this

---

26. Aune, *Literary Environment*, 159. Martyn emphasizes the oral communication of the letter in the congregation, but it is unnecessary to approach the content of the letter by restricting its ability to speak only to the lowest common denominator of what can be grasped on the first hearing. Surely it is conceivable that an important and weighty letter by Paul is not only heard once, but read many times and discussed.

27. Eastman, *Recovering Paul's Mother Tongue*, 133-34. The fact that some scholars include 5:1 in the passage that begins at 4:21 and some with the passage that follows reflects the *Janus* character of the verse (see next section).

"yoke"—placing the hope of right-relatedness on the Law (5:4)—has the consequence of losing the benefit of Christ (5:2) that amounts to falling away from grace (5:4; cf. 1:6). By contrast, Paul presents the Spirit and faith as the true means for waiting for the "hope of right-relatedness" (5:5). Furthermore, he explains that circumcision or uncircumcision count for nothing in the new reality of Christ, in which the only thing that matters is faith that expresses itself in love (5:6), which signals the direction Paul will take the argument from 5:13 onwards.[28] But before Paul moves to his positive argument, he again places the Galatians at the point of decision between obeying the truth and the "leaven" of the "distorted gospel" (5:7-12). This time Paul signals his confidence that the Galatians will side with the truth (5:10), and explains how the Galatians are to live in the freedom of Christ.[29]

The theme of freedom that was brought to the fore in Gal 4:21—5:1 is the point of departure in the parenetic section of 5:13—6:10. Accordingly, Engberg-Pedersen argues that 4:21-31 facilitates the move towards "the positive notion of freedom (from the Law, 5:1)."[30] Gal 4:21-31 facilitates this move, as it simultaneously "gather[s] up the previous argument in terms of the precise notion of freedom," which leads up to the summary of the negative argument in 5:2-12, and also "serves as a pointed entry into the 'parenetic' section of 5:13—6:10" where freedom *from* the Law is focused on "freedom *for* this and that."[31]

I follow Engberg-Pedersen's lead, as I trace how the themes in 4:21—5:1 play out in 5:13—6:10. In Gal 5:13-15, Paul warns that freedom should not be used as an opportunity for the flesh (5:13; cf. 3:3; 4:24, 29). Instead, it should be, ironically, lived out in "servitude" (*douleuō*) to one another through love (5:13). In fact, loving one's neighbor as oneself amounts to a fulfillment of the Law (5:14). Thus, Paul indicates that, even as he opposes the demand of circumcision and Law observance, he simultaneously upholds the Law, or, as Barclay puts it, Paul understands that carrying out the love command "actually fulfils what the Torah envisaged."[32] Initially the Law is fulfilled by love, but as Paul develops the thought, he highlights the Spirit as the means by which the intention of the Law is reached (5:18, 23). Hence, he exhorts the Galatians to walk by the Spirit and not according to flesh (5:16-17). Those who practice the works of the flesh will not

28. Cf. Vouga, *An die Galater*, 124.

29. The connection between 5:13—6:10 and the earlier part of the letter has been much discussed (see Barclay, *Obeying the Truth*, 1-35). I develop my understanding here in structural terms, and in ch. 6 with a more theological focus.

30. Engberg-Pedersen, *Paul and the Stoics*, 133.

31. Engberg-Pedersen, *Paul and the Stoics*, 133-34.

32. Barclay, *Paul and the Gift*, 431; discussed more in ch. 6.

inherit the "Kingdom of God" (5:18–21), but instead "reap corruption" (6:8). Those who belong to Christ have crucified the flesh (5:24), live by the Spirit exhibiting its fruits (5:22–25), and "reap eternal life" (6:8). In Gal 5:26—6:10, Paul applies the descriptions of life in the Spirit directly to the Galatians' communal life,[33] and in doing so defines fulfilling the Law in terms of fulfilling the "law of Christ" (6:2; discussed in chapters 5 and 6). Thus, the freedom that Paul calls the Galatians to align with is now defined in terms of Christ, Spirit, and service of love. In contrast, life according to the flesh is connected to the demand of Law observance, as the last paragraph of the letter indicates.

In the final paragraph of the letter (6:11–18), Paul first assigns the troublemakers' demand for circumcision to the side of the flesh. Paul states that his opponents actually do not keep the Law, but only seek a good standing, or an occasion to boast, by the circumcision of the Galatians' flesh (6:12–13). Ironically, rather than crucifying their flesh (5:24), Paul interprets the troublemakers' motive to be the avoidance of persecution for the sake of the cross (6:12). Furthermore, Paul separates himself from the troublemakers exactly in relation to the cross of Christ, which is the sole focus of Paul's boasting (6:14). The cross marks not only Paul's break with the flesh, but also with the cosmos (6:14; cosmos having here the sense of how the world is organized/perceived). His cosmos is reconfigured; he awards no weight to circumcision or uncircumcision in the reality of the "new creation" (*kainē ktisis*) (6:15). Paul blesses those who follow this standard (*kanōn*) with peace, and yet, instead of proclaiming a curse, as he did on the "troublemakers" (1:8–9), he calls for mercy on the "Israel of God" (6:16; discussed in chapter 6). Finally, Paul requests that the Galatians would no longer burden him, but recognize him as the servant of the crucified Christ (6:17). His final greeting highlights grace as the common ground for Paul and the Galatians to be God's people (6:18).

In summary, the key theme of freedom in Gal 4:21—5:1 becomes the point of departure for the parenetic section that articulates a positive argument about what it means to live in freedom. The antithetical relationship between flesh and Spirit that first appeared in 3:3, and was part of the characteristics of the two different "genealogies" in 4:21—5:1, becomes the central framework for defining the way of life in freedom. The relationship between Law observance and faith in Christ, which has been the central point of contention throughout the letter that was also addressed in 4:21—5:1, is further developed. On the one hand, the antithetical relationship

---

33. Cf. Barclay: "[i]t is striking how many of these qualities [fruit of the Spirit in 5:22–23] are given concrete form in the communal maxims that follow (5:26—6:10)" (*Paul and the Gift*, 430).

between the demand of circumcision (and implied Law observance) and the grace of Christ is upheld, but, on the other hand, Paul now demonstrates that it is actually through faith in Christ that the Law is fulfilled by those who serve one another in love by the Spirit. Finally, the issue of inheritance that was configured in 4:29-30 by the two representative sons—the one born of the Spirit and the one born of the flesh—is developed in the same terms of Spirit and flesh in relation to inheriting the Kingdom of God and eternal life (5:23; 6:8), or being outside of this inheritance and reaping corruption (5:23; 6:8). Hence, 4:21—5:1 is a pivotal passage that facilitates the development of the argument from what has preceded to how Paul finishes it: "[4:21—5:1] connects the themes of identity in 3:6-4:7 with the concerns for behavior in the Galatian congregations in 5:13-6:10";[34] and "the argument about 'genetic identity' in 4:21-5:1 anticipates the ethical outworking of that identity in 5:1-6:10."[35]

Structural Analysis of Galatians 4:21—5:1

In this section, I analyze the structure of Gal 4:21—5:1 in terms of the flow of thought, allegorical correspondences, integration of Scripture, and thematic connections.

My structural analysis of Gal 4:21—5:1 follows a rough division, in which the passage can be understood to progress in three stages:[36]

1. Gal 4:21-23 introduces the passage and lays out why and how the Abraham narrative is drawn to speak to the situation at hand.

2. Gal 4:24-28 is the central section that offers the allegory proper,[37] i.e., establishes the allegorical correspondences.

3. Gal 4:29—5:1 develops the allegory to an exhortation that calls for a decision.

The initial question in 4:21—tell me you who want to be under the Law [*nomos*], do you not listen/understand the law [*nomos*]?—introduces the concern of the passage that connects it directly with the occasion of the letter: the danger that the Galatians go "under the Law" via circumcision

---

34. Eastman, *Recovering Paul's Mother Tongue*, 136.

35. Eastman, *Recovering Paul's Mother Tongue*, 135.

36. Cf. Davis, "Allegorically Speaking," 171-74. De Boer has a similar division, but he locates v. 28 in the third rather than the second section: 1) 4:21-23; 2) 4:24-27; and 3) 4:28—5:1 (*Galatians*, 288).

37. Cf. Koch, *Die Schrift*, 204.

(5:2–12; 6:11–13).³⁸ The question also introduces Paul's strategy to counter this misguided desire; ironically, he appeals to the "law."³⁹ The appeal to "listen to the law" indicates that the struggle for the Galatians' devotion is fought largely in the field of scriptural interpretation.⁴⁰ Paul begins the appeal to Scripture (*gegraptai gar*) by a schematic summary from the narrative of the birth of Abraham's two sons (4:22–23) that highlights the dominating themes of the passage:

1. In relation to status; the two mothers present the *slave-free* dichotomy: one is a slave woman (*paidiskē*)⁴¹ and the other is a free woman (*eleuthera*) (4:22).

2. In relation to generation; the two sons present two contrastive ways of generation: the birth of the son from the slave woman is according to *flesh* (*kata sarka*), whereas the birth of the son from the free woman is through *promise* (*di' epangelias*) (4:23).

After the introductory notes, Paul moves on to make allegorical correspondences (*hatina estin allēgoroumena*) (4:24) between the narrative of the two births and present realities.⁴² The two mothers (and implied two different kinds of births), Paul says, are about "two covenants" (*hautai gar eisin duo diathēkai*) (4:24). The structure of the presentation of the two covenants resembles a chiastic flow of thought:⁴³

---

38. Cf. de Boer, *Galatians*, 290. The question in 4:21 is realistic rather than ironic (cf. Barclay, *Obeying the Truth*, 62–63; pace Wilson, *Curse of the Law*, 40–42).

39. See my discussion in ch. 5 on Paul's use of *nomos* in this passage, and for the reason why I translate the first mention of "law" with the capital L and the second with the lower-case l. For a general discussion on the variety in Paul's use of the term *nomos*, see Räisänen, "'Law' of Faith and the Spirit," and Räisänen, "Paul's Word-Play on 'νόμος.'" For a rhetorically sensitive approach to Paul's use of *nomos* in Galatians, see Thurén, *Derhetorizing Paul*, 73–94.

40. Listening to the law connotes an appeal to right interpretation (see Bligh, *Galatians*, 396; Rohde, *an die Galater*, 192; Moo, *Galatians*, 297).

41. *Paidiskē* is a common term used in reference to Hagar in the LXX Genesis narrative.

42. For discussion on *allēgoroumena*, see ch. 5.

43. Bachmann's *Ringkomposition* of 4:21—5:1 resembles mine in the section that I focus on. He also parallels lines from v. 24 and v. 28, although he suggests that slavery and promise are the corresponding concepts (*Anti-Judaism in Galatians?*, 92). Other perceptions of the chiastic structure of the passage also place the "present Jerusalem" and the "Jerusalem above" at the center (e.g., Sellin, "Hagar und Sara," 64–66; Willitts, "Isa 54,1 in Gal 4,24b–27," 198; Longenecker, *Galatians*, 213).

   A Sinai, begetting to slavery (v. 24a; one is from Mount Sinai that bears children to slavery)

      B Hagar + explanatory note (v. 24b–25a; this is Hagar. For [Hagar-] Sinai mountain is in Arabia)[44]

         C Present Jerusalem, slavery (v. 25b; it corresponds with the present Jerusalem, for she is in slavery with her children)

         C' Jerusalem above, freedom (v. 26a; but the Jerusalem above is free)

      B' Our mother + explanatory quotation of Isa 54:1 (v. 26b–27; she is our mother, for it is written: rejoice o' barren one who does not bear children; break forth and shout, the one who does not have labor pains; for the barren one has more children than the one who has a husband)

   A' Promise, children (v. 28; now you, brothers, are children of promise like Isaac)

This structure highlights that the pivotal point is the contrast between the "present Jerusalem" and the "Jerusalem above." But it also helps to identify the two covenants, especially the other covenant that is non-explicit,[45] in terms of the Sinai-covenant and the covenant of "promise."[46]

The first covenant, Sinai/Law, has a double allegorical correspondence. The first level of correspondence is with Hagar (*hētis estin hagar*) (4:24b). This is initially established by Paul's assertion that the Sinai covenant (Law) leads to slavery (4:24), which corresponds with the realities he has associated with Hagar, the "slave woman" (*paidiskē*) (4:22–23).[47] At this point, Paul adds an explanatory note (4:25a) that capitalizes on the geographical connection between Hagar, Sinai, and Arabia. This demonstrates Paul's command of a common feature in the allegorical technique that invites an engagement with

---

44. See Appendix for text critical discussion on this line.

45. Standhartinger claims that Paul fails to present any other covenant ("Zur Freiheit," 297). The other covenant is not explicitly mentioned, or clearly introduced with the expected *men . . . de* construction, unless the *de* in 4:26 or 28 is counted; cf. Carlson's suggestion that the *de* in 4:26 indicates the beginning of the second covenant, but notes that "it does not present a precisely parallel construction to the μὲν clause" ("'For Sinai,'" 85). Since the *men . . . de* construction is not decisive, it is the structure of the passage, the chiastic flow of thought, that guides the reader to make the identification. Recognizing the covenants as Law and promise is supported by Paul's earlier designation of the promise as being a covenant that is in tension with the Law in 3:15–18.

46. Cf. Bachmann, *Anti-Judaism in Galatians?*, 92. Pace Sellin who pairs 4:24b–25a (Hagar-Sinai) with 4:27 (Isa 54:1) ("Hagar und Sara," 66).

47. Cf. de Boer, *Galatians*, 299.

the deeper meaning of Scripture (see chapters 5 and 6). Paul then develops the allegorical line/column (*systoikhei*) of the first covenant of the Law (Sinai) and Hagar with the "present Jerusalem" (*nyn ierousalēm*) (4:25b). Again, this correspondence is explained by the "fact" that the "present Jerusalem" is in slavery with her children (4:25b). Thus, Standhartinger rightly observes that the concept of slavery binds together this first covenantal line (covenant from Sinai, Hagar, and present Jerusalem).[48]

In a chiastic fashion, Paul begins the second allegorical line of the other covenant from a contrast with the end point of the line of the first covenant. He contrasts the "present Jerusalem" with the "Jerusalem above" (*anō ierousalēm*) that is free (4:26a). The expected next move would be a connection from "Jerusalem above" to the free woman, Sarah, but Paul does not go there. This omission is to be noted for its possible significance in Paul's theological logic (see chapter 6). Instead, Paul identifies the "Jerusalem above" as "our mother" (4:26b). Furthermore, the reason for this identification is given in the explanatory note (*gegraptai gar*) that is a verbatim quotation of the LXX rendering of Isa 54:1 (4:27). The quotation presents the "mother" Paul is talking about, and gives the reason why she is the "mother" of the believers in Jesus. The quotation highlights the "miraculous" birth of many children to a barren and desolate woman—her children are more numerous than those of the one who has a husband. Paul finishes the allegorical line of the other covenant by moving from the many children of the barren woman to identifying the Galatians as the children of promise like Isaac (4:28). With this move, Paul completes the chiastic presentation of the two covenants.[49] But 4:28 functions also as a transitional line. By referring to Isaac, Paul returns back to the Abraham narrative, but now with the focus

---

48. Standhartinger, "Zur Freiheit," 297. Cf. Wolter, "Das Israelproblem," 12. Moo also suggests that the *gar* in 4:25b could be taken as causative: "the Hagar Sinai mountain represents the present Jerusalem, *because* it (like Hagar) is in slavery" (*Galatians*, 304; emphasis original).

49. Cf. Koch who understands 4:28 to flow logically from the preceding argumentation as the result (*Ergebnis*) (*Die Schrift*, 209); also Dunn: "verse 28 effectively rounds off and concludes the exposition" (*Galatians*, 256). Burton also takes the *de* in a continuative sense (*Galatians*, 265). Some take 4:28 as beginning a new stage with *de* signifying a shift to a new section ("now"), and the *hymeis* beginning the direct address (e.g., Moo, *Galatians*, 308). In a tightly knit and condensed argument, it seems best to avoid hard and fast boundaries. Gal 4:28 is best understood as a *Janus*—looking backwards and forwards. Besides preparing for what follows, 4:28 completes the allegorical correspondences in vv. 24–28 by connecting the mother with her children—it explicitly designates the Galatians as "children of the promise" that is logically connected to their identification with their mother, the "Jerusalem above." Furthermore, the designation "children of *promise*" (and not of Spirit, cf. 4:29) looks backwards to the son of the "free woman" who was generated by promise (4:23).

shifting from the two mothers to the two sons and two modes of generation. This prepares for the exhortative section (4:29—5:1) that works out of the contrast Paul set between the two covenants.

In Gal 4:29, Paul begins to apply the allegory to the present "conflict" in Galatia with the final exhortation in view. Just as then the one born according to flesh "persecuted" (*diōkō*) the one born according to Spirit, so also now (4:29). That Paul chooses to depict the conflict in terms of flesh and Spirit is again an important signal of his theological framework. Here, the Spirit replaces the earlier category of promise (4:23, 28), indicating that these two are closely related in Paul's theological logic (see chapter 6). Paul uses a slightly modified quotation from the Abraham narrative (LXX Gen 21:10) to sound his concluding exhortation: "cast out the slave woman and her son" (4:30a).[50] Because Hagar (the slave woman) corresponds with the covenant of Sinai, Ishmael (the one born according to flesh) represents those who base their existence on the Law. Thus, continuing in allegorical mode, Paul applies the scriptural command not as a literal command to expel the "troublemakers" from the congregations, but more so to reject what they represent.[51] He calls the Galatians to stand firm in their identity as children of promise like Isaac, and to "expel" their desire (and to resist the pressure) to come "under the Law" that has been identified with Hagar/Ishmael.[52] The quotation also gives the reason for the command, and thus presents the choice in terms of acquiring inheritance: "for by no means shall the son of the slave woman inherit with the son of the free" (4:30b). Hence, in 4:29–30, Paul brings the two contrastive covenants—"genealogical lines"—to their two contrastive ends in relation to the inheritance. The allegorical line from "Hagar"/Sinai produces children of the flesh—children of the "present Jerusalem"—and leads to slavery and *exclusion* from the inheritance, whereas the line from the "free mother" produces children of promise and Spirit, and leads to freedom and *inclusion* in the inheritance.

---

50. Paul changes *my son Isaac* (*tou huiou mou isaak*) to *the son of the free woman* (*tou huiou tēs eleutheras*) to emphasize the theme of freedom, and to make it the voice of Scripture rather than of Sarah.

51. Cf. Di Mattei, "Paul's Allegory," 121.

52. Cf. Stanhartinger, "Zur Freiheit," 300. De Boer is ambiguous in how concrete terms the decision should be understood: literal expulsion of the "new preachers," or "the Galatians are to reject the message and the missionary efforts of the new preachers active in Galatia" (*Galatians*, 308). I favor the latter, since it fits better the flow of thought that continues in 4:31—5:1, but I agree with Wright that the cited scriptural command has also the potential of issuing a disciplinary social act: "'[y]ou must *reject* the alternative teaching, and *eject* those who are teaching it'" (*PFG*, 1137; emphasis original).

In Gal 4:31, Paul adds an emphatic note to the exhortation. With the stark incompatibility of the two sons—two covenantal lines—and with the exclusion of the son of the flesh/slave from the inheritance in view, Paul reinforces the Galatian believers' identity by emphasizing first that they do not belong to the "slave woman," but are children of the "free woman" (4:31). The "free woman," at this point, is not simply a reference to Sarah, as the title has been attached to the allegorical referents of the "Jerusalem above" and the barren-made-fruitful woman of Isa 54:1 (see chapter 6).[53] Furthermore, the flow of thought (indicated by *dio*)[54] suggests that it is the prior experience of the inheritance by the Galatians (by the promise [4:23, 28], and Spirit [4:29]) that shapes the logic that identifies them with this "free woman." The emphatic note struck in 4:31 is played in reverse in the last verse of the passage where Paul rounds up the argument with a concluding statement that emphasizes first the freedom to which Christ has liberated the believers, and, due to that reality (*oun*), sounds the command not to submit to a "yoke of slavery" (5:1).[55] This command develops the earlier "allegorical" scriptural exhortation (4:30), and puts the decision in stark terms to the Galatians who desire to come "under the Law" (4:21): they are to stand firm in the freedom Christ has given, and not be led to slavery by coming "under the Law."[56]

The scholarly opinion is divided whether to include 5:1 in this passage (e.g., Barclay, Martyn, Wright) or with the following (e.g., Betz, Dunn, Hansen). There are at least three reasons why I think 5:1 is more naturally connected to what precedes it, and yet it also acts as a transitional verse for the continuation of the argument:

1. There is no indication of a break from what precedes it, but rather, the break comes in 5:2 with the particle *ide* (look).

---

53. Cf. de Boer: "[b]elievers in Christ ('we') are thus children of 'the free woman,' allegorically understood as this Jerusalem above (v.26)" (*Galatians*, 308).

54. *Dio* indicates an inference that Paul is drawing. Betz thinks it draws a conclusion to the whole argument of the *probatio* (*Galatians*, 251), but most see it as drawing together the argument of this passage (e.g., Longenecker, *Galatians*, 218; Mußner, *Der Galaterbrief*, 333; Oepke, *an die Galater*, 152–53). I think it might even be more specifically focused on drawing together vv. 29–30, although with reference to the preceding verses. The main thing is that vv. 29–30 should not be seen as parenthetical (pace de Boer, *Galatians*, 306–9), because that would fail to follow the flow of thought that the identity of the Galatians can be reinforced in 4:31 because it has been configured around the "inheritance" in 4:30.

55. Cf. Vouga on 5:1: "Die Logik verbindet Indikativ u. Imperativ [the logic binds together indicative and imperative]" (*An die Galater*, 120).

56. Cf. Wilk, *Die Bedeutung*, 90.

2. The use of the first person plural in 5:1a connects it intimately with the claim in 4:31 and keeps the flow.
3. With its emphasis on freedom and slavery, 5:1 is thematically connected to 4:21–31 rather than to what immediately follows in 5:2–12.

In conclusion, my structural analysis of Gal 4:21—5:1 has followed how Paul constructs allegorically two contrasting "covenants." The first is the covenant from Sinai that corresponds to Hagar/Ishmael and the "present Jerusalem," and it is characterized with the themes of slavery and flesh. The second covenant is that of promise, and it corresponds to the mother "Jerusalem above" and the barren-made-fruitful woman of Isa 54:1, and it is characterized with the themes of freedom and the Spirit. The second covenant is ultimately defined in relation to Christ, and both covenants are finally configured around inheritance. Hence, I aim to capture in chapters 3–6 the vision and logic that underlies these two covenantal lines, as I ask in particular:

- How can Paul make the Law/Sinai correspond with Hagar?
- How are the Law and flesh related with the "present Jerusalem" and slavery?
- How do the themes of promise, Spirit, and Christ work together in generating the children of the "Jerusalem above" that is free?
- What does Paul refer to by talking about slavery and freedom?
- What is the inheritance?

The structural analysis has also indicated that the central point of the argument of Gal 4:21—5:1 revolves around the "present Jerusalem" and the "Jerusalem above." The Jerusalem above is the starting point of the other covenant and the Galatians' identification with it. The Galatians are to embrace their identity both as belonging to the "Jerusalem above" and as being "children of promise" like Isaac. Hence, I ask:

- What do the "Jerusalem above" and the "present Jerusalem" refer to?
- What does the promise in 4:28 refer to?
- How can Paul call the Galatian believers children of promise "like Isaac"?

The two key identifications signal also the two explicit scriptural intertexts that are woven into the flow of the argument. Paul draws from the narrative of the births of Abraham's two sons (Gen 11–22) by schematically summarizing features from it, and quoting Gen 21:10 in Gal 4:30. The other explicit intertext is the quotation of Isa 54:1 in Gal 4:27 that is structurally situated in the middle of the two key identifications of the Galatian believers. Hence, I probe after the hermeneutical dimension in Paul's theological vision and logic with questions that relate to the intertexts:

- How do the narrative of the births of Abraham's two sons and the Isaianic vision of restoration, encapsulated in Isa 54:1, function in Paul's vision and logic?
- What is the relationship between these two intertexts?

Chapters 3–4 of this book give an in-depth analysis of the theological potential in the two intertexts, and chapter 5 explores the hermeneutic in Paul's re-appropriation of the potential of these texts. In chapter 6, the results of those investigations are applied to an intertextual reading of Gal 4:21—5:1 to capture Paul's theological vision and logic in the letter as a whole.

3

The Theological Potential in the Abraham Narrative

The Method

I COME TO GENESIS with Pauline interests in mind. This has at least three implications. First, it directs my attention to elements in the narrative that relate to Paul's interests in Galatians in order to facilitate a robust and in-depth intertextual reading of Gal 4:21—5:1 in chapter 6. Accordingly, my analysis of the Abraham narrative is centered on the *births of Abraham's two sons*. I also analyze the theme of *the promise of blessing to all the nations*, and the issue about *circumcision and the identity of the people of God* in relation to Ishmael and Isaac. My aim, however, is not to exercise a flat Pauline reading of the text of Genesis, but to respect its integrity in order to discern how Paul utilizes the potential of the text, i.e., does Paul go with or against the grain of the text?

Second, although I recognize that there were many ways in which Jews were reading the Abraham narrative before and around Paul's time, I do not engage in either a comparative study between Paul and other Second Temple Jewish texts (except in a limited way with Philo's allegorical practice in chapter 5), or an exploration of other aspects of the narrative with regard to other Jewish interests. I only mention here two points where Paul's interests appear to be distinctive. First, Paul focuses on Abraham's faith as the grounds for his right-relatedness with God, and distinguishes it from Law observance (Gal 3:1–18; cf. Rom 4); whereas some other Jewish interpreters were interested to present Abraham as an example of a Torah observant Jew. Thus, both the writer of Jubilees and Philo attempt to explain the chronological discrepancy in the claim that Abraham followed the Law of Moses *before* the time of Moses in their own distinctive ways. The book of Jubilees presents the Law in "heavenly" terms (transcending Mosaic confines) to argue that it was accessible to Abraham before it was given to Moses at Sinai.¹ Philo uses Abraham's conformity to the Law as evidence that the Mosaic Law conforms to the unwritten law of nature that was already available to Abraham (*Abr.* 3–6; 60–61; *Opif.* 3). A second example of Paul's distinctive interest is his emphasis on the Abrahamic promise of blessing to all the nations; whereas there is no reception history of Gen 12:3 in the Dead Sea Scrolls, which is most likely due to a conscious outlook that excluded the Gentiles from the covenantal blessings (this outlook is also shared in other Jewish texts, e.g., Jubilees) and not because of a silence of evidence.²

The third implication of approaching the Abraham narrative with Pauline interests is the assumption that Paul was not aware of questions about different compositional strands of the Pentateuch.³ Thus, my analysis operates on the "final form" of the text that is witnessed primarily in the LXX, but also in the MT.⁴ Paul quotes Gen 21:10 in Gal 4:30 from the LXX (with his own modifications), but the possibility must be entertained that Paul can also operate with Hebrew (cf. Acts 21:37—22:1 portrayal of Paul as being bilingual),⁵ and occasionally demonstrates, possibly his own, Hebraic revisions of the Greek text.⁶ It is plausible that Paul, as a self-

---

1. The Law is released from Mosaic confines in Jubilees with the repeated emphasis on it existing in the heavenly tablets, e.g., law of circumcision (Jub. 15:25), and it being mediated by angelic beings (e.g., Jub. 1:27—2:33 to Moses; 4:18 to Enoch). In Jub. 12:25–27 Abraham is enabled to understand and speak Hebrew, the language of creation, to read the books of his fathers. Thus, in Jub. 21:10 Abraham accredits his knowledge of the laws to the reading of the words of Enoch and Noah. Jub. 4:17–18 describes how Enoch received revelation concerning calendrical observances. Chs. 6–7 describe the laws that were made known to Noah. Thus, the Law predated Moses, at least in regard to the aspects that Jubilees highlights (calendrical observances, circumcision, food laws).

2. Popović, "Abraham and the Nations in the Dead Sea Scrolls," 102–3.

3. Although source critical questions do not guide my investigation, I appreciate the observations of the approach. Source critical analysis points to features of the text (similarities between accounts, tensions in the text, etc.) that are important to recognize even when the focus is on the final form of the text.

4. I recognize that the LXX is not a simple entity or a stable text. I use LXX here as a shorthand for the fluid tradition of the Greek translations (Old Greek) of the Hebrew Bible, a work that began in mid 300 BCE. I follow the LXX Göttingen edition for best available access to the Old Greek text that Paul possibly used. The MT (in the BHS) is the most comprehensive witness to the possible Hebrew text that was available to Paul, but I recognize that the MT might reflect a different Hebrew text (*Vorlage*) to that of the LXX translator, and to what Paul used. I have not included in my analysis texts from Qumran or the Targums, but I do occasionally note their contribution to the discussion.

5. Cf. Harmon, *She Must*, 25.

6. For discussion, see Stanley (*Paul and the Language of Scripture*) who maintains

confessed Pharisee, was trained with the Hebrew Scriptures (Gal 1:13-14; Phil 3:5-6; cf. Acts 22:3; 23:6; 26:4-5),[7] and thus, although my analysis is focused on the Greek text that Paul uses in Galatians, I also consult the Hebrew. My aim is to follow Paul's thought to the matrix of Scripture that he has engaged (Greek and Hebrew), and not only to the text that he is using (Greek) in his communication in the Gentile mission. Thus, I note the relevant differences between the LXX and the MT as I analyze the theological potential in the Abraham narrative.[8]

Since my focus is on the final form of the text of Genesis 11-22, I approach it with insights gained from narrative criticism. I present here some features of the narrative approach that are important for my analysis.

Berlin compares narrative to art and to the task of representation, in which *relationships* rather than absolutes matter: "[t]here is no correct size for painting a house or a flower. It depends on what else is in the picture, and where in the picture it is."[9] Thus, relationships are the clues for interpretation.[10] Berlin supplies several insights for how biblical narratives set up the relationships that should guide its interpretation:

a. *Narrative analogy*—the reading of one story in terms of another.[11] A prevalent feature in my analysis of the Abraham narrative is to establish relationships between accounts that elucidate one another (e.g., chapters 12 // 22; 16 // 21). I also note analogies that extend beyond the Abraham narrative.

---

that Paul used existing Hebraic revisions (also Koch, "Quotations," 223-40, especially pages 238-40). Hengel suggests that Paul made himself the revised text he worked from (*Septuagint as Christian Scripture*, 83, 89). Whether Paul used an already revised Greek text, or made his own revisions is beyond the scope of this research. Nevertheless, it is important to recognize that Paul mainly operates with the Greek, but also potentially had the resource to read Hebrew.

7. Cf. Davies, *Paul and Rabbinic Judaism*, 1-16. Paul's reading of Scripture in Hebrew is a debated question, which is left open by many scholars (see discussions in Horn, *Paulus Handbuch*, 66-75, 479-82).

8. I offer in the body of my text mostly quotations from the LXX, but include the MT when the Hebrew words become important in the discussion. Otherwise, I note significant differences with the Hebrew text in the footnotes. My own sense is that the LXX translator of Genesis attempted a very literal translation, but nevertheless could not retain the features that only the Hebrew language facilitates. This is supported by evidence that the LXX reading accords occasionally closely with the Hebrew text preserved in Qumran. Thus, it is possible that the LXX translator did not have the exact same *Vorlage* as the MT. See an example in Thiessen, "Text of Genesis 17:14," 628-29.

9. Berlin, *Poetics*, 135.
10. Berlin, *Poetics*, 136.
11. Berlin, *Poetics*, 136.

b. *Character contrasts*—"[c]haracters, especially main characters, in the Bible tend not to be absolutes. Our perception and evaluation of them comes through contrasts with other characters, with their earlier selves, or with the reader's expectation."[12] This is crucial for analyzing the significance of Ishmael in relation to Isaac. Also, the development of Abraham's character, and the contrast with the people of Babel is important in order to capture the narrative point about Abraham's relationship to God and his significance for humanity.

c. *Repetition*, and variations on it—"it calls attention to the similarity of two things or utterances, and may also be calling attention to their differences."[13] This relates to capturing the narrative point of view.[14]

Alter elaborates on the idea of repetition and proposes "a scale of repetitive structuring and focusing devices" that run from smaller elements to larger ones: *Leitwort*, motif, theme, sequence of actions, and type scenes.[15] The following are relevant in my analysis:

1. *Leitwort*—repetition that explores the semantic range and different forms of the word-root; includes word-play that involves phonetic relatives. This is important in capturing the significance of Isaac's birth that "plays" with his name.

2. *Theme*—a leading idea that "is made evident in some recurring pattern, and that is often associated with one or more *Leitwörter*" or with a motif (a recurring concrete image, sensory quality, action, or object).[16] This is relevant in my analysis of the theme of blessing to the nations that includes a recurring pattern in the promise of the great nation and blessing to all the nations, and which is connected with the two *Leitwörter* blessing and seed.

3. *Sequence of action*—a pattern of action with "some intensification or increment from one occurrence to the other, usually concluding either in climax or a reversal."[17] This is important in connecting Abra-

---

12. Berlin, *Poetics*, 136.

13. Berlin, *Poetics*, 136. Alter adds emphasis on the differences: "what you have to look for more frequently is the small but revealing differences in the seeming similarities, the nodes of emergent new meanings in the pattern of regular expectations created by explicit repetition" (*Art of Biblical Narrative*, 97). Thus, e.g., the differences in the repeated promise of the blessing formula are important to note (e.g., in you; in your seed).

14. Berlin, *Poetics*, 136.
15. Alter, *Art of Biblical Narrative*, 95–96.
16. Alter, *Art of Biblical Narrative*, 95.
17. Alter, *Art of Biblical Narrative*, 96.

ham with what precedes him (Babel), but also within the Abraham narrative to discern the distinctions between the covenants (Gen 15 and 17+22) that have a certain pattern of action (establishing the covenant followed by ratification that includes a sacrifice).

Berlin also points to the biblical narrative "technique of leaving gaps,"[18] and connects it to the artistic principle where "the suggestion of a thing may be more convincing than a detailed portrayal of it."[19] This suggestive technique invites the reader to fill in the picture.[20] Besides being a technique to make the representation more convincingly realistic, it also lends the potential of the text for the "painting" of various kinds of "pictures." While recognizing the potential of other kinds of pictures, I paint a picture in the following analysis that highlights the births of Abraham's two sons, Ishmael and Isaac, as the focal point for the interpretation of other important themes of the narrative. This is done to uncover the theological potential in the narrative for Paul's application in Gal 4:21—5:1. In doing this, I do not claim to give the right reading or the historically understood original meaning of Genesis, but I aim to elucidate the potential of the text that is relevant when reading Paul.

The Big Picture

The calling of Abraham is a pivotal moment in the book of Genesis and also in the whole of Scripture.[21] It can be viewed as the inception of new creation—the beginning of a movement to generate a new humanity. To capture the significance of Abraham's call, it must be placed first in the context of the preceding narrative. Cassuto draws out the significance in the connection between Abraham and Noah:

> According to the genealogy in Gen. xi, Abram belongs to the tenth generation of the line of Shem the son of Noah. Just as in the tenth generation after Adam there arose Noah, a wholly righteous man who was privileged to become the father of the new humanity after the Flood, so in the tenth generation after

---

18. Berlin, *Poetics*, 137.
19. Berlin, *Poetics*, 136.
20. Berlin, *Poetics*, 137.
21. Von Rad, *Genesis*, 149. Also Williamson, *Abraham, Israel and the Nations*, 220. Although their names are changed to Abraham and Sarah in Gen 17, I use them consistenly throughout for clarity's sake.

Noah, Abram was born, the chosen of the Lord who was to become the father of a spiritually renewed mankind [sic].[22]

The need for the "spiritual renewal of humanity" comes to the fore, as the Abraham narrative emerges from the fallout of the tower of Babel—humanity's autonomous attempt to make a great name for itself, to reach the heavens and build a human community independent of God (11:1–4).[23] This results not in a flourishing society, but in disintegration—humanity is not only alienated from God, but also from each other (11:5–9): "[l]inguistic differentiation is now seen as expressive of non-communication, an aspect of alienation."[24] This is portrayed as a judgment of God on sinful rebellion. As von Rad eloquently expresses, the narrative leading up to Abraham raises an urgent question: "Is God's relationship to the nations now finally broken; is God's gracious forbearance now exhausted; has God rejected the nations in wrath forever?"[25]

Levenson observes that the pattern of "human rebellion followed by divine punishment, which is then tempered by divine forbearance" is broken "with the Tower of Babel, the last narrative before the introduction of Abram."[26] Instead of including "a note of grace to leaven the dire sentence of international incomprehension and universal exile," what follows offers "a new beginning" that is "not simply a tempering of the note of judgment but a reversal of it."[27] Thus, the promise to Abraham in Gen 12:1–3 (I will make you into a great nation; I will bless you and make your name great; you will be a blessing; all the families of the earth shall be blessed in you) can be viewed as a promise of a re-creation of humanity: "the theme of blessing, underscored fourfold in the poem above, reverses the theme of punishment and curse that dominates from the story of Adam and Eve through that of the Tower of Babel. What is more, God promises to do for Abraham what the builders of that tower catastrophically failed to do for themselves—to grant him a great name (compare 11:4)."[28] Thus, Abraham becomes the "patriarchal figure" in the promise to bring blessing to humanity. In contrast to the independent

---

22. Cassuto, *Genesis*, 291.
23. Cf. Grüneberg, *Abraham, Blessing and the Nations*, 131.
24. Blenkinsopp, *Creation, Un-Creation, Re-Creation*, 165.
25. Von Rad, *Genesis*, 149.
26. Levenson, *Inheriting Abraham*, 19.
27. Levenson, *Inheriting Abraham*, 19. However, Grüneberg notes that the narrative does not seem to envision here a reversal of the dispersion of the nations and the restoration of "humanity's original unity," because Abraham is going to become another nation and blessing will come "to the nations in their משפחת" (*Abraham, Blessing and the Nations*, 140). This highlights the need to follow the development of this theme (see below).
28. Levenson, *Inheriting Abraham*, 19.

human attempt to build human society, Abraham is to be the beginning of the new humanity *made by God*. The first lines of the Abraham narrative introduce what the rest of the narrative underlines: the promise and program set in motion in Abraham is an act *of God*.[29]

At the heart of this promise and program is the expectation of progeny, "seed," to carry the promise to its fulfillment. But, as the genealogical introduction of the narrative indicates, this is going to create tension in the fulfillment of the promise: Abraham's wife is barren (11:30)! Hence, Levenson points out that "[t]he man whom God summons with the lofty call of Genesis 12:1–3 is an exceedingly unlikely candidate to father the 'great nation' therein promised."[30] With this, we come to the central theme of the Abraham narrative that is about the births of the two sons: "[t]he Abraham cycle focuses primarily on the question of whether and how Abraham will have descendants."[31] The question of "seed" is also bound up with the questions of how the promise of the "great nation" and the blessing to all the nations will be brought about.

The Births of Ishmael and Isaac

The question that has cast a dark shadow over the promised blessed future for Abraham and the world comes to full expression in Gen 15: Who will inherit from Abraham? How will the promise be carried forward (15:2–3)? The problem has been apparent for the reader since the mention of Sarah's barrenness in 11:30. Abraham has no progeny of his own, and no prospect of having one. The option of transferring the inheritance to Lot, Abraham's nephew, appeared on the horizon until the parting of their ways in Gen 13.[32] In 15:2–3, Abraham bemoans that as the situation stands—him being childless—it will be his servant Eliezer who will inherit from him. The Lord, however, is clear that it will not be the servant but a son who comes from his own body that will be his heir (15:4). As if the promise of a son was not enough, the Lord promises a multitude of descendants as numerous as the stars in the sky (15:5). Despite the promise being against nature and beyond the realm of human possibility because of Sarah, Abraham receives

---

29. Levenson observes that Gen 12:1–3 "foreshadows a key fact about the 'great nation' that will emerge from him: namely, that in this and other biblical texts, its existence is due to the special providence of God rather that the natural human processes of human reproduction and population growth" (*Inheriting Abraham*, 21).

30. Levenson, *Inheriting Abraham*, 21.

31. Grüneberg, *Abraham, Blessing and the Nations*, 9.

32. Cf. Cassuto, *Genesis*, 366.

the promise of descendants in recognition that this is totally dependent on God (and Abraham believed God) (15:6a). This dependence (faith) is what God is looking for; it is the grounds for his right-relatedness with God (*eis dikaiosynēn*) (15:6b): "God has indicated his plan for history, namely, to make of Abraham a great people; Abraham 'has firmly assented' to that, i.e., he took it seriously and adjusted to it. In so doing he adopted, according to God's judgment, the only correct relationship to God."[33] With this, the question about Abraham's heir seems as settled as the promise of the land that is confirmed by an unconditional covenant (15:7–21). But a new twist is added to the fulfillment of the promise that begins at Gen 16.

The Birth of Ishmael

The problem that stood in the way of the fulfillment of the promise of descendants still remained: Sarah had not given birth to a child even after ten years had passed in the promised land (16:3). As the couple had earlier turned to Egypt for help in time of famine (12:10–20),[34] so also now they turn to an Egyptian, Sarah's handmaid Hagar (most likely acquired during their stay in Egypt, cf. Gen 12:16), in their need for a son from Abraham (16:1).[35] In both cases, there is no indication that the moves were divinely initiated or approved,[36] and in light of the past experience in Egypt, this move seems perilous. This time it is Sarah who is in charge, suggesting a perfectly reasonable, theologically argued, and apparently a selfless solution to Abraham's dilemma: "look, the Lord had prevented me from giving birth; therefore have sexual relations with my slave-girl (*paidiskē*) in order that you may beget children from her" (16:2).[37] The suggestion seems in

---

33. Von Rad, *Genesis*, 180.

34. This is an incident that prefigures Israel in Egypt and her exodus with great possessions (Gen 42:1–3; 45:5–11; Exod 12:35–38). Cf. Cassuto, *Genesis*, 334, 336; Levenson, *Death and Resurrection*, 86.

35. Egypt in the Old Testament connotes "house of bondage" (Exod 20:2), "land of oppression" (Exod 3:9), place to be liberated from and not to return to (Deut 17:16) (Noort, "Created in the Image of the Son," 39). But it is also a land of refuge in time of famine (Gen 41:57—42:2; 45:5–11).

36. In a parallel scene, Isaac is deliberately commanded to stay in the promised land with assurance of blessing and a reminder of Abraham's later obedience (Gen 26:1–5).

37. The closing and opening of wombs is a divine prerogative and a recurring theme in the patriarchal narratives that highlights the narrative point of divine "election" and generative power in the formation of the people (cf. Gen 25:21; 29:31; 30:1–2). Sarah's situation is echoed in Rachel's situation (Gen 30:1–3), where Jacob's words bring out the divine prerogative: "Am I myself in the place of God, who has deprived you of the fruit of the womb?" (30:2b).

line with the promise of progeny that has been thus far specified only to be from Abraham, but not particularly from Sarah (15:4). Levenson suggests that in light of the promise at this point of the story, the actions of Abraham and Sarah can be regarded even as a "deed of faithful response," in which they can be viewed "willingly playing their role in the divine-human synergy through which the astonishing providential design will be realized."[38] Abraham agrees with the plan, Sarah gives Hagar as wife to Abraham, and he has sexual relations with her resulting in her conceiving (16:4a). But with the apparently valid arrangement (cf. Gen 30) there comes an immediate complication: tension between the two women—Hagar looks down on Sarah (16:4b). This is the first indication that obtaining an heir from the "slave woman" would bring about unforeseen consequences that only increase in the course of the narrative.

The tension is temporarily resolved, as Abraham hands power to Sarah, and she treats Hagar harshly, resulting in her fleeing from Sarah (16:5-6). But God meets Hagar in the wilderness. An angel of the Lord instructs her to return to Sarah (16:7-9). He also conveys a promise to Hagar: "I will greatly multiply your seed/descendants, and they cannot be counted due to the multitude" (16:10), and that she will bear a son, Ishmael (16:11). Since this promise to Hagar is given in the context of the birth of Abraham's and Hagar's son Ishmael, and since it resembles the one given earlier to Abraham (Gen 13:16 and 15:5), Syrén argues that "Ishmael is, in effect, integrated into Abraham's family and is seen to share in the promise made to the patriarch."[39] So it seems, but in fact, the narrative begins here a "play" on the role of Ishmael in relation to the promise of a great nation from Abraham (12:2), a "play" that the narrative extends up to chapter 21. Hence, the question why Ishmael is brought and kept in the narrative becomes one of the central features in my analysis of the Abraham story.

But even in this hopeful prospect there is tension; the son of Abraham from Hagar will live in hostility with his kinsmen—he shall be a country/wild man [*agroikos anthrōpos*]; his hands shall be against all, the hands of all against him, he shall dwell opposite to all of his brothers (Gen 16:12; cf. 25:18).[40] Nevertheless, it is here in Hagar's womb in the wilderness that the

---

38. Levenson, *Death and Resurrection*, 92.

39. Syrén, *Forsaken First-Born*, 18. However, as von Rad says: "there is not a word about the great promise to Abraham" (*Genesis*, 189). True, there is no explicit reference to the Abrahamic promise, but the language of descendants that cannot be numbered does suggest that some "play" is intended between Ishmael and the promise to Abraham.

40. The Hebrew is even more metaphoric here describing Ishmael as a "wild donkey" (*pere'*). Hence, the interpretation of this verse divides commentators in terms of

son receives his name—he is to be called Ishmael to signify that the Lord had heard Hagar's oppression (16:11b). Ishmael bears in his name the reality of oppression, but also the hope of God attending to it (Ishmael = God hears). After this encounter, Hagar returns and bears a son to Abraham, and Abraham honors Hagar's revelation by naming the son Ishmael (16:15). Like the earlier account of Abraham and Sarah in Egypt, so also this incident prefigures Israel later being in Egypt; paradoxically, Israel's matriarch's harsh treatment of Hagar prefigures the harsh treatment of Israel by Egypt.[41] Thus, the birth of Ishmael, although in a limited way, prefigures the oppression and servitude of Israel and simultaneously the hopeful reality that God attends to the oppression of his people.

But why does God not resolve the tension with this occasion and let Hagar go? This incident already anticipates the final expulsion in Gen 21, and thus begs the question: Why allow it to be repeated? What role does Ishmael have in the narrative that requires his enduring presence all the way to chapter 21? I argue that it is to bring clarity by contrast to what ultimately demarcates the child of promise, and thus also the people to be identified with him.

The Birth of Isaac

Thirteen years after the birth of Ishmael, when Abraham is 99 years old, God affirms and further defines the promise of descendants. God comes to make a covenant with Abraham regarding his offspring and their relationship to God as his people (17:1–21). After the communication of the covenant that promises God's identification with Abraham's descendants, the moment comes for the crucial aspect of this promise to be revealed: this special people will come from the son born from Sarah (17:15–21)![42] This

---

how the relationship is understood, whether hostile, neutral, or positive (see Syrén, *Forsaken First-Born*, 23).

41. Cf. Trible: "[i]ronically the verb depicts here the suffering of a lone Egyptian woman in Canaan, the land of her bondage to the Hebrews. Sarai afflicts Hagar.... Hagar becomes the suffering servant, indeed the precursor of Israel's plight under Pharaoh." Hagar flees from Sarai "even as Israel will flee from Pharaoh" ("Ominous Beginnings," 40). As Trible indicates, the prefigurative function of this episode is also established by a word connection in Hebrew; the same word for oppression (*'nh*) is used of Hagar's oppression and later of the oppression of Israel in Egypt (Exod 4:31). The conceptual connection is present also in the LXX, but the word connection functions only in the Hebrew. There is also a connection with the word "see," as Hagar names God as the one who saw her (*'el ro'i*), and in Exod 4:31 God saw (*ra'ah*) the afflictions of the Israelites.

42. Although there is mention of Abraham's old age, the focus is on the absurdity of

specification of the promise to Sarah is signaled in her name change from Sarai to Sarah (17:15). God promises to bless her, and thus she will give birth to Abraham's son (17:16a). The absurdity in the focus of the promise on Sarah is expressed in Abraham's laughter (and Abraham fell to his face and laughed [he laughed is in Hebrew: *yitskhaq*]; 17:17a): "God often fulfils God's plans by making a mockery of human expectations."[43] It is also expressed in the request that Ishmael could live before God (17:18). This indicates that Abraham had expected, and still maintained that Ishmael could be enough to fulfill the promise about descendants, because the new twist to the fulfillment of the promise was inconceivable to him (17:17b).[44] But God is adamant that Ishmael is not the means for the fulfillment of the promise. Sarah will bear him a son and his name will be Isaac (= he laughs, *yitskhaq*), and it is to him and to the people from him that the covenant is applied (17:19). Nevertheless, God honors Abraham's request and promises to bless Ishmael with fruitfulness (I will cause him to increase, and I will multiply him greatly)—echoing the initial promise to Hagar that is now focused on Ishmael (17:20). The promise regarding Ishmael is even more specific; he will give rise to a "great nation" and father twelve tribes (twelve peoples [*ethnē*] he will beget, and I will give/appoint him as a great nation [*ethnos mega*]; 17:20).[45] Again, the blessing on Ishmael resembles the promise of *the* "great nation" to Abraham (12:2). However, it is repeated that the covenant is only established with Isaac (17:21a). This tension between Ishmael and Isaac in the prospect and promise of the "great nation" opens the potential that their contrast helps to define the identity of God's people (discussed below).

Finally, 23 years after the initial promise of descendants (12:2–3), the fulfillment of that promise is given a due date: Isaac will be born in a year (17:21b)![46] But the narrative is not ready to leap the year. The significance of

---

the birth from Sarah. Abraham's old age is not an obstacle, since he was able to father Ishmael and also later six more sons through Keturah (25:1–4)!

43. Kaminsky, "Humor and the Theology of Hope," 373.

44. Cf. von Rad: "Abraham attempts to side-step what is incomprehensible to him and to direct God's interest (typically!) to what is already certainty, i.e., to Ishmael" (*Genesis*, 198); see also Westermann, *Genesis*, 2:268; Wenham, *Genesis 16–50*, 26.

45. The LXX portrays Ishmael as a "father" of twelve tribes and a great nation, whereas the MT refers to princes or tribal leaders (*nesi'im*) and a great nation (see Wenham, *Genesis 16–50*, 27; Westermann, *Genesis*, 2:270). In Gen 25:13–16 *ethnos* is used to denote Ishmael's twelve sons/tribes. Thus, on the concrete level, they are clearly separate from the twelve sons of Jacob, but on the narrative level there seems to be an intentional contrast to the identity of Israel.

46. See Wenham on the Hebrew expression here for "next year" (*Genesis 16–50*, 47–48).

the birth of Isaac is given more weight and context. Hence, in the next move, the promise of a son from Sarah is repeated and delivered to Sarah herself (18:1–15). God comes to meet Abraham with a message to Sarah (18:9). Sarah is inside the tent but hears the message that she will bear a son next year this season (18:10). Echoing Abraham's earlier response, Sarah also laughs (18:12). The laughter gives expression to the total absurdity of the promise—not only is Sarah still barren, she is also past the time a woman can in any case give birth (18:11–13).[47] The promise has been emphatically stretched beyond any human possibility. This is where the theological crux of the birth of Isaac is revealed—the birth of Isaac is an act *of God*; what is humanly impossible is not impossible with God (18:14). Moreover, while there is absolutely no human possibility in the fulfillment of the promise, the narrative has also demonstrated right after the initial promissory call (12:10–20), and will do so again immediately before the fulfillment of the explicit promise of the son from Sarah (20:1–18), that human activity outside of faith puts the promise only in peril. The contrast highlights the central point: only faith accords with the promise (cf. 15:6 and 22:15–18).

There are still two events that separate this final word of promise from its fulfillment.[48] The first is directly linked with the giving of the final promise, as it is given on the same journey when God is heading towards Sodom and Gomorrah to inspect its iniquity (18:16–21), and execute judgment (18:22—19:29). God chooses to reveal to Abraham the intent of the journey, since he carries the promise of blessing to all nations (18:18). Like the promise in 12:2–3, so also this promise of blessing to the nations is given in the context of the reality of sin and judgment, and invests the birth of Isaac with theological significance for all of humanity (cf. 22:18). This is a reminder that, although Isaac is to inherit the covenant about a special people of God, the scope and purpose of it is to communicate blessing for all the peoples, the "spiritual renewal of humanity" (see discussion below).

The second event between the final promise of the birth of Sarah's son and its fulfillment resembles the earlier Egyptian detour in 12:10–20, but also offers a contrast to the destruction of the unrighteous city of Sodom. Again, out of fear—not of faith—Abraham deceives the men in Gerar concerning his wife Sarah, saying that she is her sister (20:2a, 11). This act of unbelief puts Sarah and the promise in peril; Abimelech the king of Gerar takes her to

---

47. Cf. Wenham, *Genesis 16–50*, 47–48.

48. Alter notes that this "delay" or "interruption" between the annunciation and the fulfillment is unique among other similar accounts that include barrenness-annunciation-fulfillment patterns (Gen 25:19–25; Judg 13; 1 Sam 1; 2 Kgs 4:8–17) ("Sodom as Nexus," 149).

himself (20:2b).⁴⁹ God comes to the rescue, again, and appears to Abimelech in a dream revealing the full truth of Sarah's identity (20:3). With surprising moves, the narrative places Abraham in a negative and Abimelech in a positive light. Abraham thought no one fears God in Gerar—he "assumes that Gerar is another Sodom"⁵⁰—and thus lied due to his "fear of men" nearly causing the destruction of the place (20:9–11),⁵¹ whereas Abimelech had acted in ignorance, and was prevented by God from the actual sin of "touching Sarah" (20:4–6). Abimelech fears God and corrects the situation and reprimands Abraham (20:7–9). Nevertheless, Abraham is recognized as a prophet, and his prayer opens the closed wombs of Abimelech's wives (20:7, 17–18). This incident highlights that Abraham has nothing to add to the fulfillment of the promise of the son from Sarah; his action has nearly forfeited the promise, and, although shown to be a possibility, his prayer has not opened Sarah's womb (cf. 25:21; Isaac's prayer opens Rebekah's womb).

Finally, after 24 years, the day arrives for the long-awaited fulfillment of the promise of a descendant to inherit from Abraham. Isaac is born to Abraham when he is a hundred years old (21:5). The narrative has reached the point where the theology invested in Isaac's birth is pregnant enough (pun intended) to deliver the point: the birth of Isaac is an act *of God*. It proceeds from the power of God's promise: "and the Lord visited Sarah, as he had said, and the Lord did to Sarah as he had spoken, and Sarah bore Abraham a son in his old age at the appointed time as the Lord had said to him" (21:1–2).⁵² The theology is also invested in the boy's name; Abraham names the son of the promise, born of Sarah, Isaac—he laughs (21:3).⁵³ Sarah's response to Isaac's birth completes the significance of the name: "God has made laughter for me, for whoever hears of this will rejoice

---

49. The placement of this event seems very unlikely in line with "historical" sequence, since Sarah is at this point 90 years old and hardly so attractive that Abraham would fear other men to kill him to get her. This highlights that the deliberate narrative positioning of this event here has a point to make.

50. Alter, "Sodom as Nexus," 156.

51. Bruckner notes the irony in Abraham's thought that no one "fears God," when it is actually he himself who "fears men" rather than God (*Implied Law*, 180).

52. The repetition: "as he said," "as he spoke," and "as he spoke," places the emphasis heavily on the promissory act. The lack of mention that Abraham had sexual relations with Sarah (cf. 16:4) also highlights this as an act of God rather than man, although 21:2 specifies that Sarah bore this child *to Abraham*. Philo capitalizes on the "divine begetting of Isaac," as he uses the example of Sarah's giving of birth in his argument that God begets virtues, but gives what he has begotten to the one who would receive (*Cher.* 43–45).

53. Isaac is the only patriarch whose name is not changed. This emphasizes that it is the theology connected with the birth of Isaac that is of significance in his role in the founding of the "great nation."

with me" (21:6).⁵⁴ Thus, the laughter that initially signaled disbelief in the human impossibility of the promise (17:17 and 18:12-13) has now turned into rejoicing due to the act of God. Kaminsky expresses well the theological significance of "laughter" in the narrative:

> One of the major themes in Genesis is God's promises to the patriarchs. There are times when humans are expected to trust in God's promises even when they seem unrealistic or even impossible. Inasmuch as God's promises require the patriarchs to develop a hope that rejects a common-sense worldview, one should not be surprised to find humor in these narratives. . . . And most importantly, it is in the laughter evoked by Isaac that one finds the strength to believe, even when trust in God's promises seems absurd.⁵⁵

Isaac is the son of promise, and his name communicates both absolute human insufficiency and total divine sufficiency that is to shape the character of the people that are to be generated by the promise that is extended to Isaac's "seed" (17:19; 21:12). The "Isaac people" are to be "children of laughter"—people who recognize the insufficiency of human potential in their existence as the people of God, and thus depend solely on the promise of God—they live from faith. This is what Abraham exemplified already in relation to the promise of descendants in 15:6, and demonstrates in the extreme in the final climactic episode in the narrative of the birth of Isaac (22:1-19).

Ishmael Is Excluded

Now Abraham has two sons from two mothers: Ishmael from Hagar and Isaac from Sarah. The tension that was already between Hagar and Sarah (16:4) is now, as was predicted (16:12), reflected between Ishmael and Isaac. At a banquet for the occasion of Isaac's weaning, Sarah notices Ishmael treating Isaac in a contemptuous way that arouses her alarm (21:9).⁵⁶ Thus,

---

54. The Hebrew form of this expression (*kol hashomea' yitskhaq li*) could also be translated with a derogatory sense: "everyone who hears about this will laugh at me." But the context supports the LXX translator's choice to refer to rejoicing with her.

55. Kaminsky, "Humor and the Theology of Hope," 373-74.

56. Trible: "the 'laughing' may suggest usurpation. For Sarah, Ishmael's laughing poses a threat because, by word association, Ishmael is 'Isaacing'. The son of Hagar plays the role of the son of Sarah" ("Ominous Beginnings," 45). This is possible, but there are also other word connections that bring out the negative connotation. The Hebrew word for laughter is used here in the Piel participle form (*metsakheq*), which means to jest/mock. The Piel stem is used also in Gen 19:14 when Lot speaks to his sons-in-law

echoing the earlier incident with Hagar, she asks Abraham: "cast out this slave-girl and her son; for the son of this slave-girl shall not inherit with my son Isaac" (21:10). It is a harsh request, and causes great distress to Abraham (21:11). But it is inevitable. God confirms that Sarah is right—the two sons cannot inherit together; it is only in Isaac that the heirs to the Abrahamic promise are called/named (*kaleō*) (21:12; cf. 17:19 and 25:5–6 in relation to the other sons of Abraham). The absolute incongruity between the child born of human initiative and the child born of the power of God's promise is highlighted in relation to the identity of God's people. However, even though Ishmael is excluded from the covenant, and he and Hagar are expelled from Abraham's household, God affirms that Ishmael will be made into a "great nation" because he is also a son of Abraham (21:13). Thus, the narrative extends the "play" with Ishmael as an alternative construal of the "great nation" up to this point. But the distinction is clear: the covenant people, the true "great nation," is counted from Isaac alone (21:12). Nevertheless, God looks after the needs of the expelled mother and child (21:14–21): "God is not only with Isaac, but also with the wretched Ishmael!"[57]

The Climax: Abraham's Faith and the Near Sacrifice of Isaac

The description of the birth of Isaac in Gen 21 is surprisingly succinct; after all the waiting and suspense, his birth is narrated with only a few, although theologically weighty words. This is in contrast to Gen 22, where the narrative progression slows down and descriptions are detailed and emotional. It is with good reason that this chapter is regarded as the climax, or peak, of the Abraham narrative.[58] It is in the near sacrifice of Isaac that the significance of the promise of Isaac and the faith of Abraham come to sharp focus. Abraham's faith is ultimately defined in relation to the son of promise on the mountain in Moriah.[59] The faith that connects Abraham with the promise has already been present at the beginning of the narrative in Abraham's

---

about the need to escape, and they think he is as one who "jests/mocks." The observed word connections work only in the Hebrew. The LXX uses two different words in its translation of *metsaheq*: *geloiazō* in 19:14; *paizō* in 21:9.

57. Syrén, *Forsaken First-Born*, 44.

58. E.g., Moberly, *Bible, Theology, and Faith*, 72.

59. Levenson objects to the reading of the test of Abraham being about his faith, because he perceives that a traditional Lutheran reading severs faith from action (*Death and Resurrection*, 125–26). But, as my analysis below demonstrates, these two need not be separated, but are joined together as belonging to a life lived in dependence on the sufficiency of God.

obedient response to the command to go to the land that will be shown him, making a break with the past (12:1–4). It is demonstrated in its completion in Abraham's response to the final command to go to the yet-to-be-specified mountain to make an apparent break with the future (22:2–3).[60] In between these two commands is the explicit moment where Abraham's faith is defined in relation to the promise of progeny, and receives a favorable verdict from God (15:4–6). The connection between the promise of a son, and the request to sacrifice that son of promise invites the interpretation of Gen 22 as a further and fuller expression of the faith of Abraham.

After the miraculous, long awaited birth of Isaac, and the expulsion of Ishmael, Abraham is commanded to go to a mountain in Moriah to sacrifice his (only) beloved son (22:1–2).[61] The dynamics for creating a new humanity come into the spotlight on this mountain in the figures of Abraham and Isaac (the focus here is on how Abraham's faith relates to this; I complete the analysis under the next two major headings from other perspectives). First, it is important to recognize that the "test of Abraham" is not just about any child sacrifice, but that it is only meaningful as it relates to Isaac, the son of promise:[62] "Isaac is the child of promise. In him every saving thing that God has promised to do is invested, and guaranteed. The point here is not a natural gift, not even the highest, but rather the disappearance from Abraham's life of the whole promise."[63] Thus, it is striking that Abraham responds to God's command to go sacrifice Isaac without grumbling or hesitation (22:3).[64] There seems no doubt that Abraham is ready for this test (cf. 22:10–11). He has learned in the course of the narrative to trust God in the unexpected ways of his promise. When Isaac unknowingly asks about the sacrifice, Abraham answers in faith: "God will see for himself the lamb for the offering" (22:8). In this trust in the God who "sees better," Abraham

---

60. Levenson argues similarly for the connection between Gen 12 and 22 with additional notes on the similarity in the command (12:2 cf. 22:2) and in the intensification of "the break" (*Death and Resurrection*, 128; cf. Cassuto, *Genesis*, 310).

61. The description of Abraham's relationship with Isaac in 22:2 highlights the unique role he plays. The LXX focuses on Abraham's special love for Isaac (*ton agapēton, hon ēgapēsas*), but, in addition to being beloved, the MT has Isaac as Abraham's *only* (*yekhid*) son. This might be with reference to Ishmael's expulsion, but also to the exclusivity of the promise that is focused on Isaac (17:19; 21:12).

62. Cf. von Rad, *Genesis*, 244.

63. Von Rad, *Genesis*, 244.

64. Levenson argues that the sacrifice of Isaac in Gen 22 is to be read in light of the expulsion of Ishmael in Gen 21 (*Death and Resurrection*, 104–9). I perceive some development. In Gen 21, Abraham objects to Sarah's request to expel Ishmael and Hagar, because it seems too harsh and even ethically wrong to him (21:11, especially the MT). But here, Abraham expresses no objections.

is ready to sacrifice his son even in the face of the absurdity of the command (22:10).⁶⁵ On the one hand, Abraham has learned that taking matters into his own hands, acting on the basis of what a human sees, has resulted only in danger and conflict (Egypt, Hagar, Abimelech). On the other hand, Abraham has seen God's power at work with the impossible promise (11:30; 15:4-5; 17:15-21; 18:9-15; 21:1-7). Thus, he is ready to face the absurdity of the command: to hand Isaac over as dead to the God who gave life to the son from the dead womb of Sarah.⁶⁶ Abraham trusts God to continue the promise of blessing even in the face of the death of the son of promise. Only faith survives in the place of paradox.⁶⁷

Like earlier in 15:6, so also now, Abraham's faith is explicitly commented upon. First, God expresses that it is by Abraham's readiness to sacrifice Isaac that he knows that Abraham *fears* him (22:12). The "fear of future" (15:1-3) and the "fear of men" (20:2, 11) have now turned into the "fear of God." This "fear of God" is an expression of Abraham's faith.⁶⁸ His "fear" expresses his complete dependence on God; he is ready to trust God even when there would be good reason to fear the consequences. This "fear" makes him free to follow through with God's command. Thus, secondly, Abraham's faith is expressed in terms of *obedience* (22:16 "because *you did* this thing"; 22:18 "because *you obeyed* my voice"). The initial faith that Abraham had in receiving the promise (15:6) is the same faith he now needs to live in the fulfillment of the promise. It is a life lived in continuous dependence on the sufficiency of the God of the promise—he needs to finish like he started. The faith that Abraham expresses in the near sacrifice of Isaac also receives the reaffirmation of the promise of blessing (22:17-18). It is to this theme of the promised blessing that I turn next.

---

65. Moberly recognizes that Abraham's words "represent a fundamental trust in God as the context within which adherence to God's will is worked out" (*Bible, Theology, and Faith*, 96). Also: "His response shows the logic of trust in its most sharp and paradoxical form" (120).

66. Pace Levenson, who argues that the essence of the test is to see that Abraham loves God more than Isaac, that Isaac has not become an idol to him (*Death and Resurrection*, 126-28).

67. Although Levenson does not view faith as the key to Abraham's actions (*Death and Resurrection*, 141), he recognizes well the paradoxes of the episode: "[o]ne paradox of the aqedah is that it is Abraham's willingness to give up Isaac that insures the fulfilment of the promise that depends on Isaac. The other paradox is this: though Abraham does not give up his son through sacrifice, he gives him up nonetheless—to the God who gave Isaac life, ordered him slaughtered, and finally grants him his exalted role in the divine plan" (142).

68. Cf. Moberly's argument that "fear of God" is "*the* primary term within the Old Testament for depicting a true and appropriate human response to God," and is "equivalent to 'faith' in Christian parlance" (*Bible, Theology, and Faith*, 79).

Abraham and the Promise of Blessing that Extends to All the Nations

The Abraham narrative proper begins with these pivotal words (Gen 12:1-3):

> "And the Lord said to Abraham: go out from your land, and out from your kinsmen, and out from your father's house into the land that I will show to you.
>
> A And I will make you into a great nation.
>
>   B And I will bless you.
>
>   C And I will make your name great.
>
>   C' And you shall be blessed.[69]
>
>   B' And I will bless those who bless you, and those[70] who curse you I will curse.
>
> A' And all the tribes of the earth will be blessed in you."[71]

These words begin with a command, turn into a promise, and are saturated with blessing. Abraham is to leave his native land to receive the new land that will be shown him; Abraham is to make a break from his kindred to

---

69. In the MT, clause C' begins with the conjunction *waw* + imperative, and is followed by the noun blessing (*weheyeh berakhah*). This is read in different ways; some as a second command (be a blessing); some as an emphatic consequence clause (so that you will affect blessing) (Williamson, *Abraham, Israel and the Nations*, 221). I follow Grüneberg's reading: "the force of the imperative is not to issue a command, but to state further the divine purpose" (*Abraham, Blessing and the Nations*, 146). In any case, the Hebrew signals already here (C') a turn from Abraham being blessed (B) to Abraham becoming a blessing (B'-A'). The LXX has the future verb and an adjective here (you shall be blessed), and turns to the idea of Abraham communicating blessing in the next clause.

70. The MT has here a singular form: "the one who takes you lightly."

71. The LXX has translated the Hebrew with a future passive (*eneulogēthēsontai*; the Greek can also have a middle force). This is the sense that Paul also reads in the promise (Gal 3:8). There is considerable debate as to the proper translation and sense of the Hebrew Niphal form of the verb here and in 18:18, and the Hitpael form in 22:18. The debate has a linguistic level, but the significance is acutely theological; how Israel's role is conceived: instrumental (mediating the blessing), or more substantive (a model people). The linguistic debate is whether there is a passive or a reflexive sense in the verbal forms used for blessing (the middle sense is closely connected to the passive). For an argument for taking it as a reflexive, see Moberly, *Bible, Theology, and Faith*, 123-24; and for the passive, see Grüneberg, *Abraham, Blessing and the Nations*, 65, 177-79, 183-84, 220. For discussion on distinguishing the significance of the use of the Niphal in 12:3 and 18:18 (also 28:14) and the Hitpael in 22:18 (also 26:4), see Williamson, *Abraham, Israel and the Nations*, 227-28.

become the beginning of a new people that will be made out of him. The promise of making Abraham into a great nation precedes the word of blessing, which is otherwise the prominent note. This order can be to emphasize that the promises extend "well beyond Abraham's own life and lifetime," as the promise points to the origins of the nation of Israel.[72] But the order can also indicate a carefully crafted structure, in which I perceive a rough chiasmus.[73] This suggests that the first and last line (A and A') are to be read together—they are the two major dimensions of the promise that the narrative develops. The structure also indicates that Abraham's name being made great (C) and him being blessed (C') are integral in the movement towards his role in mediating blessing to all the nations.[74]

The first movement in the promise is focused on blessing Abraham (B–C'). Although the promise of the great nation (A) precedes the blessing (B), it is logically dependent on it.[75] The blessing reaches both to what precedes and to what follows—it is the enabling source for the promise that Abraham is to be made into a great nation, and that his name is to be made great (C). Thus, Abraham is the antitype of the people of Babel who were building a "great nation" (city) and making their name great (tower) independent of God.

The second movement of the promise is focused on how Abraham will become a blessing (B'–A').[76] Others will "inherit" blessing in relation to him; those who bless him will be blessed by God, while those who curse him will

---

72. Thus Grüneberg (*Abraham, Blessing and the Nations*, 162–63). He also suggests that the lack of an explicit promise of land here might be "to prioritise the people over the land: possession of the land is not a goal in itself, but only insofar as it facilitates the fulfilment of the other promises" (164).

73. Although the poetic quality and carefully crafted structure of 12:1–3 is well recognized (e.g., Alter, *Genesis*, 51; Cassuto, *Genesis*, 312, 315; Wenham, *Genesis 1–15*, 270; Williamson, *Abraham, Israel and the Nations*, 228–29), the possible chiastic structure of vv. 2–3 is not. This might be due to the lack of a clear center, and the fact that B' holds together the two "and" clauses rather than separating them to give a list of seven promises. My reading is not dependent on the chiasmus, since the features that it highlights are also confirmed in the development of the narrative.

74. Commentators usually discuss the meaning of making the name great in terms of fame or reputation in connection with royal ideology where the king's reputation is tied to his subjects' greatness (e.g., Wenham, *Genesis 1–15*, 275–76; Westermann, *Genesis*, 2:150). But a focused analysis on what actually happens to Abram's name rather than his fame points to the development of the theme in Gen 17 that supports my view that making Abram's name great (Abraham) is part of the movement towards the blessing of all the nations.

75. Cf. Westermann, *Genesis*, 2:149.

76. Von Rad expresses the movement in scope thus: "[t]his blessing concerns Abraham first of all; but it also concerns those on the outside who adopt a definite attitude toward this blessing" (*Genesis*, 155).

be cursed by God: "God now brings salvation and judgment into history, and man's [sic] judgment and salvation will be determined by the attitude he adopts toward this work which God intends to do in history."[77] Ultimately, the goal of the promise is that all the tribes/families[78] of the earth will be blessed in Abraham: "God's action proclaimed in the promise to Abraham is not limited to him and his posterity, but reaches its goal only when it includes all the families of the earth."[79]

Thus, Gen 12:1–3 has introduced the main trajectories for the rest of the narrative to develop: the promise and blessing for the formation of a great nation, and the promise of blessing that is to be mediated to all the nations.[80] My analysis focuses on how these two are related.

In Gen 15, the focus is on the blessing for the formation of the great nation. The first part of the chapter (15:1–6) addresses the question of the heir (15:3–4), the key to unlock the promise of a multitude of descendants (15:5) who will inherit the land promised to Abraham's "seed" (12:7; 13:15–17), which is the focus of the second section of the chapter (15:7–21).[81] The promise of descendants and land address together the issue of the great nation.[82] Although Abraham responds to the promise of descendants with faith (15:6), the promise is not settled here but continues its life in the complex narrative development that intertwines the two dimensions of the promise of blessing (great nation and blessing to all the nations). This is not the case with the promise of land; the "unilateral covenant" concerning the land in 15:7–21 seems to settle the question—it will surely be given to Abraham's posterity, although with a delay.[83] The prophetic divine speech

---

77. Von Rad, *Genesis*, 155.

78. The LXX choice of *phylai* (tribes) or in Hebrew *mishpekhot* (families) deserves attention. Grüneberg demonstrates how the Hebrew term can be used to refer to a family, tribe, or whole nation (*Abraham, Blessing and the Nations*, 185). Since the words refer back to the "description of the world's population" in Gen 10, they most likely refer to large units; "perhaps the nations in units defined by consanguinity" (185). The main point is "to make clear that the promise concerns other people however their communities are organised" (186).

79. Westermann, *Genesis*, 2:152. Cassuto: "[w]e have here the first allusion to the concept of universalism inherent in Israel's faith, which would subsequently be developed in the teaching of the prophets" (*Genesis*, 315).

80. Cf. Williamson, *Abraham, Israel and the Nations*, 18. This sets the narrative framework for what follows, although the focus is "mainly on the first stage in the outworking of this programmatic agenda: the establishment of a special line of descendants through which God's promises of nationhood and international blessing will find fulfilment" (18–19).

81. Cf. Williamson, *Abraham, Israel and the Nations*, 123.

82. Cf. Williamson, *Abraham, Israel and the Nations*, 135.

83. There are no obligations put on Abraham, and only God "walks" between the

to Abraham in 15:12–16[84] extends the narrative beyond Abraham to Israel's experience of servitude in Egypt and the exodus,[85] giving the narrative a broader horizon of meaning that supports the discernment of prefigurative elements in it (see ch. 5).

The covenant established in Gen 15 developed the promise of the blessing of the great nation, but left the other trajectory of blessing to all the nations untouched, creating an expectation for its later development.[86] This is what we find in Gen 17 where both trajectories of the promised blessing are present.[87] Abraham is asked to walk with God and be blameless (17:1) as a prerequisite of the covenant God is about to make with him (17:2a).[88] The requirement is followed by a promise of increase (17:2b).

The promissory aspect of the covenant is highlighted, as the initial promise in 17:2 is repeated and further defined: "And, as for me, look, my covenant is with you, and you will be a father of a multitude of nations" (17:4). Abraham's new name is the "sign" of the promise; Abram becomes Abraham—the "father of multitudes" (17:5).[89] The promise is further intensified, as God promises to increase Abraham greatly (LXX) / make him extremely fruitful (MT) (17:6a); indeed, he is to be made into nations (*kai thēsō se eis ethnē*), and kings will proceed from him (17:6b). The intensification of the promise echoes the original blessing on humanity to be fruitful, increase, and rule the earth (Gen 1:28). Hence, this promise (as a development of 12:2–3) suggests that in the making of Abraham's name great, he is designated as a "father" of a regenerated humanity that

---

cut pieces in the ratification ritual (Williamson, *Abraham, Israel and the Nations*, 138).

84. The prophetic divine speech is indicated by the expression of "ecstasy (LXX: *ekstasis*) / deep sleep (MT: *tardemah*) fell to Abraham," and "it was spoken (MT: he spoke) to Abraham."

85. Cf. Levenson: "[i]n the oracle amidst the covenant making ceremony (Gen 15:13–16), in sum, YHWH provides Abram with the interpretation of his own life. Abram has not only been living in anticipation of his unconceived and inconceivable progeny; he has also been proleptically living their life in his" (*Death and Resurrection*, 88).

86. Cf. Williamson, *Abraham, Israel and the Nations*, 140.

87. Cf. Williamson, *Abraham, Israel and the Nations*, 143.

88. Williamson addresses the debate on how the "two covenants" of Gen 15 and 17 are related. The options have been to view them as a development of one single covenant (two stages; ratified and reaffirmed; two different accounts of the same covenant), or as two distinct covenants (*Abraham, Israel and the Nations*, 21). His own reading recognizes that the two are "theologically distinct," but related covenants (25, 212). The introduction to the covenant in Gen 17 is given in the future tense (LXX: *thēsomai*) / imperfect cohortative (MT: *'ettenah*), and hence does not refer back to the covenant already established (145).

89. The meaning of the name comes from a wordplay in Hebrew between *'av-hamon* and *'avraham*.

inherits blessing—a "new Adam" for a new humanity.[90] Since Abraham's great name is a contrast to the "great name" of the builders of Babel, this promise suggests also that the divided humanity will find common ground and blessing via Abraham.[91]

The movement in 17:1–6 has been from the one to the many—from Abraham to a multitude of nations. It was focused on the promissory aspect of the covenant and left its mark in the name of Abraham. But then the narrative makes a sudden shift. The covenant is specified to Abraham's "seed" as a perpetual covenant, and includes the promise of a special relationship between these descendants and God, and the possession of the land of Canaan (17:7–8). This aspect of the covenant relates to the making of the "great nation" from Abraham (a development of 12:2 and 15:1–21). But this perpetual covenant with the "great nation"—a people that God specially identifies with—comes with the strict obligation to keep it by circumcising every male (17:9–10). Thus, circumcision becomes the sign of the covenant that identifies the "great nation" (17:11), a people separate from other peoples.[92] The covenant is to be marked in the flesh (*sarx*) of the males (17:13), and every male that is not marked by circumcision is outside of this covenant (17:14).

The covenant in Gen 17 presents an apparent tension; Abraham is to be a father of a multitude of nations, but only one special people is to be marked as the covenant people.[93] This tension has the potential for distinguishing these two aspects as two covenants: a covenant of promise that

90. Cf. Williamson, *Abraham, Israel and the Nations*, 163. Similarly, Wenham, who also notes that "whereas Adam and Noah were simply commanded 'be fruitful' (qal imperative), God makes Abraham a promise, 'I shall make you fruitful' (hiphil)" (*Genesis 16–50*, 22).

91. To fully appreciate the meaning of Abraham being the "father of many nations" we must wait for its further development in the narrative (see discussion below on Gen 17:16 and 35:11).

92. There is discussion on what is the "sign" role of circumcision. Williamson defines it as a cognition sign—a mnemonic devise—and refutes the idea that it could function as an identity marker, since other nations around Israel practiced circumcision also, and it would not be a readily perceived sign for the outsiders (*Abraham, Israel and the Nations*, 178–81). I agree that circumcision functions as a reminder for Israel of her covenant, but do not follow that it excludes its function also as a boundary marker, since Gen 17 connects it integrally with the formation of a "special people." Jubilees understands that circumcision is what makes Israel separate from the Gentiles (15:25–34); Jub. 15:34 expresses it in the negative: "[a]nd they have provoked and blasphemed inasmuch as they have not done the ordinance of this law because they have made themselves like the gentiles to be removed and be uprooted from the land" (English translation from Charlesworth). The focus of separating Israel from other nations is expressed also at Sinai in the introduction to the giving of the Law (Exod 19:5).

93. Cf. Watson: "the name and the sign are at odds with each other" (*PHF*, 195).

relates to all the nations, and a covenant of circumcision that relates to the "great nation." The double specification for establishing a covenant—first in relation to Abraham's role as the father of many nations (17:4), and then in relation to Abraham's "seed" (17:7)—give textual and contextual warrant for designating them as two distinct and yet interrelated covenants.

The tension is present also in the promise of blessing to Sarah. Echoing the promise to Abraham in Gen 17:1-6, Sarai's name is changed to Sarah (17:15). She is explicitly blessed (*eulogēsō de autēn*) so that she will bear a son, who is in turn to be blessed (*kai eulogēsō auton*) so that nations and kings of nations will proceed from him (17:16).[94] Thus, the new Adam receives the new Eve—Abraham and Sarah are together the designated parents of the new humanity that includes the many nations. Since Sarah (via Isaac) is designated the "mother of many nations," it further defines the meaning of the promise that Abraham will be the "father of many nations": "[o]ne does not grasp the meaning of this promise if one thinks primarily of the Ishmaelites, Edomites, and sons of Keturah (ch. 25.1 ff.); for the descendants about whom these words speak are not to be sought among those who are outside God's covenant, even less since later the same promise is made to Sarah (v.16)."[95] Hence, it becomes apparent that the sense of the "fatherhood" is something other than physical. Williamson argues that the "father of a multitude of nations" is best understood in terms of Abraham being the "mediator of divine blessing."[96] The metaphorical sense is supported especially

---

94. The MT has feminine pronouns in both blessing clauses connecting them with Sarah, whereas the LXX (Rahlfs), the Vulgate, and Syriac have the masculine connected with the second blessing phrase (see BHS apparatus). The Göttingen edition of the LXX has the feminine pronouns in both, but lacks convincing reasons for it: "[t]he majority tradition cannot be correct since the only masculine referent in this section is Abraam who is not referred to at all in a verse entirely devoted to Sarra" (Wevers, *Notes on the Greek Text of Genesis*, 237). This evaluation misses the focus on Isaac who is known to be masculine even though spoken of as *teknon* that is neuter. These different renderings reflect either fluctuation in the text or the challenge of following the complex moves of the text. Nevertheless, the sense of the text is sufficiently clear: "Sarah is brought into the promise, thus preparing the way for the special place of Isaac over against Ishmael" (Westermann, *Genesis*, 2:267).

95. Von Rad, *Genesis*, 194-95. Similarly, Watson, *PHF*, 193.

96. Williamson, *Abraham, Israel and the Nations*, 158. He supports this by tracing the non-biological usage of the term in the Hebrew Bible (e.g., in Gen 45:8 Joseph is the "father of Pharaoh" in a context of Joseph mediating blessing, i.e., preserving life; in Judg 17:10; 18:19 Micah's personal Levite priest being his "father"; in Isa 9:5 the Messiah as "Everlasting Father"; in Job 29:16 Job as the "father of the needy"), and the non-literal usage of the term in reference to the fatherhood of God (e.g., Deut 32:6; Isa 63:16; Jer 3:4, 19; Mal 2:10; Ps 68:6; Ps 89:27; 1 Chr 22:10) (*Abraham, Israel and the Nations*, 158nn47-48). Williamson infers that "there is no *a priori* reason to restrict the international community associated with Abraham to those who are able to trace their

when 17:1–6, 15–21 is read as a development of the promise in 12:2–3 where there is a close connection between the making of Abraham's *name* great and him becoming a blessing, eventually to all the nations.

The Genesis narrative continues to develop the theme of the "fatherhood of Abraham" in terms of him "mediating blessing" to the nations. In Gen 18, the content and purpose of the blessing is further defined. The twofold promise—great nation and all the nations—is reiterated to Abraham (Abraham will become a great and populous [MT: mighty] nation, and all the nations [*panta ta ethnē*; MT: *kol goye*] of the earth will be blessed in him) (18:18) in the context of God moving towards Sodom and Gomorrah to inspect their sin and execute judgement (18:16–21). Abraham is allowed insight into the purposes of God, partly because of the promise that Abraham will be a blessing to all the nations (18:17–18)—he is drawn into the episode to facilitate initial reflection on his role in mediating blessing. Abraham was chosen to be the servant of God (*abraam tou paidos mou*) (18:17), the father of the great nation, and the mediator of blessing to all the nations (18:18), with the knowledge that he will teach his descendants, and they will follow the way of the Lord by doing righteousness and justice (18:19).[97] Wenham notes the significance of this: "its [the promise's] fuller purpose is now stated for the first time: to create a God-fearing community."[98] As a servant of God he also intercedes for the salvation of the city (18:22–33), although it is only Lot that is eventually saved because of Abraham (19:29). Nevertheless, this incident reflects the same reality that occasions the initial promise in 12:2–3: humanity is in need of regeneration because of its sin.[99]

---

genealogical lineage back to the patriarch himself" (*Abraham, Israel and the Nations*, 158.) Also, Watson: "[i]t is all the more remarkable that in Genesis 17 the innumerability motif breaks out of this narrative containment, as the descendants like the dust of the earth or the stars in the sky come to be identified not with the people of Israel but with the 'many nations' of which Abraham is now said to be the father" (*PHF*, 192). Watson connects the fathering of many nations with the promise of blessing to all the families of the earth in Gen 12:3 (193).

97. Cf. Williamson, *Abraham, Israel and the Nations*, 182. The LXX highlights a conditional note, as the promise in 18:18 is predicated on Abraham's actions in 18:19 (for I knew [*ēdein gar*] that). The MT indicates that Abraham was chosen (*ki yeda'tiw*, for I knew him, i.e., chose him) for the purpose (*lema'an*, so that) of teaching and following the ways of the Lord. Nevertheless, also the MT has a conditional note at the end of v. 19: "so that the Lord will bring about to Abraham what he spoke/promised to him."

98. Wenham, *Genesis 16–50*, 50. Bruckner further states that God's purpose in involving Abraham "as a participant in determining justice in this case" is related to training Abraham so that he "will learn to teach this 'way' of determining justice and living righteously" (*Implied Law*, 128).

99. Both the Babel (Gen 11:5–9) and Sodom episodes have God "coming down" to see the situation, and execute judgment on sinful humanity.

The next occasion that develops the theme of mediating blessing to all the nations focuses it on Abraham's "seed." After Abraham has passed the test that required readiness from him to sacrifice Isaac—the son of promise—he receives back not only the son, but also a further affirmation of the promises given earlier (Gen 12, 15, 17, and 18): "I will surely bless you and greatly multiply your seed as the stars of the sky and the sand at the shore of the sea; and your seed will inherit the cities of enemies. And all the nations of the earth shall be blessed in your seed, because you obeyed my voice" (22:17-18). Echoing the conditional character of the twofold promise in 17:1-21 and 18:18-19, the promise of blessing that will generate the great nation, as well as the promise that all the nations will be blessed in Abraham's "seed," is connected to Abraham's obedience (22:16, 18).[100] Williamson argues that the covenant established in Gen 17 is finally ratified in 22:15-18 by the solemn oath of God that follows the sacrifice of the ram (cf. covenant ratification by sacrifice in 15:9-18), and is predicated upon the proved "blamelessness" (17:1) of Abraham in his "fear of God."[101] Whether this is a ratification of the covenant initiated in Gen 17 or its further development, this final reaffirmation of the promise of blessing to all the nations brings together the two dimensions of the promise in 12:2-3, and the covenants in Gen 15 and 17, as *all the nations* are to be blessed *in your seed*.[102]

100. Moberly points out the significance that this is not the first time the promise has been given to Abraham: "Abraham by his obedience has not qualified to be the recipient of blessing, because the promise of blessing had been given to him already" ("Earliest Commentary on the Akedah," 320). He also proposes a creative way to perceive the role of Abraham's obedience in the fulfillment of the promise of blessing: "[a] promise which previously was grounded solely in the will and purpose of YHWH is transformed so that it is now grounded both in the will of YHWH and in the obedience of Abraham. It is not that the divine promise has become contingent upon Abraham's obedience, but that Abraham's obedience has been incorporated into the divine promise. Henceforth Israel owes its existence not just to YHWH but also to Abraham" (320-21).

101. Williamson, *Abraham, Israel and the Nations*, 245-47.

102. Space does not permit the exploration of the potential in Genesis to facilitate Paul's move to refer to Christ as the singular seed of Abraham (Gal 3:16). I offer here some pointers for further investigation. The possibility of reading the "seed" in 22:18 with a singular sense is already opened by the singular pronominal suffix in the Hebrew word for enemies in Gen 22:17 (see Alexander, "Further Observations," 363-67; and Williamson, *Abraham, Israel and the Nations*, 248-50). Thus, the one "seed," who is promised victory over his enemies (22:17b), is distinguished from the manifold "seed" in 22:17a. If this is so, then the blessing for all the nations that follows is most naturally tied to this one "seed" of Abraham. The singular "seed" reading in 22:18 receives support from the allusion to this verse in Ps 72:17 that refers to a royal individual. This royal tone is not foreign to the purview of Genesis. The victorious "seed" in Gen 22:17b can already be viewed as looking forward to a royal figure, and the promises in 17:6, 16 refer to kings coming from Abraham and Sarah/Isaac. Furthermore, in Gen 49:10, the tribe of Judah is identified with the prospect of royal lineage that has implications for the nations that

The further development of the theme of mediating blessing to all the nations in Genesis continues to tie it closely with the "seed" of Abraham—the covenant people of God. When the Abrahamic promise is conveyed to Jacob in Gen 35, it clearly echoes the earlier promise (17:6) to Abraham: "God said to him, I am your God, increase and multiply; nations (LXX: *ethnē*) / nation (MT: *goy*) and gatherings of nations (LXX: *synagōgai ethnōn*, MT: *qehal goyim*) will come out of you, and kings will come out of your loins" (35:11).[103] The striking similarity in context and content between 35:10–12 and 17:4–6, 16 invites them to be read together.[104] The peculiar designation that out of Jacob will come *gatherings of nations* suggests to Lee that "both the physical descendants of Jacob as a nation and a multitude of nations will be associated with Israel."[105] This, together with the idea of Israel's expansion to the whole world in Gen 28:13–14, opens the possibility that the role of Abraham and his "seed" in mediating blessing to all the nations ultimately consists of the nations' inclusion in God's people.[106] To follow the implications of the theological potential that this contains for Paul's vision for Gentile inclusion in his letter to the Galatians must wait for the exploration of how this theme is developed in Isaiah's vision of restoration (see next chapter), but it also requires a focused inquiry on the identity of the people of God that the contrast between Ishmael and Isaac highlights. It is to this that I turn next.

---

opens the possibility for a messianic interpretation (Wenham, *Genesis 16–50*, 478).

103. In Hebrew, the first instance of this promise in Gen 28:3 and the recounting of this promise by Jacob to Joseph in Gen 48:4, has different wording (*qehal 'ammim*). The LXX uses the same designation in all the references. None of these are typical references to the twelve tribes of Israel.

104. Cf. von Rad, *Genesis*, 334; Westermann, *Genesis*, 2:552. Jacob's name change to Israel just prior to the promise resembles the case with Abraham. Also, the name used of God (*'el shadday*) is the same.

105. Lee, *Blessing of Abraham*, 85. In her earlier work, Lee formulated this connection even stronger: "[a]s early as in Genesis, 'Israel' as the 'people of God' is portrayed as consisting of the physical descendants of Jacob—the nation of Israel—and a multitude of nations" ("גוים in Genesis 35:11," 474). Lee also proposes that 35:11 has an eschatological dimension that is captured in the prophets' vision of the nations' gathering to the restored Israel (474–80). I develop this dimension in ch. 4, and the potential it opens up for Paul in chs. 5 and 6.

106. Scott notes Gen 28:13–14 as an example of Old Testament texts where "the land promised as an inheritance to Abraham and his seed extends beyond the borders of Canaan to include the whole world" (*Paul and the Nations*, 62–63). The idea of Israel spreading beyond its borders suggests the nations' inclusion in it (cf. Rom 4:13–18 where Paul reflects on Abraham being the "father of many nations," and interprets Abraham / his "seed" having received a promise that he would inherit the "cosmos").

Circumcision and the Identity of the People of God

I have now offered close readings of most of the material in the Abraham narrative. Based on that work, I engage here a discussion on the topic that is of key interest to Paul in his letter to the Galatians: circumcision and the identity of the people of God.

Genesis 17 is the key chapter for this discussion. I have followed the movements of Gen 17 above, and demonstrated that it is woven with cross-stitches; there is no simple line that defines the covenant of circumcision. The people that would comprise the covenant people are to be counted from Isaac (17:19, 21), but Ishmael is also in the story. In 17:18, Abraham asks the hermeneutically key question about Ishmael living before God, i.e., would Ishmael not do? At this point, the promise of Isaac, and thus the continuation of the covenant, seemed impossible. Hence Abraham's laughter and request that Ishmael would do. In response, while removing Ishmael from the covenant, God also describes Ishmael's future in terms that come strikingly close to the description of the intended covenant people from Isaac. He is to become into a "great nation" and a father of 12 tribes (17:20). He is also circumcised according to the requirements of the covenant. In fact, his circumcision is emphasized more than Abraham's (Ishmael's circumcision is recounted three times in vv. 23, 25, 26; cf. Abraham's only twice in vv. 24 and 26). And yet he does not count! He is excluded from the covenant, and later expelled from Abraham's household so that there would be no mistake as to who is the heir to the Abrahamic promise of *the* "great nation" (21:12).

The tension in the narrative concerning the role of Ishmael as the "circumcised outsider" has evoked differing explanations. Williamson approaches the problem by rephrasing it: "perhaps the question we should be asking is not: 'In what sense was Ishmael excluded from the covenant?' but rather, 'In what sense did this covenant relate uniquely to Isaac?'"[107] For Williamson, the key is the "perpetual covenant" with Isaac; Ishmael "was himself included within the covenant community," but "this covenantal status was not explicitly extended to his progeny, as is clearly so in the case of Isaac."[108] The weakness in this view is that Ishmael himself is not in fact regarded as part of the covenant community, as his expulsion demonstrates.

Thiessen offers another solution that perceives timing as the central point of the circumcision legislation—Ishmael is circumcised wrongly in his thirteenth year, whereas Isaac at the proper eighth day.[109] Furthermore,

---

107. Williamson, *Abraham, Israel and the Nations*, 161.

108. Williamson, *Abraham, Israel and the Nations*, 162.

109. Thiessen recognizes that the timing of circumcision is not the only thing that separates the two sons, but it is the factor that is decisive, since the other aspects are

Thiessen argues that the circumcision legislation is a priestly author's insertion into the narrative with a specific concern:

> Through the category of sacred time, the priestly writer solves the problem created by according covenantal significance to circumcision in a region in which Israel was confronted by the existence of non-Israelite circumcision. The reference to Ishmael's circumcision is not a mistake that unwittingly *undermines the rite's covenantal importance*; rather, it serves as the author's attempt to address the well known fact that non-Israelites, in particular those thought to be descendants of Ishmael, also practice circumcision, and to distinguish their circumcision from Israelite circumcision.[110]

Thiessen recognizes that Ishmael's circumcision can potentially "undermine the rite's covenantal importance." To avoid that conclusion, Ishmael's circumcision must be invalidated on the basis that it does not meet the eighth-day requirement. But the argument is not strong. There is no indication in the narrative that it was wrong to circumcise Ishmael and the other male members of Abraham's household as a response to the given legislation. In fact, the opposite is true—it would have been wrong not to circumcise them. Never in the narrative is Ishmael's wrong-dated circumcision the reason for his expulsion.[111] Another weakness in the argument is the fact that Abraham is also circumcised at a wrong age: 99! Thiessen admits that "no completely satisfactory explanation for this difficulty exists, presumably the priestly writer was not greatly concerned with this problem: no one questioned whether Abraham belonged within the covenant."[112] This wobble in the argument reveals the weakness in the approach: it is asking after the priestly writer's concerns and not looking for narrative intent.[113]

"no fault of his own" (offspring of Hagar, the Egyptian slave, and Ishmael's birth "issues from the uncircumcised penis of *Abram*"), and cannot be remedied (*Contesting Conversion*, 39). This is simply contradictory. Ishmael's circumcision in the thirteenth year is also "no fault of his own," it is done at the moment the legislation is given.

110. Thiessen, *Contesting Conversion*, 35.

111. If the dating of the circumcision is integral to its validity, it would also invalidate the circumcision of the whole generation of Israelites who conquered the promised land (Josh 5:1–8).

112. Thiessen, *Contesting Conversion*, 38.

113. Thiessen presents a possible reading of the material, although I do not find it convincing on the level of narrative intent. The reading he proposes is represented in some strands of Jewish tradition, especially in the book of Jubilees, which Thiessen understands as being written as a reaction to the Hellenizers of Judaism during the Hasmonean period that opened the possibility for Gentiles to "convert" to Judaism via the rite of circumcision: "[f]or the author of *Jubilees*, however, conversion was

Syrén approaches the problem/potential posed by Ishmael's circumcision similarly to Thiessen, but with different conclusions. He perceives an inherent tension between Ishmael's exclusion (17:19–21) and inclusion (17:23–27).[114] Both represent a "retrojection of later conditions in Israel back into the lifetime of Abraham."[115] The exclusive material "would then be an understandable reaction by a redactor concerned about the purity of Israel," whereas the inclusive material would represent concern for "circumcision as an absolute prerequisite for being counted among the true children of Abraham. Through circumcision the marginal groups were allowed into the religious community of Israel."[116] Syrén then postulates that these concerns would have been acute "in the period of the restoration, in which the many conflicts between the various strands within the Jewish community are given different emphases in different biblical books. . . . The question of national identity became urgent."[117] The question of national identity was not only forced by foreign influence, but also by the reality of the different groups within Israel: the people who remained in the land of Judah and those outside in exile/diaspora.[118] Whether or not this explains the genesis of the Ishmael tradition, Syrén's analysis demonstrates the potential of the Ishmael material for defining the identity of Israel. Thus, although Syrén operates mainly with a source-critical framework, he comes close to my understanding of the narrative intent for the role of Ishmael: "[i]t is through the two sons of Abraham that the division will take place that is necessary for the nation of Israel to emerge."[119] This emergence of Israel is aided by the comparison with Ishmael:

> The comparison with Israel is underlined further by the prediction in v. 20 that 'a great nation' will arise from Ishmael and that he will be 'a father of twelve princes'—just as Isaac will father a nation of twelve tribes through his son Jacob. . . . Ishmael will

---

impossible. *Jubilees* links law observance inextricably with birth and therefore with genealogy, insisting that eighth-day circumcision is the principal indicator of Jewish identity" (*Contesting Conversion*, 85; see discussion on 67–86).

114. Syrén, *Forsaken First-Born*, 40–41.
115. Syrén, *Forsaken First-Born*, 40–41.
116. Syrén, *Forsaken First-Born*, 40–41.
117. Syrén, *Forsaken First-Born*, 58. The book of Ezra is, for Syrén, an example of a *halachic* application of Ishmael's expulsion in its concern to preserve the purity of Israel when challenged by intermarriage (61–65).
118. Syrén, *Forsaken First-Born*, 58–59.
119. Syrén, *Forsaken First-Born*, 37.

form a second and separate nation beside Israel; an 'Israel', as it were, without a Promised Land.[120]

Furthermore, Syrén suggests that the story of Hagar and Ishmael in the wilderness (21:14–21) "evokes memories of Israel's own past" in the desert wanderings.[121] Nevertheless, the distinction between Ishmael and Isaac remains: "Israel's time in the desert was only a station on the way from Egypt to the Promised Land; Ishmael was to remain in the desert, to make it his home."[122]

I agree with Syrén that the narrative gives Ishmael the role of contrast, but differ with him as to the point of the contrast. I do not perceive the contrast in terms of the Land, but in terms of how the people of God are generated and sustained. It is a contrast that is designed to highlight the theological understanding of the identity and character of God's people. Ishmael represents an alternative way of construing what it means to be "Israel." If Ishmael would do, as Abraham asked, he would represent descendants according to "flesh": he is Abraham's physical son (emphasized in 21:13), he is circumcised (emphasized in 17:23–26), and he fathers a great nation. He is everything else except not being Isaac; and the one thing that separates Ishmael from Isaac is a different mother, and thus a different manner of birth. The difference is in what generates the two sons: a "natural" arrangement that relies on human potential, or an outrageous promise that is totally dependent on divine performance. Ishmael does not represent the character of the people that God was generating—the Israel *of God*. That central characteristic is only highlighted in relation to Isaac—the child of promise.

The first signpost for this was given at 11:30 where Sarah's barrenness alerts the reader to expect something that transcends the natural. Levenson's reflection on the character of God's people captures the significance of this:

> Just before the story of the Tower of Babel, we find a table listing the seventy peoples who emerged from Noah's three sons. That Israel, which emerges only afterward, is not one of these early nations is a matter of the highest significance, underlining the fundamentally different character of the new nation, not only born later but emerging as a result of a highly unlikely promise. . . . the new people comes into existence only through God's promise to Abram, a childless man with a barren wife. Israel was never secular, so to speak; it never had an identity

---

120. Syrén, *Forsaken First-Born*, 37–38.
121. Syrén, *Forsaken First-Born*, 49.
122. Syrén, *Forsaken First-Born*, 50.

> unconnected to the God who called it into existence in the beginning and who has graciously sustained it ever after. . . . the Hebrew Bible consistently assumes a unique dependence of the special people upon God.[123]

But, as Levenson continues his reflections, he ends up with a paradox:

> That Abram is commanded to break with his father at the beginning of his story—and to give up his son at the end of it . . . —tells us that the "great nation" of which he is the promised progenitor is not simply another ethnic group, to be added to the seventy nations cataloged in Genesis 10. Instead, it is something more like a religious community, a collective founded on shared faith rather than on descent. Yet the fact that the promised heir, from whom this nation is to descend, comes into being not from Abram's preaching—for he preaches nothing in Genesis—but from his own loins suggests something very different. It suggests that the "great nation" is *not* a community founded upon a creed or a religious experience. Rather, it is a natural family. . . . a natural family with a supernatural mandate.[124]

It is precisely because of this apparent tension in the narrative—a natural family yet not just another ethnic group—that the interpretation of the theology of the people of God in light of the contrast between Isaac and Ishmael offers clarity to reach beyond the tension to the essence of what characterizes the true people of God. Ishmael represents natural descent and even conformity to the covenant requirement of circumcision, but yet the people of God are not to be identified with him. Although Levenson is correct in that the people do not emerge out of Abraham's preaching, he misses what ultimately differentiates Isaac from Ishmael: promise and faith. Isaac is generated by the power of the promise, to which Abraham's faith is the only response that receives divine approval (15:6), and also the reaffirmation of the promise for the emergence of a people whose identity is to include all the peoples in the blessing (22:15–18; 35:11; see discussion above). This is the "Isaac-people"—the "children of laughter"—who are a re-created humanity brought into existence and sustained by the power of God's promise.

---

123. Levenson, *Inheriting Abraham*, 21–22.
124. Levenson, *Inheriting Abraham*, 23–24.

Conclusions

The aim of this chapter has been to explore the theological potential in the Abraham narrative with regard to the themes that are of interest to Paul in Galatians. The analysis has not been a comprehensive exploration of the meaning potential in the Abraham narrative, nor has it included a comparative study of different Jewish readings. I have simply attempted to follow the lead of Paul's special interests to be able to explore how the text of Genesis resonates with Paul's convictions. The purpose has been to gain material for a robust and in-depth intertextual reading of Gal 4:21—5:1 in chapter 6.

The Abraham narrative emerges from the context of the aftermath of the tower of Babel. The tower of Babel represents a rebellious human attempt to build community (city, tower, great name) independent of God. This is judged by God and results in further alienation—peoples are separated. The call of Abraham in 12:1–3 launches an opposite project to that at Babel. *God* begins with Abraham a new creative act to generate a new humanity: he is going to bless Abraham, and to generate a great nation out of him that would ultimately mediate blessing to all the nations. Although the narrative in Gen 11–22 is about Abraham, the central theme in the call and promise are the descendants. The promise of descendants raises the question of the heir: Who is going to inherit the promised blessing to Abraham (15:1–6; 17; 21)? Thus, the births of Abraham's two sons—potential heirs—form the theological nexus of the narrative.

The births of the two sons are crafted into the narrative to provide a contrast. The main contrast between Ishmael and Isaac is the manner of their births. Both are sons of Abraham, both are circumcised, and both are involved in the formation of alternative "great nations." But the one thing that separates them is their different mothers. Ishmael is born out of Hagar, Sarah's Egyptian slave girl. Isaac is born from Abraham's wife Sarah who is barren and beyond the age of childbirth. The birth of Ishmael does not require divine intervention. The birth of Isaac is totally an act of God; he is generated by the power of the promise. The narrative highlights the contrast intentionally, and presents it as divinely orchestrated. Since God had closed Sarah's womb (16:2), the need for Hagar arose. When Hagar and the son in her womb could have been lost from sight, God brings them back. In fact, Ishmael is kept in the narrative until the climactic moment on the mountain in Moriah. The reason is to display on the mountain what is the means and purpose of God in generating a new humanity.

One aspect in the process of generating a new humanity is Abraham's faith that is defined in relation to the promise of a son. Both of the two central texts about Abraham's response to God (15:1–6; 22:1–18) suggest that faith is about dependence on the sufficiency of God. This quality is also highlighted by means of contrast. The birth of Ishmael does not require dependence on God. The birth of Isaac is totally dependent on God. Furthermore, the birth of Isaac does not only require dependence on God, it generates it. The promise of Isaac is deliberately delayed to the point of complete exclusion of any human potential in its fulfillment. The absurdity of the promise evokes laughter. Laughter signals the recognition of the insufficiency of human potential to produce what God wants. The priority of the promise over faith highlights the need for the emptying of the human potential in order for it to be realigned. Isaac's birth is not generated by faith. In fact, the narrative demonstrates Abraham's lack of faith just prior to the birth of Isaac. Abraham has no merit to claim in the birth of the son of promise. The promise evokes Abraham's faith that is ready for the test in Moriah. Abraham's experience of the power of God's absurd promise prepares him for the paradox of the command to offer Isaac. Abraham demonstrates faith—dependence on the sufficiency of God—in obedience.

The promise to Abraham has two dimensions: the formation of the great nation and blessing to all the nations (12:2–3). Genesis 15 focuses on the promise of the great nation, whereas Gen 17 develops both dimensions. The promissory aspect of the covenant in Gen 17 focuses on Abraham's name change that signifies his role as the "father of a multitude of nations," which is best taken as a metaphorical designation of his role as the mediator of blessing. This interpretation was already indicated in the initial giving of the promise where the making of Abraham's name great leads to him becoming a blessing (12:2–3). I followed the development of this promise in Gen 17:4–6, 16; 18:18; 22:15–18; and also 35:11, and argued that the promise of blessing to all the nations is intertwined with the promise of the great nation. In fact, the blessing can be understood in terms of the nations' inclusion in the great nation—the people of God.

Isaac and Ishmael offer a contrast to capture the theology of the people of God. Ishmael represents an alternative way to construe the identity of the "great nation" (16:10; 17:20; 21:13). The alternative view focuses on physical descent and circumcision. But the fact that Ishmael is excluded from the covenant people relativizes the importance of physical descent and circumcision as the ultimate means of identifying the people of God. If they were not sufficient for Ishmael to be included, they cannot be the essence, and thus can possibly be relativized. This has the potential for the opening of the covenant to people outside of physical lineage to Abraham, Isaac, and Jacob. It also opens the possibility that circumcision is not the ultimate mark of the people included. What matters more is to be like Isaac. Isaac represents the "Israel of God"—the people that is generated by the power of God's promise.

Although Isaac is also Abraham's son, he is more a child of promise. Abraham could not father him; it was an act of God. Sarah could not give him birth; God gave life to Sarah's dead womb, and thus revealed the creative power of his promise—the people of God are a "new creation."

4

The Theological Potential in Isaiah's Vision of Restoration

The Method

THE IMPORTANCE OF THE Abraham narrative for Paul's conception of the gospel is very clear in the argument of Galatians. This is not the case with the book of Isaiah. However, increasing attention has been given to the role the book of Isaiah plays in Paul's sense of mission and his theology in general,[1] and also in the letter to the Galatians in particular.[2] Paul quotes Isaiah (54:1) only once in Galatians (4:27), but I understand, together with Hays and Harmon, that this is only the tip of the iceberg as far as the presence of the book of Isaiah in Galatians is concerned. Yet to discern the Isaianic influence in Paul's theological vision and logic in Galatians, it is best to begin from where it is explicit, and move from there to where it is more allusive. Thus, I focus my analysis of the theological potential in Isaiah's vision of restoration on Isa 54:1.

As was the case with the Abraham narrative in the previous chapter, so also now I approach the text of Isaiah with Pauline interests. This means that I explore the meaning potential of Isa 54:1 for Pauline application. Accordingly, I select and analyze themes that are related to Isa 54:1 in its immediate context and that are of interest to Pauline motifs in Galatians. The purpose is to build a foundation for a robust and in-depth intertextual reading of Gal 4:21—5:1 in chapter 6. My focus also limits the scope of my study; I do not engage in a comparative analysis between Paul's use of Isaiah and other Jewish interpretations. To be sure, there were many ways in which Second Temple Jews were reading Isaiah, but, within the constraints of this book, I cannot widen my focus to analyze the text with other Jewish interests in

---

1. E.g., Hays, *Conversion*, 25–49; Wagner, *Heralds of the Good News*; Wilk, *Die Bedeutung*.
2. E.g., Harmon, *She Must*.

mind. I only mention here a few examples of other Jewish appropriations of the meaning potential in Isaiah.

The book of Isaiah does not play a major role for Philo, but, with a rare reference to Isa 54:1, Philo perceives that the barren woman who was made fruitful has an allegorical level of meaning that is about the purification of the soul (*Praem.* 158–160). Shum's study of *Paul's Use of Isaiah in Romans* includes an analysis of the use of Isaiah in the Sibylline Oracles and the Dead Sea Scrolls.[3] He gives examples of the use of Isaiah in the Third and Fifth books of the Sibylline Oracles that originate most likely from the Jewish community in Alexandria. One of the most prevalent themes from Isaiah that Shum detects in both books is related to divine punishment of the wicked (e.g., Isa 14:12–15 is alluded to in Sib. Or. 3:100, 360; 5:72; and Isa 66:16 is alluded to in Sib. Or. 3:287, 542–544, 672–673; 5:375–380).[4] The Third book contains also allusions to the Isaianic eschatological vision of peace, which is understood by the Sibyl in terms of cessation of wars and a state of social and political stability (e.g., Isa 11:6–9 and 65:25 alluded to in Sib. Or. 3:788–795), and allusions to Isaianic material about a positive fate for the nations (e.g., Isa 49:1 and 51:5 are alluded to in lines 710–731).[5]

The book of Isaiah had an important role for the Qumran community, which is evidenced by the twenty to twenty-four manuscripts that have been found that incorporate the book of Isaiah wholly or partially, and the numerous explicit and implicit references to it in the other writings.[6] The Qumran community appropriated Isaiah for the construction of their sectarian identity, and for the role they believed to have in preparing the final visitation of the Lord (e.g., the use of Isa 40:3 in 1QS 8:1–16a [quoted in 8:14]).[7] Themes of judgment and destruction from Isaiah were applied to other nations as well as to non-sectarian Jews (e.g., Isa 24:17–18 in CD 4:13–20),[8] whereas themes about the faithful remnant were applied to the sectarians themselves (e.g., Isa 11:11 in 1QH 14:8).[9] Also, the messianic passage from Isa 11:1–5 influenced the sectarians' expectations concerning the coming of Israel's Messiah who would lead them as the "Sons of Light" to fight the eschatological battle, in which they would be vindicated

3. Shum, *Paul's Use of Isaiah*, 38–172.
4. Shum, *Paul's Use of Isaiah*, 54–95.
5. Shum, *Paul's Use of Isaiah*, 54–80, 93–95. Shum accredits the difference between the outlook of the Third and Fifth books to the different socio-political situations they originate from (94–95).
6. Shum, *Paul's Use of Isaiah*, 102.
7. Shum, *Paul's Use of Isaiah*, 111–16.
8. Shum, *Paul's Use of Isaiah*, 127–29, 171.
9. Shum, *Paul's Use of Isaiah*, 151, 171.

and the unfaithful Jews and foreign nations would be punished (e.g., 1QSb, 4Q285, 4QpIsa^a).[10]

The above examples highlight the variety of ways, in which Jewish readers appropriated the potential in Isaiah with different interests and agendas. In the following, I discuss my approach to exploring the theological potential of Isaiah's vision of restoration, as encapsulated by Isa 54:1, for Paul's application in Gal 4:21—5:1.

One of the main weaknesses in analyzing the impact of Paul's quotation of Isa 54:1 in Gal 4:27 has been the under-appreciation or inadequate analysis of the immediate and thematic context of Isa 54:1. Eastman, Harmon, and Jobes have charted the way towards a more engaged analysis of the Isaianic context.[11] Jobes has done most in incorporating a thematic dimension in her intertextual approach, but her emphasis on locating the meaning in the intertextual space *in between the related texts* (Genesis, Isaiah, and Galatians) points out both the promise and potential weakness in the intertextual approach. The promise is evident; forging connections between the scriptural texts and Paul's text provides a rich theological matrix for configuring Paul's understanding of the Christ-event and its implications. The weakness is more subtle; it resides in the temptation to develop the texts' meaning potential in the space *between the texts* without a thorough analysis of the interacting *texts themselves*. This can result, on the one hand, in a perception of discrepancy between Paul's use of the texts of Scripture and their original context, i.e., deeming Paul's reading as radical or as "extraordinary hermeneutical inversion."[12] This runs the risk of having missed the potential of the text for Paul's "radical" reading. On the other hand, a lack of depth in the analysis of the scriptural intertexts can also lead to readings that smooth the connections between the texts of Scripture and Paul's text without engaging the difficulties the material presents to Pauline application (e.g., Isaiah's vision of Gentile inclusion is not only positive), or without reflecting on the process of how the potential in the intertexts is reappropriated (e.g., how the historical experience of exile becomes a matrix for Paul's theological reflection). To avoid these weaknesses in the intertextual approach, I have undertaken an in-depth analysis of the Abraham narrative in chapter 3, and focus here on a thematic analysis of the Isaianic vision of

---

10. Shum, *Paul's Use of Isaiah*, 171.

11. Eastman, *Recovering Paul's Mother Tongue*; Harmon, *She Must*; Jobes, "Jerusalem, Our Mother."

12. Hays, *Echoes of Scripture*, 120. Stanley makes a stronger claim that anyone in Paul's audience who would have had the capabilities to check the context of the quotations would have been unconvinced by Paul's argument based on those texts (*Arguing with Scripture*, 125–26, 130–35).

restoration. Furthermore, I analyze in chapter 5 Paul's hermeneutical practice, and reflect on the dynamics in Paul's reappropriation of the potential in these intertexts. In analyzing the theological potential that Paul's quotation of Isa 54:1 connects to, I am guided by the conviction that only a step by step approach that first identifies the themes that are present in the immediate context of Isa 54:1, and then performs an analysis of these themes in the *intratextual dynamic within the book of Isaiah* can facilitate a nuanced handling of the material, and elucidate the possibilities Isa 54:1 offers for Paul's application. I now explain my method in more detail.

Hays duly notes that Paul was not aware of the modern critical division of Isaiah (1–39, 40–55, 56–66)[13] that has often caused the reading of the sections as separate works.[14] The focus on the literary unity of Isaiah gives emphasis to internal connections within the book. Accordingly, it fosters the use of synchronic analysis that regards the text as a coherent unity and looks for suitable intertexts (internally and externally), not to demonstrate dependence of the text on other material (diachronic reading), but to practice interpretation, in which meaning emerges from the connections between the intertexts—the intertextual matrix.[15] The connections are not established by simple linguistic techniques alone (synonyms and parallel expressions need to be accounted for also), but by a careful analysis of the content and function of the textual units in the book.[16] Laato summarizes the synchronic approach thus, "a prophetic book is understood as a contexture—a collection of different texts—which has three qualities: contextuality (the place of the text in the collection), intertextuality (the relationship between the texts in the collection), and the resultant texture of resonance and meaning."[17]

My analysis of the context of Isa 54:1 is synchronic, aiming to discern what *intratextual* resonances are present in the themes of the vision of

13. Hays, *Conversion*, 26. Also, Sawyer points out that there was only "one Isaiah" until the nineteenth century, and hence "it can be misleading to talk, as many modern writers do, about Paul's use of 'Deutero-Isaiah' or 'the Servant Songs' or the 'Isaiah Apocalypse' or the like" (*Fifth Gospel*, 22–23). Scholarship on Isaiah has a growing trend to approach it as a unified whole rather than a strictly divided collection of different sources (see, e.g., Williamson, "Recent Issues"; Williamson, *Variations*; Sawyer, "Daughter of Zion," 89–107). Even with this trend, it is still mostly recognized that underlying the final form of the text of Isaiah is a complex process of compilation.

14. Laato describes the historical-critical view thus: "*different* texts from *different* historical periods composed by *different* authors and edited in *different* redactional layers of the book by *different* redactors" ("About Zion," 2).

15. Laato, "About Zion," 7.

16. Laato, "About Zion," 5.

17. Laato, "About Zion," 7.

restoration that are derived from the immediate context of Isa 54:1.[18] I first determine and analyze the immediate context of Isa 54:1, and then proceed to the thematic intratextual analysis. I analyze Paul's use of Isaiah primarily based on the LXX (Göttingen), but also compare the LXX with the MT to note when there are important implications for following either the Greek or the Hebrew text (see discussion at the beginning of chapter 3). In approaching Isaiah with Pauline interests, I do not attempt to give the "right reading" or the historically understood "original meaning" of Isaiah, instead I aim to elucidate the potential of the text that is relevant when reading Paul.

Before executing the above method, I discuss two questions that relate to the validity of performing an intratextual thematic analysis of Isaiah 54:1 to elucidate Paul's engagement with Isaiah. First, did Paul read Isaiah as a whole? The collected force of the analysis of Wilk, Wagner, Hays, and Harmon with their lists of citations, allusions, echoes, and thematic parallels convincingly demonstrate that Paul is aware of and uses texts from the whole book of Isaiah. Hence, it is plausible that Paul is drawing from the potential of the whole book of Isaiah, as it contributes to the themes of the vision of restoration in the context of Isa 54:1. But, second, how plausible is it that Paul's citing of Isa 54:1 evokes a thematic intratextual matrix? In other words, do we have evidence for Paul's thematic reading of Scripture? Hays argues that Paul's "explicit citations are merely the tip of the iceberg; they point to a larger mass just under the surface, Paul's comprehensive construal of Isaiah as a coherent witness to the gospel."[19] For Hays, this construal takes the shape of a narrative: "Paul reads Isaiah as having narrated beforehand the events that have at last been set in motion in Paul's generation through the death and resurrection of Jesus."[20] Paul's narrative construal of Isaiah strongly suggests thematic awareness. Wagner is on the same lines: "Paul's use of Isa. 54:1 reveals an awareness of the function of this passage in its wider setting in Isaiah. Again, it is the wider contours of Isaiah's prophecies, and not just particular phrases or sentences, that have shaped Paul's understanding and presentation of the Gospel in important ways."[21] Horbury develops this

18. I use the term "intratextual" to denote textual connections *within* the book of Isaiah.

19. Hays, *Conversion*, 27. Dodd already argued that New Testament authors, Paul included, used quotations as pointers to the larger originating context (*According to the Scriptures*).

20. Hays, *Conversion*, 45.

21. Wagner, "Isaiah in Romans and Galatians," 130. Sawyer also suggests that, if there is evidence of one passage being fundamental to Paul (he suggests Isa 49:1–13 "or the like"), "this means that anything else Isaiah said—in the whole book that bears his name—was probably read or remembered or interpreted in that light, and given special significance" (*Fifth Gospel*, 23).

contextual awareness more specifically in terms of Paul reading thematically connected passages together: "Paul's Isaianic Zion testimonies in Gal 4.27 and Rom. 11.26-7 are unlikely to have been quoted without awareness of other similar oracles; each will have evoked for him not just a single passage, but a group of Zion oracles, especially those in the later chapters of Isaiah, and the whole biblical topic of Zion."[22] Hence, there is a sense that Paul can read Scripture, including Isaiah, thematically.

Paul's thematic reading of Scripture is readily perceived in places where there is concentrated focus on texts of Scripture. The letter to the Romans is one prime example where texts from different books of the Scriptures of Israel are connected, as they relate to the same theme. Wagner has analyzed Paul's connection of Isaiah and Deuteronomy on three occasions in Romans (10:19-21; 11:8; 15:9-12), and describes their connection as a "joint testimony" or "harmonious chorus," nevertheless in a dynamic relationship that is transformative to the understanding of both thematically connected texts.[23] Paul's thematic reading of Scripture can be perceived also in Galatians. In Gal 3:6-14, Paul develops the theme of right-relatedness by faith, and connects quotations from Genesis (15:6 in Gal 3:6; 18:18 in Gal 3:8), Deuteronomy (27:26 in Gal 3:10; 21:23 in Gal 3:13), Habakkuk (2:4 in Gal 3:11), Leviticus (18:5 in Gal 3:12), and an allusion to Isaiah (44:3 in Gal 3:14, see chapter 6) in his flow of thought.

Paul's thematic reading of the prophets, and especially Isaiah, can be demonstrated in Rom 9:24-33 where he marshals evidence to explain that God has called not only the Jews but also the Gentiles to belong to the "vessels of mercy" destined for glory (9:23). First, he uses the voice of Hosea to argue for Gentile inclusion: God makes the non-people his people (Rom 9:25-26; quoting Hos 2:25 and 2:1). Then he uses Isaiah to speak to the theme of Israel's inclusion in the "vessels of mercy," but in the present only as the "remnant" (Rom 9:27-29; quoting Isa 10:22; 28:22; and 1:9). Finally, Paul explains the dilemma arising from the Gentiles obtaining right-relatedness and Israel's (as a whole) failure to obtain it in terms of the necessity of faith, which Isaiah already indicates (Rom 9:30-33; quoting a conflation of Isa 28:16 and 8:14). Thus, when Paul chooses to quote a strategic verse from Isaiah (54:1) in Gal 4:27, it is plausible to envision Paul as drawing from the rich thematic connections within the book of Isaiah that resonate with it.

I now undertake first an analysis of the immediate context of Isa 54:1 to discern the themes that are part of the vision of restoration that Isa 54:1 is intimately connected with. I then explore the intratextual thematic matrix

---

22. Horbury, *Messianism*, 195.
23. Wagner, "Moses and Isaiah," 102-3.

within the whole book of Isaiah to fully appreciate the theology embedded in the respective themes that correlate with Paul's interests in Galatians.

The Vision of Restoration in the Immediate Context of Isaiah 54:1

> Rejoice o' barren one who does not bear children; break forth and shout, the one who does not have labor pains; for the barren one has more children than the one who has a husband, for the Lord has spoken. (Isa 54:1)

In Isa 54:1, the Lord addresses an unidentified barren woman with a promissory exhortation to rejoice over numerous children. The exhortation to shout for joy is a sure signal that we are to listen to the sounds of deliverance and restoration (cf. Isa 12:1-6; 24:14-16; 26:19; 35:4-10; 48:20-21; 51:3, 11; 52:8-9; 60:16; 62:5; 65:18-19). In order to capture how this verse communicates Isaiah's vision of restoration, it needs to be placed in its immediate context.

Isa 54:1 is directly preceded by the description of a servant (52:13—53:12), suggesting that the deliverance and restoration described in Isa 54 is the result of the servant's work.[24] The servant appears on the scene after deliverance and restoration have been declared, and emphatically ascribed to the work of the Lord himself (52:12). The servant is introduced by a theme of astonishment (52:13-15) that leads to the opening of chapter 53: "Lord, who has believed our report/message (*akoē*)? And to whom has the arm of the Lord been revealed?" (53:1). Here the servant acts as the arm of the Lord (cf. 52:10, the Lord shall reveal his holy arm before all the nations) in bringing about the promised restoration.[25] But the amazement continues: he had no form of glory and beauty (53:2), rather, he was despised and dishonored; he was in calamity/wounds and knew how to bear sicknesses (53:3). The amazement intensifies, as it turns out that this servant's suffering is actually for others: he bears *our* sins (*houtos tas hamartias hēmōn pherei*) and suffers pain for *us* (*peri hēmōn*) (53:4); he was wounded because of *our* lawlessness, made weak/sick because of *our* sins (53:5). Furthermore, the punishment on him is to bring peace to *us*, and his wounds bring *us* healing (53:5); he is the servant arm of the Lord that gathers the stray sheep,

---

24. Cf. Koole, *Isaiah 49-55*, 347.

25. Williamson argues that it appears that it is God himself who accomplishes the task of the servant, but the movement from the arm of the Lord in 51:5 to the arm of the Lord in 53:1 (referring to the servant) indicates that, although it is ultimately God, he uses a mediator in accomplishing his purpose (*Variations*, 164).

and who was given by the Lord for the sins of *us* (*tais hamartiais hēmōn*) (53:6). The "us" are defined as the people of the Lord (*tou laou mou*) (53:8), who will also be the long-living "seed" (*sperma makrobion*) of the servant (53:10). Childs explains that the voice of the "us" in Isa 53:1–11a represents those within Israel that have come to understand and believe by divine *revelation* "derived from the arm of Yahweh."[26] The declaration of the servant's innocence and his death being due to the lawlessness of God's people (53:8) underscores the vicarious nature of his work. The "we" turns into many, as the results of the servant's work are presented. He is righteous and justifies by serving well the many (*dikaiōsai dikaion eu douleuonta pollois*) (53:11); he will bear their sins, and because of that inherit many (*klēronomēsei pollous*) (53:12). The inheritance of the servant is the many "seeds" that he has generated by his vicarious suffering.

The description of the servant's work being for the many leads to the vision of restoration in Isa 54, in which the barren woman is promised many children (*polla ta tekna*) (54:1); the many "seeds" in 53:10–12 turn out to be the children born to the barren woman.[27] Consequently, she is asked to broaden her tent (54:2), because of the need to spread out, as her numerous "seed" will inherit the nations (*to sperma sou ethnē klēronomēsei*)[28] (54:3), suggesting also that the servant's inheritance of the multitude of "seeds" expands to include people of other nations. The reference to a barren woman, the setting of a tent, and the promise of numerous offspring inheriting nations evoke also connections with the matriarch Sarah, the Abrahamic promise of many descendants, and the promise of blessing that reaches the nations (Gen 12:2; 15:5; 18:18; see chapter 3).[29]

In Isa 54:1, the barren woman is said to have more children than the married one. This comparison is a puzzle: who is the married woman? Numerous suggestions have been offered in the history of interpretation (Babylon, Rome, synagogue, etc.),[30] but the imagery of the two women is actually

---

26. Childs, *Isaiah*, 411, 413–14; Childs suggests that this indicates that "the response to the servant would divide the people of Israel into two groups, those who believe and those who oppose" (414); see discussion below.

27. Cf. Koole, *Isaiah 49–55*, 352; Goldingay, *Message of Isaiah 40–55*, 524. Gignilliat argues for "strong thematic coherence" between Isa 53 and 54, and points to the following parallel themes: "seed (53:10; 54:3); the many (52:14–15; 53:11–12; 54:1); righteousness (53:11; 54:14) and peace (53:5; 54:10)" ("Singing Women," 8); cf. Bligh who observes the connection of the servant's "seed" in 53:10 and the description of the barren woman's "seed" in 54:1–10 (*Galatians*, 151).

28. The Hebrew word for inherit (*yarash*) could also be read negatively in terms of the "seed" dispossessing the nations.

29. Goldingay, *Message of Isaiah 40–55*, 525; Brueggemann, *Isaiah*, 151.

30. See Koole, *Isaiah 49–55*, 352–53.

best taken in terms of both referring to Jerusalem in different stages: before exile, during exile, and in the future.[31] This is supported by the immediate context where the "story of Jerusalem" is told in terms of an abandoned (widowed, *chēreia*) woman's shame (implying that she has been married) that is transformed by God's (implied husband) reception of her in mercy (54:4-8, see below). Burton captures the imagery well: "[t]he barren woman is Jerusalem in the absence of the exiles, the woman that hath a husband is Jerusalem before the exile; and the comparison signifies that her prosperity after the return from exile was to exceed that which she had enjoyed before the captivity."[32] As both women refer to Jerusalem, there is theological significance in the fact that she has more children after her barrenness rather than as a result of her being always married. This suggests that it is through Israel's abandonment/alienation, rather than her undisturbed covenantal existence (always married to the Lord), that the numerous children are produced—the regeneration of the people of God extends its scope to include the nations (cf. Isa 66:9; see discussion below).

The passage continues to address the abandoned woman's shame due to her "unmarried" and desolate state (54:4). She is not to be afraid, because the Lord is the one who makes her, and the God of Israel himself will redeem her (54:5). He forsook her for a while in wrath, but delivers her in great and everlasting mercy (*kai meta eleous megalou eleēsō se . . . kai en eleei aiōniō eleēsō se*) (54:7-8).[33] This promise of mercy triumphing over wrath is patterned on God's oath to Noah and guarantees lasting peace: "nor shall the covenant of your peace by no means be removed" (54:10). Levenson also notes that "[the] reference to Noah and the great flood in Isa 54:9-10 . . . frames this return of the lost children in the context of cosmic renewal."[34]

The following verses shift the imagery from the woman to the rebuilding of a city (54:11-17), which confirms that the woman and the city correspond to the same reality of restoration. But, as Goldingay points out, the imagery of the woman implies that the focus of restoration is not simply on the rebuilding of a city of stone, but on a *city of people*.[35] Accordingly,

---

31. Cf. Willitts, "Isa 54,1 in Gal 4,24b-27," 195-96. Pace Wolter who suggests that the "other woman" is merely a rhetorical device without any specific extratextual reference to emphasize the extraordinary character of the announcement to the barren woman ("Die Unfruchtbare Frau," 107).

32. Burton, *Galatians*, 264.

33. The MT is more explicit about the marriage imagery, as it designates God as the woman's husband: "the one who made you is the one who marries you" (MT 54:5, *ki bo'alayikh 'osayikh*).

34. Levenson, *Resurrection and the Restoration of Israel*, 148.

35. Goldingay, *Message of Isaiah 40-55*, 521.

after the description of the city's rebuilding with precious stones (54:11–12), the focus is on her inhabitants. Her sons are taught by God and dwell in peace (54:13). This newly formed community of people is built by God in righteousness (54:14), and are called to live in accordance with its character in keeping away from unrighteousness/injustice (*adikou*; MT has oppression, *'osheq*) (54:14). Horbury notes that the language of "creating" (*egō ktizō se; egō de ektisa se*) in the description of the restoration of the city/people (54:16) suggests that the themes of new creation and the restoration of Zion/Jerusalem are closely associated.[36]

The theme of the nations' being included in Israel's restoration is continued in 54:15, as "proselytes" (*prosēlytoi*) shall come to her on account of the Lord and flee to her for refuge.[37] The people in the restored city are the Lord's servants who have the refuge of the city as their inheritance (*estin klēronomia tois therapeuousin kyrion*; MT: *zo't nakhalat 'avde yhwh*) (54:17). The LXX wording in 54:17 (*tois therapeuousin*) does not provide a word link to the servant in 52:13—53:12 like the MT does, but nevertheless, there is a conceptual link: the servant of the Lord has produced the many children of the barren woman who are presented here as the servants of the Lord, and the righteous ones (*kai hymeis esesthe moi dikaioi*) (54:17).[38] The LXX (not the MT) does provide another link: the servant inherits (*klēronomēsei*) many (53:12), and the many servants receive an inheritance as a result of the servant's work (54:17). Hence, the concepts of righteousness, inheritance, and the vision of a restored people of God come together in Isa 54:17.

Goldingay perceives that Isa 54 begins the concluding section to Isa 40–55, the final act of the drama of deliverance.[39] Uhlig echoes this sentiment, and understands Isa 54–55 to contain the message of Isa 40–55 in a nutshell, in which Isa 54 announces the restoration of Zion, and Isa 55 summons the

---

36. Horbury, *Messianism*, 214.

37. The MT is very different here, most likely reflecting the complexity of the Hebrew text and variation in reading an un-pointed text.

38. The MT wording, *zo't nakhalat 'avde yhwh wetsidqatam me'itti*, does not designate the servants as the righteous ones, but portrays both the inheritance and righteousness of the servants (both inheritance and righteousness refer back to the *zo't*) as referring back to the promise of protection against accusing/judging voices in 54:17, and also forward (for the syntactical function of *zo't* to facilitate this, see Williams, *Williams' Hebrew Syntax*, 49) to the provision of "waters" in 55:1. Hence, the restoration reality is the inheritance and the righteousness of God's newly formed people. This points to the need to explore the concepts of righteousness and inheritance in Paul in light of the matrix of the restoration vision in Isaiah.

39. Goldingay, *Message of Isaiah 40–55*, 522.

exiles to come and return to the Lord.[40] Hence, I include in the context of 54:1 the development of the vision to its conclusion in Isa 55.

The promise of restoration in Isa 54 is followed by the invitation for the thirsty to come to the water (55:1), a common symbol for the Spirit in Isaiah.[41] This invitation is for the thirsty, but as Childs points out, it can be viewed as directed to the servants of the Lord in 54:17 further extending their inheritance: "to embrace to the full the new divine world order that has just been described in 54:9ff."[42] Those who do not have capital are invited to feast and, paradoxically, to buy wine and fat without a price (55:1). This is a gift of grace that has the intention "to subvert the standard view of covenant as expressed in classical form in Deuteronomy," in which "God's intervention on behalf of his people is contingent on their moral performance."[43]

Responding to the Lord (to the invitation to "drink and eat" in 55:1–2) opens a new future for the servants of the Lord. God will make with them an everlasting "Davidic like covenant" (*kai diathēsomai hymin diathēkēn aiōnion, ta hosia dauid*) (55:3), a move that indicates "the theology of kingship is democratized."[44] The content of this covenant is about being a witness to the nations. As David was made a witness to the nations,[45] so also now the restored people shall be called on by nations that did not know her (55:5), and they will run to her for refuge because of the work of God in her glorification (55:4–5). Thus, the servants receive their calling: "they are to call nations, not previously known, who will respond to this invitation, not because of Israel's power or intrinsic worth, but because of God that they now reflect."[46]

Isaiah 55 ends with a recapitulation of the message of Isa 40–54.[47] It sounds a call to seek and return to God in repentance to receive mercy and forgiveness (55:6–7). The wicked are to forsake their ways and unrighteous thoughts, because the Lord's thoughts are not theirs and their ways are not his (55:7–8), which echoes the new thing the Lord is doing and the theme of amazement in the introduction of the servant in 52:13—53:12.

40. Uhlig, "Too Hard to Understand?," 76.
41. Cf. Blenkinsopp, *Isaiah 40–55*, 369. See discussion below.
42. Childs, *Isaiah*, 434.
43. Blenkinsopp, *Isaiah 40–55*, 369.
44. Goldingay, *Message of Isaiah 40–55*, 547.
45. Childs argues that this is "a prophetic construct used to depict David's true vocation according to the original, theological purpose of God for his anointed one.... David's true role as God's chosen is presented as a witness to God's wonders (Ps 89:6–7)" (*Isaiah*, 435).
46. Childs, *Isaiah*, 436.
47. Blenkinsopp, *Isaiah 40–55*, 371.

The summons turns into a promise; the Lord's word—the promise of restoration—is sure and shall accomplish what it has been sent for (55:10-11). The performative power of the promise is compared to the rain that waters the ground and makes it bear fruit (55:10).[48] Hence, the generative power of the promise is expressed with imagery of water transforming barren land—imagery that connects with the work of the Spirit in Isaiah (see discussion below) and with transforming the barrenness of the woman in 54:1 to bear a multitude of children. Blenkinsopp captures the essence of Isa 55:6-11 well: "the prophetic word recorded here [referring to Isa 40-54] is efficacious, it will bring about what it proclaims, but it does not operate according to normal human calculations."[49] Echoing the rejoicing related to the birth of the many children from the barren woman, the redeemed and restored people will go out with rejoicing and be taught (LXX) / led (MT) in joy (LXX) / peace (MT) (55:12). Furthermore, restoration is pictured as a new creation event—the people are welcomed by mountains, hills, and trees to a land that is transformed, resembling the reversal of a curse and return of paradise (55:12-13).[50]

At this point, my conclusions are succinct, since fuller reflections follow the next step of thematic intratextual analysis. I have argued above that Isa 54:1 belongs intimately to the context of the vision of restoration set in Isa 52:13—55:13.[51] The following list presents the themes of this vision as they have emerged from this context:

1. Restoration is the result of the *servant's work* that produces a community of *servants* (52:13—53:12; 54:17).

2. Restoration is pictured as an event where a *barren woman gives birth to many children* (54:1).

3. Restoration causes the need to *enlarge* the tent/city, because of the many children that include the *nations* (54:2-3, 15 LXX).

4. Restoration is about the *remarrying* of an abandoned woman (54:4-8).

5. Restoration is pictured as the rebuilding of a *city* (54:11-12).

---

48. The words used here for the water causing the earth to bear fruit (LXX: *ektiktō*; MT: *holidah*) have the same roots as the words used in 54:1 for the woman who has not borne children (LXX: *tiktō*; MT: *yalad*).

49. Blenkinsopp, *Isaiah 40-55*, 371.

50. Koole, *Isaiah 49-55*, 445; also Blenkinsopp, *Isaiah 40-55*, 372-73.

51. Cf. Goldingay who treats the same section (52:13—55:13) as one unit with the title: "Yhwh's Act of Restoration and Transformation" (*Message of Isaiah 40-55*, 461). I discovered this only after my own analysis to determine the proper context for 54:1.

6. Restoration is an act of God's *mercy*, and it brings *peace* as well as produces *righteousness* (54:7–17).
7. Restoration includes an invitation to *drink of the water—symbol of the Spirit*—that the Lord provides (55:1).
8. Restoration includes an invitation to *feast freely* as a response to God's grace (55:1).
9. Restoration includes an invitation to be *taught by God* to have life (55:2–3).
10. Restoration renews a *covenant* that is about witness to the nations (55:3–5).
11. Restoration includes an invitation to *return to God* in repentance (55:6–9).
12. Restoration is *a promise with performative power* that causes a transformation described in terms of *"new creation"* (55:10–13).

I choose five themes from the above list for the next step of an intratextual thematic analysis. These are chosen, because they directly relate with the themes in Gal 4:21—5:1:

- The barren woman giving birth (cf. Gal 4:27).
- The theme of the rebuilding of the city (cf. Gal 4:26).
- The invitation to drink of the waters, as a reference to the Spirit (cf. Gal 4:29).
- The theme of the servant (cf. Gal 5:1) and many servants.
- The many children and the nations' inclusion (cf. Gal 4:26, 28, 31).

Other relevant themes that relate to the concerns in Galatians are also taken into account (e.g., Abrahamic promise, mercy/grace, Law, new creation, kingdom of God, etc.), as they appear in conjunction with the chosen main themes.

Intratextual Thematic Analysis of the Vision of Restoration in Isaiah

With the picture of restoration envisaged in the context of Isa 54:1 (52:13—55:13), it is possible to undertake a thematic intratextual analysis of the themes of restoration in the whole book of Isaiah that also connect integrally with the themes in Gal 4:21—5:1. This is done to appreciate the rich theological potential that is embedded in the intertextual matrix that Paul invites us to explore by his citing of Isa 54:1 in Gal 4:27.[52]

The Structure of the Book of Isaiah

Before plunging into the synchronic analysis of the varied and diverse material of the book of Isaiah, I present here an analysis of the structure of the whole with some important insights from a diachronic perspective.[53]

The standard way of dividing the material in Isaiah is to view it in three parts: chapters 1–39, 40–55, and 56–66.[54] There are historical-critical reasons for dividing the material thus, but also literary ones. Chapters 1–39 are grounded in the historical prophetic ministry of Isaiah (the name Isaiah appears only in this section), and the section is set in the historical framework from the time of King Uzziah to Hezekiah.[55] Chapters 34–39 are transitional; they connect with the previous chapters (1–33), and prepare (predict the Babylonian exile) for the message of the following section.[56] Chapters 40–66 present the message of Isaiah to an implied audience that lives in a different historical period to what was implied in 1–39; although the Babylonian exile was already implied in 1–39, it is only in 40–66 that the people are addressed to leave Babylon and return to Judah.[57] In chapters 56–66, the message is addressed in a context of partial or complicated fulfillment of the promises and hopes of restoration; it is implied that some have returned, but problems remain with regard to the whole scope of the vision of restoration.[58] Laato encapsulates this internal movement in the book of Isaiah succinctly: "Isaiah 40–55 proclaims that the time is now at hand when the programme of Isaiah 1–39 will come in fulfilment . . . However, Isaiah 56–66 extends this

---

52. I imagine the process thus: when Paul cites the strategic verse of Isa 54:1, he picks up a bright flower that stands out on the field. The petals of the flower are the themes that emerge in the immediate context of 54:1. As the flower is picked, it comes with its roots that are intertwined and form the intratextual thematic matrix that provides the rich theological "nutrients" for the flower—the vision of restoration in Isa 52:13—55:13.

53. Although my focus is primarily on the final form of the text and on a synchronic analysis, the diachronic dimension adds depth (cf. Childs, *Introduction*, 76).

54. The Qumran community has left evidence of an attractive alternative structuring of the book of Isaiah in two parts: 1–33 and 34–66, the two mirroring each other thematically (see Brooke, "On Isaiah in Qumran," 77–81).

55. Laato, *"About Zion,"* 45–46.

56. Laato, *"About Zion,"* 45.

57. Laato, *"About Zion,"* 49–50.

58. Laato, *"About Zion,"* 50; cf. Williamson, "Recent Issues," 37–38.

hermeneutic programme of Isaiah 40–55 by transforming the fulfilment of the promised salvation to a future time when the people has come loyal to Yhwh."[59] Furthermore, Laato suggests that the connection between the two major sections (1–39 and 40–66) is best understood by a typological model: the proclamation of the prophet Isaiah in a certain ideological-historical situation (1–39) provides a paradigm for the future generations (40–66).[60]

Understanding the nature of the connections within the sections of the book of Isaiah as typological—reappropriating a paradigm in a new historical setting—fosters a dynamic analysis of the thematic connections. In this reappropriation, some themes can evolve, e.g., royal ideology is reinterpreted as concerning the servant.[61] However, since Zion-theology retains its predominance, it suggests that the fate of Jerusalem/Zion is a central theme throughout the book (1:1 and 2:1 introduce it; Jerusalem is mentioned 49 times and Zion 47 times by name; they are also referred to in many other places with other names and images).[62] Childs expresses the internal connections in Isaiah in terms of intratextuality: "[t]he growth of larger composition has often been shaped by the use of a conscious resonance with a previous core of oral or written texts."[63] The intratextual reapplication is not clearly a one-directional movement from beginning towards the end, which complicates interpretation of sequential trajectories.[64] With this understanding of the whole book of Isaiah, I proceed to the intratextual thematic analysis of the vision of restoration communicated by Isa 52:13—55:13.

Barren Woman Giving Birth

Isa 54:1 paints the picture of restoration in terms of a barren woman giving birth to many children. To appreciate the theology of this imagery, I seek to find intratextual resonances in the identity of the woman and the process of giving birth to children (the identity of the many children is discussed later below).

The immediate context suggests that the woman is closely connected with the image of the restoration of a city (54:11–17). This connection is confirmed in Isa 51:17 where Jerusalem (in exile) is addressed as a woman

59. Laato, "About Zion," 168.
60. Laato, "About Zion," 60–61; cf. Uhlig, "Too Hard to Understand?," 72.
61. Laato, "About Zion," 62.
62. Laato, "About Zion," 62–64.
63. Childs, *Isaiah*, 4.
64. Childs, *Isaiah*, 4.

who has drunk the cup of God's wrath, and none among her sons whom she has borne can guide her (51:18), because they lie faint under the wrath of the Lord (51:20). Identifying the woman with the city is also established through the marriage imagery in 54:4–8, which is present also in Isa 62. Chapter 62 refers to Zion (62:1–2) who is not to be called forsaken anymore, neither her land desolate (*erēmos*), but she is called "my delight" and the land "inhabited" (LXX) / "married" (MT) (62:4). Her sons will dwell in marriage with her, and the Lord rejoices over her as a bridegroom (62:5). Thus, the image of the woman giving birth (54:1) is associated with Jerusalem/Zion being restored.

But there is more to the image than just a direct equation of the woman with Jerusalem/Zion. In Isa 26, the inhabitants of Judah sing an "eschatological song," in which the community of the faithful is situated between the times: "the old is passing; the new has not yet come in its fullness."[65] It is in this tension and frustration of expectancy that the community compares itself to a failed giving of birth:[66] "we conceived and had labor pains and gave birth. We did not produce a wind/spirit of salvation on the earth" (26:18).[67] But the note of frustration is contrasted and exceeded by divine promise: "the dead shall rise and those in the tombs shall be raised" (26:19). This is seen as a classical salvation oracle (*Heilsorakel*) of divine reassurance that salvation will come—a promise that transcends all the other promises.[68] Although there is debate whether the text envisions only the rebirth of the nation, or also individual resurrection from the dead, Childs argues that the main point is clear: "the ultimate status of the believing community of Israel, which lives at an intersection of two dispensations within God's economy, is not determined by the rules of the old age. The sign of the new is not that pain and misery cease, but that the promised life in God's kingdom extends even beyond the grave."[69]

The note of human frustration and the need for divine intervention in salvation/restoration is sounded also in the transitional section of the book. Isaiah 36–37 narrates the Assyrian threat and how the Lord foils it.

---

65. Childs, *Isaiah*, 190–91.

66. Childs, *Isaiah*, 191.

67. The LXX witness is not unison. Rahlfs gives a positive note: *pneuma sōtērias sou epoiēsamen*; but Göttingen edition has it as: *pneuma sōtērias ouk epoiēsamen*. The MT is similar to the Göttingen: *kemu yaladnu ruakh yeshu'ot bal-na'aseh erets*. I follow the Göttingen edition here, since it reflects most likely the original Greek and accords more closely with the Hebrew. The other versions can be understood as smoothing out the negative connotation in the community's ability to produce salvation.

68. Childs, *Isaiah*, 191.

69. Childs, *Isaiah*, 192.

As Hezekiah sends a message regarding the Assyrian threat to Isaiah, he describes the distress and hopelessness with an image that contrasts with the one in 54:1: "birth pains have come to the one giving birth to children, but she does not have strength to give birth" (37:3). Human "strength" fails to bring deliverance in the face of an overwhelming threat—there is no strength to deliver the children. In contrast, the Lord promises deliverance for the remnant in Jerusalem (37:28-35). With this emphasis, the initial historical ministry of the prophet Isaiah closes, and becomes the typological paradigm for the vision of future deliverance and restoration.

As we come to the second major section of the book of Isaiah, the image of the woman giving birth receives more dimensions and a more positive note of promise. The Lord is depicted going out like a mighty man of war to deliver his people (42:13-16). In the midst of this description of deliverance, the Lord says he has endured like a woman in labor pains (*ekarterēsa hōs hē tiktousa*) (42:14; cf. 45:10).[70] God is depicted here as a woman in the process of giving birth, as he brings deliverance. This image of God generating a people is to be placed in contrast to the beginning of the book of Isaiah where the Lord exclaims a sad realization that the children he begat (*gennaō*) and raised have rejected him (1:2; cf. 48:8);[71] they have not known or understood God (1:3), and thus have become a sinful and degenerate people who provoked the anger of the Lord (1:4).[72] But anger is not the final note; the promise of restoration is an act of God's mercy that brings new hope (cf. 40:1-2; 54:7-10). God's commitment to regenerate a people is reflected in the following texts that develop the theme further.

In the beginning of Isa 44, Israel is to gain hope for the future from her origins. She is addressed as God's servant whom God formed from the womb (*ho poiēsas se kai ho plasas se ek koilias*) (44:1-2)—a possible reference to the birth of Isaac from Sarah.[73] At the end of the chapter, Is-

---

70. The MT is even stronger in its description of God in labor: "like a woman giving birth I groan, I pant and gasp at the same time" (*kayoledah 'ef'eh 'eshom we'esh'af yakhad*).

71. The MT does not use the term begat, but instead descriptions of raising children up and exalting them (*banim giddalti weromamti*) that might be to emphasize the privileged status of Israel among the nations.

72. The MT does not speak of anger, but focuses on the people having despised the Holy One of Israel and having become totally alienated (*ni'atsu et-qedosh yisra'el nazoru 'akhor*).

73. There are various views as to what event in Israel's history this refers to. Blenkinsopp suggests that this refers to the birth of Jacob (*Isaiah 40-55*, 233). Westermann connects verse two with the exodus, but with reference to the creation account (*Isaiah 40-66*, 135). Koole does not tie the interpretation to one single event in Israel's history: "the verbal forms relate not only to Israel's first beginning but to her entire history. . . .

rael is asked to recognize the work of God in the (prophetic) present / (eschatological) future: God is the one who redeems her and is re-forming her from the womb (*ho plassōn se ek koilias*) (44:24).[74] The Lord's address to daughter Babylon in Isa 47 provides a contrast to the promise of restoration to Israel. Babylon's destruction is depicted with the image of being made a widow and losing children (47:7–11)—a counter image to the barren woman giving birth to children, and an abandoned woman being married in Isa 54:1–7.

In Isa 49, a servant speaks to coastlands and people afar. The servant's name was called from the womb of his/her mother (49:1), referring to Israel's call to be the Lord's servant (49:3).[75] Later in the passage, the Lord says that a servant will bring Jacob back and gather Israel (49:5). Hence, the Lord challenges Zion who thinks the Lord has forsaken and forgotten her (49:14), and asks whether a woman would forget her nursing child. Even if she would, the Lord would not forget (49:15). There is even more amazement, as her sons, who had been lost/destroyed, will say that the place is too narrow (49:20). Then Zion wonders in words that echo Isa 54:1–7: "Who has begotten me these? Now, I was childless and a widow, so who has raised these for me? Now, I was left/forsaken alone, so from where did I have these?" (49:21). The Lord answers that it is he who signals the nations and peoples to bring her sons and daughters (49:22–23). Thus, Isa 44 and 49 together suggest that Israel's initial call to existence and her future restoration are closely connected in the theological matrix of Isaiah: "[t]he revitalization of the downtrodden and despondent people is clearly patterned on the old legends [Abrahamic promise and Jacob] of their having to come into being against all odds, historical and

---

God not only chose his people but also brought it into being and preserved it . . . This was evident in the history of the patriarchs, the Exodus, the settlement in Canaan, in short, in the entire history in which the people was able to maintain itself by the will of God" (*Isaiah 40–48*, 358). Koole's approach is attractive, but I discern the strongest connection with the initial paradigmatic birth of Isaac from the barren womb of Sarah, because of the strong resonances to the Abrahamic tradition in 44:3 (seed, blessing). The LXX rendering of *ya'aqov wiyshurun* as *iakōb kai ho ēgapēmenos israēl* in 44:2 also supports the connection with the Abraham narrative and the identification of the people with Isaac—the beloved son (LXX Gen 22:2)—or with Abraham (*hon ēgapēsa*) in Isa 41:8.

74. The image of God as the "mother" is present also in Isa 46:3–4.

75. Koole notes that the womb of the mother in 49:1 has been identified with Sarah in the history of interpretation (*Isaiah 49–55*, 7). This is not clear in this text, but as 51:2 makes an explicit connection to Sarah, it is possible to have an allusion to Sarah also here.

natural."⁷⁶ The possible echo to the birth of Isaac from the barren womb of Sarah is brought to the surface in Isa 51.⁷⁷

Isaiah 51 addresses the people who align themselves with the servant from Isa 49 (see discussion below). They are first to look to God as the ultimate source of their existence (MT 51:1b).⁷⁸ Then they are to look to Abraham their father and to Sarah who bore them (*emblepsate eis abraam ton patera hymōn, kai eis sarran tēn ōdinousan hymas*) (51:2).⁷⁹ As Noort aptly summarizes, "in Isa 51:1–3, everything is focused on the rebirth of the people, exemplified by the names of Abraham and Sarah."⁸⁰ They are encouraged, because as Abraham was but one when he was called and the Lord blessed and multiplied him (from the barren womb of Sarah) (51:2), so also now the Lord is able to transform Zion's desolate/barren places (*ta erēma autēs*) into a paradise of the Lord (51:3; cf. 54:1 where *erēmos* is used of the barrenness of the woman). Callaway captures the significance of this: "[t]he way in which Yahweh called the single man Abraham and made him into a nation, and chose the barren Sarah to become the mother of all Israel is the paradigm for the way in which he will recreate the nation out of the desolate band of exiles which is now Israel."⁸¹ Sarah is "theologically" the woman who has given birth to the people aligning themselves with the servant of Isa 49:5–9.⁸² Although the focus is on Abraham, the reminder invokes the miraculous realization of the promise of many offspring to Abraham through the barren womb of Sarah. The vision of

---

76. Levenson, *Resurrection and the Restoration of Israel*, 145.

77. Also, Isa 48:18–19 suggests that restoration is understood in connection with the promise to Abraham about many descendants.

78. The LXX and MT render 51:1b differently. The LXX uses the active voice: look to the solid rock you hewed (*hēn elatomēsate*), whereas the MT has the passive voice (Pual): look to the rock from which you were hewn (*khutsavtem*). The MT points to the ultimate origin of the people in God as their Rock, an echo of Deut 32:4, 15, 18, 30–31 (cf. Blenkinsopp who recognizes the link to Deut 32, but prefers to identify the rock and quarry with the "ancestral couple" [*Isaiah 40–55*, 326]). The LXX does not use the term rock in Deut 32, but speaks only of God. This might explain partly why LXX Isa renders 51:1 in a way that misses the connection with Deut 32.

79. Blenkinsopp notes that this is the only place besides Genesis that Sarah is mentioned by name (*Isaiah 40–55*, 326). He also perceives that Isaiah represents two traditions in the ancestry of Israel: Jacob as the father (perceived from Isa 40–48), and Abraham the father and Sarah the mother of the people (cf. Isa 29:22; 41:8).

80. Noort, "Abraham and the Nations," 10.

81. Callaway, *Sing, O Barren One*, 62.

82. Cf. Noort: "Zion's motherhood is visualized by the matriarch *par excellence*, Sarah, once barren. In a combination of past and present, the matriarch bears the new Israel . . . , here addressed" ("Abraham and the Nations," 11).

restoration, as transformation of barrenness, is intimately connected with the miraculous birth of Isaac.

In Isa 66, God's act of deliverance is pictured as a woman who gave birth before she was in labor; before her pain came she delivered a son (66:7). This event refers to Zion's restoration: "Zion was in labor pains and gave birth to her children," and is marveled at as an unheard thing: "Did the earth give birth (MT: was the earth birthed) in one day; was a nation born in one moment?" (66:8). Childs encapsulates the effect of this imagery: "God has accomplished the totally unexpected."[83] It also provides a fitting climax to the development of the imagery of a woman giving birth, as it "makes the point that the restoration of Jerusalem will come about by direct divine action."[84] Blenkinsopp discerns resemblance in this with the miraculous birth of Isaac.[85] But the questions probe deeper. The Lord asks: "Was it not I who made the woman who gives birth, and who is barren (*ouk idou egō gennōsan kai steiran epoiēsa*)?" (66:9).[86] The implied answer is that the Lord has ultimately caused the punishment of exile (barrenness), and redemption/restoration (giving birth to children). This advances my initial interpretation of Isa 54:1 as a reflection on God's paradoxical working in Israel's experience: the Lord "caused" the barrenness of Israel so that her restoration in mercy would generate more children, as the nations are included in the people of God. I return to this theme in my last intratextual thematic analysis in this section.

A Tale of Two Cities

The barren woman giving birth in Isa 54:1 is connected with the restoration of Jerusalem; the picture of a woman giving birth turns into a vision of a restored city (54:11–14). The exhortation for the woman to broaden her tent (54:2) also echoes an earlier description of Zion/Jerusalem as a secure tent (33:20).[87] I turn next to the resonances of the restoration of the city in the intratextual matrix of the whole book.

---

83. Childs, *Isaiah*, 541.

84. Blenkinsopp, *Isaiah 56–66*, 305.

85. Blenkinsopp, *Isaiah 56–66*, 305–6. Blenkinsopp perceives that the Abrahamic promise of descendants, land, and blessings underlies much of Isa 40–66. I agree, as this surfaces clearly in Isa 49, 51, and 54.

86. The MT expresses this differently: "Is it not I who causes to give birth and shuts (*'im-'ani hammolid we'atsarti*)?"

87. Cf. Horbury, *Messianism*, 219.

Isaiah 1 and 2 constitute a framing scene for the rest of the book; it is a "tale of two cities"—from the Jerusalem before exile to the restored Jerusalem. This tale is encapsulated in 54:1 in the figures of the barren woman who is promised more children (restored Jerusalem) than the woman with a husband (Jerusalem before exile).[88] Isaiah 1 speaks of Jerusalem's future in open (the city has not yet been destroyed) and conditional terms (repentance can prevent destruction), but it culminates in promises for restoration after the purging punishment of the Lord (1:24-28). The punishment of exile (1:7-8; being forsaken and desolation) is due to lawlessness—a failure to heed the Law (1:4-17). Yet the horizon beyond the punishment portrays Zion as a city of righteousness (*polis dikaiosynēs*) and a faithful "mother-city" (*mētropolis pistē ziōn*) (1:26). The LXX rendering *mētropolis* is a rare use of the term, and could be used here to elevate "Zion to the mother-city for which the exile heart yearns,"[89] or as a reflection on the significance of the city as the locus of identification for the community. The designation of the city as a "mother-city" provides also a word picture that connects the symbol of the woman with the city.

Isaiah 2 continues the note of future restoration, as it starts with an elevated vision of the restored Zion/Jerusalem:

> For in the last days the mountain of the Lord will be manifest, and the house of God will be on the tops of the mountains and exalted far above the hills, and all the nations will come to it. And many nations shall go and say: come, let us go up to the mountain of the Lord and into the house of the God of Jacob, and he will declare to us his way, and we will walk in it. For the law shall come out of Zion, and the word of the Lord from Jerusalem. (2:2-3)

This is a vision the LXX ascribes to the last days (*eschatais hēmerais*).[90] Zion is pictured as the mountain of the Lord that is now made manifest, presumably in new significance. The house of the Lord is on the highest of the mountains, and it is exalted far above (*hyperanō*) the hills. This geographical note is to be taken with theological significance: "we must not understand biblical geography as a statement of scientific nature. . . . geography is simply

---

88. Cf. Willitts, "Isa 54,1 in Gal 4,24b-27," 192-97. He credits the term "tale of two cities" to Dumbrell, *End of the Beginning*. I suspect also an echo from Charles Dickens's *A Tale of Two Cities* (1859).

89. Baer, "'It's All about Us!,'" 41-42.

90. Cf. Childs: "[i]t speaks of God's time, different in kind from ordinary time, and it signals immediately that there is no simple linear continuity between Israel's historical existence and the entrance of God's kingdom" (*Isaiah*, 29).

a visible form of theology."[91] The theology conveyed by this "mythic" imagery in connection with other "mythic" connotations in Zion theology are summed up by Levenson: "Zion as the place from which the world was created, as the point from which the primal ray of light emanated, and as the only mountain to stand above the deluge, is also the highest point in the highest land, the center of the center, from which all the rest of reality takes its bearings."[92] Childs also connects this imagery with creation and with the function of orienting reality; the vision of Zion's transformation resembles ancient Canaanite mythopoetic imagery, and reflects the theme of "new creation," but now bearing "the marks of God's original intention of primordial harmony of the universe (Gen 2:10ff.)."[93]

This future "new creation" reality invites all the nations (*panta ta ethnē*) and many peoples (*ethnē polla*). They are pictured coming into it to be taught by God (Isa 2:3). Childs understands this statement to emphasize that "the nations come not to be proselytized into the Hebrew religion — the concept of human religion is foreign to the text — but to learn from God."[94] Levenson also understands that a reference to Torah here resembles Mal 2:6-7, and "refers to revealed instruction, oracles, and not to the Pentateuch."[95] This is supported in the text by the move from the law (*nomos*) from Zion to the word of the Lord (*logos kyriou*) from Jerusalem (2:3).

Isaiah 4 presents a vision of the day when the inhabitants (daughters) of Jerusalem/Zion (mother) have been washed and cleansed (4:3-4). It pictures

91. Levenson, *Sinai and Zion*, 116.

92. Levenson, *Sinai and Zion*, 135.

93. Childs, *Isaiah*, 29-30. Levenson points also to the rabbinic tradition, in which Mount Zion was understood as the navel of the earth, "the point from which creation proceeded" (*Sinai and Zion*, 118).

94. Childs, *Isaiah*, 30. There is much debate about the role and content of the Torah in this: Is it referring to the Mosaic Torah or the prophetic teaching independent of the Law of Moses? Childs avoids this polarization and suggests that "the Mosaic Torah itself increasingly received its full meaning from the divine reality witnessed to by the prophets." This meant that the prophetic polemic both "kept in check" all legalistic moves and "blocked all attempts to mitigate the full force of the divine will that was given a concrete form at Sinai." Childs summarizes this relationship thus: "both law and the prophetic proclamation were expanded in terms of a deepening grasp of God's reality, but neither was subordinated in principle to the other." Significantly, the LXX uses here the term *nomos*, which Paul uses in Gal 4:21 to refer to both the Mosaic Law and to the Scripture in a wider sense (see chapter 5). Blenkinsopp understands the vision of Isa 2:2-4 very differently: "[it] envisages Jerusalem as preeminent among the nations, the *religious* capital of the world to which Gentiles will come attracted by the high ethical ideals embodied in the *Jewish law*" (*Isaiah 1-39*, 203; emphasis added). Both are possible readings, but the aim here is to explore the meaning potential of the text that Paul could have utilized.

95. Levenson, *Sinai and Zion*, 126.

the Lord coming to Zion and it being covered by a cloud during day and by fire during night, echoing the exodus experience (4:5). Integral to this restoration of Zion is the return of God's glory (4:5)—his presence among the people. But, as Childs notes: "the sign of God's gracious presence is no longer confined to the Holy of Holies with its access only to the high priest, but the entire mountain is overshadowed as a sacred sanctuary."[96]

Isaiah 24 presents the restoration of Zion in terms of cosmic redemption: "the eschatological focus of these chapters [24–27] has raised their sights to the ultimate purpose of God in portraying the cosmological judgment of the world and its final glorious restoration."[97] After depictions of judgment (24:1–22), the Lord is seen to reign on Mount Zion and in Jerusalem with his glory (24:23). Again, Zion and Jerusalem are intimately connected, and its restoration is about the reign of God over the faithful remnant from both Israel and the nations (24:6): "this climax also signals the beginning of God's new order and its effect on the faithful of the world, both among Israel and the nations."[98] The vision flows into Isa 26 where the city is pictured protected by the surrounding walls of salvation (26:1). In Isa 27, the Lord gathers his people and they will come and worship the Lord on the holy mountain at Jerusalem (27:13). Restoration of Zion/Jerusalem in the "apocalyptic" section of Isaiah is about the ultimate eschatological restoration of the reign of God over his saved people.

In Isa 44, Cyrus is specified as the one fulfilling God's purposes in the rebuilding of Jerusalem (44:26–28). Due to opposition and questioning of God's choice, God affirms that he has chosen Cyrus, and makes his way level so that he shall build Jerusalem and set the exiles free (45:13). When Cyrus is pictured in the restoration of Israel, the content is more specific and the language is concrete (build my city, return the exiles) rather than metaphoric.

In Isa 51, the ransomed of the Lord are described as returning to Zion with singing and joy (51:11). Furthermore, it is the community of the people that constitute Zion: "you will say to Zion, you are my people" (51:16). In Isa 52, Zion is called to awake, and Jerusalem is designated as the holy city (52:1). It is because of the holiness of the city that no uncircumcised or

---

96. Childs, *Isaiah*, 37.

97. Childs, *Isaiah*, 173. It is in this sense (focus on final eschatological judgment and entrance of the kingdom of God) that Childs agrees to call this section apocalyptic, but at the same time he does not perceive the Isaianic writer to "leave the realm of history," or to be concerned with "mysteries known only to the initiated or to hidden numbers pointing to heavenly secrets that call for a special interpreter"—elements usually associated with apocalyptic.

98. Childs, *Isaiah*, 181.

unclean person shall come into her anymore (52:1).⁹⁹ Captive Zion will have a day when she hears the good news of salvation: "your God reigns" (52:7). The watchmen sing for joy as they see the Lord having mercy on Zion (*eleēsē kyrios tēn ziōn*) (52:8).¹⁰⁰ Westermann captures the mood well: "what for so long a time Israel had been unable to believe or comprehend now turns out to be a real thing that men can plainly see."¹⁰¹ Desolate/barren Jerusalem (*ta erēma ierousalēm*) is to break forth into singing because the Lord has had mercy (*eleeō*) on her and has delivered her (52:9; cf. 54:1).

Isaiah 60, reflecting on the promise of restoration from the perspective of a return from exile with yet unfulfilled expectations of full restoration, describes the time when Jerusalem is to shine (*phōtizou phōtizou, ierousalēm*) for her light has come, and the glory of the Lord is upon her (60:1).¹⁰² This language of light and glory describes a "theophany, in which God reveals himself in the victory over his enemies and the salvation of his people."¹⁰³ The nations that are under darkness shall come to her light (60:3). Jerusalem is to gaze at all her children that have been gathered from afar (60:4). Jerusalem's fate is turned and she is to be called the City of the Lord, Zion of the Holy One of Israel (60:14). The description of the new building materials (60:17; cf. the more heightened language in Isa 54:11–12) highlights the contrast between the old and the new, and the use of hyperbolic language envisions a new eschatological city of God.¹⁰⁴ The eschatological note is taken further, since there is no more need for the light of the sun, as the Lord is her light and glory (60:19). But it also refers to the new reality where

---

99. The negative note on the uncircumcised/unclean seems to be highly contextual, as Blenkinsopp explains: "[Jerusalem] must no longer be defiled by the presence of foreign conquerors" (*Isaiah 40–55*, 340). Childs connects the holy city with the divine name and explains the prohibition thus: "the uncircumcised and unclean will not be allowed in the city to profane the name of God" (*Isaiah*, 405). Thus, the focus here is more on holiness than on the actual practice of circumcision. The scenario could be very different, if the "uncircumcised" were not the invaders, but actual participants in the redemption, and furthermore, if they would be "sanctified" by the Lord by some other means than circumcision.

100. MT speaks of the return of the Lord to Zion here (*beshuv yhwh tsion*).

101. Westermann, *Isaiah 40–66*, 251.

102. The LXX has Jerusalem named here, whereas the MT does not. This reflects most likely the LXX translators mode to translate the sense, with "helps" for the reader, rather than give a literal translation—"a natural insertion" (Ottley, *Book of Isaiah According to the Septuagint*, 365).

103. Koole, *Isaiah 56–66*, 222.

104. Childs summarizes the note well: "the new Jerusalem is not a rebuilt earthly city, but the entrance of the divine kingdom of God, the creation of a new heaven and earth" (*Isaiah*, 500).

"everything will literally be seen in a different light."[105] The ordinary light has not been enough for the blind people; true light—revelation—comes from God: "he is the light himself."[106] This picture of the restoration of Jerusalem envisions it in a new eschatological reality, in which salvation and the presence of the Lord is the glory and light of the new restored people that encompasses both the gathered children of Israel and nations that are attracted to it by her light. The note of eschatological restoration of Jerusalem—the new thing God is going to do—is heightened in Isa 65 in the promise of new heavens and new earth (*estai gar ho ouranos kainos kai hē gē kainē*) (65:17) that includes a restored Jerusalem and her people: "look, I make Jerusalem as gladness and my people as a joy" (65:18).[107] This is a nexus that is already present in Isa 54:11–17.

In conclusion, the imagery of the barren woman being made fruitful evokes a "tale of two cities" that is about the restoration of the desolate Jerusalem—alienated people—into a glorious future metropolis—a "mother-city"—that functions as a symbol, or a place of identification, for the new community that includes people from other nations. The restoration of Jerusalem has an eschatological horizon, and it is essentially about restoring the presence and rule (kingdom) of God among the people. Furthermore, the elevation of Zion, and the establishment of the new Jerusalem above any other city transposes the event to a cosmic level that is described with language of new creation.

The Spirit and Fruitfulness

The vision of restoration in Isa 52:13—55:13 includes an invitation to drink of waters provided by the Lord (55:1). The desolation/exile of God's people has been described in Isaiah in terms of a garden that has no water (1:30) and a people who are thirsty (5:13). In the vision of restoration in Isaiah, this condition is remedied by the gift of water. The imagery of the water is rich and multivalent, but contains an important link with the Spirit. This is perceived in the language about turning wilderness into fruitful land by means of water and the Spirit.

In Isa 32, it is the *Spirit* that is poured on the people that will turn wilderness (*erēmos*) into fruitful land (32:15), whereas in Isa 35 the promise of God's salvation is pictured as the wilderness blossoming (35:1–7) that

---

105. Koole, *Isaiah 56–66*, 218.

106. Koole, *Isaiah 56–66*, 218.

107. Horbury notes the connection between "new creation" and the expectation of a future temple/city (*Messianism*, 204).

involves *water* flowing in the wilderness and streams in the desert (35:6–7). This link that parallels water and the Spirit is present in other texts also. Furthermore, the water transforming barren land (*erēmos*) into fruitfulness is intimately connected with the transformation of the barrenness (*erēmos*) of the woman in Isa 54:1. The Spirit is the agent of restoration in transforming the desolation, and thus it is also plausible to view the Spirit at work in generating the many children in Isa 54:1. This connection is confirmed in the following analysis.

In Isa 41, Israel is comforted by recalling her choosing as the offspring of Abraham (*sperma abraam*) (41:8). Then Israel is promised God's help as the redeemer (41:13–14). The ensuing restoration is described by the providence of abundant water that transforms the thirsty land (41:18). This connection between the offspring/seed of Abraham and the "waters" that signal restoration is strengthened and expressed also in terms of the Spirit in Isa 44.

Isaiah 44 addresses Israel as God's servant, whom God formed from the womb (44:1–2), echoing the origins of the people in the birth of Isaac from Sarah (see discussion above), but now focusing on God's regenerative activity in the restoration of the new people that is elaborated in 44:3–5. She is not to fear, for God will give water for the thirsty (*hoti egō dōsō hydōr en dipsei*), to those walking in the dry places (44:3). The metaphor of the water is opened up by the proclamation that God will pour his Spirit upon Israel's offspring/seed (*epithēsō to pneuma mou epi to sperma sou*), which in turn conveys the Lord's blessing on Israel's children (*kai tas eulogias mou epi ta tekna sou*) (44:3).[108] This is a key moment in understanding the role of the Spirit in the formation of the new people of God. First, it confirms that the rich use of the water metaphor in Isaiah can be taken to refer to the Spirit of the Lord. Second, it connects the Spirit, seed, children, and blessing in a theologically significant way.

The generative role of the Spirit in the formation of the new people of God is further elaborated, as the pouring of the Spirit produces the restored people of God who "spring up like grass" and "willows by the streams" (44:4). These people identify as the Lord's own, and name themselves after Jacob-Israel (*houtos erei tou theou eimi, kai houtos boēsetai epi tō onomati iakōb, kai heteros epigrapsei tou theou eimi, epi tō onomati israēl*) (44:5). Blenkinsopp asserts that the descriptions in 44:5 "can only be understood as proselytes . . . who have joined themselves to Yahveh."[109] Hence, this pas-

---

108. Lee understands the parallelism between the Spirit and blessing to develop the thought and not simply as two lines that are equated, i.e., the Spirit being the blessing (*Blessing of Abraham*, 115–16).

109. Blenkinsopp, *Isaiah 40–55*, 233. Cf. Koole, *Isaiah 40–48*, 366. Also Ma: "[i]t is certainly unnatural for any Israelite born to have a need to call himself Jacob, or to add

sage claims that the provision of the Spirit is integral in the formation and identification of the restored people of God that includes people from other nations. This connects with the Abrahamic promise in Gen 12:3; 18:18; 22:18; and its development in 35:11. Thus, Lee is correct in perceiving here a prophetic envisioning of the fulfillment of the Abrahamic promise of blessing to the nations: "[t]he promise in Gen 35:11, which is a development of the Abrahamic blessing for the nations, that, Jacob, who was renamed Israel, shall become 'a nation and a company of nations,' is finally fulfilled at the eschatological restoration of Israel."[110]

Isaiah 63 is another important text that talks about the Spirit in the life of God's people.[111] As the days of old (exodus) are remembered, the Spirit's role is recognized as an integral part in the life of the people. The Lord saved his people from affliction,[112] because of his love and compassion, but the people disobeyed and provoked his Holy Spirit, and therefore, by opposing God, he became their enemy (63:10). The memories of old provoke a further question: Where is the one who set the Holy Spirit among them (63:11), who gave the Spirit that led his people (63:14)?[113] This question acts as a lament of the present condition, in which "divine involvement at the present time" is absent.[114] The Spirit is remembered as the hallmark of God's people. Surprisingly, when the people now in need of divine assistance ask for the Lord to look upon them in mercy (63:15), they appeal to him directly as the father (*sy gar hēmōn ei patēr*) (63:16). Even if the patriarchs (Abraham and Israel/Jacob) would not recognize them, the Lord is asked to be the father of a people (63:16) who have become as if not his people (*egenometha hōs to ap' archēs, hote ouk ērxas hēmōn oude epeklēthē to onoma sou eph' hēmas*) (63:19).[115] This is a confession of a people who sense that their unfaithful-

---

the name Israel to his own. The speakers must be non-Israelites who witness the work of the life-giving spirit within Israel and are convinced by the absoluteness of Yahweh and the turn to him" (*Until the Spirit Comes*, 87).

110. Lee, *Blessing of Abraham*, 194; cf. Childs, *Isaiah*, 230. Blenkinsopp: "the Abrahamic blessing runs like a strong undercurrent throughout this entire second part of the book" (*Isaiah 40–55*, 233).

111. On the significance of Isa 63 in the development of the understanding of the Holy Spirit in Israel's Scripture, see Blenkinsopp, *Isaiah 56–66*, 261.

112. LXX is emphatic that it was not an angel *ou presbys oude angelos, all' autos kyrios* (63:9), whereas the MT designates it as an angel *umal'akh panayw hoshi'am*.

113. Cf. Blenkinsopp: "the first step toward restoring the broken relationship between people and their God is to remember" (*Isaiah 56–66*, 261).

114. Blenkinsopp, *Isaiah 56–66*, 261.

115. The MT has a different tone here (shifting from us to them), as it seems to lament a more fundamental problem with Israel: "we are from ancient times, [but] you did not rule them, nor was your name called upon them [ownership]" (*hayinu me'olam*

ness would not allow them to be recognized as offspring of Abraham or the people of Israel. As Koole notes, "this means that the congregation in its present situation can no longer appeal to its natural ancestry . . . this requires a new covenant."[116] It is a call for a new beginning, deliverance, and re-formation of a people who need the mercy of the Father and the restored presence of his Spirit to become the true people of God.

The Servant and Generating the Community of Servants

As I note in my analysis of the immediate context of Isa 54:1, it is the servant in 52:13—53:12 that brings about the restoration pictured in chapters 54-55. I also point out that the servant's work generates the many children of the barren woman who are later described as the community of servants in 54:17.[117]

Before I take up the texts that directly speak of the servant or many servants, I briefly discuss the movement in Isaiah from the expectation of a messianic figure to the servant. Isaiah 11 introduces an expectation of a future "Davidic" king (11:1) who is anointed by the Spirit (11:2-3) to execute the saving justice of God (11:4). His justice brings about conditions of unprecedented peace that are pictured like a new creation: the wolf grazing with the lamb, etc. (11:5-9). Moreover, the "new creation" conditions are the result of the entire earth having been filled with the knowledge of the Lord (11:9). This vision of restoration in Isa 11 shares in the same pattern as 54:1 in its context; the future "Davidic messiah" brings about restoration in peace and the knowledge of God.

But what happens to this expectation of the Davidic messiah? Williamson observes that God's kingship comes to the fore in the latter part of the book, and human kingship disappears, as far as Israel is concerned.[118] Furthermore, the covenant with David's house is understood to have been extended/transferred to all Israel according to Isa 55:3—the movement of "democratization of the monarchy."[119] But this is limited in its context

---

lo'-mashalta bam lo'-niqra' shimkha 'alehem).

116. Koole, *Isaiah 56-66*, 378.
117. Cf. Laato, "About Zion," 156, 160-61.
118. Williamson, *Variations*, 4.
119. Williamson, *Variations*, 5, 7-8; commenting on 55:3-5: "the covenant with David is here potentially transferred to the people as a whole" (117). Cf. Goldingay, *Message of Isaiah 40-55*, 97. Fishbane also notices in Isa 55:1-5 "a nationalization of the promises to David as formulated in Ps.89" (*Biblical Interpretation*, 495).

(55:4–5) to refer to the role of a witness to the nations.[120] Hence, the pattern of God–king–people is transformed to God–people–nations.[121] It is in this transition that Israel begins to be called the servant, a title that was used of the king in Israel (cf. Ps 89).[122] This connection between the kingly role and the servant is reflected in the presentation of the servant in Isa 42:1–4 in "royal guise."[123] Although there is movement from the role of the king to the people becoming the servant, the vision of the king and his task continues through this transition. This is anchored in the vision of God as king in Isa 6.[124] Thus, the role of the servant (collective people) is to witness—to represent—the interests of God the King in the ultimate vision of restoration that is about a new "ideal society" that consists of faithfulness, righteousness, and peace.[125]

With this understanding of the transition from the role of the king to the people as the servant, I turn to the analysis of the texts about the servant. In Isa 41, Israel is comforted by recalling her calling: "you are Israel, my servant (*pais mou*) Jacob whom I chose, the seed of Abraham whom I loved" (41:8). Israel is designated here as the servant, being the offspring of Abraham and God's chosen one. The next verse directs attention to the future reality of restoration—a prophetic reality that historical reality must catch up with:[126] Israel is the servant that was gathered from the uttermost parts of the earth (41:9). She is not to be afraid for she has been redeemed and made secure (41:10–14).

The description of Israel as God's servant continues in Isa 42.[127] Now, in addition to Israel being designated as the chosen servant of the Lord, she is pictured as anointed by the Spirit (*edōka to pneuma mou ep' auton*) to bring justice (*krisis*) to the nations (42:1),[128] echoing the description of

---

120. Williamson, *Variations*, 119.
121. Williamson, *Variations*, 123–24.
122. Williamson, *Variations*, 129.
123. Williamson, *Variations*, 132–34.
124. Williamson, *Variations*, 9.
125. Williamson, *Variations*, 20.
126. Cf. Goldingay, *Message of Isaiah 40–55*, 103.

127. The LXX translator makes the identity of the servant clear by the terms Jacob and Israel (*iakōb ho pais mou, antilēmpsomai autou; israēl ho eklektos mou*) (42:1) that do not appear in the MT. This is most likely due to the translator's attempt to translate by giving the sense of the text rather than a slavish literal translation. The context from Isa 41 supplies these designations.

128. Ekblad's analysis concludes that "the LXX presents κρίσις as justice and the victory of righteousness in a world of injustice and darkness" (*Isaiah's Servant Poems*, 278).

the "Davidic messiah" in Isa 11.[129] In a surprising move, the servant delivers justice not by a mighty display of power but in meekness (42:2-3). She/he will shine forth and not be broken in the task of establishing justice on the earth, and his law becomes the hope of the nations (*epi tō nomō autou ethnē elpiousin*) (42:4).[130] Justice is the note that dominates the description of the servant's work in 42:1-4, and Koole defines the justice envisioned here as "the realization of God's rule, the advent of the kingdom in which God is recognized, obeyed and praised."[131] The Lord promises to uphold his servant and give him as a covenant for a race/people (*eis diathēkēn genous* / MT: *'am*), a light to the nations (*eis phōs ethnōn*); to open blind eyes and bring out those in bonds who sit in darkness (42:6-7). This description of the servant's task is ascribed to Israel, but as an ideal.[132] The development in the theme of the servant unfolds how this ideal vision is reached. However, the description of the servant's task to open blind eyes and release captives in 42:6-7 already anticipates that the servant in Isa 42 somehow also serves Israel's restoration. Hence, the ideal picture of Israel as the servant in Isa 42 is complicated, which prepares for the development of the theme in Isa 49, and ultimately in Isa 53.

After the servant's description in Isa 42, the Lord is depicted going out like a mighty man of war (42:13) to deliver his people; to lead the blind in a way they do not know and turn darkness into light (42:13-16). The blind people in darkness turn out to be those who have turned away from the Lord to worship idols (42:17). In fact, the glorious depiction of the servant has turned into a picture of the servant being blind and deaf; though Israel has seen, she has not observed, has eyes but has not perceived (42:18-20). Furthermore, she is blind and deaf because she has not understood that

129. This description of the servant renders the possibility of interpreting it in a Messianic sense (Koole, *Isaiah 40-48*, 210). This is possible, but I resist the "quick" identification of 42:1-9 with a Messiah, and rather follow the development of the theme that provides a "narrative scheme" for identifying the servant in relation to Israel.

130. Thus the Göttingen edition that corresponds with the MT (*uletorato 'iim yeyakhelu*). Rahlfs has *epi tō onomati autou*.

131. Koole, *Isaiah 40-48*, 208.

132. Blenkinsopp argues that the servant in 42:1-9 refers to Cyrus, but also recognizes that it could be about an "ideal Israel" or an individual who speaks and acts for Israel (*Isaiah 40-55*, 210-11). I prefer to follow the LXX translator's example in identifying the servant in 42:1-9 from its literary context. Cf. Childs: "for anyone who takes the larger literary context seriously, there can be no avoiding the obvious implication that *in some way* Israel is the servant who is named in 42:1" (*Isaiah*, 325; emphasis original). However, Childs recognizes that this opens "enormous interpretive problems." Hence, it is appealing to identify here a servant who has a function towards Israel rather than being Israel herself. Nevertheless, it is worth pursuing the more difficult task of following the lead of the LXX, and inquire how the servant in 42 can be identified as Israel.

exile was the Lord's doing on account of her sin—her resistance to walk in his ways and to listen to his Law (42:23-25).

But this is not the end of Israel's story as the servant. The scene shifts again to the theological reality of restoration—Israel is not to fear for the Lord has redeemed her and called her by name to be his (43:1). Because of his love for her, the Lord gathers and calls his people from the ends of the earth (43:4-6). God establishes the blind and deaf people as his witness—his servant—who is now to know, believe, and understand that it is only the Lord who saves (43:8-12). They are called not to remember former things, but behold the new thing God is doing—redemption and restoration (43:18-20). Despite Israel's burdening of the Lord with her sin (43:24),[133] the Lord promises forgiveness (43:25; cf. 44:21-22). Furthermore, the restoration of Israel as God's servant is the result of the Spirit being poured on her offspring (44:1-5; see discussion above).

Hence, in this intriguing section of Isa 41-44, the servant is designated as Israel, but she only becomes the true servant who fulfills her calling as God's "Spirit anointed witness" to the nations (Isa 42:1-9) after God has delivered her from her own blindness, deafness, and imprisonment in darkness, and has re-formed her by the Spirit.[134]

In the process of restoring Israel to her true calling as God's servant, Cyrus is named as a historical figure who was anointed for the task of restoring the people (44:28—45:13). Hence, God uses another "servant"—an anointed figure—for the sake of the servant Israel (*heneken iakōb tou paidos mou kai israēl tou eklektou mou egō kalesō se*) (45:4).[135] But the positive reception of Cyrus—a Gentile king—as an agent of restoration is not obvious (45:9-10). God, who made the earth and humankind, declares to have raised Cyrus for the task of restoring his people (45:12-13). Cyrus's role towards Israel is a historical precedent that highlights the need for another "servant" to serve the purpose of restoring Israel to become the servant. After Isa 48, Cyrus fades from the purview of the book to make room for the "suffering servant."[136] Nevertheless, he provides a paradigm for what follows.

---

133. The meaning of the LXX is obscure here: *en tais hamartiais sou kai en tais adikiais sou proestēn sou*. The MT is more explicit that the sins and iniquities have burdened the Lord: *he'vadtani bekhatto'wtekha hoga'tani ba'awonoteka*.

134. Cf. Laato, who claims that "according to 42:1 and 61:1 Yhwh's Spirit rests upon his loyal servant. Isa 59:21 promises that this Spirit will come upon all the righteous who share in the covenant that the loyal servant will establish" (*"About Zion,"* 167-68).

135. However, as Goldingay points out, the actual term "servant" is not used of Cyrus, as it is kept for "figures with a part to play in other aspects of Yhwh's purpose than the ones involving Cyrus" (*Message of Isaiah 40-55*, 368).

136. Childs, *Isaiah*, 352.

Williamson argues that Isa 49 is a pivotal chapter where there is a transfer of the servant's role from Israel to someone else, and a shift in context and tone from 40–48 to 49–55.[137] After Israel has been designated as the Lord's servant in 49:1-3 (*kai eipe moi, doulos mou ei sy, israēl*) (49:3),[138] surprisingly, the servant in 49:5-9 has the task to gather Israel back to God (*tou stēsai tas phylas iakōb kai tēn diasporan tou israēl epistrepsai*), and offer light and salvation to the ends of the earth (*tetheika se eis phōs ethnōn tou einai se eis sōtērian heōs eschatou tēs gēs*) (49:6). Furthermore, the servant is given as a covenant to the nations (*edōka se eis diathēkēn ethnōn*)[139] (49:8) to deliver them from their bonds, and bring them out of darkness (49:9). In between these "two" servants, is an expression of a sense of failure or frustration in the servant's work (*kenōs ekopiasa kai eis mataion kai eis outhen edōka tēn ischyn mou*) (49:4a), that moves to a more hopeful tone of expectation (*dia touto hē krisis mou para kyriō, kai ho ponos mou enantion tou theou mou*) (49:4b). This movement from the servant in 49:1-3 to the servant in 49:5-9 and onwards via verse 4 has caused much puzzle.[140] Whether or not the

---

137. Williamson, *Variations*, 147–52. I do not agree with Williamson's suggestion that the servant's role has been transferred to the prophet or a group that has responded to his message. I prefer not to engage in speculative historical reconstruction, but rather focus on what can be understood by following the text—a transferral of the task to another servant whose identity is not given (cf. Childs, *Isaiah*, 385).

138. Some argue that rather than Israel being designated as the servant here, it is the new servant who is designated as Israel, and thus the whole description is about this new servant without a transfer taking place within the movement in 49:1–9 (e.g., Childs, *Isaiah*, 384; Williamson, *Variations*, 151). The difference comes from reading "Israel" with different syntactical meanings (the MT and LXX are similar here). It can be read as a vocative "O Israel"; or in apposition: "you are my servant, Israel"; or as predicative: "you are my servant, you are Israel" (Childs, *Isaiah*, 384). I perceive it in apposition for contextual reasons (see below).

139. The LXX assigns the servant as a covenant to the *nations* (*ethnē*), whereas the MT designates the covenant to the *people* ('*am*). This is an interesting move by a translator that is sometimes accused of a nationalistic agenda (see, e.g., Baer, "'It's All about Us!'").

140. The difficulty in the perceived contradiction between v. 3 and vv. 5–6 has caused some earlier commentators even to delete Israel from v. 3 without real textual evidence (e.g., Westermann, *Isaiah 40–66*, 209). Childs (*Isaiah*, 383–85), Koole (*Isaiah 49–55*, 11–13), and Williamson (*Variations*, 150–51) argue that it is the same servant in both vv. 1–3 and 5–9, who is a new servant that is designated as Israel (but not replacing Israel). I still perceive that 49:1–9 includes the transition from Israel as the servant to another servant. The weakness in my reading is the content of v. 4 that expresses frustration that could imply an attempt at trying to be the right kind of servant but seeing no results, in contrast to the failure of Israel to be the servant due to her sin that has been made clear in the previous passages. But it could also be understood as Israel's failure, or sense of frustration in bringing about her own restoration (cf. Isa 37:3; 49:14), which is then addressed in the following verses that introduce a new servant that can accomplish it, and the larger task to communicate salvation to the nations. Hence, I

movement from one servant (Israel) to another takes place within 49:1–9 or is presupposed in it, what is important for our purpose, is to note that the servant's role is transferred from Israel to someone else closely identified with her. As Ekblad concludes: "the LXX of Isaiah 49:1–7 is an extremely enigmatic text. Its Greek translators sought to take seriously the title of the servant often attributed to Israel. At the same time they wrestled deeply with the impossibility of the servant, (or perhaps some other figure alluded to by the text), actually being Israel."[141]

I have earlier offered an analysis on how the servant's work in Isa 52:13—53:12 leads to the vision of restoration in Isa 54. I now situate it in the overall narrative scheme of the servant in Isaiah. This passage has attracted a lot of attention and differing proposals for the identification of the servant.[142] My reading of Isa 52:13—53:12 follows the movement that ascribes the role of the servant to someone other than Israel for the purpose of the restoration of Israel, which has implications for the nations. As the "narrative of the servant" in Isa 41-44 demonstrates, Israel needs God's deliverance from bondage and sin to become the servant she is meant to be. She cannot serve herself in this purpose. In Isa 45, God's act of deliverance is given a historical precedent in Cyrus—he is God's agent to serve the purpose of restoring the servant Israel. Both Cyrus and the servant in 52:13—53:12 are received by a sense of astonishment. In addition, I suggest that Isa 49 (especially the LXX) encapsulates the narrative scheme: the failure of the servant Israel to bring about her own restoration occasions the designation of "another servant" to the task of her restoration, and to extend salvation to the nations. It is in this context that the servant in 52:13—53:12 is introduced. This is *the* servant who acts on God's behalf (the "arm of the Lord," cf. 52:10) to bear the sins of the people, and to bring about restoration of a new community of servants that is envisioned in Isa 54. Hence, Isa 54:1 encapsulates the narrative of restoration that is centered on the servant.

---

perceive that this passage summarizes the narrative of the servant Israel who needs another servant to restore her and take salvation to the nations (Isa 41–44 and 45).

141. Ekblad, *Isaiah's Servant Poems*, 122.

142. Heskett collects a helpful review of the different suggestions for the identity of the servant in Isa 52:13—53:12: the servant as Israel; individual distinct from Israel; Moses; Cyrus; Prophet Second Isaiah; Messianic figure (*Messianism within the Scriptural Scroll of Isaiah*, 133–52). Seitz adds to the list the option that Isa 52:13—53:12 is about personified Zion (*Zion's Final Destiny*, 203–5). The diversity can partially be explained by variety in approaches, e.g., is it aimed at historical reconstruction? Is the passage read as a separate "servant song" in connection with the other "servant songs," or in the context of the whole book of Isaiah?

This is highlighted in the following analysis of the movement from the one servant to the many servants.[143]

The shift from the one servant to the many servants begins in Isa 54:17.[144] It is characteristic of the last section of the book of Isaiah to speak of servants in the plural rather than of a singular servant in conjunction with making a sharp distinction within Israel between the responsive faithful and the disobedient.[145] Hence, Williamson speaks of a move from a "collective singular" to a "plurality of individuals"; not the nation as a whole, but those who seek the Lord are the servants of the Lord.[146] Yet the many servants are not only from among Israel. In Isa 56, the foreigners who "attach" themselves to the Lord to serve him (*tois allogenesi tois proskeimenois kyriō douleuein autō*) are to be his male and female servants (*einai autō eis doulous kai doulas*) (56:6).[147] They have free access to the house of prayer for all the nations on the holy mountain (56:7).

The greatest concentration of the language of "many servants" is in Isa 65. But first, the LXX states that it is because of a singular servant that the Lord will not destroy all the people (*houtōs poiēsō heneken tou douleuontos moi, toutou heneken ou mē apolesō pantas*) (65:8).[148] Hence, there is hope that the descendants of Jacob and Judah, or moreover God's chosen ones and servants, will inherit the holy mountain to dwell there (65:9). Following the LXX, we have again in Isa 65 the pattern of a servant generating the "seed" that are the servants who inherit future restoration. Furthermore, as Koole perceptively points out, "the emphasis is not on national privilege but on individual election and personal servanthood."[149] This fact is highlighted as, in contrast, those who forsake the Lord and disregard the holy mountain will be destroyed (65:11-12). This distinction between the servants and the ones being destroyed comes to sharp focus in 65:13-14 with pronouncements of blessings on those who serve the Lord

---

143. Isa 61:1-7 is another text about an "anointed figure." The description of his task (61:1-2) is full of echoes from the anointed "Davidic messiah" in Isa 11, and the servant in Isa 41-44, 45, 49, and 52:13—53:12: "a character who somehow gathers to himself every available role in deutero-Isaiah related to the work of announcing and inaugurating God's salvation" (Williamson, *Variations*, 184).

144. Cf. Blenkinsopp: "[Isa 54:17] serves to introduce a major theme in the last section and functions as an important editorial link between sections" (*Isaiah 40-55*, 366).

145. Cf. Williamson, *Variations*, 192.

146. Williamson, *Variations*, 194.

147. The MT does not distinguish between male and female servants.

148. The MT has the plural pointing with a first-person singular suffix *'avaday* (my servants). It is not difficult to imagine the LXX translator rendering it as a singular servant from an un-pointed Hebrew text.

149. Koole, *Isaiah 56-66*, 431.

and "curses" on those who have forsaken the Lord.[150] Those who are under destruction leave their "name" to the chosen ones as a reminder of the destiny of those who forsake the Lord (65:15). The chosen ones are the servants who will receive a "new name" (*onoma kainon*) (65:15; cf. 62:2), and inherit a "new creation" reality (65:17-25). The giving of a new name is "symbolic of a new epoch" that continues the trajectory of restoration as the new thing that God does (e.g., 43:18-19), with this section envisioning an eschatological scenario that moves the destiny of the servants "from the historical to the metahistorical plane."[151]

These observations about the generation of the plurality of servants indicate the direction of the next section where I deepen the discussion concerning the identity of the many children of the barren-made-fruitful woman in Isa 54:1 with focused attention on the nations' inclusion.

The Identity of the Many Children and the Nations' Inclusion

In the vision of restoration in Isa 54, the many children of the barren woman cause the need to enlarge her tent (54:1-2), and her offspring will inherit the nations (54:3). As the vision develops to the imagery of the city, proselytes/strangers are said to come to the restored city because of God (54:15 LXX). In the following, I analyze the identity of the many children with focus on the complex theme of the inclusion of the nations.

In Isa 1, Judah/Jerusalem is initially rebuked for her rebellion (1:1-4), and her land is depicted as desolate and devoured (1:7-8). If the Lord had not left some offspring, Jerusalem's fate would have been like that of Sodom and Gomorrah (1:9). Jerusalem's close comparison with the sinful cities continues with the address to leaders of Sodom and people of Gomorrah that refer to the leaders and inhabitants of Jerusalem/Judah (1:10). This connection "dissolves any distinction between Israel and the nations based on superior righteousness."[152] The discrepancy in Judah's sin and continued life of worship is revealed (1:11-15) and followed by a call to repentance (1:16-17). The offer of forgiveness and the call to obedience would result in "eating the good of the land" (1:18-19), but if she refuses and rebels, she shall be "eaten by the sword" (1:20). Hence, inclusion in restoration is conditional even for the people of Judah. Furthermore, although Zion

---

150. Cf. Laato: "Isa 65:13-15 makes a final distinction between the two groups; the groups of 'my servants' and the groups of 'you' who have abandoned Yhwh and his proclamation of salvation" (*"About Zion,"* 163).

151. Blenkinsopp, *Isaiah 56-66*, 281-83.

152. Ekblad, *Isaiah's Servant Poems*, 283.

shall be saved, those who forsake the Lord shall perish and be put to shame because of idolatry (1:27-31), highlighting the division within Israel with respect to salvation and judgment.[153] Where Isa 1 narrows the line of inclusion within Israel, Isa 2 widens it to encompass the nations. As Zion is restored and exalted above all other mountains, all the nations are pictured coming to her to be taught by the Lord (2:2-3). Thus, the vision of restoration in the opening chapters of Isaiah makes it clear that inclusion in the restored community is not obvious for the Israelite, and opens the prospect for people of other nations to be also included.

Isaiah 19 describes God's judgments on Egypt and its turning to the Lord (19:1-22). Furthermore, people from Assyria and Egypt, who have turned to the Lord, are joined in the blessing of Israel (implying her restoration) as God's people (*eulogēmenos ho laos mou ho en aigyptō kai ho en assyriois kai hē klēronomia mou israēl*) (19:25).[154] The LXX rendering highlights that it is not the nations as a whole, but those who have turned to the Lord that are reckoned to be included in God's people.

The "apocalyptic section" of Isaiah describes the restoration of Israel with universal and cosmic consequences. The Lord, who reigns from Zion, judges the impious and evil people, and elevates the poor and oppressed (24:23—25:5). Isa 25 describes the Lord making a "feast" (the word for feast is lacking in the LXX, but is in the MT: *mishteh*) for all the nations on Zion (25:6). On that day, people rejoice in God's salvation (25:9), but at the expense of the Moabites whose pride has been brought low (25:10-12). Isaiah 26 states that the people who keep righteousness and faith, and have hoped in the Lord, will enter the city (26:2-4). In contrast, the oppressors of Israel, the ungodly and impious, are destroyed (26:10-15, 21). Isaiah 27 places the emphasis on the gathering of the scattered and oppressed people of Israel from among the nations (*hymeis de synagagete tous huious israēl kata hena hena*) (27:12). They will come and worship the Lord on the holy mountain at

---

153. Blenkinsopp, *Isaiah 1-39*, 187.

154. The LXX could just mean that the blessing is to "my inheritance Israel" ("my people who are in Egypt and in Assyria, indeed my inheritance Israel"), and not necessarily Egyptians and Assyrians. Thus Seeligmann: "the countries Egypt and Assyria, as the recipients of God's blessing, in the Hebrew text have been replaced in the Greek by the diaspora groups in Egypt and Mesopotamia" (*Septuagint Version of Isaiah*, 117). But this is unlikely due to the context that describes Egyptians turning to the Lord. It is better to view the translator specifying that it is not the nations as a whole, but only those in them that have turned to the Lord. The option remains also to read the sense as: "blessed be my people who are in Egypt and in Assyria, indeed they are my inheritance Israel." Nevertheless, the MT remains much stronger and explicit in stating that Egypt is God's people and Assyria the work of his hands (*barukh 'ammi mitsrayim uma'ashe yaday 'ashur wenakhalati yisra'el*).

Jerusalem (27:13). Hence, the "apocalyptic vision" of restoration emphasizes the salvation of God's oppressed people Israel, and the nations are placed primarily under judgment. But these categories are not purely nationalistic, as the focus of salvation is on the oppressed people who have hoped in God, and judgment is on the boastful and ungodly oppressors.

In the context of restoring Israel to be God's servant, the restored people in Isa 43 are the scattered offspring of Israel who are being regathered (43:1–7). As Cyrus is designated the anointed agent of Israel's deliverance and restoration, the aim is that other nations recognize that there is no other God but the Lord (45:6). Furthermore, people of other nations—former slave-owners—become Israel's slaves in chains, recognizing that God is in Israel (45:14).[155] All who oppose God shall be put to shame, but Israel is saved with everlasting salvation (45:16–17). However, invitation to salvation is extended to the ends of the earth (*epistraphēte pros me kai sōthēsesthe, hoi ap' eschatou tēs gēs*) (45:22). Indeed, righteousness will proceed from the mouth of the Lord like words that shall not return back (45:23). The words of righteousness are proven effectual in the future reality (cf. 55:11) when every knee shall bow before the Lord and every tongue confess to God (45:23).[156] As Blenkinsopp remarks, Isaiah is not a universalist when presenting a universal offer of salvation—it is not an offer of "unconditional universal salvation, without some form of confession of faith."[157] The content of the confession is a recognition of dependence on God; righteousness and glory are ascribed to him, and, while shame comes to those who separate themselves from the Lord (45:24), all those who have turned to the Lord are made righteous by the Lord (*apo kyriou dikaiōthēsontai*), indeed all the seed of Israel (those who have joined in the confession) is glorified (45:25).[158] In this vision of restoration, monotheism and the universal offer of salvation are connected. The people being saved are the ones who recognize the sovereignty of God. In contrast, those who oppose or separate themselves from God are excluded. These categories of inclusion and exclusion transcend national/ethnic boundaries, and have the potential to create a new community of a shared confession.

155. Cf. Koole, *Isaiah 40–48*, 463.

156. Cf. Childs, *Isaiah*, 297. There is question whether the word of righteousness is a word of promise or command; and whether the confession is willing or forced (see Blenkinsopp, *Isaiah 40–55*, 262–63). I understand that v. 22 sets the tone to be about an invitation for salvation, and hence, I read the next verses to be about the promise of righteousness and the willing response of those who have turned to the Lord.

157. Blenkinsopp, *Isaiah 40–55*, 257.

158. Cf. Childs: "the 'offspring of Israel' is now defined in terms of those who find in God their righteousness and strength" (*Isaiah*, 356).

The vision of restoration in Isa 49 resembles the note in 54:2-3: when the Lord delivers and restores Zion, she will be too crowded for her inhabitants (49:19-20). Zion wonders where all the people have come from (49:21). The Lord answers that it is he who signals the nations to bring her sons and daughters (49:22). Foreign kings and queens have been "foster fathers and mothers" who now bow down to Zion (49:23). Then Zion knows that the Lord is the Lord, and those who wait for him shall not be put to shame (49:23). The Lord will surely save Zion's children and judge her oppressors (49:25-26). Here the focus is on gathering the sons and daughters of Zion, and the nations are subservient to that purpose. This is an example of the "common promise that Israel's humbling by the nations will be systematically reversed."[159]

Isaiah 51 addresses those who pursue righteousness and seek the Lord (*akousate mou, hoi diōkontes to dikaion kai zētountes ton kyrion*) (51:1), i.e., the people aligning themselves with the servant introduced in Isa 49, whom those who fear the Lord have been asked to listen to (*tis en hymin ho phoboumenos ton kyrion? akousatō tēs phōnēs tou paidos autou*) (50:10).[160] As Koole summarizes, "decisive now is the relationship with the person and work of the Servant, 50:10f."[161] They are to look to Abraham their father and to Sarah who bore them, with the reminder that Abraham was but one when he was called that the Lord might bless and multiply him (51:2). The Lord will send out his law and justice as a light to the peoples (51:4; cf. 2:3). As the Lord's salvation goes out, the nations and islands hope for him and wait for his "arm" (51:5). Thus, in line with the Abrahamic promise, as the Lord restores Zion, the saving "arm" of the Lord is extended to the nations.

Isaiah 56 begins a new section, in which the hope of restoration is reflected on in the context of partial/complicated fulfillment. The Lord promises to bring to his holy mountain all those who keep the Sabbath and his covenant (56:1-7). This includes the stranger and eunuch (56:3). The eunuch, who keeps the Sabbath and covenant, is promised an especially esteemed position in the house of the Lord (56:4-5). The foreigner, who attaches himself to the Lord to serve him is promised a place as a servant (56:6). Thus, the Lord's house shall be called the house of prayer for all

---

159. Goldingay, *Message of Isaiah 40-55*, 392.

160. Blenkinsopp notes the connection from 50:10 to 51:1, but interprets the servant as the prophet, and hence perceives the addressees as "the well disposed among the prophet's audience addressed in the previous passage" (*Isaiah 40-55*, 325).

161. Koole, *Isaiah 49-55*, 138. Koole concludes: "in the drama of chs. 40-55, after the opposition to the divine word in 42:18ff.; 45:9ff.; 48:1ff., a division emerges within Israel, which goes together with the prospect of universal salvation." Childs is also emphatic on the identification of the people with the servant (*Isaiah*, 402).

peoples/nations (*ethnē*) (56:7). This vision of people from all nations joining in the worship of Israel's God is the result of God's act of restoration that consists of the gathering of the dispersed of Israel and an "added gathering"—most likely of people from other nations (*eipen kyrios ho synagōn tous diesparmenous israēl, hoti synaxō ep' auton synagōgēn*) (56:8).[162] Following these verses, Childs concludes: "the point is made decisively that the 'servants' can include foreigners and outcasts who line themselves with the law of God over against the rebels and sinners within and without Israel who continue to resist his will."[163] Callaway presses the point even further: "[t]he prophet challenges the accepted categories of blessed and cursed, elect and outcast; precisely he who is excluded from worship turns out to be the one who receives the blessing. The 'barren' one who keeps the law is in fact the fruitful one."[164]

Where Isa 56 blurred the categories for who can be included in the people of God, Isa 58 complicates the line of what it means to be the faithful/righteous restored people of God. It begins by an emphatic command to declare the sins of Israel to them (58:1). Yet these are people who seem to do righteousness (*hōs laos dikaiosynēn pepoiēkō*) (58:2). Hence, they ask: Why does God not look to our fasting and humbling (58:3)? The Lord answers that their fasting is not of the kind he is looking for—their action is self-seeking and oppressive to others (58:3). He then outlines the content of real fasting: caring for those in need (58:6–7), and if the people would practice this, their restoration would be real (58:8–12).[165] The focus then shifts to the true practice of Sabbath (58:13). The people are called to abandon their own self-seeking practice, and to truly hallow the day, and delight in the Lord's Sabbath, and thus trust (LXX) / delight (MT) in the Lord (58:14).[166] If they do this, they will be given/fed the inheritance of Jacob—the provision of the land (58:14). Hence, it is not an outward

162. The MT is more obscure on 56:8: *'od 'aqabbets 'alayw leniqbatsayw* (literally translated: still/again/adding I will gather to/upon him [to] his gathered ones). In any case, the previous verse suggests that this "added gathering" consists of people from other nations.

163. Childs, *Isaiah*, 458.

164. Callaway, *Sing, O Barren One*, 92–93.

165. Fishbane argues that this is not about social concern in self-referential terms, but about the reapplication of the rules and regulations concerning the Day of Atonement (Lev 16; 23:24–32) (*Biblical Interpretation*, 305).

166. Koole notes the contrast between the "delighting in the Sabbath" and the torments and mourning rituals of the fasting (58:5), and the self-seeking enriching of the self (58:13) (*Isaiah 56–66*, 156). The point is, according to Koole, that "the value of these activities can be played down, because well-being and salvation are not brought about by man himself but by God's blessing."

observance of the Law that satisfies the Lord and secures the inheritance of restoration. God desires a people who trust in him and live in true accordance with righteousness and compassion.

In Isa 60, Jerusalem is called to shine the light of the glory of the Lord. It includes the dimension of mediating divine revelation to others.[167] This light is set in contrast to the darkness upon the nations of the world—the absence of salvation (60:2a).[168] As the glory of God is manifested and concentrated on the new restored Jerusalem (60:2b), the nations are not left in darkness but shall come to her light—"the salvation of fellowship with God"[169]—echoing the vision in Isa 2:2–3.[170] In fact, the people from other nations can be understood as being included among the children of the new restored Jerusalem (*ide synēgmena ta tekna sou*) (60:4; cf. 56:8).[171] This reading is supported by the development of the thought in the following verses. With the returning of the children of Jerusalem comes also the wealth of the nations (60:5–6) that is brought joyfully with proclamation of the good news of the Lord's salvation (*to sōtērion kyriou euangeliountai*) (60:6)[172]—the nations' transition from darkness to light (60:3). The nations' offerings include acceptable sacrifices in the Lord's house of prayer (60:7; cf. 56:7 and 66:23). The nations also bring back the dispersed of Israel (60:8–9), which is an act of eschatological reversal from wrath to mercy, from being destroyed by foreign nations to having the foreigners build the city walls up again (60:10).[173] The nations'

---

167. Koole, *Isaiah 56–66*, 223.

168. Koole, *Isaiah 56–66*, 224; cf. Childs, *Isaiah*, 496.

169. Koole, *Isaiah 56–66*, 225; cf. Laato, "About Zion," 155.

170. See Fishbane (*Biblical Interpretation*, 498) for a demonstration of Isa 60 picking up of the themes from 2:1–4 (cf. Childs, *Isaiah*, 496). Koole notes that some juxtapose "the pilgrimage of the nations" in Isa 2 with the picture of "Israel's position of power" in Isa 60 (*Isaiah 56–66*, 225). This is understandable in light of vv. 10–16, but does not take seriously enough the emphasis on the nations' being drawn to the light of God's salvation, and the difference made between the peoples that come in and those that refuse (vv. 12–14).

171. There is debate whether the children of Jerusalem/Zion here refer to the nations or the dispersed of Israel (see Koole, *Isaiah 56–66*, 226). Koole argues that both are in view when this verse is taken in its context (vv. 4b and 9b referring to the dispersed of Israel; 5b and 6 to the nations). I agree, although I perceive more focus on the returning of the dispersed of Israel, but nevertheless including the nations in that process and in salvation (cf. 60:3, 6). It is possible to understand the nations being included in *all* the children of Jerusalem, but it is not clear. For Blenkinsopp the passage is primarily about the "repatriation of diaspora Jews," and the nations are in a subservient role (*Isaiah 56–66*, 212–16), but he neglects any notions of the nations' joyful entry and participation in salvation.

172. The MT has the nations proclaiming the praises of the Lord: *tehillot yhwh*.

173. Blenkinsopp, *Isaiah 56–66*, 214 (cf. Koole, *Isaiah 56–66*, 238). Childs argues

involvement in the restored city receives even more nuances, as some come in with their wealth (60:11), and others are humbled, or face destruction, because they were either former oppressors (60:14), or now refuse to serve the restored Jerusalem/Zion (60:12).[174] Hence, the vision of restoration in Isa 60 opens the gates of the restored Jerusalem wide open for the people of other nations to enter into God's light and salvation, but their inclusion in salvation is not self-evident. The emphasis on eschatological reversal places the nations in a subservient role to Israel's regathering, as former oppressors become the new servants, and those who refuse to submit to the "new" Jerusalem are destroyed. Thus, although the gates of the restored Jerusalem have been opened, they remain shut for those who refuse to recognize its glory. Consequently, the categories for inclusion or exclusion transcend national boundaries, as Childs concludes, "the polarity, which is consistent throughout Third Isaiah, is between those who turn to Yahweh, including foreigners, and those who resist God's will . . . judgment is decreed for those peoples, including Israelites, who oppose God's salvation."[175]

Characteristically for the last section of the book of Isaiah, after the hopes of salvation set forth in Isa 62, the people cry out to God in despair, as the city is in desolation (63:15; 64:9–10). In all this, the people think the Lord has kept silent (64:11). But the Lord answers in Isa 65, and declares that he became visible and was found by those who did not seek him; he said "here I am" to a nation that did not call my name (*eipa idou eimi, tō ethnei hoi ouk ekalesan to onoma mou*) (65:1)[176]—referring to the people of Israel who have just declared that they were as if not his people (63:19). The Lord says he has stretched his hand all day long to a disobedient and rebellious people who walk in their sin (65:2). This vision of restoration provides a paradigmatic move: the Lord reveals himself to a non-people—to a sinful,

---

that to view the picture (in vv. 8–9) as "crude postexilic nationalism" misses the theocentric theological point, in which "Zion is understood as the restored divine city" and "its splendor is identified with the rendering of honor to God" (*Isaiah*, 497). To prevent a one-sided reading of the roles in restoration, Isa 61 describes those who mourn for Zion rebuilding the ancient ruins (61:4), in contrast to the foreigners in 60:12. Blenkinsopp attributes the discrepancy in the description of the rebuilding of the walls (60:12; 61:4; 62:6) to the lack of unity in authorship (*Isaiah 56–66*, 214). But speculations on authorship are unnecessary, as it can be due to reflecting on different emphases on the future restoration.

174. Koole points out that the *huioi tapeinōsantōn se kai paroxynantōn se* in 60:14 does not necessarily refer only to people from other nations, but can also include the oppression within Israel that has been exposed in 58:6–10 and implied in 60:18 (*Isaiah 56–66*, 245).

175. Childs, *Isaiah*, 498.

176. MT has the passive voice (Pual): *'el-goy lo'-qora' bishmi* ("to a people that was not called by my name").

rebellious, and idolatrous people. This refers to Israel, but also offers a possible point of identification for other "non-peoples."

In Isa 66, the Lord articulates what he is looking for: not a temple, but for the humble that tremble at his words (66:1-2). In contrast, God will repay those who offer sacrifices in vain, because they did not hear him (66:3-4). All those who love Jerusalem are to rejoice with her (66:10). The Lord will provide comfort to those who worship/serve him (66:13-14). In contrast, the Lord comes in fire against those who disobey him, and the idolaters shall be destroyed (66:14-17). Here, the focus is on Israel, but with a distinction within—the Lord looks with acceptance at the humble that listen to him, but is against those who disobey him.

In the concluding section of Isa 66:18-24 that provides a "summary of eschatological themes that occur throughout the entire book of Isaiah,"[177] the Lord comes to gather all the nations (*synagagein panta ta ethnē kai tas glōssas*) to see his glory (66:18).[178] Then he sends people from among the saved (those from among the nations that were gathered, as described in the previous verse)[179] to proclaim God's glory to the nations who have not heard God's name or seen his glory (66:19). They will bring "your brothers" from all the nations (*axousi tous adelphous hymōn ek pantōn tōn ethnōn*) as a gift to the Lord (66:20), most likely referring to the dispersed of Israel.[180] Nevertheless, the ultimate aim of this multidimensional gathering is that "all flesh" (*pasa sarx*) shall come to worship in Jerusalem (66:23). In contrast, those who transgress against the Lord do not make it to the holy mountain but lie destroyed on the ground (66:24) as a warning sign and a reminder that "Isaiah is the book which preaches salvation and also penitence."[181] Although the final concluding section maintains the categories of Israel and the nations, the restored community dissolves the distinction, as it is comprised of people from the nations and Israel who respond to the proclamation of God's self-disclosure (glory), and as all flesh join in the worship of the one God.

As Schultz has pointed out, the canonical framing of the book of Isaiah by the parallel sections of chapters 1-2 and 65-66 is an important

---

177. Childs, *Isaiah*, 542.

178. Koole notes that in the history of interpretation the purpose of this gathering of the nations has been seen as "the divinely intended attack on the holy city by Gog and Magog, which would end in their destruction," but argues that this view is not supported by the use of gathering language in the second main section of Isaiah, where it is "always in a favorable sense" (*Isaiah 56-66*, 517-18).

179. Cf. Blenkinsopp, *Isaiah 56-66*, 314; Koole *Isaiah 56-66*, 520.

180. Koole, *Isaiah 56-66*, 523.

181. Koole, *Isaiah 56-66*, 531.

hermeneutical key for navigating the complexity in the material about the nations' role in Israel's restoration.[182] This guides the reading of Isaiah to a more universal direction, because the beginning and end envision an "unhindered access of Gentiles from many nations to divine instruction and to the worship of Yahweh in the temple."[183]

Besides the guide from the canonical framing of the book, I perceive that the key to reading Isaiah in relation to the nations is its nuanced view of inclusion in the restored community that transcends the traditional dichotomy of a nationalistic versus universalistic focus. As I have demonstrated in the analysis of several texts, the categories of those being saved and those being excluded transcend the national categories of Israel or the nations. Hence, I agree with Williamson who claims that the last two chapters in Isaiah signal a major transition (not just in Isaiah, but in the whole of Israel's Scripture), in which the identity of the people of God is being identified theologically rather than nationally.[184] The Lord looks both in Israel and among the nations to those who hear his word and respond (Isa 66). Also, the new restored humanity consists of those who join in the confession that God alone gives righteousness and glory to those who turn to him (Isa 45). It is those who oppose him in Israel and among the nations that face judgment. Furthermore, Israel's deliverance from exile is presented as an act of mercy and compassion rather than an act of obligation that God has towards his special people. The statement in Isa 65:1 about God appearing to a people who were not in the state of being his people, referring to Israel (63:19), brings hope also to others who are not originally God's people. Hence, when the nations see this act of mercy and the Lord's glory in it, they are drawn to its light. Israel's salvation and restoration can be viewed as a paradigmatic event that opens the way for other similarly sinful people to receive mercy and be included in the people of God. This, I perceive, is the theological potential Isaiah offers. Also, the book appeals to Abraham as a paradigm of God's ability to form his people again from the "barrenness" of her desolation. In accordance with the Abrahamic promise, the blessing of inclusion in the restored people of God is extended to all the nations by the servant of the Lord—the "arm" of God's salvation.

---

182. Schultz, "Nationalism and Universalism in Isaiah," 131. For a similar approach, see Laato ("*About Zion*," 163–64) and Childs (*Isaiah*, 22).

183. Schultz, "Nationalism and Universalism in Isaiah," 143.

184. Williamson, *Variations*, 194–95.

Conclusions

The aim of this chapter has been to explore the theological potential in Isaiah's vision of restoration, as it is encapsulated by Isa 54:1 in its immediate context, with regard to the themes that correlate with Paul's interests in Gal 4:21—5:1. The analysis has not been a comprehensive exploration of the meaning potential of Isaiah nor a comparative study of its appropriation by different Jewish interpreters. I have simply attempted to follow the lead of Paul's special interests to explore how the Isaianic textual matrix resonates with Paul's convictions. The purpose has been to gain textual proficiency with the pertinent material in the book of Isaiah for a robust and in-depth intertextual reading of Gal 4:21—5:1 in chapter 6 of this book.

My analysis of the immediate context and the thematic intratextual matrix of Isa 54:1 has demonstrated that the verse Paul quotes in Gal 4:27 is "pregnant" (pun intended) with theological themes that run through the book of Isaiah. The barren woman giving birth to many children entails its own narrative of restoration as God's regenerative activity to form a new people of God—re-create humanity (Isa 1:2; 42; 44; 49; 51; 66). It is also integrally connected with the "narrative of the servant" (Isa 11; 41–44; 45; 49; 52:13—53:12; 54:17; 56; 61; 65) and the provision of the Spirit (Isa 44; 55; 63) that are both placed in key roles in the generation of the "many children" who are identified as "children of Sarah" (Isa 51:2; 44; 54:1) and as the restored community of the "Jerusalem above" (Isa 2; 24–27; 51–52; 54:11–13; 60; 66).

The barren woman with many children is intimately connected with the vision of restoring a desolate city to new glory. The vision of the "Jerusalem above" in Isa 2 sets in motion the expectation of the coming of God's kingdom (Isa 24–27; 52). It is about a new community of people that live in the presence of God (Isa 2; 4; 66), and are taught to live in his ways (Isa 2; 54:13; 66) to reflect and represent the character of God—justice and mercy (Isa 42; 54:14; 58; 66)—for the light and ongoing redemption of the world (Isa 42; 66). The "Jerusalem above" is the "mother city" of all who have received the revelation of the servant of the Lord (Isa 52:10; 53:1), and have come in their thirst to drink of the waters (Isa 44:3–5; 55:1)—the Spirit—that the Lord gives as a gift of grace (Isa 55:1). Those who enter the city have also entered the reality of "new creation" (Isa 43; 55; 66).

The identification of the barren woman's many children wrestles with the theme of the nations' inclusion. The material is diverse and resonates with different and sometimes conflicting voices. The canonical form of Isaiah provides landmarks to navigate the crosscurrents. The beginning (Isa 1–2) and end of the book (Isa 65–66) mark the route that dissolves the dichotomy between the nationalistic and universalistic dimensions. The "many children"—the regenerated people of God—are ultimately neither Israelites nor people of other nations, but people that have turned to the Lord from their own ways (Isa 1; 19; 55; 66), and have responded with humility and trust to the offer of salvation (Isa 55; 66)—they depend on God for righteousness and glory (Isa 45). But, more importantly, it is the "narrative of the servant" that defines the "many children" who inherit the promise of restoration—their existence and identity are derived from their relationship to the servant (Isa 49–51; 53–54; 61) and the Spirit (Isa 44; 63). Isaiah's vision of the restored community is not so much about the *who* (Israelites and/or the nations), as it is about the *how* (God's generative activity via the servant and Spirit)—it is the *how* that determines the *who*.

The vision of restoration is intimately connected with the Abrahamic promise (Isa 29:22, 44; 48; 51; 54). Restoration, as the generation of a new humanity, is understood as the fulfillment of the program set in motion with Abraham—many descendants and blessing that extends to the nations (see chapter 3). Isa 54:1 echoes the first movement of the birth of Isaac from barren Sarah, and connects it with the hope and reality of restoration that includes the nations within the scope of divine blessing. The echo of the Abrahamic promise of blessing is heard in the frequent reference to all the nations being included in restoration (e.g., Isa 2:2; 25:6; 56:7; 66:18). Nevertheless, the regenerated people ultimately appeal to God, rather than to Abraham, as their Father (Isa 63), since they owe their existence to his mercy (Isa 54; 55; 63) and direct divine action (Isa 66) rather than their ancestral heritage or any other sense of fittingness and worth.

5

Paul's Allegorical Practice in Galatians 4:21—5:1

I AM NOW IN a position to analyze Paul's hermeneutic, as I address in this chapter the questions of how and why Paul conducts his allegorical reading of Scripture in Gal 4:21—5:1. To set Paul's allegorical practice into a theoretical framework and a historical context, I discuss first the phenomenon of allegory in the Hellenistic and Jewish worlds before and around the time of Paul with special reference to the famous allegorist Philo of Alexandria. In my actual analysis of Paul's allegorical practice, I also draw on some insights from studies on rabbinic interpretation (midrash). In the latter part of this chapter, I lay a foundation for understanding how Paul appropriates scriptural intertexts in his letter to the Galatians.

Context for Paul's Allegorical Practice

Defining allegory is not a simple matter, since there is no one type of allegory, but more of a spectrum.[1] Due to this variety, the purpose in discussing allegory here is not to impose a tightly defined category on Paul, but to discuss some general features of allegory that establishes a theoretical framework and a historical context for analyzing Paul's allegorical practice.

The term "allegory" stems from Greek, composed of the words *allos* ("other") and *agoreuein* ("to speak in public"), giving the sense of "other speaking."[2] From this is derived the classical definition of allegory: to say something other than what one seems to say.[3] The actual Greek noun *allēgoria* came to use in the Roman period, and was still regarded as a new term by Plutarch at the end of the first century CE (*Quamodo adolescens poetas audire*

---

1. Young, "Allegory," 112. Because of the wide spectrum in allegorical practice, typology is also best understood as "simply one species of allegory . . . a certain subpractice" (Dawson, *Allegorical Readers*, 16).

2. Dawson, *Allegorical Readers*, 2.

3. Dawson, *Allegorical Readers*, 3; Whitman, *Interpretation and Allegory*, 2.

debeat, Stephanus 19e–f).[4] But the roots of the allegorical mode of thinking go further back (at least to the fourth century BCE), and it is related to terms such as "symbol," *hyponoia* ("under-meaning"), and "enigma."[5] As a literary trope, it is closely related to metaphor, and it is sometimes described as an extended metaphor,[6] or composed of metaphors.[7] What distinguishes allegory from metaphor, Dawson explains, is its narrative dimension.[8] Narrative also distinguishes allegory from personification (*prosopopoeia* that "endows non-human entities ... with human attributes") and etymology (searching out "the history of a word or name by distinguishing its components and tracing them back to their primordial forms in some ancestral language for the purpose of discovering an original or fundamental meaning") that are often part of allegory, but not of themselves allegory.[9] All of these—metaphor, personification, and etymology—are "tools of the allegorist," but "only when the allegorist uses such tools to compose or interpret a narrative do we have allegory."[10] With these general notes on allegory, I now turn to discuss the practice of allegorical interpretation, or *allegoresis*.

The Relationship between Text and Allegorical Interpretation

There are two related aspects to the practice of "other speaking": allegorical composition and allegorical interpretation (allegoresis). Allegorical composition denotes "writing with double meaning," whereas allegoresis is about "explaining a work, or a figure in myth, or any created entity, as if there were an other sense to which it referred, that is presuming the work or figure to be encoded with meaning intended by the author or a higher spiritual authority."[11] Berek makes a more pointed distinction between these two modes of allegory in terms of intentionality. He understands that allegorical composition is intentionally allegorical, whereas allegoresis is the

---

4. Copeland and Struck, *Cambridge Companion to Allegory*, 2. See also discussion in Brisson, *How Philosophers Saved Myths*, 56–61.

5. Copeland and Struck, *Cambridge Companion to Allegory*, 2; Brisson, *How Philosophers Saved Myths*, 58–59.

6. Copeland and Struck, *Cambridge Companion to Allegory*, 2.

7. Dawson, *Allegorical Readers*, 5.

8. Dawson, *Allegorical Readers*, 3–5.

9. Dawson, *Allegorical Readers*, 6.

10. Dawson, *Allegorical Readers*, 7.

11. Copeland and Struck, *Cambridge Companion to Allegory*, 1–2. Sellin also understands that allegoresis is based on the assumption that the text is allegorical (*Allegorie*, 12).

"allegorizing of a text whose author's intention did not clearly call for such interpretation."[12] However, the relationship between the text and its allegoresis requires a more nuanced approach, in which even the concepts of authorial intention and meaning in text need to be opened up. It is not to be assumed that an allegorical interpreter conceptualizes "the author" in a similar way to historical critical scholarship. As the quotation above from the *Cambridge Companion to Allegory* already suggests, the interpreter might presume that the allegorical meaning of a text is intended by a higher spiritual authority rather than the human author whose name the text bears. Or, as is the case with Philo, the conception of what an author intended might differ from modern notions (see discussion below). Modern scholarship also recognizes that it is difficult to make claims about the intentions of "the author," since they are not accessible to later interpreters beyond the level of the text, and even there they are not self-evident.[13] Thus, even with a focus on the text, it is problematic to talk simply about interpretation as a "procedure that uncovers meaning hidden in text," or "drawing forth the meaning it somehow 'contains.'"[14] Rather, a text is subject to a range of readings that are opened by the rich semantic potential of any text, and depend on the readers' own contexts and interests.[15] Hence, I focus my analysis of Paul's allegoresis in Gal 4:21—5:1 on the relationship between the meaning potential of the scriptural intertexts and Paul's reading of them without making claims about authorial intentions concerning the intertexts.

Whitman describes the relationship between text and its allegorical reading in terms of *correspondence* and *divergence*. Allegory, Whitman claims, is based on the tension between the apparent ("literal") and actual meanings ("allegorical") that are simultaneously comparable to one another, and yet must diverge.[16] Thus, allegorical interpretation of a text establishes a correspondence between an apparent meaning of the text and the claimed actual meaning that contains necessarily a level of obliqueness that requires a "series of divergences or transfers," by which the "allegorical interpretation

---

12. Berek, "Interpretation," 123.

13. See, e.g., Young's discussion on the difficulty in making the distinction between "compositional allegory and allegorical interpretation," in which the main problem is the "weight this puts on authorial intention and the difficulty, in some cases, of identifying the 'plain sense'" ("Allegory," 112).

14. Dawson, *Allegorical Readers*, 5.

15. Cf. Dawson, *Allegorical Readers*, 5; also Whitman, *Interpretation and Allegory*, 34–35; and Sellin, *Allegorie*, 18. However, Berek's point is still valid that *genre* is an indication of authorial intention ("Interpretation," 119).

16. Whitman, *Interpretation and Allegory*, 2.

repeatedly departs from the apparent meaning of the text, reinterpreting it in order to sustain a correspondence."[17]

Young has developed Whitman's insights further, and states that "the crucial differences between forms of allegorical reading lie in the way in which the correspondences and divergences are conceived."[18] She describes ancient conceptions about language, and how they elucidate the "different perceptions of how a text might represent or refer to something other than itself."[19] This representation, Young observes, "may occur through genuine likeness or analogy, an 'ikon' or image, or it may occur by a symbol, something unlike which stands for the reality."[20] Thus, Young distinguishes between *ikonic* and *symbolic* allegory: "[i]konic allegory would find a higher degree of correspondence between the various features of the text, the passage or narrative as a whole reflecting or mirroring in the narrative structure the 'undersense' adduced,"[21] whereas, "[s]ymbolic exegesis would tend to focus on particular verbal 'tokens' which consistently signify specific heavenly realities in the scriptures taken as a whole, but at the level of particular passages may produce a more piecemeal and apparently arbitrary meaning."[22] These categories are more helpful to my purposes than, e.g., the distinction between allegory and typology, since they succinctly capture the nature of the relationship between text and its allegoresis in terms of varying degrees of correspondence and divergence.

The analysis of the relationship between the text and its allegoresis can be developed a step further to probe at the interpreter's theological/ideological program. Barr distinguishes between two systems at play in allegoresis: the text and the "system into which the interpretation runs out," which he names as the *resultant system*.[23] Rather than methodological questions, Barr argues, it is the questions about the resultant systems that distinguish different allegorical interpretations.[24] Hence, Barr first asks, whether the resultant system is resultant at all; is it "entirely known before the interpreter begins";[25] or is it derived to some degree from the text?[26] In Paul's

17. Whitman, *Interpretation and Allegory*, 3–4.
18. Young, "Allegory," 113.
19. Young, "Allegory," 114.
20. Young, "Allegory," 114.
21. Young, "Allegory," 114.
22. Young, "Allegory," 114.
23. Barr, *Old and New in Interpretation*, 108.
24. Barr, *Old and New in Interpretation*, 108.
25. Barr, *Old and New in Interpretation*, 108.
26. Borek perceives that allegoresis is totally guided by an already established frame

case, it is related to the question whether the Scriptures he interacts with in Gal 4:21—5:1 are formative for his theology or only auxiliary. Second, and a related question asks, whether the resultant system is *homogeneous* or *heterogeneous*; does the interpretation belong to the same or different "world of thought"?[27] A heterogeneous resultant system is usually "drawn from quite alien areas of thought," whereas a homogeneous system can be understood as "grown up" from the textual matrix it interprets.[28] Where the heterogeneous system can be criticized for being a foreign imposition on a text, the homogeneous system can be probed as to whether or not what it contains is found in the text it interprets, or is only supported generally by the larger textual matrix it seeks to draw from.[29]

The Sociocultural Function of Allegory

It is possible to take the question of how allegory is related to the author's theological/ideological program to another level: What is the sociocultural function of allegory? What is it designed to achieve?

One view of allegory understands it as a mode of interpretation that attempts to save a text: "[t]he impulse to allegoresis is conservative in the root sense of the word: an impulse to conserve or preserve a high valuation on text and ideas that apparently contradict one another without being forced to acknowledge an inconsistency in one's beliefs."[30] Berek gives as an example of this the Greeks' treatment of Homer when his writings were found to contain inadequate or scandalous philosophy.[31] He then makes a claim with regard to Scripture: "[i]n the case of Scripture especially, the impulse to conservation expresses itself in large part as an impulse towards perceiving internal consistency. . . . figural interpretation is in large measure designed to reinterpret Old Testament narrative and doctrine in the light of a new dispensation that gives the appearance of contradicting it."[32] Dawson also recognizes this mode in allegory, and describes it in terms of

---

("Interpretation," 125), whereas Barr allows some room for both: "[t]he fact that the resultant system is in some way 'known' beforehand may not necessarily alter the fact that the organization and development of this system may be noticeably affected through it being 'found' as the meaning of a particular text" (*Old and New in Interpretation*, 109).

27. Barr, *Old and New in Interpretation*, 115–16.
28. Barr, *Old and New in Interpretation*, 116.
29. Barr, *Old and New in Interpretation*, 116.
30. Berek, "Interpretation," 124.
31. Berek, "Interpretation," 124; cf. Sandmel, *Philo of Alexandria*, 19.
32. Berek, "Interpretation," 125.

"domesticating a text," i.e., bringing a text to line up with cultural expectations by neutralizing "the culturally deviant meanings of the literal text, replacing them with culturally obvious meanings."³³ But rather than allegory being solely a conservative agent, Dawson proposes that it can also function as a culturally revisionary force.

Dawson's approach asks how allegory functions not only "as a way of reading texts, but as a way of using that reading to reinterpret culture and society."³⁴ He understands that "[a]ncient allegorical compositions and interpretations constituted fields on which struggles between competitive proposals for thought and action took place."³⁵ At the heart of this competition stands the question of what constitutes the *literal reading*. Dawson suggests that rather than being an inherent quality of the text, the idea of a literal sense is "the product of a conventional, customary reading," and as such it "is simply an honorific title given to a kind of meaning that is culturally expected and automatically recognized by readers."³⁶ An allegorical reading, by its definition ("other speaking"), is designed to challenge the customary reading, as the meaning it proposes to the text receives "its identity precisely by its contrast with this customary or expected meaning."³⁷ But while this allegorical "something else" is a challenge to the reigning literal sense, it is also potentially a newly emerging literal sense for the reading community that accepts it as the new obvious reading—the "actual" rather than the "other" meaning.³⁸ This revision of the literal sense has the potential of being a "*counterhegemonic force*" that aims to change prevailing cultural ideals or "reigning assumptions."³⁹ Dawson identifies that these forces are present when "a religious community struggles with itself, as emerging forces seek to subvert or overthrow well-entrenched traditional points of view."⁴⁰

---

33. Dawson, *Allegorical Readers*, 10.
34. Dawson, *Allegorical Readers*, 1.
35. Dawson, *Allegorical Readers*, 2.
36. Dawson, *Allegorical Readers*, 8. Barr allows the text more independence, and argues that it is exactly a written text that "created and held open the possibility of real change," because, as a written text, "it was given to succeeding generations." Hence, although certain readings could have gained dominance, the text could offer the potential for challenge: "the text remains as a potential witness against the interpretation unless the text is actually rewritten to fit the interpretation, and the original text lost or destroyed. The mere existence of the text therefore keeps open the possibility of a challenge to its accepted interpretation" (*Old and New in Interpretation*, 137).
37. Dawson, *Allegorical Readers*, 8.
38. Dawson, *Allegorical Readers*, 8.
39. Dawson, *Allegorical Readers*, 9.
40. Dawson, *Allegorical Readers*, 9–10.

I propose that Paul's allegoresis in Gal 4:21—5:1 functions both in a conservative mode and as a counterhegemonic force. It is conservative in its attempt to demonstrate internal consistency between the Scriptures of Israel and the new act of God in Christ and the Spirit that is embracing also the Gentiles. But Paul's allegorical interpretation is also counterhegemonic, as it challenges traditional interpretations of the Abraham narrative vis-à-vis Israel and the Gentiles.[41] The tension between conservation and subversion is reflected in the opening question of Gal 4:21—5:1, which at the same time appeals to the authority of the Scripture (law) and challenges the way it is being heard. The new subversive reading Paul is offering does not necessarily originate from the pressure to answer the opposition,[42] but rather emerges from his own revelatory experience (Gal 1:11–16) and consequent rereading of Scripture. Analyzing how Paul operates in reading the "law" allegorically to express his understanding of the gospel opens to us the theological vision and logic in his defense for constructing a new social reality of the "children of promise" that comprises the "Jerusalem above" community.

Philo's Allegorical Practice

To be able to appreciate the distinctive features in Paul's allegorical practice, I analyze first the work of a famous Jewish exegete and allegorist, Philo (c. 20 BCE to c. 50 CE). He lived in Alexandria around the time of Paul as part of a historical Jewish community that had a large measure of autonomy, e.g., in terms of allowing them to follow the Jewish Law.[43] Philo's involvement and loyalty to his Jewish community is reflected in his role of leading the delegation of Jews that was sent to Rome from Alexandria in 40 CE to plead their cause (Philo writes about this in *Against Flaccus* and *On the Embassy*

---

41. Bruce expresses the sense of Paul's subversive reading thus: "[i]n the present 'allegory', however, there is a forcible inversion of the analogy . . . the argument here is up against the historical fact that Isaac was the ancestor of the Jews, whereas Ishmael's descendants were Gentiles" (*Galatians*, 218).

42. This view is reflected in the influential essay by Barrett: "[i]t [Paul's use of the Hagar-Sarah narrative] stands in the epistle because his opponents had used it and he could not escape it" ("Allegory of Abraham, Sarah, and Hagar," 10; see also de Boer, *Galatians*, 286–87; Longenecker, *Galatians*, 199–200; Martyn, *Galatians*, 449–50). Whether or not there is an element of response, it is important to recognize that Paul does not go to the Genesis narrative because he is forced to deal with it. I demonstrate in chs. 5–6 that both Genesis and Isaiah are foundational and formative texts for Paul's theology.

43. Sandmel, *Philo of Alexandria*, 6–7. For a fuller discussion on Jews in Alexandria, see Barclay, *Jews in the Mediterranean Diaspora*, 19–81.

to Gaius).⁴⁴ Philo was also thoroughly Greek. He had received a broad Greek education that is evidenced by his excellent use of Greek language, literary forms and rhetoric, and his in-depth knowledge of Greek thought.⁴⁵ The way Philo navigates these two worlds, Jewish and Greek, creates the dynamic to Philo's allegorical practice, which is evidenced in his extensive body of written work that mainly consist of biblical exposition in the forms of commentary, retelling of biblical narratives, and questions and answers.⁴⁶

Philo's comments on Abraham's departure from Chaldea towards the promised land in obedience to the divine call in Gen 12:1, are illustrative of his approach: "[t]he aforesaid emigrations, if one is to be guided by the literal expressions of the scripture, were performed by a wise man; but if we look to the laws of allegory (*hoi en allēgoria nomoi*), by a soul devoted to virtue and busied in the search after the true God" (*Abr.* 68; translation by Yonge). This example describes how Philo distinguishes between the literal and the allegorical level of meaning in the text of Scripture. As an observant Jew, who believed that the prescriptions of the Torah were to be kept in their details (*Migr.* 89–94), Philo does not use allegory primarily to do away with the literal level.⁴⁷

The following example from Philo's comments on the same event of Abraham's migration opens up the system that his allegorical interpretation runs out to:

> Therefore, having now given both explanations, the literal one as concerning the man, and the allegorical (*hyponoia*) one relating to the soul, we have shown that both the man and the mind are deserving of love; inasmuch as the one is obedient to the sacred oracles, and because of their influence submits to be torn away from things which it is hard to part; and the mind deserves to be loved because it has not submitted to be forever deceived and to abide permanently with the essences perceptible by the outward senses, thinking the visible world the greatest and first of gods, but soaring upwards with its reason it has beheld another nature better than that which is visible, that, namely, which is appreciable only by the intellect; and also that being who is at the same time the Creator and ruler of both (*Abr.* 88; translation by Yonge).

---

44. Nickelsburg, "Philo among Greeks, Jews and Christians," 57.
45. Nickelsburg, "Philo among Greeks, Jews and Christians," 57.
46. Borgen, "Philo of Alexandria as Exegete," 114–43.
47. Borgen, "Philo of Alexandria as Exegete," 55.

Here Philo makes distinctions between the man and the soul; between the visible, sense perceptible world (*ho horatos kosmos*), and the other nature (*physis*) that is apprehended by the intellect (*noētos*). This approach displays the deep-seated influence of Greek philosophy in Philo's reading of Israel's Scriptures, but with the conviction that the God of Israel is the Creator of both the visible and noetic worlds. Sandmel's description is apt: Philo is a "sort of Platonist" and also a "kind of Stoic," as he represents "the first major blend of Judaism and Hellenism."[48]

Greek philosophy provides Philo with the ontological framework that underlies his allegorical practice: "Philo's allegorical method was rooted in a theory of (Stoically revised) Platonic ontology."[49] Greek philosophy also shapes what Sandmel calls Philo's "grand Allegory," a unifying system, into which individual allegorical items fit.[50] The "grand Allegory" has to do with Philo's conception of a spiritual journey towards perfection that corresponds with the narrative shape of the Pentateuch that is transposed to "an account of the contemporary, personal experience of every man [sic]."[51] The content of the spiritual journey is derived from Greek thought, as described by Sandmel: "[m]an's [sic] higher mind, if properly used, can so regiment the senses and passions that the soul can be freed from bodily domination. Spiritual perfection is the successful arrival by an individual to the point at which his soul is completely freed from the baleful influence of his body."[52] Sandmel perceives that the universalizing of the biblical accounts so that they concern the contemporary experience of all humans amounts to the dissolving of history in Scripture.[53] This seems like an overstatement, since Philo recognizes that the literal level in Scripture describes real historical accounts of Israel's past (cf. *Abr.* 68 and 88).[54] Nevertheless, Philo's focus on the noetic vision necessarily transcends history, and thus Philo's allegoresis does not have a history of salvation, or a promise-fulfillment framework.

Philo's allegoresis incorporates Platonic and Stoic exegetical methods, which were already part of the tradition of Alexandrian Jews such as Aristobulus and Pseudo-Aristeas.[55] However, even though there is a formal

---

48. Sandmel, *Philo of Alexandria*, 4.

49. Nordgaard Svendsen, *Allegory Transformed*, 39; see 28–36 for a full discussion on how Platonism and Stoicism are reflected in Philo.

50. Sandmel, *Philo of Alexandria*, 24.

51. Sandmel, *Philo of Alexandria*, 24.

52. Sandmel, *Philo of Alexandria*, 25.

53. Sandmel, *Philo of Alexandria*, 24–25.

54. Nordgaard Svendsen, *Allegory Transformed*, 38–39.

55. Sterling, "Place of Philo," 32–34.

similarity between Stoic and Philonic allegory, there is also an important difference. The need to seek for a deeper meaning in the text was connected, for the Stoics, with the need to go behind the literal level of the Greek poets to uncover a wisdom that the poets themselves were unaware of. For Philo, it was about capturing the original Mosaic vision that was *intentionally* invested in the text: "[i]n his [Philo's] opinion, Moses the author of the Pentateuch, had achieved the summit of philosophical insight and was fully aware of the truths he enclosed within his writings."[56] Moses's authority and authorship, Philonically conceived, stand thus at the center of Philo's allegorical approach.[57] Philo perceives that Moses reached the noetic vision that is embedded in his writing (*Mos.* 1:158). Allegoresis gives Philo the ability to uncover this vision from the scriptural text. This allegorical ability is also predicated on Philo's own revelatory experiences or ascents of the soul (*Migr.* 34–35; *Spec.* 3.1–6; *Somn.* 2.250–54; *Cher.* 27–28).[58]

The way Philo perceives Moses and the content of the allegorical meaning in the Torah amounts to what Nordgaard Svendsen calls a reversal of intellectual history. By ascribing to Moses the original noetic vision that precedes all of the Greek philosophers by centuries, Philo, following Aristobulus, actually claims that "Greek philosophers picked up inspiration from the law-giver and copied his insights into their works" (e.g., *Leg.* 1:108; *Her.* 214; *Prob.* 57; *Somn.* 1.58).[59] To support his claim for the priority and superiority of Mosaic revelation, Philo argues that the Greek philosophers' disagreements are due to the inadequacy of human cognition to penetrate true wisdom, which was given to Moses by divine revelation (*Her.* 246–248).[60]

Dawson connects Philo's strategy to subsume Greek philosophy into the field of Mosaic revelation to the sociocultural function of his allegoresis, in which "Moses' writing could thus become the basis for a revisionary stance toward the dominant, Hellenistic culture."[61] This revisionary stance has a double aim: to guide highly Hellenized Jews to be faithful in the practice of Judaism that is paradoxically also "the most authentic way to

---

56. Nordgaard Svendsen, *Allegory Transformed*, 38.

57. Cf. Nickelsburg's argument that Philo's focus on the five books of Moses "reflects the centrality of the Torah in the Jewish religion in general, but also indicates Philo's high regard for Moses as the supreme revealer of God and God's will" ("Philo among Greeks, Jews and Christians," 56).

58. Borgen, "Philo of Alexandria as Exegete," 121–22. See also a detailed discussion on these texts in Wan, "Charismatic Exegesis," 54–71.

59. Nordgaard Svendsen, *Allegory Transformed*, 48. See also Dawson, *Allegorical Readers*, 109–12.

60. Nordgaard Svendsen, *Allegory Transformed*, 49.

61. Dawson, *Allegorical Readers*, 73.

be Greek,"⁶² and to demonstrate to critics of Judaism, such as Apion, "that the Jewish people was not intellectually degenerate. . . . and that the Jewish people's loyalty towards their peculiar customs was not an expression of philosophical inanity."⁶³ Thus, on the sociocultural level, Philo did not aim to make Judaism more Hellenistic, but to make Hellenism more Jewish. This is reflected in Philo's tendency to define "universal Hellenistic ideals in terms of Jewish particularity," e.g., connecting the problem of the passions distorting reason to the problem of not following the Jewish Law.⁶⁴ Philo's universal "eschatological vision" is also defined in terms of Jewish particularity, as he anticipates a time when the Jewish Law, which is "stamped with the seal of nature itself" (*Mos.* 2.14), will eclipse other nations' own customs just as the "light of the sun obscures that of the stars" (*Mos.* 2.43–44).⁶⁵ Dawson concludes:

> Rather than an effort to transform Jewish texts and history into Greco-Roman philosophy and sociopolitical structures, Philo's work was a bold hermeneutical and sociopolitical bid for the right of Jews to define authentic Hellenism. Rather than simply giving scripture "other" meanings, Philo reads scripture as Moses' rewritten version of the host culture's meanings. The resulting reinscription of the world was brought about by Philo's allegorical reading of Jewish scripture, a reading through which he announced that all authentic intellectual and cultural wisdom, as well as the plot of world history, had been first written by Moses.⁶⁶

Dawson's conclusion seems apt with regard to the sociocultural function of Philo's allegorical practice. But, when analyzing the actual hermeneutic in Philo's allegorical reading of Israel's Scriptures, Sandmel's assessment rings true: "by resorting to the use of allegory, he is enabled to read Platonic and Stoic ideas into Scripture."⁶⁷ Thus, Philo's attainment of Greek philosophical insights (by education and personal "revelatory" experience) lead him to find, allegorically, the noetic vision in the text of Scripture. This philosophically constructed resultant system does not grow out from the text but is actually the presupposition that he operates with. However, Philo would himself claim that his philosophical system

---

62. Dawson, *Allegorical Readers*, 118.
63. Nordgaard Svendsen, *Allegory Transformed*, 48.
64. Dawson, *Allegorical Readers*, 120.
65. Dawson, *Allegorical Readers*, 122.
66. Dawson, *Allegorical Readers*, 126.
67. Sandmel, *Philo of Alexandria*, 28.

is homogenous with the world of thought in the Scriptures, since Moses's revelation is in his view the original true wisdom that Greek philosophy emulates.[68] Whether or not Philo's system is homogenous with the Scriptures depends on accepting or rejecting this premise.

With regard to correspondence and divergence between Philo's allegorical meaning and the text of Scripture, it seems that correspondence is found mainly on the level of narrative sequence,[69] but his philosophical system diverges significantly on the level of the content and themes that the narrative itself is concerned with.[70] The way Philo operates with the Abraham narrative is a good example of this. The narrative sequence about Sarah's role in giving Hagar to Abraham, and then asking her to be expelled, is important for Philo's construction of the role of encyclical studies in the spiritual journey of the soul towards true virtue:

> But we must give our belief to another woman, such as it was ordained that Sarah should be, Sarah being in a figure the governing virtue; and the wise Abraham was guided by her, when she recommended him such actions as were good. For before this time, when he was not yet perfect, but even before his name was changed, he gave his attention to subjects of lofty philosophical speculation; and she, knowing that he could not produce anything out of perfect virtue, counselled him to raise children out of her handmaid, that is to say out of encyclical instruction, out of Agar, which name being interpreted means a dwelling near; for he who meditates dwelling in perfect virtue, before his name is enrolled among the citizens of that state, dwells among the encyclical studies, in order that through their instrumentality he may make his approaches at liberty towards perfect virtue. After that, when he saw that he was now become perfect, and was now able to become a father, although he himself was full of gratitude towards those studies, by means of which he had been recommended to virtue, and thought it hard to renounce them; he was well inclined to be appeased by an oracle from God which laid this command on him. "In everything which Sarah says, do

---

68. Cf. Sandmel: "[b]ut Philo would never have admitted reading Plato into Scripture; he would have insisted that the Platonism and Stoicism came out of Scripture" (*Philo of Alexandria*, 28).

69. Cf. Sandmel: "[t]he adhesive that binds together what Philo presents allegorically is the narrative nature of the Pentateuch" (*Philo of Alexandria*, 24).

70. Cf. Sandmel: "Philo uses allegory beyond what he can deduce from Scripture and connect with it. He also uses allegory to invest meanings he can read into Scripture so as to find there the proof for the often novel and profound insights that are his" (*Philo of Alexandria*, 28).

thou obey her voice." Let that be a law to every one of us to do whatever seems good to virtue; for if we are willing to submit to everything which virtue recommends we shall be happy. (*Leg.* 3:244–245; translation by Yonge)

Philo manages the transformations of meaning from the literal to the allegorical level with techniques, such as etymology (as is the case above with Hagar's name), finding hidden meaning in numbers (see the example below), and by latching on to details of the text.[71]

Philo's allegorical reading has also a level of intertextuality, or what Dawson calls "'intratextual allegorization' in which he strives to validate scriptural meaning in some sense by scripture rather than by his imagination or by Stoic philosophical doctrine alone."[72] Geljon and Runia describe the intertextual dimension similarly as offering proof for Philo's interpretation: "interpreting the biblical verse that forms his starting point, he will quote another biblical text as proof of his interpretation."[73] Moreover, they perceive that Philo's stringing together of scriptural verses is the structural "skeleton" for his elaborate interpretive moves.[74] However, this "skeleton" arguably receives its "flesh" largely from Philo's Hellenistic matrix.

Philo's discussion on Gen 4:15 is a comprehensive example of Philo's strategies to manage the divergences between the literal and allegorical sense that includes Philo's "intertextual" technique or structure of interpretation.[75] Philo begins from the detail in the text about Cain and the "sevenfold punishment" to move to the allegorical meaning of the five senses and two organs, and then supports his idea of the purification of the senses in subjection to the Jewish Law by reading this text "intertextually" with the story of Noah and the deluge:

> And God says, he "who slays Cain shall suffer sevenfold." But I do not know what analogy this real meaning of this expression bears to the literal interpretation of it, "He shall suffer sevenfold." For he has not said what is to be sevenfold, nor has he described the sort of penalty, nor by what means such penalty is excused or paid. Therefore, one must suppose that all these things are said figuratively (*tropikōteron*) and allegorically (*di' hyponoiōn*); and perhaps what God means to set before us here is something of this sort. The irrational part of the soul is divided into seven

---

71. Cf. Borgen, "Philo of Alexandria as Exegete," 122–25.
72. Dawson, *Allegorical Readers*, 105.
73. Geljon and Runia, *Philo of Alexandria*, 16.
74. Geljon and Runia, *Philo of Alexandria*, 10–16.
75. Cf. Dawson, *Allegorical Readers*, 104–5.

parts, the senses of seeing, of smelling, of hearing, of tasting, and of touch, the organs of speech, and the organs of generation. If, therefore, any one were to slay the eighth, that is to say, Cain, the ruler of them all, he would also paralyse all the seven.... when the Creator determined to purify the earth by means of water, and that the soul should receive purification of all its unspeakable offences, having washed off and effaced its pollutions after the fashion of a holy purification, he recommended him who was found to be a just man ... to enter into the ark, that is to say, into the vessel containing the soul, namely, the body, and to lead into it "seven of all clean beasts, male and female," thinking it proper that virtuous reason should employ all the pure parts of the irrational portion of man. And this injunction which the lawgiver laid down, is of necessity applicable to all wise men; for they have their sense of sight purified, their sense of hearing thoroughly examined, and so on with all the rest of their outward senses. Accordingly, they have the faculty of speech free from all spot or stain, and their appetites which prompt them to indulge the passions in a state of due subjection to the law. (*Det.* 166–171; translation by Yonge)

In conclusion, Philo's allegorical practice is a combination of scriptural reflection (close literal reading) with a strong centrality of the Torah (and Mosaic authorship) and its interpretation from the perspective of Greek philosophical thought. For Philo, the allegorical meaning does not always negate the literal, but, since the allegorical level aims to make the meaning contemporaneous and universal to all humans, it transcends history. The ability to penetrate the allegorical level of meaning is claimed to be based partly on Philo's revelatory experiences, ascents of the soul, that correspond with Philo's conception of the Mosaic noetic vision. However, a critical analysis would struggle to follow the claim that Philo's resultant philosophical system stems from the text. There is also an element of intertextual construction in Philo's allegoresis, although it seems that the allegorical meaning is not derived from the matrix of scriptural intertexts, but rather from the Greek philosophical tradition that is reframed within Jewish particularity.

I have provided an analysis of Philo's allegorical practice as a point of departure to appreciate the distinctive features in Paul's approach. I will argue below that as with Philo, so also with Paul, a claimed revelatory experience occasions or enables the discerning of the allegorical level of meaning in the text of Scripture that departs from a conventional literal reading. But whereas the allegorical meaning in Philo's system seems to represent a different world of thought to that of the Scriptures, Paul is actually interested in the themes and content of the scriptural text, and focused on appropriating the scriptural promises to the new situation occasioned by the Christ-event. This is also why Paul operates more on a historical level with the fulfillment of God's promises and the implications of that for the Jews and Gentiles. For Philo, the historical level is not pertinent, since what matters more is the meaning that transcends the contingencies of time and place. Nevertheless, Philo is not a pure Platonist, as he upholds the significance of the historical people of the Jews with their particular laws, and has a sense of eschatological destiny for the Law in relation to other nations. Paul is also engaged in configuring the role of the Mosaic Law in the new eschatological age. But where Philo uses the argument about the congruity of the Jewish Law with the Greek ideal of natural order to expect the universal practice of the Law in its concrete form, Paul can be seen to transform the meaning of the Law and its fulfillment in a more radical way. Ironically, I demonstrate in chapter 6 how Paul uses the resources in Israel's own tradition, the Scriptures, to defend his vision and logic that removes the Law from the center stage and yet finds fulfillment for what the Law intended but could not itself deliver. Furthermore, I argue below that intertextuality, which functions like the structural "skeleton," or as validation/proof of interpretation in Philo's allegorical practice, is more substantive for meaning making in Paul's allegoresis. Yet, just like the Hellenistic noetic vision extends the revelatory field beyond the Scriptures for Philo, so also does the revelatory Christ experience expand the "intertextual field" for Paul. I now turn to how Paul conceives this, and how it shapes his allegorical practice.

Paul's Allegorical Practice and Intertextuality

The opening question in Gal 4:21, "You who want to be under the Law, do you not hear the law?," is a call to adopt the right interpretative practice in order to relate rightly to the Mosaic Law (see chapter 2). What follows from this question is crucial for capturing Paul's hermeneutical strategy, since Paul goes on to model the hermeneutic he wants his readers to adopt (cf. 4:12).[76] Paul's explicit statement about his own practice being allegorical (4:24) provides the entry point for analyzing his hermeneutic here.

Boyarin has argued that Paul's allegorical mode of reading Scripture is indicative of his theological program (see ch. 1). Boyarin's Paul has a Hellenistic vision that is predicated on the flesh-spirit duality, where the body is

---

76. Cf. Watson: "he is inviting them to participate with him in a responsible interpretation of this [Genesis] text" (*PHF*, 190).

particular but spirit universal.⁷⁷ Similarly, Boyarin claims that Paul's hermeneutic is dualistic, and thus allegorical; language is composed of outer material signs (signifiers) and inner spiritual significations.⁷⁸ Although Boyarin's construction of Paul's hermeneutic would apply better to Philo than to Paul, I begin my discussion on Paul's allegoresis from his claims.

Boyarin understands Paul's allegorical interpretation as a movement away from the level of the text (signifier) to a reality beyond it (signified). This is in sharp contrast with his understanding of the rabbinic mode of interpretation (midrash). The contrast Boyarin sets up between these two modes of interpretation is a helpful analytical tool for approaching the nature of Paul's allegorical practice. Boyarin claims that rabbinic midrash is intertextual rather than allegorical.⁷⁹ In other words, midrash is an intertextual reading that makes meaning on the level of texts rather than using the texts as pointers to meaning on another level.⁸⁰ Boyarin connects the rabbinic preference for intertextuality over allegory to the status of the Torah as the ultimate reference point: "[f]or the Rabbis of the midrash, the highest reality, other than God Himself, of course, is the Torah—that is, a text, not an abstract idea."⁸¹ However, a more nuanced understanding of the concept of the Torah in rabbinic interpretation actually opens the idea of intertextuality in ways that resemble Paul's allegorical practice.

Bruns asserts that midrash is engaged in *contemporizing* the Torah: "[t]he sense of Torah is the sense in which it applies to the life and conduct of those who live under its power"; and "[t]he text is always contemporary with its readers or listeners, that is, always oriented towards the time and circumstances of the interpreter."⁸² This results in the *extension of the concept of the Torah* to include the interpretative community and its traditions:

> The word Torah, and therefore its power and authority, extends itself to include not only the original books of Moses but also the Mishnah, the Talmuds and Aggadot as well. In other words, the Torah is constituted as an open canon. To be sure, the letters of the original scriptures are fixed, but they are not dead. Openness here has to be construed as the openness of what is written;

77. Boyarin, *Radical Jew*, 7.
78. Boyarin, *Radical Jew*, 7.
79. Boyarin, "Song of Songs," 226.
80. Boyarin, "Song of Songs," 223.
81. Boyarin, "Song of Songs," 226.
82. Bruns, "Hermeneutics of Midrash," 191.

that is, its applicability to the time of its interpretation, its need for actualization.[83]

The openness in the "canon" of the Torah extends the intertextual field of rabbinic interpretation to encompass not only the text of Scripture (books of Moses, the Prophets, and Writings), but also the rabbinic dialogue—"the traditions of the fathers." This is an important qualifier to Boyarin's insistence that midrash does not move beyond the text. The intertextual practice of midrash moves beyond the field of Scripture, since the rabbinic dialogue participates in some sense in the authority of the Torah. Bruns explains this in terms of the unity of the *written* and *oral* Torah:

> [Rabbinic interpretations] are modes of participation in the dialogue with Torah, such that the words of the wise as they engage the Torah cannot be isolated from the words of Torah itself. Hence the rabbinic tradition—which perhaps extends all the way back to the Pharisees and beyond them to the priestly Ezra—concerning the unity of the written and oral Torah. The meaning and authority of the word *Torah* extends itself to include not only the original Pentateuch, followed by the Prophets and Writings, but also the Mishnah, the Talmudic commentaries on the Mishnah, and the whole tradition of midrash.[84]

These two moves in the rabbinic interpretative practice (midrash)—the extension of the intertextual field and its predication on the contemporizing drive—provide a point of comparison to analyze Paul's allegorical practice in Gal 4:21—5:1.

I argue that Paul's allegorical practice is essentially intertextual, but, as with the rabbis, so also is Paul's intertextual interpretative field extended, and similarly predicated on the need to contemporize. As we observe what Paul does after his initial question in Gal 4:21, we get a sense of how Paul extends the intertextual field. To counter the Galatians' desire to come "under the Law (*nomos*)," Paul asks the Galatians to listen to what the "law" (*nomos*) really says—to interpret it right (4:21).[85] What follows this question reveals how

---

83. Bruns, "Hermeneutics of Midrash," 201. Not everyone agrees with this view, see, e.g., Porton, "Rabbinic Midrash," 198–224.

84. Bruns, "Midrash and Allegory," 632.

85. Many commentators note Paul's play with a double sense of *nomos* here, and read it so that the first instance refers to the Mosaic legislation/commands of Scripture and the second either to the Pentateuch (e.g., Bruce, *Galatians*, 215; Moo, *Galatians*, 297; Rohde, *an die Galater*, 192–93), or to Scripture as a whole (e.g., de Boer, *Galatians*, 291; Longenecker, *Galatians*, 206–7; Vouga, *An die Galater*, 115). I suggest that the full sense of Paul's second use of *nomos* here becomes clear only as we follow what he actually does.

Paul extends the sphere of the "law." For Paul, the second mention of "law" here is not simply a reference to the Torah, but a reference to the "intertextual field," or "revelatory field," in which he constructs meaning—the right understanding of the Law. Initially, it includes not only the books of Moses (narrow sense of *nomos*/Torah), but also the prophetic revelation in Isaiah (Isa 54:1 quoted in Gal 4:27).[86] But even that is not its limit. The totality of revelation that comprises the wider sense of the "law"[87] is ultimately centered on the reality of Christ that is signaled in the concluding exhortation of the passage (5:1) and eventually in reference to the "law" of Christ (*nomos tou christou*) (6:2; cf. 1 Cor 9:21).[88] Thus, Paul's allegoresis is intertextual, in which the intertextual revelatory field (wider sense of *nomos*) is extended beyond the Scripture to include the revelatory experience of Christ.

When Paul expounds his allegorical other sense of Scripture (see discussion below on the expression *hatina estin allēgoroumena* in Gal 4:24), he derives it from the extended revelatory field that he has come to embrace. In other words, Paul does not read the Abraham narrative only together with the Isaianic vision of restoration (4:27), but also in light of the generative activity of God in Christ (5:1) and the Spirit (4:29). Hence, Paul's hermeneutic has a dialogical dynamic between Scripture and experience (Paul's

---

86. The extension of the Torah to include also prophetic revelation can already be perceived in the book of Isaiah (e.g., Isa 2 and 58).

87. Cf. Eisenbaum who recognizes the possibility that, for Paul, the *nomos* "constitutes the sum of God's revelation to God's people" (*Paul Was Not a Christian*, 168).

88. The expression "law of Christ" has generated multiple views for its meaning. For discussions on the wide range of possibilities (that are not mutually exclusive) and evaluation of them, see Barclay, *Obeying the Truth*, 126–35; and de Boer, *Galatians*, 378–81. In his recent work, Barclay helpfully narrows the options for understanding the relationship between the "law of Christ" and the Torah in terms of 1) the "law of Christ" is "an allusion to the Torah, reconfigured in Christ," or 2) it represents a "Pauline wordplay, akin to his insistence in 1 Corinthians 9:20–21 that he is neither 'under the law' (ὑπὸ νόμον) nor lawless in relation to God (ἄνομος θεοῦ), but 'lawfully beholden to Christ' (ἔννομος Χριστοῦ)" (*Paul and the Gift*, 431). I see value in both views. The first rightly recognizes the hermeneutical impact of the Christ-event that maintains some level of continuity with the Torah (fulfillment) in the new reality brought about by the Christ-event. The second view rightly emphasizes the centrality of Christ in Paul's theology and ethics. Additionally, Dunn argues that the "law of Christ" also refers to the influence of Jesus's own teaching and example concerning the Torah: "Paul drew his attitude to the law from Jesus.... And it was no doubt this teaching and that example which Paul had in mind when he spoke of the 'law of Christ' (Gal 6.2)" (*Jesus, Paul, and the Gospels*, 114). This is historically plausible (Paul being aware of the Jesus tradition; cf. 1 Cor 11; 15), and complements my focus on the influence of the Christ-event reconfiguring Paul's understanding of the Law. It is also possible that the concept of the "law of Christ" has some roots in the matrix of Isaiah where it is the servant who becomes the law for the restored people (Isa 42:4) who are taught by God the new way of life in the "Jerusalem above" (Isa 2:3; 54:13).

experience of the risen Jesus [Gal 1:1, 11–16], and the Spirit in the Gentile mission [3:1–5]), in which he reads Scripture within the total revelation of God that has at its gravitational center the Christ-event. Paul believes that Scripture and the revelation of Christ belong to the same revelatory field. With this premise, he reads Scripture in light of Christ and interprets the Christ-event in light of Scripture.[89] Both forms of revelation function as signifiers that participate in the same divine reality.[90]

With this understanding of Paul's allegoresis, it is possible to argue that the resultant system (theology) in it is not heterogenous; it does not originate from or move to alien terrain, as is the case arguably with Philo's Hellenistic vision and Greek philosophy. Instead, Paul's system is homogenous, because it emerges out of the matrix of divine revelation in Scripture and in Christ—both belong to the "same world of thought." The difference from rabbinic midrash is that Paul displaces Mosaic revelation from the center of gravity by the revelation of Christ, and, rather than extending the intertextual field to include the "traditions of the fathers" (i.e., oral Torah and rabbinic dialogue), it includes the experience of Christ and the Spirit to give a promise-fulfillment shape to the intertextual field of the *nomos* (see Figure 1). Furthermore, as I will demonstrate below and in chapter 6, Paul's allegoresis is more ikonic than Philo's, because the allegorical meaning is facilitated to a greater measure by the meaning potential in the Abraham narrative itself, especially as it is read within the enlarged intertextual field. Hence, convictions concerning the nature of the Christ-event ultimately determine whether Paul's resultant system is homogenous or heterogenous with Israel's Scriptures.

---

89. Cf. Watson, *PHF*, 15–16.

90. Cf. Childs: "Scripture is a divine vehicle bearing testimony to theological reality. Its truth is thus not tied to its linguistic form, but it can be extended to embrace a fuller divine reality only partially manifested in the original form" (*Church's Guide for Reading Paul*, 190).

Figure 1. The "Intertextual Fields" in Rabbinic Midrash and in Paul's Allegoresis

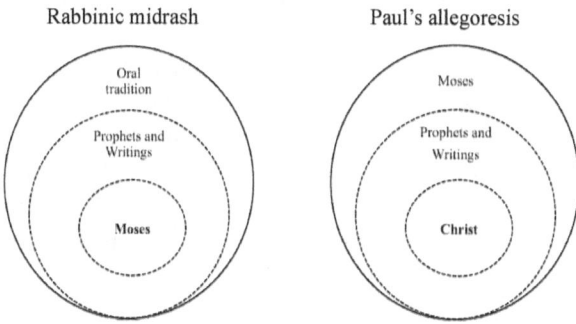

The extension of Paul's intertextual interpretative field stems from the necessity to contemporize. But unlike the open-endedness of the rabbinic contemporizing, or Philo's universal contemporizing, Paul operates in the mode of *Pesher* that is associated with the Qumran community,[91] in which "the text is related to one moment only, a moment thought of as occurring near the end of time."[92] Paul's emphasis on the revelatory experience of Christ (*apokalypsis iēsou christou*) (Gal 1:11–16) is an indication of his understanding of his place in time for hearing the Scripture. The cross and resurrection of Jesus form the nexus for the tension between the "present evil age" (1:4) and the "new creation" (6:14–15). The Christ-event has taken place, for Paul, at the "fullness of time" (4:4), and it occasions a turn in time that gives a new angle for interpreting Scripture.[93] Paul hears the Scripture now in the context of the in-breaking of the new creation that on one level (anthropology/cosmology) results in a sharp break between the new age and the present evil age (apocalyptic emphasis), but on another level (divine action/purpose)[94] retains a sense of continuity—the new is understood as

---

91. For discussion on the different Jewish interpretive practices in the first century, see Longenecker, *Biblical Exegesis*, 6–35.

92. Bruns, "Midrash and Allegory," 634; also Longenecker, *Biblical Exegesis*, 25.

93. Dunn understands the "fullness of time" with a covenantal emphasis as an "eschatological climax" (*Galatians*, 214), whereas Martyn takes it with an apocalyptic emphasis as indicating a "stepping on the scene," or a "punctiliar liberation" (*Galatians*, 389). These categories can be confusing, since both continuity and discontinuity are present in Paul on different levels.

94. I like Wischmeyer's preference for using the concept *die Geschichte Gottes mit der Menschheit* (The history of God with humankind) rather than *Heilsgeschichte* (salvation history) ("Wie kommt Abraham?," 135), because it captures better Paul's emphasis on divine action in the continuity of his purposes.

a fulfillment of the promises given in the old age (covenantal emphasis).[95] Both the Abrahamic promise of blessing to all nations (Gen 12:3; 22:18) and the Isaianic promise of restoration (Isa 54:1), envisaged as new creation (e.g., Isa 43; 54:11–12; 65), are now being realized in Christ and the Spirit (Gal 3:8, 14, 29; 4:4–7, 29; 5:1; 6:14–15). The alignment of Scripture and the experience of Christ and the Spirit is predicated on this perceived promise-fulfillment matrix.[96] Since both the promise and its fulfillment are configured as part of the same divine action, they are also part of the same divine revelatory field. The perception that the Christ-event participates in the same divine revelation that Paul attributes to Scripture is evidenced in the way Paul conflates time; the revelation of the gospel of Christ was already foreseen by Scripture (*proidousa de hē graphē*), and pre-proclaimed (*proeuēngelisato*) in the promise to Abraham (Gal 3:8). Time is not understood simply as linear historical progression; the past, present, and future can be conflated within the same divine reality, as the future gospel of Christ was already present in the past promise to Abraham.

I have now argued that Paul's allegorical mode is essentially intertextual. I substantiate this claim further by analyzing how the intertexts lend themselves to Paul's allegorical application. I first consolidate the sense of a prefigurative potential in the Abraham narrative that emerged during my analysis in chapter 3, and note the significance in Isaiah's re-appropriation of the pattern of the Abrahamic promise in its theological program. This leads to a discussion on the hermeneutical role of the Isaianic vision of restoration in Paul's allegoresis.

The Broader Horizon of Meaning in the Abraham Narrative

The only instance in the LXX and the New Testament where the word allegory is used occurs in Gal 4:24 (*hatina estin allēgoroumena*), and its meaning here is debated. The present passive participial form of the verb *allēgoreō*

---

95. This is the essence of apocalyptic for Wright, who combines both the apocalyptic and the covenantal emphases in referring to the "apocalyptic nature of Paul's covenantal theology" ("Gospel and Theology," 91). I agree with Wright that it is essential to understand that the coming of the new does not come out of the blue or to destroy everything old, but, as in Isaiah, the new creation is the fulfillment of God's covenantal promise.

96. Dawson's critique of Boyarin highlights that Boyarin misses Paul's insistence that the divine action in Christ accounts for the fulfillment of the divine promise in Scripture: "[w]hile 'promise' might describe the pledge of an agent to perform a future action, in Boyarin's reading it becomes a term used to denote the abstract meaning of a textual signifier" (*Christian Figural Reading*, 25).

has been taken either with an emphasis on text reception as a reference to Paul's allegorical reading (these things are now interpreted allegorically),[97] or with an emphasis on text production as a reference to the quality of the text (these things are written allegorically).[98] Both di Mattei and Sellin have argued from Greek sources that the best sense of the passive participle is the latter.[99] Yet the latter does not exclude the former, which can be understood to follow from the latter. Hence, I think that it is best to take the statement in Gal 4:24 with both senses; Paul claims that his allegorical reading is actually predicated on the allegorical dimension in the text. In other words, Paul is making allegorical correspondences with the Abraham narrative, because he believes the text has inherent (divinely endowed) potential to speak beyond its initial horizon (cf. Gal 3:8). Attributing an allegorical level of meaning to a scriptural text that does not claim to be allegorical can seem arbitrary or forced, but, as my analysis of the Abraham narrative has indicated, Paul's approach might actually be in tune with the character of the text that is already constructed with a broader horizon of meaning.[100]

During my analysis of the Abraham narrative in ch. 3, I noted its prefigurative potential (e.g., Hagar's oppression by Sarah, and God attending to it, prefigures, ironically, Israel's oppression in Egypt). This is one of the elements that invests the text with potential to speak beyond its initial confines. One trigger that alerts us to this potential is the prophetic vision given to Abraham about the future of the people that includes servitude and consequent release and return to the land (Gen 15:12–21). Many scholars have recognized this prefigurative potential of the Abraham narrative. Cassuto perceives that the composition of the Abraham narrative had the motive to teach, among other things, "how the events of Abraham's life paralleled the destiny of the people of Israel, in the sense that the experiences of the sires prefigured those of the scions; and how the reader may conclude from this that the history of the Israelites was not the result of chance, but the execution of plans that were predetermined from the beginning by God's will and were foreshadowed from the first in the events that befell the primogenitor

---

97. E.g., Longenecker, *Galatians*, 208–10.

98. E.g., Oepke, *an die Galater*, 148; Mußner, *Der Galaterbrief*, 139; Burton, *Galatians*, 253–57. Burton makes an important qualification here: "[t]he assertion pertains not to the original sense of the passage, what the writer meant when he wrote it, nor to the current or proper interpretation of the words, but to the character of the utterances as they stand in the scripture" (253). This lines up with Paul's framing of an individual passage as the voice of Scripture in Gal 4:30.

99. Di Mattei, "Paul's Allegory," 106–9; Sellin, "Hagar und Sara," 66–67.

100. Cf. Watson's note that "an 'allegorical dimension' is already built into the Genesis redaction, in the form of an overarching theological perspective on the traditional narrative material" (*PHF*, 189n48).

of the people."[101] Levenson echoes the same sentiment: "[a]s the father of the Jewish people, he [Abraham] is not simply their biological progenitor . . . , he is also the founder of Judaism itself—the first Jew, as it were—and the man whose life in some mysterious ways pre-enacts the experience of the Jewish people, who are his descendants and who are to walk in trails he blazed."[102] Kawashima agrees that the narrative does not present Abraham merely as a biological progenitor of the people ("as ancestral cause to national effect"), but has a "non-historical, non causal" dimension by which he symbolizes or prefigures Israel's life.[103] He detects that this prefigurative dimension has affinities with allegory: "[t]o the extent that the Patriarchal History reflects certain historical realities of, say, preexilic Israel, one might loosely compare it to political allegory, or at least discern within it a number of vaguely allegorical elements."[104]

But how are the "vaguely allegorical elements" present in the narrative? How do they lend themselves to re-appropriation and extension of meaning? Alter offers a tool for analyzing this in his treatment of the function of the Sodom episode in the Abraham narrative and beyond:

> [T]he way the Sodom episode reaches back multifariously into the Abraham narrative, and further still to the Deluge and ultimately to the creation story, and forward to the future history of Israel, suggest that there is elaborate if irregular *design* in this large complex of stories. It might be better to think of it less as structure than as *finely patterned texture*, in which seemingly disparate pieces are woven together, with juxtaposed segments producing among them *a pattern that will be repeated elsewhere with complicated variations*.[105]

Alter expresses the allegorical element in the narrative in terms of a "finely patterned texture" that offers "a pattern" that is repeated (with variations). He stresses the importance of recognizing the "patterns of motifs, symbols, and themes, keywords, key phrases, and plots," or else "we are likely to under-read the individual episodes and grasp at best imperfectly the *broader horizon of meaning* towards which the biblical writers mean to lead us."[106] This is a helpful insight for thinking about the way Paul appropriates the Abraham narrative allegorically. Paul is interested in the

---

101. Cassuto, *Genesis*, 299–300.
102. Levenson, *Inheriting Abraham*, 3.
103. Kawashima, "Literary Analysis," 90.
104. Kawashima, "Literary Analysis," 90.
105. Alter, "Sodom as Nexus," 159; emphasis added.
106. Alter, "Sodom as Nexus," 159–60; emphasis added.

"pattern" in the birth of Abraham's two sons (Gal 4:22–24, 28–29), as he follows the broader horizon of meaning to which the text points in terms of the identity of God's people (see ch. 3). Hence, Paul's allegorical engagement with the text is in tune with the narrative's "finely patterned texture." Furthermore, I argue below that Paul utilizes the Abraham narrative's broader horizon of meaning by reading it with a text that has done exactly the same, namely Isaiah, and situates the Christ-event on that matrix to capture its significance for all humanity.[107]

We can further develop the idea of the "broader horizon of meaning" in the Abrahamic narrative with Childs, as he explains it in terms of prophecy and eschatology that stretches the promise-fulfillment pattern beyond the confines of its initial setting in Genesis to a wider canonical context:

> [W]ithin the canonical context of the book of Genesis the promises to the patriarchs have been clearly assigned a different role [to that of imminent fulfilment]. This new interpretation has been realized by means of several explicit passages (15:13) and by the larger framework into which the promises have been ordered. The divine words of assurance have been set within *an eschatological pattern of prophecy and fulfilment* which now stretches from Abraham to Joshua. The promises function only as a prelude to the coming exodus, and *extend into the distant future*. The canonical effect of this new role for the ancient patriarchal promises is far reaching. All the individual stories of the Fathers have now been *framed within the bracket of eschatology*.[108]

This eschatological potential of the Abrahamic promise is realized in the book of Isaiah where it is re-appropriated within the vision, or promise, of restoration (e.g., Isa 51:1–2; 54:1–3). Isaiah reinterprets the Abrahamic promise of a multitude of descendants like sand on the shore in terms of the remnant (Isa 10:20–23; cf. Paul quoting it in Rom 9:27–28),[109] and the promise of blessing to all the nations (Gen 12:3; 18:18; 22:18) in terms of all the nations being within the scope of the restored people of God (e.g., Isa 2:2; 25:6; 56:7; 66:18; see chapter 4). In fact, this connection strengthens the conclusion that the vision of restoration in Isaiah is not simply about the restoration of Israel, but is situated within the larger narrative of Scripture

---

107. Cf. Di Mattei: "[t]he function of Paul's allegorical use of the Genesis narrative therefore is thus [*sic*] also in imitation of how Paul might have envisioned Isaiah using the same narrative" ("Paul's Allegory," 119).

108. Childs, *Introduction*, 151.

109. See Blenkinsopp, *Opening the Sealed Book*, 205, 227–30. I did not focus on the idea of the remnant in my own analysis of Isaiah.

and the purpose of God for the re-creation of humanity. Furthermore, the allegorical potential in the pattern of a barren woman giving birth contrary to nature in Genesis (Sarah giving birth to Isaac) is repeated in Isaiah in the theme of the barren woman giving birth to many children as a symbol of restoration that includes the Gentiles. Thus, Paul's claim about the allegorical quality of the Abraham narrative can be understood partly as an extension of the eschatological pattern of prophecy and fulfillment that is facilitated by Isaiah's re-appropriation of the Abrahamic promise that is being realized in the (re)generation of the people of God by the gift of Christ and the Spirit. But the eschatological reading of the Abrahamic promise with an Isaianic lens should not be done at the expense of neglecting the theological potential in the Abraham narrative itself. My attempt is to hold these two together, as I understand that Paul reads the Abraham narrative *together with* Isaiah's vision of restoration in the new situation brought about by the revelation of Christ—*both* carry theological weight for Paul.

The nature of scholarship is such that one can hardly focus on all the relevant aspects at the same time in analyzing a text, which is true also of this work. Hence, there are many studies on Galatians in general, and on 4:21—5:1 in particular, that focus either on the role of the Abraham narrative,[110] or on the role of Isaiah in Paul's hermeneutic/theology.[111] Both Hansen's and Thiessen's works represent a one-sided focus on the Abraham narrative to the exclusion of the Isaianic matrix.[112] The consequence of coming to Gal 4:21—5:1 with a heavy emphasis on the Genesis narrative is in its inability to adequately account for the central pivotal point about the two Jerusalems (4:25-26). Neglecting the role that the Isaianic vision of restoration has in the passage results also in a configuration of Paul's theological vision and logic only in terms of the Abrahamic promise. Rather than viewing Isa 54:1 as an add-on text to support the argument that is primarily controlled by the Abraham narrative, there has been increasing focus on the role of Isa 54:1 as a hermeneutical key.[113] The problem with this is an over-enthusiasm to elevate Isaiah's voice with the consequence of not attending enough to the

---

110. E.g., Emerson, "Arbitrary Allegory"; Fowl, "Who Can Read Abraham's Story?"; Gignilliat, "Paul, Allegory"; Hansen, *Abraham in Galatians*; Punt, "Revealing Rereading. Part 1"; Punt, "Revealing Rereading. Part 2"; Thiessen, *Paul and the Gentile Problem*.

111. E.g., Brawley, "Contextuality, Intertextuality"; Byrne, "Jerusalems Above and Below"; de Boer, "Paul's Quotation of Isaiah 54.1"; Di Mattei, "Paul's Allegory"; Eastman, *Recovering Paul's Mother Tongue*, 137–60; Harmon, *She Must*; Jobes, "Jerusalem, Our Mother"; Willitts, "Isa 54,1 in Gal 4,24b–27."

112. Hansen, *Abraham in Galatians*; Thiessen, *Paul and the Gentile Problem*.

113. E.g., de Boer, "Paul's Quotation of Isaiah 54.1"; Di Mattei, "Paul's Allegory"; Eastman, *Recovering Paul's Mother Tongue*, 137–60; Harmon, *She Must*; Jobes, "Jerusalem, Our Mother"; Willitts, "Isa 54,1 in Gal 4,24b–27."

potential in the Abraham narrative. The unique contribution of this book is to analyze Paul's allegoresis in Gal 4:21—5:1 with a robust approach that accords due weight to each involved text (see chapter 6).

The Broader Horizon of Meaning in the Exile-Restoration Paradigm in Isaiah

I noted in my structural analysis of Gal 4:21—5:1 the strategic positioning of Paul's quotation of Isa 54:1 in relation to the two key identifications of the Galatian believers: belonging to the "Jerusalem above" and being "children of promise like Isaac." I discuss here the potential of the exile-restoration paradigm that is present in Isa 54:1 for Paul's re-appropriation in the "fullness of time."

As I analyzed the vision of restoration in the book of Isaiah in chapter 4, I joined the view that perceives movement within the book, in which the initial prophetic message of Isaiah is re-appropriated in new contexts. The new contexts are reflected in the three main sections of the book (1–39 pre-exilic; 40–55 exile / promise of return; 56–66 after exile / partial return), and yet the re-appropriated material is not limited to its respective sections, since elements of the later developments have also been brought to bear on the earlier material in the process of the formation of the final form of the book (e.g., Isa 2). The main thing about the movement is its eschatologizing thrust.[114] This is especially evident in the framing of the book (Isa 1–2 and 65–66), by which the vision of restoration is moved to another level that is not fixed directly to the initial historical experience of exile and partial return. The eschatologizing of the Isaianic vision of restoration and the symbolic language used to represent it opens its broader horizon of meaning for theological re-appropriation. I presently develop both of these claims.

Blenkinsopp has explored how the "detachment of the exile from its historical moorings" and its "symbolic representation" contribute to its function as a locus of theological reflection.[115] He argues that, with these two developments, the exile and promise of restoration in Isaiah provided the matrix for different Jewish sectarian groups to configure their identity:

114. For Blenkinsopp, one indication of the eschatologizing thrust in Isaiah is the formula "'on that day,' which redirects them [oracles on Egypt in Isa 19] to a future very different from the unsatisfactory present" (*Opening the Sealed Book*, 7). This eschatologizing is not unique to Isaiah, but is present in the whole corpus of the prophets (Isaiah, Jeremiah, Ezekiel, and the twelve) (see Blenkinsopp, *Opening the Sealed Book*, 5–6).

115. Blenkinsopp, *Opening the Sealed Book*, 231; also: "[i]t is a curious fact that, while the biblical narrative provides practically no information on the exile as a historical episode, the exile as symbolic representation, as idea, is fully developed" (230).

> Exile from which a few return as the core of a new people is the Isaianic concept which proved to be most productive and generative for the future. . . . It anticipates the creation of a new people to prepare for the final intervention of God in the affairs of Israel and human affairs in general, the final showdown. . . . it is therefore open to becoming quite explicitly an eschatological concept. As such, it provided a powerful impulse not only to the development of a sectarian and apocalyptic way of thinking, evident already in the book of Isaiah itself, but also to the actual formation of eschatological and apocalyptic sects throughout the period of the Second Temple.[116]

Similarly, the symbolic representation of Isaiah's exile-restoration paradigm can be understood as providing a "cognitive map" for the early Christian movement to make sense of the Christ-event and its implications.[117] I use the idea of the "cognitive map," as I draw together material from my analysis of Isaiah and explore how the exile-restoration paradigm is symbolically represented in it, which in turn offers a matrix for Paul's theological reflection.

The one metaphor used of the exile-restoration paradigm that is explicitly present in Gal 4:21—5:1 is the barren woman giving birth from Isa 54:1. As I argued in my analysis of Isaiah, the two women in Isa 54:1 represent the pre-exilic Jerusalem and the promised restored Jerusalem. Thus, the "tale of two cities" and the imagery of rebuilding the city (Isa 54:11-12 and related texts)—a vision for the restored Jerusalem (e.g., Isa 2)—are intimately connected with the barren woman giving birth, and potentially correspond with Paul's two Jerusalems in Gal 4:25-26 (see chapter 6). The representative function of Jerusalem/Zion is more complex, since the idea of rebuilding a city is on one level about a concrete reality and not about symbolic representation. But, as I observed in my analysis of Isaiah, the language used of the new restored city elevates it to a symbolic level. The city functions as a symbolic representation of the restored presence and rule of God among the new restored community. Furthermore, the heightened language used in association with the restored Jerusalem gives it affinity with the idea of new creation (Isa 54:11-12; 65). Hence, the reference to two Jerusalems and to the barren-made-fruitful woman in Gal 4:21—5:1 can be understood as re-appropriations of the Isaianic exile-restoration paradigm. But there is a double distance to the historical experience of the exile and partial return: first, there is *theological interpretation in the book of Isaiah*

---

116. Blenkinsopp, *Opening the Sealed Book*, 226-27.

117. Blenkinsopp, *Opening the Sealed Book*, 136; emphasis added. Blenkinsopp believes this dependence on Isaiah goes back to Jesus himself (136-37).

that is represented in the symbolic language it uses; and second, there is *Paul's theological reflection on the symbols in Isaiah* and their re-appropriation in the new situation occasioned by the Christ-event.

The theological interpretation in Isaiah extends also into the condition that leads to exile. The concrete events of exile and partial return become a matrix for reflection that addresses deeper realities than the immediate problems of the devastation of the city and the exile of the people. The problem that leads to exile is sin, as defined in relation to the Law and prophetic revelation (Isa 1:2–17; 42:24–25; 48:18–19; 58; 59; cf. Rom 3:9–18). Blindness and obduracy are related to sin (Isa 6; 41–43; 48:1–8). These keep the people in captivity/slavery outside of the inheritance of the restoration reality. It is the narrative of the servant that brings together this level of theological reflection; the suffering servant in Isa 53 deals with the people's sin in order to deliver and restore the blind and captive Israel to be the servant she is called to be (Isa 42; 49). However, the theological interpretation in Isaiah reaches its most potent category in describing the exilic condition as death and restoration as resurrection (Isa 26:18–19). The categories that are used in Isaiah to reflect on the crisis of exile and the hope of restoration offer a complex matrix where the symbolic and concrete levels are blurred.

As Levenson traces the background of Jewish theology on resurrection partly to the language and theology of restoration, he points out the important interconnectedness between the different symbols/metaphors (I use these interchangeably) that are used of exile and restoration, and also between the symbolic level and its reference to reality:

> Barrenness, exile, loss of children, abandonment by one's husband (either through divorce or through death), estrangement from God, death—all could function as metaphors for the others in the list. To these must be added slavery, of course, which often appears in connection with them, especially with death.[118]

> To us, it is natural to describe the language of widowhood and remarriage, of the loss of the divine husband and his miraculous, triumphant return, and of the restoration of vanished children (or the birth of their replacements) as metaphorical, as I have indeed done above. For Israel or Zion is not literally a wife, their God does not literally die, and the return from exile and repopulation of the Promised Land is not a matter of literal birth. Sometimes, however, this distinction of the literal and the metaphorical can lead us astray, causing us to miss the deep interconnections internal to ancient Israel's culture but foreign

118. Levenson, *Resurrection and the Restoration of Israel*, 161.

> to us. The sources in the Hebrew Bible . . . have a definition of death and of life broader than ours. That is why they can see exile, for example, as death and repatriation as life . . . death and life in the Hebrew Bible are often best seen as relational events and are for the selfsame reason inseparable from the personal circumstances of those described as living or as dead.[119]

Levenson's analysis of the interconnectedness of the metaphors and their relation to reality in terms of the embedded relational element is instructive. He uses it primarily to emphasize the social relatedness of the individual for understanding the language of death and life, but I think the observation also points to the unifying element underlying the symbolic language about exile and restoration in general. In essence, the exile-restoration paradigm refers to a condition of being inside or outside in relation to promised "inheritance" (Isa 53:11–13; 54:3, 17). This is true also in relation to God (exile as God-forsakenness),[120] but even that is expressed with reference to inheritance of the land or the city—being in or out of the land/city reflects the people's relationship with God.[121]

Morales has also argued that the representative language of death and resurrection for the exile-restoration paradigm (Morales focuses here on the book of Ezekiel) is what Paul capitalizes on, especially via the reality of the resurrection of Jesus and the giving of the Spirit:

> Paul appeals to the Spirit as a sign of the inauguration of the restoration of Israel promised by the prophets and anticipated by some during the second temple period. Paul's interpretation however, does not simply reproduce these expectations, but rather radically transforms them through the death and resurrection of Jesus. Just as the resurrection of Jesus completes the transformation of the metaphorical language of Ezekiel from a symbol of return from exile into literal, bodily resurrection, so, too, does it complete the transformation of the language of the

---

119. Levenson, *Resurrection and the Restoration of Israel*, 154.

120. Blenkinsopp: "[t]he dark side of the experience of exile can be expressed metaphorically in many different ways. In biblical texts, the Babylonian exile is the time of Godforsakenness, the time when the God of Israel moved away from his people" (*Opening the Sealed Book*, 242). Blenkinsopp examines here particularly Isa 54:7–8 (243).

121. The relational language of covenant (Isa 49:8 the servant as covenant; 54:10 covenant of peace; 55:3 Davidic covenant) and righteousness (Isa 54:13–14, 17) that is used about inclusion in the inheritance/restoration are also potential contacts to Paul's application of the exile-restoration paradigm.

dead bones from a symbol for the exile into a literal reference to death, the true problem with the Law.[122]

This highlights the central hermeneutical role of Christ's resurrection and the giving of the Spirit that signal the reality of restoration when they are placed on the matrix of the symbolic representation of it in Isaiah and other texts of Scripture. They also configure the "cognitive map" in the direction that makes the symbols (death-resurrection) the reality and the concrete (exile-return) the symbol. This is a dialogical hermeneutic, in which Isaiah (among others) provides the matrix to interpret the experience of the risen Christ and the Spirit as God's eschatological restoration of his people. At the same time, the reality of Christ and the Spirit push the reading of Isaiah beyond the concrete walls of Jerusalem to emphasize the generation of a new restored community.

With these observations about the eschatologizing of the vision of restoration in Isaiah and the symbolic representation of the exile-restoration paradigm, I have indicated my understanding of the hermeneutic in Paul's re-appropriation of the theological potential in Isaiah. At this point, I want to clarify one of the implications of this. When I refer to Paul using the Isaianic exile-restoration paradigm, I am not referring to a prior sense of an extended exile on a continuous narrative of Israel. Whether or not Paul or some other Jews thought that Israel was experiencing an ongoing or extended exile on a historical or symbolical level is not my point.[123] My point is that the theological interpretation about the exile and promise of restoration in Isaiah provides a theological matrix ("cognitive map") that functions as a pattern or a paradigm for Paul to re-apply to the understanding of the Christ-event and the giving of the Spirit and its implications.[124] To be sure, the Christ-event is, for Paul, the real and unique fulfillment of the Abrahamic promise of blessing in terms of the Isaianic promise of restoration (see

122. Morales, *Spirit and the Restoration of Israel*, 79.

123. Wright offers evidence that some Jews indeed thought of living in an ongoing or extended exile (*PFG*, 139–62).

124. Starling's assessment of Second Temple Jewish texts recognizes the possibility that there is not always a sense of a continuing exile, but that the exile can also function as a matrix that was "typologically" reapplied to a new situation: "[t]he pattern of citations that we have surveyed supports the view that for a variety of writers across the spectrum of Second Temple Judaism, the promises of Israel's restoration in the exilic prophets were understood as having been at best only partially fulfilled in the return under Cyrus, and that the plight of Israel in the Second Temple period could be described as a continuing exile or *typological second exile*" (*Not My People*, 33, emphasis added). I also think that the New Testament portrays different ways how the idea of exile is re-appropriated, e.g., Matthew seems to place it into a continuous narrative culminating in Christ (Matt 1:1–17).

chapter 6), and thus, this eschatological hope is being realized through the resurrection of Jesus and in the giving of the Spirit. In this sense restoration is not a pattern that is repeated in history. But it does not necessarily follow that the time before the "fulness of time"—the inauguration of restoration by Christ—is a period of an extended exile. For Paul, the Christ-event is the new center of reality that determines what constitutes alienation, and what amounts to inclusion in restoration. Being outside of Christ is the realm of alienation, whether or not that condition is understood on a continuous narrative by a sense of an ongoing exile (however conceived), and whether or not one is a Jew or a Gentile. Inclusion in the restoration people is predicated on belonging to Christ.

This kind of Christ-centered configuration of the exile-restoration paradigm is expressed in Galatians with the use of the related concepts of slavery and freedom. The (mostly Gentile) Galatians have been in the condition of slavery in their alienation from God prior to coming to faith in Christ (4:8). They are now in danger of being alienated from the grace of Christ (5:4). This would mean being *again* enslaved (5:1; 4:9–10). Alienation/slavery can be experienced both *prior* and *after* the coming of Christ, as well as coming to Christ, and is thus best understood as a realm of existence outside of Christ. In order to avoid confusion and the attribution of an ongoing/continuous sense to the exile-restoration scheme in Paul's theological reflection, I choose to refer to the alienation-restoration paradigm when discussing the exile-restoration matrix in Paul.

6

Configuring The Theological Vision and Logic of Galatians from the Vantage Point of 4:21—5:1

I HAVE ARGUED THUS far that Gal 4:21—5:1 offers a unique vantage point for configuring Paul's theological vision and logic in Galatians. I have also argued that Gal 4:21—5:1 is best read in tune with Paul's dynamic hermeneutical matrix that is formed by the experience of the risen Christ and the gift of the Spirit together with the Scriptures of Israel, especially the Abraham narrative and Isaiah. In this chapter, I demonstrate that Paul's understanding of the gospel—the good news of what God is doing in the world through Christ and the Spirit—is integrally connected with the Abrahamic promise of blessing to the nations and with Isaiah's vision of restoration, and that it can be expressed as a vision for the re-creation of humanity that has implications for both Jews and Gentiles.

Method for an Intertextual Reading of Galatians 4:21—5:1

Before I embark on my reading of Gal 4:21—5:1 and the configuration of Paul's theological vision and logic in Galatians therein, I establish here the criteria by which I evaluate the presence of the scriptural matrix in Paul's text—the intertextual relations. The aim is to have a robust method to determine how Paul draws from the theological potential in the texts he interacts with in Gal 4:21—5:1. Underlying my criteria are some of Hays's criteria for determining the presence of scriptural echoes (although I do not use the category in my discussion) in Paul's text:[1]

1. Hays, *Echoes of Scripture*, 29–32. I choose to explain only three of Hays's seven criteria at this point. Some of the criteria are discussed elsewhere (*historical plausibility*, i.e., could Paul or his recipients be thought to have picked up the references to Scripture is discussed below; also *satisfaction* is discussed below). *Availability* is not a necessary criterion in my work, since my analysis focuses only on texts that are clearly available to Paul (portions of Scripture he uses, and not, e.g., texts of Philo), and most

a. *Volume* refers to the degree of identifiability of the textual relation in terms of verbal links and similarity in syntactical patterns. The volume of the intertextual connection depends also on the prominence the intertext has in Scripture (i.e., is it an important text?) and the rhetorical stress that Paul gives it.

b. *Recurrence* refers to the frequency with which a text is cited or referred to by Paul. If there is evidence that a certain text/section of Scripture is important to Paul, detecting an intertext from the same context is more probable.

c. *Thematic coherence* has to do with the fit between the intertext and Paul's text: How does the intertext fit in Paul's argument? Do the ideas or images in the intertext illuminate Paul's text? I would also add to this the idea of *logical correspondence*, which focuses on the correspondence between the internal logic in the line of thought expressed in the intertext and in Paul's text. This last criterion of thematic coherence and logical correspondence is not simply about identifying connections, as it relies on an interpretation of the intertext and Paul's text to establish coherence or correspondence. Hence, to be able to execute my intertextual reading, I have carried out interpretations of both the Abraham narrative in Genesis and the vision of restoration in Isaiah, as well as an initial analysis of Paul's text in Galatians.

With these criteria in mind, I regard as *certain* the presence of those intertexts that are made explicit by quotations and leave no room for doubt. The next level are *very likely* (probable) intertexts that are *intimately* connected with the texts whose presence has been made explicit by quotations, and are supported by both *verbal and conceptual* links as well as thematic coherence / logical correspondence. On the third level are *likely* (plausible)

---

likely also to the recipients of his letter (access and familiarity with the LXX). *History of interpretation* is a criterion that comes up in a limited way in my discussion with relevant scholarship.

I prefer not to use the categories of allusion or echoes in my approach, since they can be misleading in relation to the focus of my analysis. As Hays explains, allusions are often connected to intentional intertextual relations (intended by the author and assumed to be recognizable by the readers), whereas an echo is a metaphor for an allusion that does not depend on intentionality (29). Hays himself makes no systematic distinction between an echo and an allusion: "*allusion* is used of obvious intertextual references, *echo* of subtler ones." Allusion can be a misleading category, since my focus is not on what scriptural connections Paul intended his readers to pick up, but on how the scriptural matrix can be perceived to inform Paul's theological vision and logic that is reflected in the text. Echo could be a useful category for the more subtle relations between the texts, but, since my focus is on a range of relations from certain to possible, I find it unnecessary.

intertexts that are *somehow* related to the explicit intertexts, and are supported by *conceptual* connections, and have thematic coherence / logical correspondence. Finally, there are *possible* influences of intertexts that lack direct evidence on the surface of the text, but operate on the level of textual substructure. Yet they have thematic coherence / logical correspondence, and are reasonable to infer due to their connection with the explicit intertexts and their ability to deepen the reading.

These criteria are about identifying textual connections, but they are not adequate for determining to what extent these texts have influenced Paul (thematic coherence / logical correspondence move in that direction), i.e., how much have the content and context of the related intertexts shaped Paul's thought? I have given some evidence at the beginning of chapter 4 that supports the view that Paul is not a superficial reader of Scripture, but that he operates contextually in tune with the thematic connections within Scripture and with the narrative shape of the material. I presently explain how this view impacts my reading of Paul.

Riffaterre has argued that the need for interpretative help from an intertext arises from "the need to fill out the text's gaps, spell out its implications and find out what rules of idiolectic grammar account for the text's departure from logic, from accepted usage . . . ."[2] Furthermore, he suggests that when an intertext is signaled by a quotation or an allusion, the intertext acts as the *key to the text's interpretation*, in which case the *context of the intertext* also becomes significant.[3] I agree, and my view on the influence of the content and context of the texts Paul interacts with is more of a maximalist than a minimalist one.[4] I perceive that Paul's thought is thoroughly immersed in Scripture, which is indicated by the high frequency and volume of its presence in Paul's letters (especially in Galatians, Romans, and the Corinthian correspondence).[5] This is why I explore the maximal theological potential in the texts of Scripture that are indicated in Paul's text in order to capture Paul's vision and follow his logic.[6] I recognize that the

2. Riffaterre, "Compulsory Reader Response," 57.
3. Riffaterre, "Compulsory Reader Response," 70.
4. See the discussion in Watson, *PHF*, 491–501.
5. Cf. Hays: "to interpret Paul discerningly, we must recognize the embeddedness of his discourse in scriptural language (or the embeddedness of scriptural language in his discourse) and explore the rhetorical and theological effects created by the intertextual relationship between his letters and their scriptural precursors" (*Conversion*, 29).
6. I recognize that Paul's context for reading Scripture seems to be all of Scripture rather than individual passages or books (e.g., he connects texts from different books as they relate to a theme). But, since certain books play an especially prominent role in Paul's thought (e.g., Genesis and Isaiah), it is reasonable to think that Paul is influenced by the theological potential that is communicated by the books as a whole.

proof of the pudding lies in the satisfaction that a reading offers, i.e., in its power to explain the text—to capture its force and flow.

With these notes on my method, I now analyze Paul's allegorical engagement with Scripture in Gal 4:21—5:1 with an intertextual reading that simultaneously configures Paul's theological vision and logic in the whole letter.

Vision of Restoration and the Alienation-Restoration Paradigm

In my structural analysis of Gal 4:21—5:1 (see ch. 2), I identified belonging to the "Jerusalem above" as one of the two key identifications (the other is "children of promise"; discussed below) that Paul assigns for the Galatian believers in Christ together with himself—she is *our* mother (4:26). It is set in contrast to the "present Jerusalem," and together they form the central pivotal point of the passage. I argue in the following that both the "present Jerusalem" and the "Jerusalem above" are intimately linked with the Isaianic matrix and point to the significance of the vision of restoration and the alienation-restoration paradigm in Paul's thought. Hence, I begin my reading of Gal 4:21—5:1 with an analysis of these two designations.

The Jerusalem Above

It is certain that the "Jerusalem above" in Gal 4:26 is related to the quotation from Isa 54:1 in the following verse that is introduced as the reason (*gegraptai gar*) for the "Jerusalem above" being the mother of the Galatian believers with Paul.[7] Since the two women in Isa 54:1 represent the "tale of two cities" that is introduced in Isa 1-2 (see ch. 4),[8] I argue that it is very likely that Paul has crafted his central point in the argument with reference to these intimately related texts and possibly with other texts that relate to the same theme in Isaiah.[9]

---

7. Cf. de Boer, *Galatians*, 302-3; Oepke, *an die Galater*, 151-52; Vouga, *An die Galater*, 115.

8. Cf. Willitts, "Isa 54,1 in Gal 4,24b-27," 192-97. Also Eastman, *Recovering Paul's Mother Tongue*, 147; Jobes, "Jerusalem, Our Mother," 310-11. Pace de Boer who argues that the two women in Isa 54:1 represent Jerusalem and Babylon, and thus provide for Paul a foil to make the "present" and "above" Jerusalems the "polar opposites" (*Galatians*, 302-4).

9. Paul's notion of a "present" and "above" Jerusalem is usually connected with the Jewish apocalyptic tradition of a heavenly Jerusalem that is the counterpart to the

The relationship between Paul's text and Isa 1–2 is established also by verbal and conceptual links. Paul's designation of the "Jerusalem above" as a *mother* (*mētēr*) resembles the description of the promised restored Jerusalem as a *mother-city* (*mētropolis*) in Isa 1:26.[10] Furthermore, the idea of Paul's Jerusalem being *above* (*anō ierousalēm*) has close correspondence with the vision of the eschatological restored Jerusalem on top of Mount Zion being *far above* (*hyperanō*) any other city/mountain in Isa 2:2.[11] These connections make it very likely that at least the "Jerusalem above" is related to the idea of the restored Jerusalem in Isaiah. But, as the quotation of Isa 54:1 suggests, it is also likely that the alienation-restoration paradigm that is present in the figures of the two women is also informing the construction of the "present Jerusalem" in slavery versus the "Jerusalem above" that is free. But before I explore the theological implications of this dimension, I present other connections between Paul's text and Isaiah that relate to the theme of the "Jerusalem above."

The New Creation

The vision of the restored Jerusalem is intimately connected with the theme of *new creation* in Isaiah (see ch. 4). The language used about the new restored city in Isa 54:11–17 resembles the language in Isa 60:17–19 and 65:17–18, and they, together with the vision in Isa 2:2–4, suggest that it is conceptualized as a "new creation" event. Hence, I argue that it is very likely that both the "Jerusalem above" in Gal 4:26 and the "new creation" in 6:15 stem from the Isaianic matrix that connects them both to the vision of restoration.[12] Not only are these two themes intimately connected in Isaiah, but the language Paul uses in association with the "new creation"

---

earthly one (e.g., Dunn, *Galatians*, 253–54; Longenecker, *Galatians*, 212–15; Moo, *Galatians*, 304–5; Mußner, *Der Galaterbrief*, 325–26). This is helpful in shedding light on one aspect of the cultural milieu that Paul is located in, but is not sufficient with regard to the *particular* matrix of Scripture Paul draws from, and the *particular way* Paul is situated in relation to this tradition.

10. Noted also by Jobes, "Jerusalem, Our Mother," 310.

11. Also Scott (*Paul and the Nations*, 132–33) and Fredriksen ("Judaism, the Circumcision of Gentiles," 532–64, especially 544–45, 564) recognize Isa 2 (and Micah 4) as part of Paul's scriptural matrix in his general vision about Gentile inclusion in the end times. I move further from these general notions by demonstrating how integrally Isa 1–2 relates with Isa 54:1, and how it impacts Paul's vision and logic.

12. Cf. Harmon, *She Must*, 218, 228–36. Pace Longenecker for whom 6:15 is a "traditional maxim" taken over by Paul to sum up his message in Galatians (*Galatians*, 295–96). Martyn connects the idea of "new creation" to the apocalyptic tradition, but recognizes that "[t]he roots of the motif lie in Isa 65:17–25" (*Galatians*, 565n64).

in Gal 6:15–16 has links to Isa 54:10 that is situated in the context of both the two women in Isa 54:1 and the description of the restoration of the city with "new creation" language in Isa 54:11–17.[13] Right after elevating the "new creation" as the new reality that relativizes the boundaries of circumcision and uncircumcision (6:15), Paul proclaims peace (*eirēnē*) on those who align with the "canon" of "new creation," and prays/hopes for mercy (*eleos*) on the "Israel of God" (*kai hosoi tō kanoni toutō stoichēsousin, eirēnē ep' autous kai eleos kai epi ton israēl tou theou*) (6:16).[14] Both peace and mercy are central in Isa 54:10 (*oude to par' emou soi eleos eklepsei oude hē diathēkē tēs eirēnēs sou ou mē metastē*). Since these two words do not occur together usually in Paul's greetings or benedictions,[15] their peculiar combination and the reference to the "Israel of God" support the view that Paul is here drawing from the language of restoration in Isaiah that is integrally related to God's dealings with Israel that has implications also for the Gentiles. Thus, both the "Jerusalem above" and "new creation" very likely have their roots in the Isaianic matrix, and both are connected to its vision of restoration.[16] Furthermore, in both Isaiah and Paul, this theologi-

---

13. Cf. Wright, *PFG*, 1150–51; Beale, "Peace and Mercy Upon the Israel of God," 204–23. I, however, do not agree with them that this indicates that the "Israel of God" refers to "the believing church" (see discussion below).

14. Scholars are divided whether 1) to separate the benediction of peace to the group that has aligned itself with the "canon" of "new creation," and the prayer for mercy to another group called the "Israel of God" (Burton, *Galatians*, 357–58; de Boer, *Galatians*, 403–5; Dunn, *Galatians*, 343–46; Eastman, "Israel and the Mercy of God," 367–95), or 2) to view them both as addressing one single entity that is the "new creation" people described also as the "Israel of God" (Betz, *Galatians*, 320–23; Longenecker, *Galatians*, 297–99; Wright, *PFG*, 1148–51). There is also a third option that views the double blessing as intended initially on the Galatians (with the hope that they will align with Paul's "canon") that is then extended also for Paul's fellow Jews as a future hope (Mußner, *Der Galaterbrief*, 416–17; he emphasizes the future form of *stoichēsousin*). I side with the first view, and sympathize with the third option. This is a minority position, but it does take full note of the peculiar syntax (third *kai*, and double use of *epi*), the choice of words (*eleos* instead of *charis*; cf. 6:18) and their ordering (peace before mercy; cf. Gal 1:3). The separation of peace and mercy reflects to me that Paul invokes peace on those who are already in the "new creation," i.e., restoration reality, and prays for mercy on those who are yet to be regenerated to enter this inheritance (cf. Bachmann's argument that *eleos* is related to "the problem of Israel" and has "'eschatological' connotations" [*Anti-Judaism in Galatians?*, 109–10]; similarly Mußner, *Der Galaterbrief*, 416). The issue here is closely tied with the identity of the "Israel of God" (see discussion on that below).

15. Bachmann, *Anti-Judaism in Galatians?*, 115–16; Eastman, "Israel and the Mercy of God," 155–56.

16. Cf. Horbury: "'new creation' in Paul should probably therefore be reckoned as another reflection of the set of interpretations and expectations concerning Zion" (*Messianism*, 214; also 192, 194).

cal vision has implications for both Israel and the Gentiles in a way that transcends these traditional boundaries—circumcision or uncircumcision do not count in the new reality of restoration (Gal 5:6; 6:15–16; for this notion in Isaiah, see ch. 4).

The Kingdom of God

I discuss here one more concept in Galatians that is closely connected with the "Jerusalem above" and the Isaianic vision of restoration: the *kingdom of God* (5:21).[17] Again, these two concepts are linked both in the text of Isaiah and in Galatians. As I have argued, Isaiah's vision of the restoration of the city is at heart about the restoration of the presence and rule of God among his regenerated people (see chapter 4). Especially, the language about the kingdom of God in Isa 52:7–9 is intimately connected with the vision of restoration in Isa 54:1, and thus I argue that it is likely that it is part of the matrix that underlies Paul's conception of the gospel in relation to the reality of the kingdom of God. The proclamation of the good news to Zion about the coming reign of God (*basileusei sou ho theos*) in Isa 52:7 is connected in its context to the tale of two cities; the good news is directed to captive Zion/Jerusalem (*hē aichmalōtos thygatēr siōn*) (Isa 52:2) who is to be transformed by God's act of mercy in delivering her (Isa 52:8–9). The language of breaking forth with joy (*rhēxatō euphrosynēn*) and the transformation of the desolate/barren Jerusalem (*ta erēma ierousalēm*) in Isa 52:9 connects the imagery of the coming of the kingdom of God closely with the infertile woman in Isa 54:1 who is also exhorted to break forth in joy (*euphranthēti; rhēxon*) as her barrenness (*erēmos*) is to be transformed into fruitfulness by God's act of mercy in delivering her (54:4–10).

Before I demonstrate how the link between Isa 52:7–9 and 54:1 is reflected in Galatians, I note the explicit presence of Isa 52:7 in Rom 10:15, where Paul applies Isaiah's words about the proclamation of the good news to his current context, in which the good news of Jesus is proclaimed both

17. Betz connects 5:21 to a shared tradition of "primitive Christian catechetical instruction," because the language about the kingdom of God is quite non-Pauline, and the sense of inheritance here ("enter into") "is in some tension with Paul's theology" (*Galatians*, 284–85). Similarly, Longenecker, *Galatians*, 258; Martyn, *Galatians*, 497–98; and de Boer, *Galatians*, 360–61. De Boer perceives a misfit between Paul's talk of inheritance in relation to the kingdom of God and what has come before, because Paul has earlier spoken about inheritance "only in connection with the fulfilment of God's promise to Abraham in the gift of the Spirit (3:18, 29; 4:1, 7, 30)" (361; cf. Vouga, *An die Galater*, 138). The perception of misfit here is quite unnecessary. I demonstrate below that all of these belong quite naturally to Paul's theology, if it is viewed from the perspective of the restoration vision in the Isaianic matrix.

to the Jews and Gentiles (Rom 10:11-13), but with special emphasis on Israel (Rom 10:1; 16-21). Hence, we know that this text is important to Paul. I perceive that the intimate connection between the coming of God's kingdom in Isa 52:7-9 and the figure of the barren-made-fruitful woman in 54:1, which is about the restoration of Jerusalem ("above"), is also reflected in Galatians.

In Gal 5:21, Paul connects his warning/prediction that those who practice the works of the flesh do not / will not inherit the kingdom of God to something that he has said before (*ha prolegō hymin kathōs proeipon*). It is very likely that the earlier moment when he had iterated the same warning occurred just moments before, as Gal 4:29-30 was read.[18] The similar concern in both of these moments in the letter makes this probable. In both, the argument is about the incompatibility between Spirit and flesh (4:29 *all' hōsper tote ho kata sarka gennētheis ediōken ton kata pneuma, houtōs kai nyn*; 5:17 *hē gar sarx epithymei kata tou pneumatos, to de pneuma kata tēs sarkos, tauta gar allēlois antikeitai*), and in both, that which is connected with flesh cannot share in the inheritance (4:30 *ou gar mē klēronomēsei ho huios tēs paidiskēs* [*sarx*]; 5:21 *hoi ta toiauta* [*ta erga tēs sarkos*] *prassontes basileian theou ou klēronomēsousin*). These correspondences do not seem accidental but rather intended, and thus indicate that Gal 4:21—5:1 already prepares for what follows in the letter, and, conversely, that the statement in 5:21 does refer back to the punchline (4:29-30) in the argument in 4:21—5:1. This link between Gal 5:21 and 4:29-30 supports the connection between the concepts of the kingdom of God and the "Jerusalem above," and suggests that both concepts describe the reality to which the "inheritance" refers.

Inheritance and Inaugurated Restoration

As I have analyzed in ch. 4, the restoration reality that is presented in the immediate context of Isa 54:1 is described in 54:17 as the *inheritance* of the Lord's servants. Furthermore, this inheritance is also connected with righteousness (right-relatedness), as it is those included in the inheritance who are also rightly related with God (*kai hymeis esesthe moi dikaioi*) (Isa 54:17). I argue that the conception of the restoration reality as the inheritance of God's righteous ones in Isaiah is also reflected in the conception

18. Commentators usually connect it with what Paul has taught the Galatians when he has been earlier with them. Longenecker recognizes the possibility that it could refer to something that Paul has said before "in the immediate context of the letter," but suggests only 1:9 as a possible candidate (*Galatians*, 258). My suggestion that Paul is referring to 4:29-30 is supported by a similar phenomenon in Gal 1:6-9, where Paul says again in 1:9 what he had already said in 1:8.

CONFIGURING THE THEOLOGICAL VISION AND LOGIC OF GALATIANS 173

of the inheritance in Gal 4:21—5:1, and coheres with the development of the theme of right-relatedness in the letter, in which it becomes defined in terms of "sonship" and inheritance (see ch. 2).

The scriptural command in Gal 4:30 is an indirect exhortation to the Galatians that portrays the decision they face in terms of "casting out" the slave woman and her son (4:30a) that allegorically represent life under the Law (see ch. 2 and further discussion below).[19] The reason for casting away the desire, and for resisting the pressure, to come under the Law is the fact that the son of the "slave woman" cannot share in the *inheritance* of the son of the "free woman" (4:30b). The exclusion of the child of the "slave woman" from the inheritance of the child of the "free woman" is also the (theo)logical reason why the Galatians, and other believers in Christ ("we"), are to identify as children of the "free woman" rather than the "slave woman" (4:31). It is important to emphasize that, at this point in the flow of thought, the "slave woman" and the "free woman" are no longer a direct reference to Hagar and Sarah in the Genesis narrative (as they still were in 4:22-23)—a point that is enforced by Paul's own modification of the Genesis quotation in 4:30 where he replaces Sarah's voice ("my son Isaac") with the reference to the "free woman" ("son of the free woman"). The Genesis narrative is being read allegorically (4:24) together with the Isaianic matrix of the two Jerusalems (4:25-27). Hence, the slave woman and the free woman are a reference to what they allegorically represent. Hagar represents the covenant from Sinai and the "present Jerusalem" (4:25). Contrary to what could be expected, Paul never names Sarah in the other covenantal line. What stands in her place is the mother "Jerusalem above" who is free (4:26), and who is described by the image in Isa 54:1 of the barren-made-fruitful woman (4:27). Sure enough, the free woman retains an association with Sarah (the importance is in the pattern of Isaac's birth from Sarah; see below), but Paul's burden is not to connect the believers to Sarah as their mother, but rather to the "Jerusalem above"—*she* is our mother. Similarly, although the inheritance in 4:30 is connected to the theme of being an heir to the Abrahamic promise (3:[8]/18-29; 4:1-7), it moves also beyond that in Paul's allegorical appropriation of the Abrahamic promise that is read

---

19. Eastman argues that the singular imperatives in 4:27 and 4:30 are not directed as commands at the Galatians, but rather "depict for the Galatians the contrasting destinies of the children of the free woman and the children of the slave" (*Recovering Paul's Mother Tongue*, 132-33). I agree with her emphasis that they depict destinies, but maintain that 4:30 not only depicts, but also indirectly calls for a decision on the Galatians' part in relation to the inheritance. This is so because at this point in the passage the biblical actors in 4:30 have allegorical referents that point to the decision the Galatians face.

together with Isaiah.[20] Consequently, I understand the logic thus: since the Galatians *have been included in the inheritance* of belonging to the restoration people as children of the "free woman"—the "Jerusalem above" that is free (4:26)—and as "children of promise," they should not identify with the slave woman—the "present Jerusalem" that leads to slavery. In other words, the Galatians are not to come under the Law because it represents the reality outside of the *inheritance* that they have already entered into as children of the "Jerusalem above." They need to recognize who they already are to know what they should not become. Hence, I claim that the "Jerusalem above" and the related concepts of the "kingdom of God" and "new creation" describe the restoration reality that is, for Paul, the inheritance of God's regenerated people.

I have now argued that the "Jerusalem above" connects Paul's theological vision to the vision of restoration in Isaiah, as it is encapsulated in Isa 54:1 with its interrelated texts. But I want to deepen the discussion by exploring whether the "Jerusalem above" in Gal 4:26 should be taken with an emphasis on the future or on the present, and whether it refers to a heavenly city or to something else in a symbolic way.[21]

Horbury has analyzed Paul's conception of the "Jerusalem above" in relation to other Jewish expectations concerning the Jerusalem prophecies in Scripture, and argues that Paul had a vision of a literal future heavenly city coming to earth. He describes how in Paul's cultural milieu the Jerusalem prophecies were "remembered in prayer and sacred song, and thought of collectively" with requests for the fulfillment of prophecy.[22] He gives evidence of such expectations in Tobit, Ecclesiasticus, the Hebrew Apostrophe to Zion from Qumran Cave 11, Sibylline Oracles, 2 Maccabees, and the Amidah (18 benedictions).[23] Horbury also perceives that Isa 2:2-4; 49:14-26; 54; 59:16—60:22; 62; 65:17-25; 66:5-24 are part of the scriptural matrix underlying such hopes.[24] Yet he reckons that Gal 4:27 is "the earliest clear witness to the notion of a heavenly Jerusalem," but "the expectation of

---

20. Cf. Eastman, *Recovering Paul's Mother Tongue*, 137-55. Others usually emphasize here the Abrahamic promise (Longenecker, *Galatians*, 218), and the connection to Sarah (Betz, *Galatians*, 251; Moo, *Galatians*, 312-13).

21. Many commentators equate the "Jerusalem above" with a heavenly Jerusalem, either as a concrete counterpart of the earthly city to be revealed in the future, or as a spiritual city (e.g., Betz, *Galatians*, 246-47; Dunn, *Galatians*, 253-54; Longenecker, *Galatians*, 213-14; Oepke, *an die Galater*, 151; see also Lincoln, *Paradise Now and Not Yet*, 9-32).

22. Horbury, *Messianism*, 192.

23. Horbury, *Messianism*, 192.

24. Horbury, *Messianism*, 192.

a divinely-prepared holy place above was already well-established in Paul's time" and is "consonant with hope for an ultimate full divine glorification of Jerusalem on earth."[25] Thus, Horbury maintains that Paul's "Jerusalem above" looks to the future: "Paul envisaged a coming messianic reign in the divinely prepared Jerusalem."[26] The future orientation of the "Jerusalem above" is expressed, in Horbury's analysis, in the contrast to "present Jerusalem" and with the links to promise and inheritance.[27]

Horbury's grasp of the Second Temple Jewish literature is impressive, but I think that a closer reading of Galatians resists such a tight correspondence between Paul's vision in the letter and other hopes for a future descent of a heavenly city. What distinguishes Paul from some other Jewish expectations is his experience and conviction that a turn in the ages has already begun (4:4), and that the awaited eschatological realities have made their way into the present, changing the configuration of the cosmos for Paul (6:14-15). It is true that Paul can have a heavenly orientation in the believers' identity, and a future expectation for a full consummation of the eschatological glory (e.g., Phil 3:20-21), but I perceive that in Galatians Paul's emphasis is on the present implications of the already inaugurated eschatological age. This is indicated in Gal 4:26 in the fact that the mother "Jerusalem above" has *already* given birth—she *is* our mother.[28] Similarly, the "new creation" has *already* become the determinative reality for Paul's view of the world/humanity, and has refocused what now counts for inclusion in the community that is shaped by the cross of Christ (6:14-16). Also, as Mußner perceptively notes, living in alignment (*stoicheō*) with the standard of the new creation (6:15-16) is connected to Paul's exhortation to align (*stoicheō*) with the reality of the Spirit (5:25), which has the implication that the Spirit signals the arrival of the new creation reality.[29] Thus, both the "Jerusalem above" and the "new creation" have a clear emphasis on the already inaugurated restoration.[30]

25. Horbury, *Messianism*, 197.

26. Horbury, *Messianism*, 218. Also Horbury, "Land, Sanctuary and Worship," 219-20.

27. Horbury, *Messianism*, 221.

28. Cf. Mußner, *Der Galaterbrief*, 326.

29. Mußner, *Der Galaterbrief*, 415-16.

30. Cf. Cosgrove: "[a]t this point cosmic and eschatological dualism intersect, so that the *present manifestation of the future*, embodied in the community itself, is understood as owing its life to the world above. Although the language of a new or restored Jerusalem is not employed, the use of Is. 54:1 suggests the thought" ("Law Has given Sarah No Children," 231; emphasis added). Also, de Boer, "Paul's Quotation," 374-75. Wagner is in general agreement with this emphasis: "Paul finds in the message of Christ that he proclaims to gentiles the realization of Isaiah's visions of redemption" ("Isaiah in

But what about the kingdom of God? Here the evidence is divided, which reflects the already-not-yet shape of Paul's eschatology. Since, as I have argued above, the kingdom of God in Gal 5:21 is intimately connected with the concerns that are present in the context of the "Jerusalem above" (flesh-Spirit, inheritance), it could be argued that it also shares in the present emphasis of the inheritance in 4:26-31. Even the future form of the verb to inherit (*klēronomēsousin*) in Gal 5:21 could be taken with an "imperatival" force (they shall not inherit) in line with the sense it has in 4:30 (the son of the slave woman shall by no means inherit [*klēronomēsei*]).[31] But this would be to neglect the other vital connection 5:21 has in the letter. The same concern about the outcome of living in line either with the Spirit or with the flesh in Gal 5:17-21 is reflected in 6:7-10, where "sowing into the flesh" results in "reaping" corruption, and "sowing into the Spirit" results in "reaping" eternal life. The moment of reaping refers to a future time that calls for perseverance in the present (6:9-10). This future oriented hope is reflected also in Paul's succinct statement about eagerly waiting for the hope of "righteousness" (*hēmeis gar pneumati ek pisteōs elpida dikaiosynēs apekdechometha*) (5:5)[32]—the hope for the completion of what has already begun with right-relatedness in terms of inclusion in the restoration reality. Hence, although the "Jerusalem above" in Gal 4:26 has a clear focus on the already inaugurated restoration reality, it does not exhaust Paul's hope for the fullness of the rule of God awaiting in the future, even in his urgent letter to the Galatians.

Romans and Galatians," 130).

31. Wallace explains that the imperatival force of the future form is usually found in the quotations of Scripture in the New Testament (reflecting a literal translation of Hebrew), but it is also known in classical Greek (*Greek Grammar beyond the Basics*, 569). See also discussion in BDF §362 and §387.

32. I agree with Betz that the condensed statement in 5:5 consists of abbreviated ideas that Paul has made earlier in the letter (*Galatians*, 261-62; cf. de Boer, *Galatians*, 315; Longenecker, *Galatians*, 228-29). The future oriented sense is found in the expression "eagerly waiting" (*apekdechomai*) that connotes eschatological anticipation in Paul (cf. Rom 8:19, 23, 25; 1 Cor 1:7; Phil 3:20) (de Boer, *Galatians*, 316; Moo, *Galatians*, 327). The genitive construction "hope of righteousness" is best taken as the hoped-for righteousness rather than the hope that comes from righteousness (Barclay, *Paul and the Gift*, 392; de Boer, *Galatians*, 316). However, there is a tension between the present and future sense in righteousness. Mußner emphasizes that both the present and future dimensions look at the one salvation in Christ (*Der Galaterbrief*, 351). I follow his lead, but modify it, as my analysis points to taking righteousness with the meaning of inclusion in the restoration people, and thus I read the hope of righteousness as the future hope of the completion of the process of restoration that has already begun (cf. 5:6; 6:15-16).

Present Jerusalem, Jerusalem Above, and the Alienation-Restoration Paradigm

As I have argued, the restored Jerusalem functions in Isaiah as a symbolic description of the restoration reality that consists of a community that experiences and represents the presence and reign of God (see chapter 4).[33] Hence, I also argue that the "Jerusalem above," with the supporting quotation from Isa 54:1, functions for Paul as a shorthand for the restoration reality described in Isaiah, into which believers in Christ have already entered as their inheritance. They have been generated into a new community, a new social reality, that needs to reflect the "new creation" identity rather than the present reality of the old cosmos with its categories for identifying the people of God (Gal 6:14–16). Because the "Jerusalem above" is closely connected with the idea of "new creation," Paul's vision of the gospel is about the re-creation of humanity that has a cosmic scope.

How does this conception of the "Jerusalem above" in Gal 4:26 help in understanding the "present Jerusalem" in 4:25? As I have indicated already, I perceive that the "present Jerusalem" and the "Jerusalem above" reflect the "tale of two cities" in Isa 54:1 and 1–2 (with related texts). Paul's "present Jerusalem" is described as being in slavery with her children (4:25), and as corresponding with the covenant from Sinai that also leads to slavery (4:24). This resembles the theological interpretation in Isaiah, where it is the Law, or more accurately *violation* of the Law, that leads to "slavery," or captivity in exile (e.g., Isa 1:2–17; 42:24–25; 48:18–19). Exile is God's act of judgment (e.g., Isa 66:9 LXX), in which the Law operates as the agent of judgment. Furthermore, failure to respond to the revelation of God's new act of restoration keeps the people outside of the full inheritance of the restoration reality (Isa 50:10; 65–66). The conceptual and logical correspondences make it likely that the alienation-restoration paradigm in Isaiah underlies Paul's construction of the "present Jerusalem" / "Jerusalem above" dichotomy. Furthermore, I argue that as in Isaiah so also in Paul the state of alienation refers to a realm outside the "inheritance," which is a realm associated with sin and slavery (see chapter 5). Thus, the "present Jerusalem" in Galatians is best approached in connection with the "present evil age" that is marked by sin (1:4) rather than with a direct equation to Judaism, or to the competing Gentile mission that claimed the support of

---

33. Schlier connects the Jerusalem above tightly with the church (*An die Galater*, 223). This is problematic, since, even though the believers in Jesus become eventually known as the church as distinct from Judaism, it is necessary to emphasize that what Paul envisions here is in continuity with the Jewish matrix, as a fulfillment of the hope of Israel that is by design larger than the Jews.

the Jerusalem church.[34] The "present Jerusalem" functions as a symbol for existence outside of the inheritance of the reality of restoration.[35] It is about the sphere of existence that is not aligned with the revelation of the Son, i.e., has not allowed Christ to define the *nomos* (see chapter 5), and thus, has not recognized/followed the implications of the coming of Christ and the giving of the Spirit that have opened the gates of the "Jerusalem above" and generated a "new creation" community.

The logic of the alienation-restoration paradigm that configures slavery and freedom in relation to the Law and inheritance is the key to reading Paul's logic in Gal 4:21—5:1, and consequently in the other passages in Galatians where the same or related concepts are discussed (especially in 4:1–7 [slavery, sonship, inheritance] and 3:10–14 [curse, righteousness, blessing, Spirit]; I discuss these texts below). To capture better how the concepts of slavery, freedom, and inheritance work together with the other themes in the framework of the two covenants in Gal 4:21—5:1, I first explore the identification of the Galatian believers as "children of promise" according to the pattern of Isaac, the connection between Hagar and Sinai, the role of Christ as the Isaianic servant in the covenant of promise, and Paul's identification with the divine generative activity in Christ, which then lead

---

34. In the identification of the "Jerusalem above" and the "present Jerusalem," I disagree with the position that is argued influentially by Martyn that they refer to two different Gentile missions: Paul's "circumcision-free" mission and the "Law-observant" mission promulgated by the Jerusalem church (Martyn, "Tale of Two Churches"; similarly de Boer, *Galatians*, 285–310). It is true that the Galatians might hear an echo from Paul's earlier reference to Jerusalem in the letter, but that would not necessarily support Martyn's argument that rests on a negative portrayal of the Jerusalem church, in which the leaders (at least James) are implicated in the activity of the "false brothers"—the circumcision party. But, rather than merging the positions of the Jerusalem church and the "false brothers," Paul keeps them separate, and emphasizes that the Jerusalem church leaders support his Gentile mission (Gal 2:1–10; although Peter is inconsistent in Antioch, 2:11–14). I do not resist ascribing a social dimension, i.e., real groups that reflect different theological views, to the two Jerusalems, but I disagree with limiting these to the social level with speculative historical reconstruction. For further critique, see Barclay, *Paul and the Gift*, 417n64.

35. That Paul is not referring to the concrete city of Jerusalem could also be indicated by the observation that he is using a different spelling of Jerusalem in 4:25–26 (*ierousalēm*) to what he uses in Gal 1:17, 18 and 2:1 in reference to the geographical Jerusalem (*ierosoluma*) (cf. Bruce, *Galatians*, 220; Longenecker, *Galatians*, 213). The spelling in 4:25–26 reflects the language of the LXX (e.g., Isa 1:1 and 2:1) that could indicate scriptural influence in Paul's designation here (cf. de Boer, *Galatians*, 297). De Boer also suggests that Paul's use of the *feminine* form over the neuter "facilitates his allegorical-typological interpretation of 'Hagar' and 'Sarah.'" We should not make too much of the different spellings, since Paul can use *ierousalēm* also in reference to the geographical Jerusalem in Rom 15:19, 25, 26, 31.

to a synthesis of my reading of Gal 4:21—5:1 and the configuration of the theological vision and logic of the letter.

Children of Promise According to the Pattern of Isaac

The logic of Paul's argument in Gal 4:26-28 can be discerned thus: those who belong to the "Jerusalem above" (4:26) are also "children of promise" (4:28), because of Isa 54:1 (4:27).[36] In other words, the children of the mother "Jerusalem above" are described also as the "children of promise" *kata* Isaac (the possible sense of *kata* is explored below), because they are children of the barren-made-fruitful woman of Isa 54:1. To be able to follow this logic, I first draw on the theological potential in the Abraham narrative for the designation of being children of promise *kata* Isaac, and then follow how the Isaianic promise of restoration facilitates ascribing a title closely connected with the identity of Israel now also to the Gentile believers in Christ.

The Pattern of Isaac's Birth and the Abrahamic-Isaianic Promise

It is certain that Paul is crafting his argument about two kinds of "children" in Gal 4:21—5:1 on the matrix of the narrative about the births of Abraham's two sons (*abraam duo huious eschen*) (4:22). To be more specific, it is very likely that the matrix of Gen 17 and related texts is pivotal for Paul's understanding of the "children of promise" *kata* Isaac and its implication for the identity of God's people.[37]

We know from Romans that Gen 17 is significant for Paul in respect to Abraham being the "father of many nations" (Rom 4:9-18). Furthermore, in Rom 9:6-9 Paul weaves together many texts related to Gen 17 that deal with the paradigm and significance of Isaac:

> For not all who are of Israel are Israel, because neither are all the children seed of Abraham, but 'in Isaac shall your seed be called/named' [reference to Gen 21:12 and related with Gen 17:15-21]. This means that the children of flesh are not the children of God, but the children of promise are reckoned as the seed. For this is the word of the promise: 'about/at this time I will return and Sarah will have a son' [reference to Gen 18:10].

---

36. Cf. Jobes, "Jerusalem, Our Mother," 302-3, 313.
37. Cf. Watson, *PHF*, 187-90.

I also argue later below that Gen 17 is very likely the primary matrix for Paul's conception of the two covenants in Gal 4:21—5:1. Hence, I focus here on how Gen 17, with related texts, informs the meaning of *kata* Isaac in the designation of the "children of promise."

As I have argued in ch. 3, Gen 17 is an important culmination point in the narrative about Abraham's two sons as they relate to the promise of the "great nation" and blessing for all the nations. The contrast between Ishmael and Isaac as two alternative construals of the great nation—Israel—is played out most clearly in Gen 17. As the promise of an heir to Abraham is specified to come from Sarah (17:15-19), Abraham laughs (17:17). The absurdity of the promise is emphasized, when it is repeated to Sarah in Gen 18 at a stage when she is not only barren but also past menopause (18:11). Hence, also Sarah laughs (18:12-15). The laughter of disbelief turns into the laughter of rejoicing when God acts to fulfill his promise and Isaac is born (21:1-7). The theme of laughter invests the son of promise with a name that has theological significance: Isaac (he laughs) (21:3-7). Isaac's name epitomizes the theology of the people of God as the "Israel *of God.*" It signifies the realization of both total human insufficiency and absolute dependence on the performative power of God's promise to generate the people of God—the people according to the pattern of Isaac are as much "children of laughter" as they are "children of promise."

Genesis 17 also explains the exclusion of Ishmael from inheriting the promise of the true "great nation" that culminates in his expulsion, on which Paul capitalizes in his citing of Gen 21:10 in Gal 4:30. Gen 17:19-20 specifies that only Isaac counts as an heir of the covenant between God and his special people (cf. 21:12) who are also trusted with the promise of blessing for all the peoples (17:15-16; 22:17-18; 35:11; 49:10). Ishmael does not count even though he is Abraham's physical seed and is circumcised (17:20-21, 25-26). Ishmael is everything that Isaac is, except that he is not a son of promise. They are born of different mothers, and it is the manner of their births that has the final verdict on who inherits the promise of the true "great nation." Ishmael is born out of "flesh"—out of theologically reasoned human potential (16:2) that can conform to requirements of physical lineage and the law of circumcision.[38] Only Isaac is generated by the power of God's promise rather than by human potential. This is what ultimately counts for the identity of God's people.

When Paul designates the Galatian believers as children of promise *kata* Isaac, he is drawing from the theological potential in the *pattern of*

---

38. Pace Thiessen, who argues that the main factor that excludes Ishmael from the covenant is his wrongly dated circumcision (see ch. 3).

Isaac's birth and its significance for inclusion in the people of God.[39] Isaac is for Paul the paradigm for being generated by the power of God's promise in contrast to Ishmael who represents generation by the "flesh" (4:23). This accords with the opening of Paul's letter that underscores the divine origin of his gospel (Gal 1:1) that is not according to human pattern (*ouk estin kata anthrōpon*) (1:11), i.e., it "is at odds with the normative conventions that govern human systems of value."[40] Furthermore, in light of the contrast to Ishmael that Paul highlights in Gal 4:21—5:1, Isaac represents the essential characteristic of the people of God that has the potential to include uncircumcised people outside of the Abrahamic physical seed as heirs of the inheritance and blessing of Abraham.[41] But it is vital at this point to follow Paul's move closely to avoid construing his logic with emphasis on continuity in the identity of the covenant people without recognizing the "rupture" that Isa 54:1 brings into the storyline.

What is crucial for Paul is the connection in the pattern of Isaac's birth and the pattern in the promise of restoration in Isa 54:1—it is the *barren* that is made fruitful. This pattern de-emphasizes natural (physical descent) or linear (undisturbed continuation of covenant) continuity, and instead emphasizes divine regenerative activity as the defining factor in the identity of the people of God. This logic is also reflected in Gal 3:26–29, where it is on the condition of being "sons" *of God* (*pantes gar huioi theou este dia tēs pisteōs en christō iēsou*) (3:26) that the Galatians can also be reckoned as "seed" of Abraham, that is, heirs according to the promise (*ei de hymeis christou, ara tou abraam sperma este, kat' epangelian klēronomoi*) (3:29).[42] The logic that defies linear continuity is encapsulated in Isa 54:1 in the

---

39. Cf. Martyn, *Galatians*, 443–44. At this point, I agree with Martyn that Paul is not drawing a linear connection from Abraham to the Galatians, but is focused on the *pattern* in Isaac's birth. For Eastman this indicates that "Paul tells his converts that their continuity with the family tree of Abraham comes solely through the continuity of promise" (*Recovering Paul's Mother Tongue*, 140). This is true, but does not exclude the role the *nomos* plays in Paul's retelling of Israel's story with the alienation-restoration paradigm that has implications also for the Galatians.

40. Barclay, *Paul and the Gift*, 355.

41. What is not essential can be relativized, since what is essential can be counted more important than the non-essential (cf. Rom 2:25–29; Phil 3:3). Unfortunately, the contrast that Paul sets between Ishmael and Isaac has been applied directly to equate the Jews with Ishmael and Gentile believers in Christ with Isaac (e.g., Rohde, *an die Galater*, 203). I argue in this chapter for a more nuanced approach.

42. Pace Thiessen's prioritizing of the genealogical connection with Abraham: "those who are in Christ, and those who are thus seed and sons of Abraham, are also sons of God (Gal 3:26). Those who receive the *pneuma* of Christ become not only sons of Abraham, but also sons of God, since Christ is both the seed of Abraham and the son of God (Gal 4:6)" (*Paul and the Gentile Problem*, 154–55).

fact that it is exactly *because the woman is barren* that she will have more children than she would have had, if she had remained as the woman who always had a husband (cf. Isa 66:7–9). This is the logic in the alienation-restoration paradigm. It is Israel's alienation and the promise of restoration that redefines her identity theologically rather than ethnically (see chapter 4). Israel's experience of alienation joins her with the nations—she is made in effect a non-people (Isa 63:19; 65:1). She cannot appeal to Abrahamic ancestry (Isa 63:16) or adherence to Law (e.g., Isa 58) as the reason for restoration. Her restoration depends on God's mercy (Isa 54:7–10; 55:1), and on her responsiveness to God's regenerative promise (Isa 50:10; 51:1; 53:1; 65:1–3; 66). The barrenness of the woman—the alienation of Israel—opens the possibility for other non-peoples to be generated from their "barrenness"—alienation—into the life of the new restored people of God. Starling's analysis of Paul's application of texts of Scripture that are initially addressed to the exiles of Israel to the Gentiles (he looks at Isa 54:1 in Gal 4:27, as well as the Scripture catena in 2 Cor 6:16–18; and Hos 1:10 and 2:23 in Rom 9:25–26 [also Isa 57:19 in Eph 2:17]),[43] supports my proposal that the alienation-restoration logic in Isa 54:1 facilitates for Paul the inclusion of Gentiles in the "children of promise."

But even more can be said about the theological potential in Isaiah to facilitate the move to name the Gentiles as "children of promise" in the pattern of Isaac. Because the designation "children of promise" follows from the Galatian believers being designated children of the "Jerusalem above" according to Isa 54:1, the *promise* in Gal 4:28 does not refer only to the initial promise to Abraham about the birth of Isaac. Rather, as the promise of the birth of Isaac is also connected to the advancement of the promised blessing to all the nations (see chapter 3), the promise here most likely refers to the Abrahamic promise of blessing to all the nations (cf. Gal 3:8) *as it is re-appropriated in Isaiah's vision of restoration*.[44] Hence, the promise refers to the composite Abraham-Isaiah promise, or composite blessing-restoration promise. As I argued in the thematic intratextual analysis of Isaiah, the vision of restoration is intimately connected with the Abrahamic promise of blessing that extends to all the nations (Gen 12:3; 18:18; 22:17–18; 35:11; the influence of these can be recognized, e.g., in Isa 41; 44; 51; 54; see ch. 5). Furthermore, the barren-made-fruitful woman is also about the vision of the restored city (Isa 2; 60; 66), in which the language of the Abrahamic promise echoes far and wide—it is all the nations (*panta*

---

43. Starling, *Not My People*.

44. Most commentators discuss the promise in 4:28 only in reference to the Abrahamic promise (e.g., Betz, *Galatians*, 249; de Boer, *Galatians*, 305–6; Dunn, *Galatians*, 255–56; Longenecker, *Galatians*, 216).

ta ethnē) that are in the scope of the "inheritance" in the restored city—the regenerated community of God's people.

It is important to re-emphasize that, although the barren-made-fruitful woman participates in the pattern of Sarah giving birth to Isaac, she is not named as Sarah by Paul. Rather, she is the "Jerusalem above" mother. Hence, the two designations of the identity of the Galatian believers (together with Paul) are intimately connected. They are "children of promise" according to the pattern of Isaac *exactly because* they are children of the barren-made-fruitful woman who are the restoration people of the "Jerusalem above." The theological implication of this is that Paul resists the view that Gentiles are to be joined to Israel according to the pattern of Ishmael—"according to the flesh"—by the means of their circumcision and adoption of the Law from Sinai (coming "under the Law"). The Gentiles are not to join the "present Jerusalem"—a realm of existence reflected in the community that is not aligned with the reality of restoration effected by Christ and the Spirit—since what matters for Paul is inclusion in the regenerated "new creation" people that is not predicated on circumcision or physical lineage from Abraham, but on divine generation (see Figure 2 below).

This is why Paul also hopes/prays that his kinsmen the Jews, whose very fleshly existence is derived out of the power of God's promise in the birth of their patriarch Isaac, would be reached by the mercy offered in Christ (Gal 6:16). Hence, Paul can designate the physical descendants of Abraham as the "Israel of God,"[45] and simultaneously hope for the mercy of restoration that would "justify" her as such, but only as his fellow Jews also respond to the promissory act of God in Christ and the Spirit (cf. Gal 2:16) that regenerates them to be, not only children of the initial promise to Abraham, but also children of the promise of restoration (see Figure 2).

---

45. The identity of the "Israel of God" is a highly debated question. For a good introduction to the alternative views, see de Boer, *Galatians*, 405–10. I agree with Bachmann (*Anti-Judaism in Galatians?*, 101–23), Barclay (*Paul and the Gift*, 418–21), and Eastman ("Israel and the Mercy of God") that the Israel of God is Paul's reference to the Jewish people (especially those still outside of Christ). The majority view is to read "Israel of God" as referring to the "new creation" people of 6:15—the believers in Christ of both Jews and Gentiles. This view is represented by Martyn and Wright (also e.g., Oepke, *an die Galater*, 204–5; Schlier, *an die Galater*, 283). For both, the decisive issue is the overall argument of the letter. I maintain that Paul's peculiar expression and choice of words in 6:16 signal that something unexpected can be expected. Paul indicates that he still has a special concern for his kinsmen in the flesh, which he opens up more fully in Rom 9–11 (cf. Mußner, *Der Galaterbrief*, 417).

Figure 2. Schematic Presentation of the Generation of the "Children of Promise"

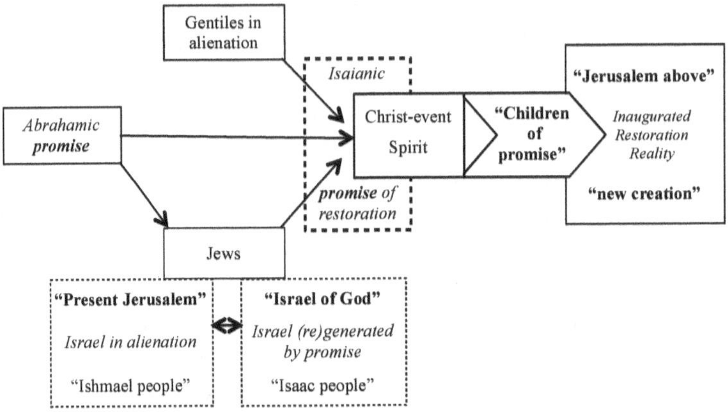

```
                    ┌──────────────┐
                    │ Gentiles in  │
                    │  alienation  │
                    └──────┬───────┘
                    ┌ ─ ─ ─│─ ─ ─ ┐
                      Isaianic                          ┌──────────────┐
                    │      ▼      │                     │"Jerusalem above"│
┌──────────────┐           ┌──────────┐  ┌──────────┐   │              │
│  Abrahamic   │──────────▶│Christ-event│▶│"Children │──▶│ Inaugurated  │
│   promise    │    │      │    of    │  │    of    │   │ Restoration  │
│              │           │  Spirit  │  │ promise" │   │   Reality    │
└──────┬───────┘    │      └──────────┘  └──────────┘   │              │
       │                   ▲                             │"new creation"│
       │            │promise of│                         └──────────────┘
       │             restoration│
       │            └ ─ ─ ─ ─ ─┘
       ▼
   ┌───────┐
   │ Jews  │
   └───────┘
┌ ─ ─ ─ ─ ─ ─ ─ ─ ┐   ┌ ─ ─ ─ ─ ─ ─ ─ ─ ┐
│"Present Jerusalem"│  │ "Israel of God"  │
│                   │⬌│                  │
│Israel in alienation│  │Israel (re)generated│
│                   │  │    by promise    │
│"Ishmael people"   │  │ "Isaac people"   │
└ ─ ─ ─ ─ ─ ─ ─ ─ ┘   └ ─ ─ ─ ─ ─ ─ ─ ─ ┘
```

This paradoxical construction of Paul's logic that the "Israel of God" refers to the physical descendants of Abraham, but at the same time she is only "justified" as such by her response to the new promissory act of God in Christ, is reflected also in Paul's logic in Gal 4:1–7.[46] There the "heir"—Israel—is at the same time recognized as a son (implied) and the heir (4:1–3), but also in need of redemption and "adoption" (4:4–5) to realize the inheritance—the restoration reality—of the sons of God (4:6–7). In other words, the heir is a "son," but also a "slave" until the "fulness of time" when his/her status can be fully realized. If Israel's status as the "son," who is the heir, is only realized by divine redemption, it is not unimaginable to perceive that Paul thinks that the "Israel of God" is proved, or better yet, regenerated to be the "Israel of God" by her response to divine mercy in Christ. Thus, Paul holds that dependence on divine promise in the offer of mercy in Christ is decisive also for the Jews in determining whether they become who they truly are (Isaac people) in their inclusion in the "new creation" people of the "Jerusalem above." A failure to respond to the divine revelation in "the Son" is a failure to live up to Israel's true character

---

46. Wright's reading of Gal 3:14 has similar logic that leads him to modify Sanders's categories: "[a]t this point the categories of 'getting in' and 'staying in,' . . . , seem to need more nuances: 'getting *back in*,' for instance, or 'staying in when it looked as though one had been ejected.' Israel's peculiar plight is that, through the exile, she has been, in one sense, still inside the covenant and, in another, outside it. Gentiles simply come in, from nowhere; Jews have their membership renewed, brought back to life, by sharing the death and resurrection of their Messiah" (*The Climax of the Covenant*, 155; emphasis original).

according to the pattern of Isaac, and thus a construction of the identity of Israel (by the Jew or the Judaizing Gentile) according to the flesh (the Ishmael alternative) that results in the status of slavery—alienation—in the "present Jerusalem" (see Figure 2 above).

Promise of Restoration and Generation by the Spirit

The above analysis about the composite character of the promise (Abraham-Isaiah) in Paul's designation of the Galatian believers' identity as "children of promise" can be further developed, as we follow closely the move that Paul makes in describing the birth of Isaac in contrast to Ishmael. Paul describes Isaac's birth first in terms of having taken place by the promise (*di' epangelias*) in contrast to the birth of Ishmael that was according to the flesh (*kata sarka*) (4:23). But, on the second occasion, Paul pits the two sons against each other in terms of the one being born according to flesh and the other according to Spirit (*kata pneuma*) (4:29). On a rhetorical level, the explication of the promise in terms of the Spirit is most likely due to the more direct application of the tension between Ishmael and Isaac to the situation with the Galatians (*houtōs kai nyn*) (4:29).[47] The Spirit is connected to the generative line of the promise with an emphasis on the incompatibility between being generated by the Spirit or by flesh. This is reminiscent of Paul's earlier emphasis on the Galatians' reception of the Spirit as the reason why they should not attempt to complement their life as God's people by the flesh (3:3) that is connected with their desire to come "under the Law" to practice the "works of the Law" (3:2). The tension between flesh and Spirit in Gal 4:29 also anticipates the major role these categories play in Gal 5:13-26 where, however, the works of the flesh do not resemble the "works of the Law," but rather corrupted practices that describe a totally opposite way of life to that lived by the Spirit (see discussion below).

In addition to the rhetorical reason, it is also significant that the reference to generation by the Spirit in Gal 4:29 follows the Isa 54:1 quotation (4:27) and the identification of the Galatian believers with the pattern of the

---

47. Cf. de Boer, *Galatians*, 306. Earlier commentators perceived the "persecution" in terms of the (unbelieving) Jews persecuting Christians (e.g., Betz, *Galatians*, 250; Rohde, *an die Galater*, 204; Schlier, *an die Galater*, 226-27; Burton already recognized that it had more to do with Paul's opponents [*Galatians*, 266]). The discussion has rightly moved away from portraying the persecution in terms of Jews vs. Christians, and focused on Paul's opponents' imposition of the Law over the Gentile Galatians (cf. Gal 5:11-12) (e.g., Longenecker, *Galatians*, 216-17; Martyn, *Galatians*, 444-45). Yet I maintain that Paul's focus is primarily on the theological level where it is connected to the polarity between Spirit and flesh that is the focus in 3:1-5 and in 5:16—6:10.

birth of Isaac (4:28). Hence, I suggest that the reference to the one generated by the Spirit functions as a reference to the "allegorical Isaac" who now represents the Galatian believers (among others). Furthermore, I reckon that this logic is facilitated by the Isaianic matrix. The logic can be summarized thus: the Galatians are identified as "children of promise" (4:28) who are generated by the Spirit (4:29), and, as such, are included in the inheritance (4:30), which means that they are also children of the "free woman" (4:31) that refers back to the mother "Jerusalem above" (4:26)—the restoration reality according to Isa 54:1. Hence, I explore the role of the Spirit in Paul's logic with the help of the Isaianic matrix that is connected with the vision of restoration in Isa 54:1.

I have argued in ch. 4 that the transformation of barrenness into fruitfulness in the image of the woman with many children in Isa 54:1 is intimately connected with the theme of the Spirit's generative activity that is often pictured in Isaiah by waters transforming barren/desolate land into fertile blossoming that resembles new creation (e.g., Isa 35:1–7; 41:18; 43:18–21). One key text in this regard is Isa 44:1–5. It is very likely that this text has influenced Paul in his conception of the Spirit mediating the Abrahamic promise of blessing to all the nations, which is understood via the Isaianic matrix as inclusion in the restored people of God. We can perceive the influence of Isa 44:1–5 initially in Gal 3:14, which then leads us to recognize its impact also in the logic of Gal 4:21—5:1.

Isaiah 44:1–5 is about regenerating Israel as God's people. It first looks back to how God formed her from the womb (44:1–2), in order to assure her of God's ability to re-form her by the Spirit (44:3–5). The pattern in the birth of Isaac (which is also repeated with variations in the birth of Jacob and his sons) is the paradigm for connecting the performative power of God's promise with the activity of the Spirit in the generation of a people. The language of providing water for the thirsty (44:3a) is explicated in the next line by the promise of placing the Spirit on Israel's seed (44:3b), which is then developed with the theme of blessing on her children (44:3c). This results in, or better yet, the blessing consists of, the children "springing up" like grass or willows by the waters (44:4). These newly generated children identify themselves as belonging to God, and take on the name Israel (44:5). This refers to the re-formation of Israel from a non-people (cf. Isa 63:10–19) that has the potential for including Gentiles, which amounts to the fulfillment of the Abrahamic promise of blessing (see ch. 4).

The thematic coherence and logical correspondence together with conceptual and verbal links between Isa 44:3 and Gal 3:14 make it very likely that Isa 44:1–5 is the matrix for Paul's concluding statement in Gal 3:14 about the blessing of Abraham reaching the Gentiles that is conceived in terms of the reception of the promised Spirit (*hina eis ta ethnē hē eulogia tou abraam genētai en christō iēsou, hina tēn epangelian tou pneumatos labōmen dia tēs pisteōs*).⁴⁸ The two key concepts of *blessing* and the *Spirit* are paralleled in the same way in Isa 44:3 and in Gal 3:14 in connection with the formation of the new people of God (the aim of the argument about the Abrahamic promise of blessing in Gal 3:8 is expressed in 3:28–29 in terms of the re-formed people of God).⁴⁹ The Isaianic connection has also the power to explain Paul's move to correlate the Abrahamic blessing with the promise of the Spirit. The promise of the Spirit is not found in the Abraham narrative itself, but it is an integral feature in the Isaianic vision of restoration that is conceived as a fulfillment of the Abrahamic promise of blessing to all the nations.⁵⁰ Furthermore, the Isaianic matrix suggests that the Spirit functions as one generative means to bring the Gentiles into the blessing of the inheritance of the restoration reality. Hence, I understand that Gal 3:14 is another moment, besides 4:21—5:1, where Paul reads the Abraham narrative together with Isaiah to arrive at the conclusion that the Abrahamic promise of blessing to all the nations is being fulfilled in the gift of the Spirit, which is both a means for and a sign of inclusion in the restored community of God's people.

48. Cf. Lee, *Blessing of Abraham*, 194; Harmon, *She Must*, 146–48; Hays, *Faith of Jesus Christ*, 182–83; Morales, *Spirit and the Restoration of Israel*, 181–83. Also, though not developed, de Boer, *Galatians*, 215; Moo, *Galatians*, 216. Pace Watson: "[t]he text [Genesis] is clearly a 'promise,' but only in the light of Christian faith and experience can the content of the promise be identified as the giving of the Spirit" (*PHF*, 176).

49. The two *hina* clauses in Gal 3:14 express the purpose/result from the statement in 3:13 (*christos hēmas exēgorasen ek tēs kataras tou nomou*). The second *hina* clause is best viewed as a co-ordinate with the first (in apposition) that does not depend on the first (as if the blessing to the Gentiles would be the prerequisite for the reception of the Spirit). Cf. Betz, *Galatians*, 152; Bruce, *Galatians*, 167; Longenecker, *Galatians*, 123; Oepke, *an die Galater*, 109; Vouga, *An die Galater*, 77. This is a case of parallelism, in which the second clause advances and enlarges the first. Hence, Paul does not simply equate the blessing and Spirit, so that the blessing would consist of the Spirit (pace de Boer, *Galatians*, 215). Rather, the Spirit is the "mediator" of the blessing that consists of "righteousness" (cf. Burton, *Galatians*, 175; Lee, *Blessing of Abraham*, 193–98; Watson, *PHF*, 173) that is defined in Galatians as generation and inclusion into the restored people of God.

50. Pace Thiessen, who dismisses the possibility that Isa 44:1–3 underlies the logic of Gal 3:14, because it is addressed to Jacob/Israel rather than Abraham, and because Paul does not explicitly refer to Isaiah here (*Paul and the Gentile Problem*, 131–32). Instead, Thiessen argues that the promise of the pneuma is found in the Abraham narrative, although implicitly, in the promise of Abraham having descendants as the stars (see ch. 1). Thiessen's proposal is possible, but hardly more plausible than understanding that Paul reads the Abraham narrative together with Isaiah, as he explicitly does in Gal 4:21—5:1.

Although Paul's argument in Gal 3:6-14 includes a catena of Scripture (Deuteronomy, Habakkuk, and Leviticus cited in Gal 3:10-13), the argument is bracketed by engagement with the Abraham narrative at the start (Gen 15:6 in Gal 3:6; Gen 12:3; 18:18 in Gal 3:8) and by the concluding statement that is very likely influenced by Isa 44:1-5 (Gal 3:14). Hence, while Paul works here with a wider contour of Scripture that is configured in terms of the promise and Law, the Isaianic matrix is again part of the pattern that describes Israel's experience and its implications for the Gentiles in terms of the alienation-restoration (here curse-blessing) paradigm configured by the gift of the Spirit.[51] Thus, due to the corresponding logic between Isa 44:1-5; Gal 3:14; and 4:21—5:1, it is very likely that Isa 44:1-5 is part of the matrix for including the Spirit in the generative line of the promise that makes the Gentile Galatians "children of promise" and members of the restored people of God—the children of the "Jerusalem above."

There is yet another text in Isaiah that I regard as a likely matrix for Paul's conception of the Spirit as one key generative agent of the restored people of God. I have analyzed in chapter 4 how the Spirit is presented as the hallmark of the people of God in Isa 63, although it is expressed via the negative experience of Israel—the lack of divine involvement is lamented in terms of the Spirit's absence. The people remember how the exodus generation provoked the Holy Spirit by disobedience turning God into their enemy (63:10), and recognize that they have now degenerated to a status that would practically disqualify them from being the special people of God (63:19). In their plight, they remember the exodus and how God had placed his Spirit among them to lead them (63:11-14). These people appeal to God's mercy to deliver and lead them to inherit even a little portion of the "holy mountain" (63:15-18). In their appeal, the people call explicitly on God as their Father to be their deliverer; they do not appeal to their Abrahamic ancestry or their pedigree as Israelites, but seek directly the mercy of the Father to restore them (*sy gar hēmōn ei patēr . . . alla sy, kyrie, pater hēmōn, rhysai hēmas*) (63:16).

---

51. For Paul's construal of the promise-Law pattern in Scripture, see Watson, PHF. For Wright's critique of Watson's promise-Law construction, see PFG, 1456-71. For Watson's discussion on the differences between his approach and Wright, see PHF, xxvi-xxxv. The core of their disagreement is in part about the existence of an overarching or underlying (covenantal) narrative (metanarrative) in Paul's reading of Israel's Scripture (see also Watson, "Is There a Story in These Texts?," 231-39). But even more it is about the shape of this narrative; whether or not there is an unbroken continuity of Israel's story to Christ. I present in this thesis a mediated position that perceives more elements in the story than Watson presently has developed (namely from the Isaianic matrix), but also finds less of a sense of an ongoing or extended exile than Wright.

I perceive that there are conceptual and logical correspondences between Isa 63:11–18 and Gal 4:4–7, which make it likely that this text in Isaiah is part of the matrix that informs Paul's understanding of the role of the Spirit in generating the restored people of God.[52] The logical and conceptual correspondence between Isaiah and Paul is reflected in the emphasis on God as the Father acting to deliver (Isa 63:16 *rhuomai*) or redeem (Gal 4:5 *exagorazō*) the alienated people (enmity and abandonment in Isaiah; slavery in Galatians) to a new status as heirs (inherit a portion of the holy mountain in Isaiah; being heirs of the restoration reality in Galatians). In contrast to the lament in Isa 63, the regenerated children of God in Galatians enjoy the Spirit's presence that affirms their status with the cry of the child: *Abba*, Father (4:6). Furthermore, Isa 63 has the potential to be applied to the Gentiles, since it offers hope for alienated people to be restored by the mercy of God without appeal to any prior sense of worth or status. Hence, it is likely that in Gal 4:4–7 Paul interweaves the Gentiles into the story of Israel's restoration with reflection on the theological potential in the Isaianic matrix that is also the case in the Spirit's role in generating the "children of promise" in Gal 4:21—5:1.

Integrating the Gentiles into the Recalibrated Story of Israel

The recalibration of the story of Israel with the alienation-restoration paradigm integrates the Gentiles into its scope, which is reflected in Paul's puzzling use of the first- and second-person plural pronouns (we, you) and verbal forms.[53] Some instances of his use of the first-person plural are straightfor-

52. Wright emphasizes the role of the exodus/new exodus narrative here (*PFG*, 656–58, 876–79). I agree, but would stress more than Wright that Paul reads the exodus narrative together with its re-appropriation in Isaiah's vision of restoration (new exodus) that has the Spirit as a key element in it. Harmon identifies an echo or thematic parallelism between Isa 63 and Paul's conception of being led by the Spirit in Gal 5:18 (*She Must*, 221–25). This supports my argument that Isa 63 is a text Paul has reflected on with regard to the Spirit's role in the life of the people of God. I recognize that the context of Greco-Roman adoption and inheritance practices must also be considered as adding meaning to Gal 4:1–7, but I cannot pursue it here. For a good treatment of this dimension, see Walters, "Paul, Adoption, and Inheritance," 42–76.

53. This is a well-recognized puzzle; see Barclay, *Paul and the Gift*, 419–20, n70–71; de Boer, *Galatians*, 209–10, 256–61; Donaldson, "'Curse of the Law,'" 94–112; Johnson Hodge, *If Sons, Then Heirs*, 70–71, 123 with n35; Martyn, *Galatians*, 334–36; Moo, *Galatians*, 211–14; Thiessen, *Paul and the Gentile Problem*, 130. The question here is whether Paul's use of the "we/us" in Gal 3:13–14; 3:23–29; 4:1–7 refers to the Jews/Jewish believers (Barclay and Donaldson), or is about Paul's identification with the Gentile believers (Johnson Hodge and Thiessen), or a reference to a universal "we" (de Boer,

ward: in Gal 1:8-9 and 2:5 it is a clear reference to Paul and his associates; in 2:15-17 it is a clear reference to Jewish believers in Christ; and in 1:4; 5:5; 5:25; and 6:9 it is a general reference to Jewish and Gentile believers in Christ. But it is more challenging to follow Paul's logic with the "we/us" in Gal 3-4. This is where the approach espoused in this book can demonstrate some level of satisfaction in terms of its ability to provide clarity.

I begin from Gal 4:21—5:1. Paul uses the second-person plural *you* to direct his address to the Galatian believers in 4:21 ("you who ... do you not"), 28 ("you are"),[54] and 5:1 ("you stand!"), but his use of the *we/us* in 4:26 ("our mother"),[55] 31 ("we are not"), and 5:1 ("Christ has set us free") connects the direct address to the Galatians with the bigger story that includes at least Paul, and most likely also other Jewish believers in Christ.[56] The inclusive "we" is an indication that the Galatian Gentile believers (not excluding the possibility that there are also Jewish believers among the congregations) are joined into the story of Israel's redemption according to the alienation-restoration paradigm. Because the Galatian believers are children of the promise of blessing and restoration according to the pattern of Isaac (4:28), they have also become participants in the "we" together with Jewish believers in Christ who are not children of the "slave woman"—belonging to the "present Jerusalem"—but whose mother is the "Jerusalem above"—belonging to the restored people of God. The underlying

---

Martyn, and Moo). The position I argue here starts from the recognition of the Jewish priority in the "we," but moves towards the universal "we," as the Jew-Gentile distinction is blurred because the Gentiles are integrated into the story of Israel retrospectively (cf. Hays, *Faith of Jesus Christ*, 108). It seems to be characteristic of the RNPP to exclude the Jews from Paul's "we." Johnson Hodge connects the use of the Gentiles + Paul "we" to the "fictive" construction of Gentile genealogy that connects them to Abraham (*If Sons, Then Heirs*, 79-91, 123 with n35). This has some resemblance to what I express in terms of Paul integrating Gentile Galatians into the story of Israel. But why should Paul's emphasis on the implications of Israel's story on the Gentiles remove the Jews from the purview of Paul's retelling of his/their own story?

54. Many manuscripts have "we" (*hēmeis*) here (e.g., ℵ, A, C, D², K, L, P, Ψ, majority text, lat, sy, bo); most likely to harmonize with the use the first-person plural in 4:26 and 31. The reading "you" (*hymeis*) is supported, e.g., by P⁴⁶, B, D*, F, G, 0261^{vid}, b, sa.

55. The apparently later addition of *pantōn* (*pantōn hēmōn*) further highlights this as an inclusive statement. The addition is attested in, e.g., ℵ², A, C³, K, L, P, majority text, vg^{mss}, sy^h. Text without *pantōn* is found in, e.g., P⁴⁶, ℵ*, B, C*, D, F, G, lat, sy$^{p.hmg}$, co.

56. Dunn takes the first-person plural in vv. 26 and 31 as including all who have been "born in accordance with the Spirit [iv.29], Jew as well as Gentile," since the new "heavenly reality" is not constrained by "ethnic and fleshly considerations" (*Galatians*, 254, 259). Betz reads the "our mother" in v. 26 as Paul's way of taking up polemically a famous Jewish dictum "and claims it for the Christians" (*Galatians*, 247-48). These examples demonstrate that there are theological implications from how Paul's use of the "we" and "you" is understood.

logic is about regenerating the restoration people that applies both to the Jews and Gentiles. With these initial insights from Gal 4:21–5:1, I now turn to other passages that play on the shifts between the Jewish "we" and the Gentile "you," and their modification by the impact of the construction of a new inclusive "we."

In Gal 3:13, the "us" who have been redeemed from the curse of the Law most naturally refers to the Jews who have been under the covenant from Sinai.[57] But it has an indirect address also to the Gentile Galatians who desire to come under the Law (4:21), since the curse of the Law applies to "as many as" live "out from the Law" (*hosoi gar ex ergōn nomou eisin, hypo kataran eisin*) (3:10).[58] Yet the "us" in 3:13 retains its primary reference to the Jews and the story of their redemption, as it is the reality of Israel's restoration that has already begun, which has occasioned the extension of the Abrahamic blessing to the Gentiles (3:14a).[59] Furthermore, the inclusion of both the Jew and Gentile in the sphere of restoration has created the new "we" who are the recipients of the promise of the Spirit on the mutually

---

57. Cf. Wright, *The Climax of the Covenant*, 143. Pace Thiessen who claims that Gal 3:10–14 is focused solely on Gentiles; the curse relates to Gentiles who attempt to keep the Law (*Paul and the Gentile Problem*, 106). However, in applying his address to "as many as" (3:10), Paul does not limit his address as neatly as the RNPP does. Also, the texts that Paul cites in discussing the curse of the Law (especially Deut 27:26 in Gal 3:10) apply directly to Israel's life under the Law and only indirectly to Gentiles desiring to come under the Law. Cf. Donaldson: "[o]nly Israel is under this curse, because only Israel is 'under law.' But because of the way in which Israel's plight is related to the universal human plight, the redemption of Israel from the curse of the law can have universal consequences" ("Curse of the Law," 105). Paul's paradigmatic speech in 2:15–21 sets the precedent for his use of the Jewish "we" (vv. 15–17), even as he aims to curb the Gentile desire to come under the Law. Cf. Donaldson: "[i]f a distinction between Jewish and Gentile groups is made in the statement of the thesis (2.15–21), we should not be surprised to find such a distinction appearing in the arguments used to support the thesis (3.1–4.7)" ("Curse of the Law," 97; cf. Barclay, *Paul and the Gift*, 419).

58. Cf. Schlier, *an die Galater*, 132.

59. Schlier resists any logical flow from a Jewish "we" to an inclusive "we" in vv. 13–14 (he only perceives that the Jews are somehow a *type* of those who are under the Law), as he emphasizes that both the Jew and Gentile are equally under the curse of the Law and in need of redemption (*an die Galater*, 136–37). This is true in relation to the outcome, but misses the underlying logic in how Paul integrates the Gentiles into the story of Israel. Bachmann is better in tune with Paul's logic, as he claims that the use of the first-person plural in reference to Jews/Jewish believers in Christ reflects Paul's "orientation toward the history of redemption, which maintains the priority of Judaism, even while he emphasizes the dependence of also the Jews (or Jewish Christians) on Christ and on forgiveness of sins (esp. 2:16–17, 20d, 21b). . . . the salvation event asserted for the Jews is expressed as the prerequisite for what—for this reason—can also be effective for the Gentiles (see esp. 3:14, 26–29; 4:6–7)" (*Anti-Judaism*, 105).

shared ground of faith in Christ (*hina tēn epangelian tou pneumatos labōmen dia tēs pisteōs*) (3:14b).⁶⁰

The movement from the redemption of the Jews to the inclusion of the Gentiles in the restoration of Israel is expressed in Gal 3:23-29 with emphasis on Gentile inclusion in the regenerated people of God. Paul first outlines the Jewish reality of life before and after Christ in terms of the "we" having been under the guardianship of the Law (*hypo nomon ephrouroumetha synkleiomenoi*) until the coming of faith in Christ that brings "righteousness" was revealed (*eis tēn mellousan pistin apokalyphthēnai . . . hina ek pisteōs dikaiōthōmen*) (3:23-25).⁶¹ Because dependence (faith) on Christ for inclusion in the restoration reality (righteousness) is true for the Jews, it is more so also for the Gentiles (that is also highlighted in 2:15-16). Hence, the Gentiles—"you"—are included in the regenerated people of God by their inclusion in Christ (3:27-29).⁶² However, the clear demarcation of the "we" (Jew) and "you" (Gentile) is blurred by the new inclusive "you all" who are the children of God through faith in Christ (*pantes gar huioi theou este dia tēs pisteōs en christō iēsou*) (3:26), that is, by their new identity that has emerged from baptism into Christ (3:27). The new identity in Christ is reflected in the new social reality that is expressed in the programmatic statement about the oneness of the re-created humanity that relativizes the boundaries, and divests of symbolic capital the status symbols of the old cosmos, the Jew-Gentile distinction included (Gal 3:28; cf. 5:6; 6:14-16).⁶³

---

60. The fact that the two *hina* clauses appear to be in apposition does not necessarily mean that the "we" in 3:14b refers only to the Gentiles in 3:14a (pace Thiessen, *Paul and the Gentile Problem*, 130). I also do not follow Wright's suggestion that the "we" in 3:14b refers specifically to Jewish believers in Christ (*The Climax of the Covenant*, 154-55). The reception of the Spirit by the Gentile believers has just been highlighted in 3:1-5, and the Spirit is one prime actor in generating the one new restored people of God (cf. Gal 4:1-7).

61. The Jewish "we" is at its clearest here, since the Gentiles have not been under the Law but are only now desiring to come under it (Gal 4:21) (cf. Barclay, *Paul and the Gift*, 419n71; pace Martyn who contends that all are somehow under the *power* of the Law [*Galatians*, 362]). De Boer is cautious in recognizing the primary Jewish reference, and simultaneous universal implication: "Paul may perhaps have Jews particularly in view, at least in the first instance, but if so he uses their situation 'under the law' to be representative of the situation of all humankind . . . " (*Galatians*, 238). I contend that the universalizing implication in Paul's use of the "we" comes rather from Paul's conviction that all are under *sin* (Gal 3:22) (see discussion below).

62. The shift to the "you" here is sometimes explained by Paul's recourse to baptismal tradition (e.g., de Boer, *Galatians*, 237, 242-47). The baptismal tradition is a possible source here, but does not exclude the possibility that Paul's use of the "you" also incorporates the Gentile Galatians to Israel's story.

63. Cf. Barclay, *Paul and the Gift*, 396-97. See also Martyn who understands 3:28 as a declaration of the death of the old cosmos, and an implied reference to the new

Similarly, as Paul retells the story of Israel in Gal 4:1-5 in terms of the heir who, while being under-aged, is compared to the status of a slave until the fullness of time, the Gentiles, who are now also counted in the "seed" of Abraham as heirs according to the pattern of the promise (3:29), are also to identify with the story *retrospectively*—the recalibrated story of Israel is now also their story.[64] Hence, the Jewish story about redemption/adoption of the "we" who have been under the Law (*hina tous hypo nomon exagorasē, hina tēn huiothesian apolabōmen*) (4:5)[65] has a wider application to represent the reality of all humanity being under the "elements of the cosmos" (*houtōs kai hēmeis, hote ēmen nēpioi, hypo ta stoicheia tou kosmou ēmetha dedoulōmenoi*) (4:3). Donaldson expresses this aspect well:

> Israel, the people of the law, thus functions as a kind of representative sample of the whole. Their plight is no different from the plight of the whole of humankind, but through the operation of the law in their situation that plight is thrown into sharp relief. Being under νόμος is a special way of being under τὰ στοιχεῖα τοῦ κόσμου, because only under the former can the true nature of the bondage to the latter be clearly seen.[66]

Even as the address is again directed to the Gentile recipients—"you" (*hoti de este huioi*) (4:6a)—both the Jew and Gentile are in the scope of the newly generated children of God—the new inclusive "we"—who have the witness of the Spirit (*exapesteilen ho theos to pneuma tou huiou autou eis tas kardias hēmōn*) (4:6b).[67]

---

creation (*Galatians*, 376-77).

64. Moo also observes the link from 3:29 to 4:1 with the word *heir*, and comments: "[b]oth situations [described in 3:24-25 and 4:1-2] illustrate the position of Israel (and by extension, the Galatians) before Christ, when they were 'under the law'" (*Galatians*, 258).

65. The two *hina* clauses in 4:5 reflect the construction in 3:14 (see discussion above), and yet in this context the second *hina* clause can be understood to depend on the first, thus creating a sequence rather than parallelism (cf. Betz, *Galatians*, 208; Bruce, *Galatians*, 197; pace de Boer who understands that the first emphasizes purpose and the second result [*Galatians*, 264]). I understand that the first *hina* clause presents redemption especially in relation to the Jews (those under the Law) that has implications also for the Gentiles, and hence the second clause represents the new restoration reality that includes both Jews and Gentiles among those who have received their status as "sons" of God (cf. Betz, *Galatians*, 208; Dunn, *Galatians*, 216-17). Others take both clauses as referring to Jews/Jewish believers (Longenecker, *Galatians*, 172), or to Jews and Gentiles together (Burton, *Galatians*, 219; de Boer, *Galatians*, 264-65; Moo, *Galatians*, 266-67).

66. Donaldson, "'Curse of the Law,'" 104.

67. The manuscript evidence reflects the potentially confusing way Paul uses the first- and second-person references, as some manuscripts (e.g., D^2, K, L, Ψ, majority text, vg^{cl}, Syriac, bo^{pt}) have in 4:6b *hymōn* instead of *hēmōn* (attested in e.g., P^{46}, ℵ, A,

Thus, the new inclusive "we" of the restoration people, and the recalibration of the story of Israel according to the alienation-restoration paradigm modify for Paul also the old categories of the Jewish "we" and Gentile "you." As the Jews are also within the scope of the address to the new "you all," so also are the Gentiles implicated in the old "we" who are no longer to derive their identity from the Law. The blurring of the old categories of the "we" and "you" is reflected in, and indeed stems from, Paul's realization of the universal scope of both the problem and the solution. Everything/one is under sin (3:22a), and no human/flesh—neither Jew nor Gentile—is made righteous by the Law, and hence all—the "we" and the "you"—depend on faith in Christ to be rightly related with God (2:16), that is, depend on the promissory act of God in Christ and the Spirit for inclusion in the restored people of God. The people of the new inclusive "we" derive their identity—"those who believe"—from their response to the promise (*hina hē epangelia ek pisteōs iēsou christou dothē tois pisteuousin*) (3:22).

I have now explored how Paul capitalizes on the pattern of Isaac's birth in the logic of Gal 4:21—5:1. I argued that Paul does *not* use it to connect the Gentile believers in Christ directly to Sarah as their mother, and thus bolster their identity in the family of Abraham. Rather, he focuses on divine generation in the line of promise that consists of the Abrahamic promise of blessing to the nations and its re-appropriation in the Isaianic promise of restoration. This defines both the *promise* as the composite Abrahamic-Isaianic promise and the *people* of promise as those who receive the blessing of Abraham in their inclusion in the restoration people envisioned with Isaiah as the "Jerusalem above" community. Thus, Paul's logic emphasizes divine generation and participation in the restoration promise as the defining factor in inheriting also the Abrahamic promise of blessing as inclusion in God's people. The Isaianic matrix also provides Paul with the resources to recognize the Spirit in the line of promise as the generative means by which God re-forms the alienated people into the regenerated people of God that includes both Jews and Gentiles—the re-created humanity. I have also demonstrated how Paul's recalibration of the story of Israel according to the vision of restoration and the logic of the alienation-restoration paradigm reshapes the old categories of the Jewish "we" and Gentile "you," and creates

---

B, C, D, F, G, P, lat, sa, bo[pt]) to harmonize with 4:6a. The other difficulty with 4:6 has to do with the sense of the *hoti* (see discussion in Betz, *Galatians*, 209–10; Longenecker, *Galatians*, 173). I agree with de Boer's reading that the *hoti* does not mean that the reception of the Spirit is somehow dependent on achieving first the status of a "son," but rather that "for Paul the sonship of believers becomes evident in the experienced fact that God sent forth the Spirit of his Son into their collective hearts" (de Boer, *Galatians*, 265). Similarly, Dunn translates the sense thus: "and in that you are sons . . . " (*Galatians*, 219).

the new inclusive "we" of the people who have responded to the divine performance of the promise. In the following, I first analyze Paul's contrastive covenantal line that capitalizes on the theological potential in the birth of Ishmael from Hagar to make it correspond with Sinai before I return to the covenant of promise as it is ultimately defined in relation to Christ.

Hagar and the Covenant from Sinai that Leads to Slavery

One of the puzzling questions in the covenantal line that proceeds from Sinai and leads to slavery (4:24) is the correspondence it has with Hagar (*hētis estin hagar*) (4:24) and with the "present Jerusalem" (*systoichei de tē nyn ierousalēm*) (4:25). To capture the logic here, I start from Paul's correlation of Sinai with Hagar by analyzing the role that the explanatory note in 4:25a plays in this allegorical correspondence before exploring how the theological potential in the Abraham narrative and Isaiah can explain it.

Both Hansen and di Mattei have suggested that an etymological argument in 4:25a is the major ground for Paul's allegorical correspondence between Hagar and Sinai (Law).[68] Although there is uncertainty about the original text form (see Appendix), my structural analysis supports the note as an intrinsic part of the text, and hence I offer an explanation about the function of the note in relation to the two strongest candidates for the possible original text form identified by Carlson: 1) *to gar sina oros estin en tē arabia*; 2) *to de hagar sina oros estin en tē arabia*.[69] As di Mattei observes, the one constant in all the variations at the beginning of this sentence is the article *to*.[70] With text form one, it refers either to the composite Sinai-mountain ("for the Sinai-mountain is in Arabia") or to Sinai ("for [the] Sinai is a mountain in Arabia"). With text form two, there is a discrepancy, since the neuter article *to* does not correspond with the natural gender of Hagar. Hence, it must refer to something other than her person. Di Mattei argues that it establishes the etymological/geographical argument between the *name* Hagar and the mountainous region to which Hagar fled that is named *Hagra* in the Targums Pseudo-Jonathan and Onkelos on Gen 16:7.[71] Furthermore, drawing on the work of McNamara, he suggests that there is a link with Sinai, which was believed in some Jewish traditions to be in the area of Petra where Hagar

---

68. Di Mattei: "The allegory of Hagar as the covenant from Sinai rests on the wordplay which Paul inherently saw in the name 'Hagar'" ("Paul's Allegory," 111–14; citation from 113); Hansen, *Abraham in Galatians*, 147–50.

69. Carlson, "For Sinai."

70. Di Mattei, "Paul's Allegory," 111.

71. Di Mattei, "Paul's Allegory," 112.

was also thought to have fled.[72] These connections are possible, but require several steps from various Jewish traditions that weaken the argument. Also, as McNamara and those who draw from his work recognize, these connections are hardly accessible to the Gentile recipients of Paul's letter (unless Paul had explicitly explained them). However, this does not mean Paul could not have been aware of them, as McNamara concludes: "[o]ne may legitimately ask if the Galatians can be expected to have understood such a reference to Jewish tradition. They probably did not. But this would not weaken the strength of the argument, since at times, particularly in moments of heightened tension, Paul seems to have written from the abundance of his own mind rather than from what his readers would be expected to know."[73] Whatever we think of the plausibility of these Jewish traditions informing Paul's connection between Hagar, Sinai, and Arabia, the one thing that seems firm in both text forms is the importance of locating at least Sinai in the region of Arabia. It is also plausible to find support for connecting Hagar with Arabia, and thus also with Sinai, from either the above mentioned Jewish traditions, or from a more straightforward logic. Since Hagar's descendants were associated with the Arabs,[74] it also provides an affinity with Hagar and Sinai, which is identified with Arabia: "Sinai is located in the Hagar country."[75]

Borgen suggests another take on how the explanatory remark in 4:25a (with text form two) functions in establishing the correspondence between Hagar and Sinai. He argues that rather than the *to* referring to the name Hagar, it functions as an "exegetical quotation mark" that refers back to the *allegorical meaning* given to Hagar in 4:24.[76] Hence, it is not primarily an etymological or geographical connection, but Hagar is used as a type—*the Hagar covenant*—for the covenant of Sinai: "[t]he equation in v.25a 'Now 'Hagar' is Mount Sinai in Arabia,' is then based on the similar nature of Hagar's identification with the covenant/the Law and Mount Sinai's identification with the Law of Moses."[77] Furthermore, Borgen uses Philo (especially *Abr.* 251) to arrive at the view that "Hagar was the type of pagan who was characterized as a Hebrew because she chose the Law as her way

---

72. Di Mattei, "Paul's Allegory," 112.

73. McNamara, *Targum and New Testament*, 476.

74. The "Hagrites" are referred to as an Arab group in 1 Chr 5:10, 19–22; 27:31; Ps 83:6 (Bruce, *Galatians*, 220).

75. Wright, "Paul, Arabia and Elijah (Galatians 1.17)," 158.

76. Borgen, "Some Hebrew and Pagan Features," 158–59.

77. Borgen, "Some Hebrew and Pagan Features," 159.

of life. Similarly, Mount Sinai, which was part of pagan Arabia, became the Mountain of the Law of Moses."[78]

I agree with Borgen that the connection between Hagar and Sinai is established on the allegorical level, in which Hagar represents the covenant of the Law. This is true with or without the explanatory note in 4:25a, and irrespective of the text form of the note, since the connection is already made in 4:24. But taking the explanatory note into account, it could be a moment where Paul displays his own geographical knowledge that he acquired during his stay in Arabia (1:17), and/or that he employs an allegorical device to "startle" his recipients with the purpose of inviting them to seek for a "deeper meaning."[79] But rather than perceiving Philo as the primary intertext for understanding *how* Hagar represents life under the Law (a pagan who chose the Law), I suggest that Paul invites his readers to seek for the deeper meaning from the theological potential in the explicitly signaled intertexts of the Abraham narrative and Isaiah. This does not exclude other possible influences on Paul, but I would make them the secondary port of call in case more explanatory power is required.

I reckon that it is very likely that Paul constructs the two covenants on the template that Gen 17 offers him. As I have demonstrated in chapter 3, the language in Gen 17 is such that the promise to Abraham about him becoming a father to many nations—mediator of blessing to all the nations—(17:1-6; cf. 12:3), can be taken as a distinct and yet related covenant from that of the covenant of circumcision that focuses on marking out the special people—the great nation (17:10-14). This juxtaposing of "two covenants" in Gen 17 resembles closely Paul's juxtaposing of promise and Law in Galatians in general (3:6—4:7), and particularly in the contrast between the two covenants in 4:21—5:1.[80] Not only are the two covenants of Gal 4:21—5:1 reflected in Gen 17, but also the polarity between Abraham's two sons is the theological key for configuring these two covenants in both Gal 4:21—5:1 and Gen 17 (with related texts). Besides these close conceptual and logical correspondences, we also know of Paul's interest in Gen 17 from Rom 4 (see above). Thus, Gen 17 is the prime candidate for Paul's construction of the two covenants in Gal 4:21—5:1.

The Sinai covenant (Exod 19:5-6) that Paul speaks of in Gal 4:24 is connected to the covenant of circumcision in Gen 17, since a central logic

---

78. Borgen, "Some Hebrew and Pagan Features," 159.

79. Cf. Davis, "Allegorically Speaking."

80. De Boer suggests something similar, yet without exploring the theological potential that this matrix opens up: "Paul evidently distinguishes the covenant of promise in Gen 15:18; 17:1-8 from the covenant of circumcision in Gen 17:9-14, regarding them as two separate covenants" (*Galatians*, 298).

in both is to mark out the special people from among the other peoples. Circumcision and the obligation to follow the Sinaitic Law are also intimately connected in Paul's understanding: "I testify again to every man who is circumcised that he is obligated to practice the whole Law" (Gal 5:3).[81] I focus first on the potential in the Genesis narrative to present Hagar and Ishmael as representatives of the covenant of circumcision/Sinai, and then connect it with the potential in Isaiah to perceive how Paul can claim that life under the Law leads to slavery.

The connection between Hagar and Sinai consists, for Paul, of the reality that both generate children for slavery (see ch. 2). Since it is possible to view Hagar's child Ishmael as an alternative construal of the identity of the "great nation" (see ch. 3), it is also possible to trace in Ishmael a construction of Israel under the covenant of circumcision. Already when Ishmael is in Hagar's womb, he represents Israel's life in slavery. Sarah's harsh treatment of Hagar results in her fleeing to the wilderness. It is there that the boy receives his name that carries both the recognition of oppression and the hope of God attending to it (Gen 16:11). This episode has the potential to prefigure Israel's slavery in Egypt (see ch. 3). Thus, we have a first indication that Hagar-Ishmael represents something of Israel's existence that is related to slavery/oppression.

But the prefigurative function of Hagar-Ishmael is developed even further. In Gen 17, it becomes clear that, although Ishmael is circumcised, and thus potentially part of the covenant of circumcision, he is nevertheless excluded from the covenant of the special people (17:16-21), and finally expelled outside of the inheritance (21:10). This has the potential to prefigure, for Paul, the reality of life under the covenant from Sinai that leads to slavery— existence outside of "inheritance." As Hagar gave birth to a son who, though a son of Abraham and circumcised, ended up outside of the inheritance, so also Sinai gives birth to a people that are Abraham's descendants and marked by circumcision, but yet can remain outside of the inheritance. The way this works for Paul as an argument that Sinai leads to slavery is predicated on the intimate connection that exists between the concept of slavery and the reality of being outside of inheritance (see ch. 5), which is also expressed in the theological logic in Gal 4:21—5:1 (cf. 4:1-7) where slavery and exclusion from

---

81. I disagree with Thiessen that the "again" (*palin*) in 5:3 refers back to 4:21-31, and with his interpretation that the requirement to perform the whole Law refers to the impossibility of the Gentiles to conform with the requirement of the eighth-day circumcision (*Paul and the Gentile Problem*, 94-95). De Boer (with Martyn and Dunn) argues convincingly that it refers back to 5:2 emphasizing the point made there (*Galatians*, 312-13; cf. Schlier, *an die Galater*, 231). It is also possible that the *palin* refers back to 3:10 (the linking word is *poieō*) and Paul's view that living out from the Law is about doing all the Law, which leads under a curse (see discussion below).

inheritance are connected in the figure of Ishmael: Hagar/Sinai gives birth to slavery—"Ishmael"—(4:24); the "son of the slave woman"—"Ishmael"—is excluded from the inheritance (4:30).

But there is even more in the connection between the figure of Hagar and the Law from Sinai. Paul emphasizes Hagar's status as a "slave woman" (*paidiskē*), and, likewise, he also refers to the Law as a "slave" custodian (*paidagōgos*; a function of a slave) (Gal 3:24).[82] As Hagar was "enslaved," so also is the Law implicated in the condition of slavery for Paul. Thus, the Law not only leads to slavery, but it is also itself "enslaved." The Law does not contain the generative potential to make alive (3:21), but rather, it is constrained by the condition of all things being under sin (*alla synekleisen hē graphē ta panta hypo hamartian*) (3:22).[83] The Law does not bring about "new creation," but is itself bound by the conditions of the "present evil age." Hence, Paul can talk about coming under the Law as being the same as coming under the basic elements of the cosmos: "when we were under-aged, we were enslaved under the basic elements of the cosmos (*stoicheia tou kosmou*) . . . . When the fulness of time came, God sent his son, born of a woman, born under the Law, so that he could redeem those who are under the Law . . . . How is it that you again turn to the weak and worthless elements (*stoicheia*), to which you want to be enslaved all over again?" (Gal 4:3-5, 9).[84] The Law and the "elements" are not the same, but the Law is bound by the condition

---

82. The *paidagōgos* was distinct from the teacher (*didaskalos*), and had only an indirect role in education in terms of protection, guardianship, and discipline (see, e.g., Betz, *Galatians*, 177-78; Bruce, *Galatians*, 182-83; de Boer, *Galatians*, 240-41; Longenecker, *Galatians*, 146-48).

83. I agree with de Boer that the *hē graphē* is a reference to the witness of Scripture (*Galatians*, 234-35), and most likely refers to a wider sense of how Paul reads Scripture. Also, I agree with de Boer that *ta panta* includes also the Law in some sense being under the power of sin (*Galatians*, 234-35), but via the logic that humanity's condition under sin compromises the Law's ability to make alive (cf. Rom 8:3). The hermeneutical-theological framework advanced in this book points to Paul's particular reading of the witness of the Scripture that includes the theological interpretation of Israel's experience of exile, which removes the possibility for anyone to claim a special status above sin (cf. Gal 2:16)—the alienation-restoration paradigm levels the playing field. Thus, as in 4:21, Paul again constrains the function of the Law, and confidence in the Law, by an extended reading of the witness of the Scripture that has Christ as the defining center (3:22b).

84. Barclay writes wisely about the connection that Paul establishes between pagan practices, the Law, and the *stoicheia*: "[h]e is not claiming that pagan worship and Torah-observance are substantially identical; nor does he identify the στοιχεῖα either with the 'non-Gods' of the pagan pantheon or with the Torah itself. He is simply stating (though this 'simply' is shocking enough) that, from his perspective, pagan religious practice and life under the rule of the Torah may be classified in the same category of subjection to the στοιχεῖα of the world" (*Paul and the Gift*, 409).

of the cosmos and humanity that is described as being enslaved to the "elements." The Law does not operate above the "elements" that are under the corruption of sin, neither can it lead out from this condition of slavery. Thus, Paul perceives that the Law is limited in its potential and its function. It cannot produce what it demands: righteousness; that is, it cannot lead into being rightly related to God in the inheritance of the freedom of the "Jerusalem above." This logic is present in Gal 4:1–7, where being under the guardianship of the Law does not lead into the inheritance; the inheritance is reached by divine agency (*dia theou*) in generating the "sons" who are made heirs by the redemption in the Son and the gift of the Spirit.

I have explored above the potential in the Abraham narrative to construe Hagar-Ishmael as prefiguring Israel's life under the Law of Sinai that can only generate children to slavery—the realm outside of the inheritance. But I do not think that Paul began there. Certainly, Paul finds in the figures of Hagar and Ishmael a matrix that corresponds with the view that the Law leads to slavery, and is bound by the conditions of slavery, but the realization of that view emerged for him from the present realities that the coming of Christ and the gift of the Spirit instigated. These realities Paul configures in terms of the "present Jerusalem" and the "Jerusalem above." Hence, I perceive that the alienation-restoration paradigm in Isaiah is the most potent for Paul's theological reflection about the role of the Law leading to slavery. Furthermore, Paul's experience of the risen Christ and the Spirit brings the focal point of the alienation-restoration paradigm to the point of Christ's death and resurrection (Gal 1:1–4; 6:14–15). Paul reads Scripture from the perspective of the revelation of the Son (1:13–14), and the sending of the Son in the fullness of time (4:4). The reality of inaugurated restoration configures existence outside of it as being the realm of alienation—slavery. Thus, Paul's understanding of the "covenant of promise" reconfigures the covenant of Sinai. I turn next to investigate Paul's understanding of the covenant of promise in relation to Christ to deepen the discussion on why Paul perceives that coming under the Law is incongruous with living in the covenant of promise.

The Role of Christ as the Isaianic Servant in the Covenant of Promise

As I argued in my structural analysis in ch. 2, the other covenant that is not named in Gal 4:21—5:1 can be identified from the chiastic structure of the passage as the covenant of promise. This is supported by Paul's explicit identification of the Abrahamic promise as a covenant in Gal 3:17. The covenant of promise in Gal 4:21—5:1 is the generative line that the Galatians are called to align with, and consequently to resist the compulsion to construct their identity according to the covenant from Sinai. The "Jerusalem above" functions as the focal point for the generative line of the promise, and Isa 54:1 links Paul's argument with Isaiah's vision of restoration. I have argued above that the promise in Gal 4:28 carries theological weight from both the Abrahamic promise of blessing to the nations and the Isaianic promise of restoration, and as such it is about the re-creation of humanity. I now develop more fully Paul's construction of the covenant of promise with reference to the role of Christ as the Isaianic servant.

I argued in the previous section that Paul very likely constructs the two covenants in Gal 4:21—5:1 on the matrix that Gen 17 provides. The covenant of promise in Gen 17 is about mediating blessing to all the nations that is focused on Isaac and the "seed" that is identified with him and his posterity in Gen 17:16; 22:17-18; 35:10-11; and 49:10 (see ch. 3). Accordingly, one dimension in Paul's conception of the covenant of promise in Galatians is related to the Abrahamic promise of blessing (Gal 3:8, 15-18) that is mediated by Christ as the "seed" of Abraham (3:16).[85] Christ is the one who ultimately defines the covenant of promise also in Gal 4:21—5:1. As I have argued in my structural analysis in ch. 2, I regard Paul's statement in Gal 5:1 to be a conclusion to the passage that begins at 4:21 (it is also a transitional verse), which points to the defining role that Christ has in the covenant of promise. Since the promise is not defined only in terms of the Abrahamic promise, but also in terms of its re-appropriation in the Isaianic vision of restoration, I argue in the following that Paul's presentation of the liberating work of Christ to be the reason to oppose the "yoke of slavery" (5:1)—the compulsion/desire to come under the Law (4:21)—is very likely configured with the help of the Isaianic servant, especially as depicted in Isa 52:13—53:12 (Isa 53 for short).

Watson offers the first level of evidence for the influence of the Isaianic servant on Paul's understanding of the work of Christ in general, as he demonstrates Paul to be indebted in language about Christ to the LXX translation of Isa 53.[86] Watson notes the textual connections between LXX

85. See my discussion in ch. 3, for some ideas how the scriptural matrix in Genesis can facilitate the move towards identifying the "seed" with a messianic figure. This can be combined with the potential in the Isaianic matrix where there is movement from the Davidic messiah to the singular servant who brings about the restoration that is conceived also as a fulfillment of the Abrahamic promise of blessing to all the nations (see ch. 4).

86. Watson speaks of the LXX translation of Isa 53 as "mistranslation," which he defines in terms of a "paraphrase" that introduces "new semantic possibilities that cannot unambiguously be derived from the Hebrew" ("Mistranslation," 215-16).

Isa 53 and Paul's letter to the Romans: Isa 52:15 is quoted in Rom 15:21; Isa 53:1 is quoted in Rom 10:16; Isa 53:12 is probably alluded to in Rom 4:25.[87] This establishes the fact that Paul can identify Christ with the servant of Isa 53 (especially by his reading of Isa 52:15). Watson also suggests that the *verbatim* quotation of the passages directly connected with the "fourth servant song" (Isa 53:1 in Rom 10:16 and Isa 54:1 in Gal 4:27) signal the great significance ascribed to Isa 53.[88] However, the main part of Watson's analysis explores how Isa 53 "served as a lexical and semantic resource or reservoir from which terms, phrases, or concepts can be freely drawn and adapted to new uses."[89] Watson is clear: "without this text [Isa 53], there would be no basis for the claim that what took place in Christ's death took place 'for us.'"[90] The evidence suggests for Watson that "Isaiah 53 was foundational for Paul's thinking and language about the death of Christ, and its foundational status is evident from the traditional terminology derived from it."[91]

Building on Watson's analysis about the general dependence of Paul's language about Christ on Isa 53, I focus here on how the connection between Christ and the Isaianic servant is present in Gal 4:21—5:1. My argument is based on conceptual connections and the corresponding logic between the connection from the servant in Isa 53 to the vision of restoration in 54:1 and from Paul's conception of the liberating work of Christ (Gal 5:1) to the generation of the children of the mother "Jerusalem above" (4:26).[92] I have

---

87. Watson, "Mistranslation," 233. He also discusses the debate whether Paul's citations, allusions, or use of language "retain links with their original scriptural contexts, or whether they are wholly integrated into their new contexts" (234). After careful analysis, Watson concludes that "it is hard to maintain that Paul's citations sever links with the original scriptural context" (240). Watson substantiates his claim by observing that Paul cites five of the twelve verses between Isa 52:5 and 53:1 (52:5, 7, 11, 15; 53:1); on one occasion, two of these are cited together (Rom 10:15–16 cites Isa 52:7 and 53:1); on another occasion (Rom 15:21), the use of Isa 52:15 is "clearly derived from its original context"; in addition, "[t]here are thematic unities in Paul's readings of these texts and of Isa 54:1."

88. Watson, "Mistranslation," 239–41.

89. Watson, "Mistranslation," 234.

90. Watson, "Mistranslation," 243.

91. Watson, "Mistranslation," 248n65. Watson's conclusion challenges the influential work of Hooker who concluded that "we found little evidence that the identification of Jesus with the Servant played any great part in the thinking of St Paul, . . . , and no proof that it was known to them at all" (Hooker, *Jesus and the Servant*, 127). Hooker's analysis included a section titled "Various words echoing the vocabulary of the fourth Song" (121–23), but was limited in scope, and lacked the thorough and sweeping analysis done by Watson.

92. Horbury looks at the Targum of Isaiah and later Christian authors who link Isa 53 and 54, and argues that "the two chapters are likely to have been read in sequence by Paul, who would then naturally understand 54 as a messianic city of restoration" (*Messianism,*

argued in ch. 4 that the servant's work in Isa 53 enables the generation of the children of the barren-made-fruitful woman of Isa 54:1. In Galatians, the freedom that Christ delivers is the foundation for the freedom of the mother "Jerusalem above" that denotes the restoration community according to the quotation of Isa 54:1 in Gal 4:27. In Isaiah, the servant deals with the sins of the people to restore them—to heal and bring them back to God (53:5–6). The *many* whose sins the servant bears to make them righteous (53:10–12) turn out to be the *many* children of the barren-made-fruitful woman of Isa 54:1. This represents a deep level of theological reflection in Isaiah, in which the servant deals with the root of the problem of alienation—sin—to bring about restoration. Similarly, Paul describes the work of Christ in Galatians in terms of him dealing with sin (1:4), delivering from curse (3:13), and transforming slaves into "sons" and heirs (4:4–7). In Gal 5:1, the freedom to which Christ sets free retains a connection to all of these aspects, yet in 5:1 the specific focus is on the freedom that Christ offers in contrast to the "yoke of slavery" that the Law is implicated in.[93] I claim that the Isaianic matrix, and especially the alienation-restoration paradigm, aids in capturing the logic that underlies this statement.

I summarize here my discussion from ch. 4 about the roles of the servant and the Law in the alienation-restoration paradigm in Isaiah. In the Isaianic matrix, the role of the servant is to deliver the blind and captive servant Israel (Isa 41–44; 49; 53) so that she can become who she is called to be, a light to the nations (Isa 42). Thus, it is another servant who sets the captive servant Israel free. This deliverance is not depicted as God's response to a Law-observant people, but it is dependent on the response of Israel and the nations to the revelation of God's salvation via the servant (53:1). The Law is not the hope of deliverance and restoration, which is an act of God's mercy (54:7–10) in the extension of the "arm" of salvation (52:10; 53:1) to undeserving people (63:19; 65:1). Hence, the Law is not a liberating agent

---

221). Others have also noted the importance of this connection for Paul, e.g., Harmon, *She Must*, 156–60; Jobes, "Jerusalem, Our Mother," 312–13; Wright, *PFG*, 1137–38.

93. The "yoke of slavery" is mostly understood in reference to the Law, possibly subverting an existing positive idiom about the "yoke of the Law" (Bruce, *Galatians*, 226–27; de Boer, *Galatians*, 309; Dunn, *Galatians*, 262–63). However, due to the word "again" in 5:1b with reference to the Galatians' experience, the Law is placed to a wider field of slavery. Thus, Longenecker (*Galatians*, 224–25) and Moo (*Galatians*, 320–21) include here *ta stoicheia tou kosmou*. Betz extends the "yoke of slavery" to include both "taking up the yoke of the Jewish Torah (5:2–12) and the corruption by the flesh (5:13–24)" (*Galatians*, 258). I prefer to use the expression "the Law is implicated in the conditions of slavery" to highlight that the Law is not the cause of slavery as such, but is itself bound by the condition of humanity (and cosmos) that is under sin (3:22). See discussion above.

but a cursing element (exile) due to the people's sin (evidenced by blindness and obduracy). The problem is sin not the Law, but the Law cannot help the blind and captive people. It is only the servant who brings deliverance from sin and bondage to regenerate the people of God.

Paul expresses a similar understanding about the role that the Law plays in the plight of Israel's alienation, and its inability to offer the hope of restoration, which is then ascribed to the work of the servant. In Gal 3:6-14, Paul constructs the role of the Law in contrast to the blessing promised to Abraham. The Law is described as a cursing agent (3:10; the Law brings curse on those who do not *do* all the Law; cf. 5:3),[94] and Christ as the one who redeemed Israel ("us") from the curse of the Law (3:13)[95]

---

94. The logic in 3:10 is difficult and debated. How does the Law procure curse on those who are "of the works of the Law" (*ex ergōn nomou*)? (See Moo, *Galatians*, 201-5.) To simplify, a traditional Reformation reading takes the *ex ergōn nomou* with the general reference to performing the commands of the Law, and constructs the logic either in terms of the whole mode of *doing* being antithetical to the way of faith in attaining righteousness (cf. 3:10b-12) (e.g., Bruce, *Galatians*, 159-61; Luther, *Galatians*, 244-47), or with the implied idea that no one actually does/can do *everything* in the Law (cf. 5:3) that amounts to a violation of the Law (e.g., Burton, *Galatians*, 164; Longenecker, *Galatians*, 117-18; Oepke, *an die Galater*, 105). The NPP reading (Dunn) takes the *ex ergōn nomou* here as a reference to those who put "too much weight on the distinctiveness of the Jews from Gentiles" and the problem being that the "restrictiveness of covenant grace" is in some sense "being false to the covenant" that amounts to putting oneself outside of the terms of the covenant, and thus under its curse (*Galatians*, 172-73). Wright emphasizes here Israel's story and the curse being on Israel as a whole rather than on individual transgressors, and that it takes the form of Israel's extended exile (*The Climax of the Covenant*, 144-48; *PFG*, 863-67; see also Scott, "'For as Many as are'"). I agree with Wright that Israel's story, including the exile, is the correct starting point here, but I also embrace aspects of the traditional reading that takes better account of the contrast Paul sets here between doing and faith (cf. 3:11-12). These are connected to Paul's flesh-Spirit antithesis (3:1-5; 4:29), and to the Ishmael-Isaac alternatives in constructing the identity of God's people (4:22-31). Hence, I perceive that Paul's deeper logic is about faith as dependence on the promise—now enacted in Christ and the Spirit—being the only mode of existence that leads to the inheritance of restoration (righteousness). Relying on the "flesh," or *doing* the Law, is thus about false confidence/boasting in natural/normal conventions of worth/status rather than depending on the gift of God in Christ (cf. Gal 6:12-14; Phil 3:3-9).

95. As with 3:10, so also here with 3:13 opinion is divided concerning what is the *curse* that Christ redeems from by becoming a *curse* for "us" / on "our" behalf. Luther's focus is on sin and judgment that Christ vicariously bears on the cross (*Galatians*, 269). Longenecker understands this as "an exchange curse" in terms of the Law's punishment on transgressors (*Galatians*, 123). Dunn moves away from the category of sin, and frames the exchange in terms of exclusion and inclusion in the people of God: "[t]o affirm that the crucified Jesus was cursed by God, therefore, was tantamount to saying that he had been put outside of the covenant, outside the people of God. Which also meant (this is the implicit corollary) that God's resurrection of Jesus signified God's acceptance of the 'outsider', the cursed law-breaker, the Gentile sinner" (*Galatians*, 178). For Wright, Christ

to enable the blessing to reach also the Gentiles via the gift of the Spirit that makes and marks the re-formed people of God (3:14; see above). As Wright and Scott have argued, the logic here fits the pattern of sin-exile-restoration, in which Christ has the crucial role of dealing with the curse of "exile" and inaugurating the restoration.[96] However, I am not convinced of the necessity to construct Paul's logic with the prior sense of an ongoing/extended exile that Christ comes to resolve, but I rather emphasize that the exile functions as a theological matrix that Paul reflects upon in light of the Christ-event. I maintain that what is more important to Paul is the theological interpretation of Israel's experience of exile (by Isaiah and others) that transposes it to a symbolic level, in which it becomes a paradigm for addressing the deeper problem with Israel and humanity that is about sin, slavery, and death—alienation from God (see chapter 5).[97] Accordingly, Paul never speaks of exile as such in Galatians, but uses categories that can be taken as reflections on the theological interpretation of it: barrenness (4:27), curse (3:10), sin (1:4), slavery (4:1-10), and death with reference to Christ (1:1-4). With this position I attempt to avoid two extremes: the emphasis on an *ongoing/extended* exile, on one side, and, on the other, the apocalyptic emphasis that perceives *no real role* for Israel's story by suggesting that Paul's categories of curse and blessing constitute the "apocalyptic antinomy that *came into being* with Christ."[98]

The contrasting role of the Law to the promise is further developed in Gal 3:21—4:7. The Law is not opposed to the promise, but simply lacks the generative power of the promise—it cannot make alive or lead into righteousness (3:21).[99] Thus, Paul perceives that the Law functioned as

---

crucified is the climactic event that deals with the curse of the exile: "[t]he crucifixion of the Messiah is, one might say, the *quintessence of* the curse of exile, and its climactic act" (*The Climax of the Covenant*, 151, emphasis original; see also *PFG*, 865–67). Again, I agree that the matrix here is Israel's story and even the paradigm of exile, but maintain that the traditional understanding of Christ's death being on account of sin can also be read from that matrix where sin is exposed in Israel's story in relation to the Law, which, by extension, also reflects the general human condition in sin (Gal 1:4; 3:22).

96. Scott, "'For as Many as Are'"; Wright, *The Climax of the Covenant*, 137–56; *PFG* 860–67.

97. Scott's quote from Ackroyd (*Exile and Restoration*, 242) suggests that he recognizes that the extended sense of exile moves it to a more symbolic level: "[h]ere [Dan 9] the exile is no longer an historic event to be dated to one period; it is much nearer to being a condition from which only the final age will bring release. Though bound to the historical reality of an exile which actually took place in the sixth century, the experience of exile *as such* had become a symbol of a period, viewed in terms of punishment but also in terms of promise . . ." ("For as Many as Are," 200; emphasis original).

98. De Boer, *Galatians*, 198, emphasis added.

99. For Paul, it is not enough that the Law prescribes provisions for atonement (as

a custodian with temporal and "soteriological" limitations until the revelation of faith (3:23–25), that is, until the promise was enacted in the coming of Christ that evokes the response of faith that leads into right-relatedness (3:22, 24); Christ generates the "sons of God" who participate in Christ (*en christō*) by faith (*dia tēs pisteōs*) in the restoration reality (3:26).[100] Paul explains the same process immediately afterwards in terms of deliverance from slavery into sonship and inheritance (4:1–7). Again, the Law is pictured as implicated under the conditions of slavery (4:1–5), and Christ is presented as the one who enacts the divine promise by redeeming those who were under the Law (Israel) with the implication that also the Gentiles have been included in the re-formed people of God who are the recipients of the Spirit, and heirs according to the pattern of the promise (4:4–7) (see above).

Paul's logic moves partly from solution to plight, as it is the resurrected Christ who reveals the true state of affairs. Christ determines for Paul the beginning and the shape of the restoration community; being in Christ makes alive and leads into the freedom of the "Jerusalem above." Thus, being outside of Christ means being outside of the inheritance of the restoration reality, and hence, being in alienation and in slavery. Due to the inability of the Law to lead into the inheritance of the "Jerusalem above," Paul designates a role for it that recognizes its limitation. The Law is not the plight, sin is. But since the Law cannot bring freedom—deliver from the "present evil age"—it is seen as implicated in the condition of slavery rather than offering the solution. Hence, although the influence of the Isaianic matrix is not made explicit in Gal 3:6–14, 21–24; and 4:1–7 that configure the role of the

---

emphasized by Sanders and the RNPP), since the fundamental problem is not the removal of sins, but the transformation of the human condition by generating the new creation life—Paul's gospel is about the re-creation of humanity that moves beyond the forgiveness of sins to "making alive" by the work of Christ and the gift of the Spirit.

100. Gal 3:22–26 is a famously difficult passage for understanding the relationship between faith and Christ. This passage is also a focal point for a "third view" on the *pistis christou* debate, which suggests that, rather than limiting the discussion to Christ being either the subject or the object of faith, both faith and Christ ("Christ-faith") are to be connected to an eschatological event that creates a new sphere of influence in which the believer in Christ participates (see Schliesser, "'Christ-Faith' as an Eschatological Event," 277–300). This view focuses on the time references in 3:23–26 ("coming" and "being revealed") that correspond with the arrival of the fullness of time and the sending of the Son in 4:4. This feeds into my own reading that emphasizes Christ as the "actor" in the narrative of divine promise (rather than in the narrative of *pistis*), and I take faith as the human response to that divine act/event. I understand that Paul's point in Galatians is about faith being the mode that connects humans to the divine performance of the promise. Thus, just like Abraham responded with faith to the divine promise (3:6), so also now the divine performance of the promise in Christ calls for a similar response of faith (3:7–9, 22).

Law and Christ similarly to the alienation-restoration paradigm in Isaiah, it is possible that the Isaianix matrix functions on the level of a substructure that surfaces in Gal 4:21—5:1.[101]

In the next section I explore Paul's identification with Christ as the Isaianic servant and its impact on Paul's mission. This gives further support for the perception of the influence of the Isaianic servant on Paul's conception of the work of Christ.[102]

Paul's Labor Pains and the Formation of New Creation Communities

I have argued above that Paul's re-proclamation of the gospel in Galatians is driven by the vision of the re-creation of humanity as it stems from the Abrahamic promise of blessing and Isaiah's vision of restoration that has been inaugurated by the generative activity of God in Christ and the Spirit. I have also demonstrated that Paul configures the work of Christ in terms of the Isaianic servant who generates the restoration community envisioned in Isa 54:1. I now explore how Paul identifies with the work of Christ, and how it shapes his mission, as I ask: What is Paul in labor pains for (4:19)?

I have argued in my structural analysis in ch. 2 that the expressions in Gal 4:19–20 signal Paul's burden for writing the letter that leads directly into 4:21—5:1, making it a passage that carries much weight in focusing Paul's communication. In Gal 4:19, Paul speaks to the Galatians as his children for whom he is again in labor pains until Christ is formed in/among them (*tekna mou, hous palin ōdinō mechris hou morphōthē christos en hymin*). As Martyn, Eastman, and Gaventa have rightly argued, the language of labor is connected to Paul's mission and to an apocalyptic vision.[103] I develop their insights further, as I explore the potential in the scriptural matrix that Paul works with when he expresses his mission, especially in relation to Jesus as the Isaianic servant.

---

101. See the elaborate, but at times stretched, argument of Harmon, *She Must*, 133–203. My presentation of Paul's argument and the correspondence it has with the logic of the alienation-restoration paradigm in Isaiah is limited, and it is by no means exclusive of the influence of the Pentateuch. Yet the pentateuchal influence is not sufficient in explaining some aspects in the logic, e.g., the role of the Spirit and Christ.

102. There is also the possibility that the association of the servant and covenant in Isaiah (42:6 and 49:8) could be part of the matrix for connecting Christ with the idea of a covenant.

103. Eastman, *Recovering Paul's Mother Tongue*, 89–126; Gaventa, "Maternity of Paul"; Gaventa, *Our Mother Saint Paul*, 29–39; Martyn, *Galatians*, 426–31.

Paul's labor pains for his children in Gal 4:19 anticipates the Isaianic image of the barren woman in 4:27 who has not had labor pains prior to giving birth to the many children.[104] Whether the woman experiences labor pains in giving birth to the many children or not is not known, but what is emphasized is the miraculous nature of her giving of birth—it is about divine generation that defies natural order (cf. Isa 66:7-9). In fact, underlying the barren woman's giving of birth are divine labor pains (Isa 42:14; cf. 45:10)[105] that are ultimately expressed in the suffering of the servant in Isa 53 (see chapter 4). The point is that the restoration children in Isa 54:1 are generated by divine action, in which the servant in Isa 53 has the defining role. As we follow this line of inquiry further in Galatians, it becomes more plausible that Paul conceives his own mission in terms of identifying with the mission of the Isaianic servant who acts out the divine labor pains that generate the restoration community.

Paul's identification with Christ the Isaianic servant does not begin by his own initiative. It is God's sovereign pleasure to reveal the Son to Paul, which reshapes Paul's own identity and his sense of mission (Gal 1:15-16).[106] The language Paul uses about the calling that issued from the revelatory experience reflects the language of the servant in Isa 49,[107] which is a passage that prepares the move towards Isa 53 where the portrait of the servant who serves Israel and the nations is developed further (see ch. 4). Paul's description of being set apart from the mother's womb and being called by grace (*ho aphorisas me ek koilias mētros mou kai kalesas dia tēs charitos autou*) (Gal 1:15), can reflect Israel's (as the initial servant) recognition of being given a name from the mother's womb (*ek koilias mētros mou ekalese to onoma mou*) (Isa 49:1). But more likely it refers to the other servant's (distinct yet related

---

104. Eastman works also with this connection, but emphasizes the difference between Paul's labor pains and the barren woman of Isa 54:1 not having pains (*Recovering Paul's Mother Tongue*, 155-60).

105. Cf. Harmon, *She Must*, 168-73. Harmon focuses here on Isa 45:7-11.

106. Stendahl initiated the modern discussion whether to describe Paul's experience described in Gal 1:15-16 as his conversion or calling ("Paul among Jews and Gentiles"). If by conversion we mean a change of religion, i.e., from Judaism to Christianity, it is not an apt description. Paul's experience is about a predetermined calling to proclaim the gospel among the Gentiles that is now put into effect (1:16). But it issues more than a calling in terms of reordering Paul's own identity. See also Chester's discussion on Paul's use of *kaleō* with reference to "conversion," or "the new role/identity created by that calling" (*Conversion at Corinth*, 59-112, quotation from 61).

107. This has been noted by many, e.g., Ciampa, *Presence and Function of Scripture*, 111-18; Harmon, *She Must*, 78-80; Wilk, *Die Bedeutung*, 397-98. It is also suggested that the language here might also echo Jeremiah's call (Jer 1:5), but, due to the prominence of the Isaianic matrix, and the rather negative tone in Jeremiah's "mission" (Jer 1:10), I think that the Isaianic matrix is primary (cf. de Boer, *Galatians*, 90-91).

to Israel; i.e., a messianic servant figure) formation from the womb to be the servant of the Lord (*ho plasas me ek koilias doulon heautō*) for the purpose of gathering Israel and being a light to the nations to bring salvation to the ends of the earth (Isa 49:5; cf. Acts 13:47). The influence of the description of the servant in Isa 49 on Paul's conception of his mission is supported also by the sense of a shared purpose in both to glorify God (Gal 1:24 *kai edoxazon en emoi ton theon*; Isa 49:3 *kai en soi doxasthēsomai*), and the shared experience of frustration in the task of the servant (Gal 4:11 *phoboumai hymas mē pōs eikē kekopiaka eis hymas*; Isa 49:4 *kai egō eipa kenōs ekopiasa kai eis mataion kai eis outhen edōka tēn ischyn mou*). Furthermore, both the servant's and Paul's missions are set in the context of the vision of restoration that is expressed with the language of generating children for a mother (Isa 49:14-23; Gal 4:19, 27) that is intimately related to Isa 54:1-3. These verbal, conceptual, and thematic correspondences make it very likely that Paul's sense of mission was shaped by the servant's task described in Isa 49. Recognizing the influence of Isa 49 on Paul's mission is supported by Paul's explicit appeal to Isa 49:8 in 2 Cor 6:2 in the context of Paul's elaborate description of his ministry that is about identifying with Christ (2 Cor 5:14-15) to be shaped to function as his ambassador (2 Cor 5:18-20).

The development in the description of the servant's mission from Isa 49 to Isa 53 is also reflected in Paul's identification with Christ and his representation of the gospel. Paul's emphasis on receiving the gospel by revelation (Gal 1:15-16) already reflects the conception of his mission in terms of identifying with the Isaianic servant in Isa 53—the "arm of the Lord" who is made known by revelation (53:1). Paul's identification with Christ, the Isaianic servant, becomes more prominent as we follow Paul's presentation of his own transformation of identity and the shape of his gospel mission. In the climax of Paul's speech in Gal 2, Paul explains how his response of faith to the revelation of the Son has made him a "new creation"—"it is no longer I who live but Christ in me" (2:20a).[108] He no longer seeks righteousness from the Law, in fact, he has died to the Law in order to live to God (2:16-19).[109] He has experienced his own "Isaac moment," in which he has been stripped from his trust in his advances in Judaism (1:13-14), that is, from all his

---

108. Barclay discusses this as the "reconstitution of the self," and explores how Paul's narration of his own transformation functions paradigmatically in the letter ("Paul's Story," 142-44).

109. Betz proposes that in Gal 2:19-20 Paul sets forth "the basic elements of his own theological position" in the form of the thesis that he will develop in the letter (*Galatians*, 121-26). Commentators generally agree that the concise statements that Paul makes in the first-person mode in Gal 2:19-20 anticipate their fuller treatment in the letter, and thus their meaning is derived in relation to our reading of those (e.g., Longenecker, *Galatians*, 91; Moo, *Galatians*, 167-72). This is also my approach.

previous tokens of status and worth—living *out of* the flesh (Ishmael)—to now, while still living *in* his Jewish body, living *out of* dependence on God: "the life I now live in the flesh, I live in faith in the Son of God who loved me and gave himself for me" (2:20b; cf. 2:16).[110] The Son of God, who, as the Isaianic servant, had given himself up on the cross due to "our" sin—Paul included—to bring deliverance from the "present evil age" (1:4), and redemption from the curse of the Law (3:13), has become the defining center in Paul's identity. Thus, the revelation of the Son has transformed Paul's identity to the extent that he not only proclaims the gospel with words, but also embodies it. The revelation of the Son *to* Paul results in the revelation of the Son *in* Paul (1:16).[111]

As Paul reminds the Galatians of their initial reception of the gospel, he reminds them of Christ being portrayed before their eyes as crucified (*hois kat' ophthalmous iēsous christos proegraphē estaurōmenos*) (3:1). The portrait of Christ crucified is on one level evoked by Paul's proclamation of Christ crucified.[112] But it is possible that the reality of the crucified Christ was also made visible in Paul's bodily presence. Paul came to the Galatians due to bodily weakness,[113] and yet they received him as Christ Jesus (4:13-14): "[t]he enfeebled Paul was, for them, a representative, even a personification, of the crucified Christ whom he placarded (3:1)."[114] Paul's

---

110. On Paul's advances in Judaism, see Ciampa, *Presence and Function of Scripture*, 106-11; de Boer, *Galatians*, 84-89. Commentators usually take the *sarx* in 2:20b as a general reference to bodily existence (e.g., Burton, *Galatians*, 138; Longenecker, *Galatians*, 93; Moo, *Galatians*, 171). I argue that Paul alludes back to where he started in 2:15-16 (note the *pasa sarx* at the end of v. 16), now highlighting that his construction of self and the world has changed so that, while he still lives in his Jewish flesh, he depends on Christ rather than any other token of status or worth (cf. Phil 3:3-9) (cf. Dunn, *Galatians*, 146).

111. The Greek expression *en emoi* can be taken with the sense *to me, in me*, or *by/through me* (see de Boer, *Galatians*, 92). I sense an intended movement in the expression here, in which the Son is first revealed *to* Paul in order to be revealed *in* Paul. Some resist the translation *in me* because they think that it refers to some form of a mystical experience, i.e., subjective revelation (e.g., de Boer, *Galatians*, 92; Mußner, *Der Galaterbrief*, 86-87). This is unnecessary, since it can also indicate that Paul comes to embody the gospel.

112. Cf. Longenecker, *Galatians*, 100-101; Moo, *Galatians*, 181-82; Rohde, *an die Galater*, 129.

113. For *di' astheneian* indicating the reason, see Schlier, *an die Galater*, 210. I think that Acts 13:14—14:22 description of Paul's "persecutions" (including stoning) driving his movements during his first visits to the Galatians could be what is referred to here.

114. Barclay, "Paul's Story," 145. There is much speculation about the nature of Paul's "weakness of the flesh" (cf. 2 Cor 12:7) (see discussions in Burton, *Galatians*, 238-39; Eastman, *Recovering Paul's Mother Tongue*, 100-108). Schlier (*an die Galater*, 210-11), Dunn (*Galatians*, 233-36), and Moo (*Galatians*, 282-86) see it as some kind

own suffering in the ministry of the gospel had marked him as the servant ("slave") of Christ (*egō gar ta stigmata tou iēsou en tō sōmati mou bastazō*) (6:17).[115] Thus, the Galatians' reception of Paul reflected their reception of the gospel of the suffering servant—Christ crucified.

In referring to the Galatians' reception of the message that Paul represented, which delivered the promise of the Spirit, Paul uses the peculiar expression *akoē pisteōs* twice (3:2 - *ex ergōn nomou to pneuma elabete ē ex akoēs pisteōs*; 3:5 - *ex ergōn nomou ē ex akoēs pisteōs*).[116] This expression resonates with the question in Isa 53:1 that has to do with believing the message that is about the revelation of the "arm of the Lord" who is the suffering servant of Isa 53 (*tis episteuse tē akoē hēmōn? kai ho brachiōn kyriou tini apekalyphthē*).[117] We know from Paul's quotation of Isa 53:1 in Rom 10:16 that this text is important for Paul in explaining the necessity of the response of faith to the gospel. In Rom 10:16–17—"But not all have been obedient [*hypēkousan*] to the gospel. For Isaiah says: 'Lord, who has believed our message [*akoē*]?' Faith is then from hearing [*akoē*], but the hearing [*akoē*] is through the word of Christ"—Paul connects *akoē* initially to the message he proclaims about Christ (passive sense), but also, as Harmon astutely observes, to the active sense of hearing the message of Christ that evokes believing (cf. Rom 10:14).[118] Hence, the definition of *akoē pisteōs* in Gal 3:2 and 3:5 is best given in light of the text it most likely refers to, Isa 53:1, and Paul's application of it elsewhere. This gives it the sense: "the hearing of the message that you believed," that points ultimately to Christ as the object of faith, but retains its focus on the active sense of hearing and believing the gospel (cf. Abraham's faith in 3:6, and the contrast between works and faith in 3:10–12).

The conceptual and thematic correspondence between Gal 3:1–5 and Isa 53 further supports my argument that the Isaianic servant informs Paul's understanding of his mission as a representation of the work of Christ. Paul represents in his mission the revelation of the Son as the Isaianic servant, and the Galatians' reception of Paul, and their faith in his message about Christ

---

of eye problem (cf. 4:14–15), whereas Eastman has argued a strong case for taking it as a reference to Paul's suffering that had left its marks on Paul (cf. 6:17). I agree with Eastman, as her view fits best with Paul's emphasis on his condition somehow representing Christ (4:14; cf. 3:1), and with the reference to the marks of Jesus on his body in 6:17.

115. Schlier points out that "the marks (*stigmata*) of Jesus" signifies Paul's identification as a "slave" of Christ, and refers to his suffering (*an die Galater*, 284–85; similarly Rohde, *an die Galater*, 279–80).

116. On the various possibilities to interpret Paul's use of *akoē pisteōs*, see de Boer, *Galatians*, 173–77; Hays, *Faith of Jesus Christ*, 124–32; and Williams, "Hearing of Faith," 82–93.

117. Cf. Jobes, "Jerusalem, Our Mother," 312–13; Harmon, *She Must*, 129–30.

118. Harmon, *She Must*, 131–32.

(cf. 3:22–26), has led them into the inheritance of the restored people of God by the generative power of the Spirit. Thus, Paul's labor pains are about participating in the work of God in Christ and the Spirit, so that the promise carried in the proclamation of the gospel can perform what God is after.

Paul is *again* in labor pains (4:19) because of the danger that the "distorted gospel" would lead the Galatians away from the generative and sustaining power of the promise—the grace of Christ (5:2–4). As Paul embodied the gospel in his initial visit among the Galatians, so also now with the letter that he writes his own narrative embodies the message he desires to communicate to the Galatians—the Galatians are to become like Paul (4:12).[119] Paul's own transformation of identity from one that was afforded to him by the Law to become a person who depends on Christ is part of the antidote to curb the Galatians' desire to come under the Law. If Paul had needed to be made alive by dying to the Law of Moses (*nomos*) by the revelation of Christ (*nomos*; the defining center of the totality of God's revelation) (*egō gar dia nomou nomō apethanon, hina theō zēsō. Christō synestaurōmai*) (2:19; cf. 6:14–15),[120] how much more are the Galatians to reject their desire to come under the Sinaitic Law by embracing fully the revelation of Christ (4:21; see chapter 5 for discussion on the double sense of *nomos*) and allow it to define the people of God. The transformation of identity and the recalibration of the law by Christ results in a new conception of community—the re-created humanity.

Christ had found form in Paul (2:19–20), and now Paul was in labor pains that Christ would also find *form* among the Galatians (4:19). The Galatians have been set free by Christ (5:1)—they have been generated into the restoration reality of the "Jerusalem above" community (4:26–27). Now they are to learn to live out from their "new creation" identity in the freedom of the restored people of God (5:13). The theological vision of restoration as a new creation reality must be translated into social practice.[121] Paul (and the Jerusalem church leaders; 2:3) had endured "labor

---

119. Cf. Barclay, "Paul's Story," 145.

120. Betz identifies 2:19a as a *crux interpretum* due to its abbreviated form that must be decoded (*Galatians*, 122). Moo identifies that especially difficult is the expression "through the law" (*Galatians*, 169). Commentators look for help from the rest of the letter, but I know only of Augustine to have recognized the similar tension set within the concept of the law (law "against" Law) in 4:21, but having utilized the potential rather differently to how I perceive it: "through the same law, understood spiritually, they might die to carnal observances of the law" (Plumer, *Augustine's Commentary on Galatians*, 149). The last line *christō synestaurōmai* supports my reading that the law by which Paul has died to the Law of Moses refers to the revelation of Christ, by which Paul's identity is remade, his hermeneutic is recalibrated, and the cosmos is reordered.

121. Cf. Barclay: "'The truth of the good news' (2:14) is ineffective unless it 'takes

pains" in his defense for the appropriate social practice that aligns with the new reality—the "truth of the Gospel"—in Jerusalem with the challenge of the "false brothers" who pressed the case for Gentile (Titus) circumcision (2:3-5), which Paul interpreted as an attempt to "enslave" those who lived in the "freedom in Christ" (2:4). He had also taken a stand for embracing the full implications of the "truth of the gospel" in Antioch against the actions of Peter, Barnabas, and other Jews who implicitly compelled (separating from table fellowship) the Gentiles to Judaize in order to be fully counted in the fellowship of the people of God (2:11-14). Now the Galatians must also align their social practice with the reality of life as the re-created humanity. Circumcision or uncircumcision are not to receive the weight they do in the way the cosmos is conceived and community constructed outside of the reality of restoration defined by the revelation of Christ (5:6; 6:14-16). What determines the identity of the restoration community is "new creation" (6:15), and what guides the new community is faith expressed in love (5:6) according to the pattern of Christ who gave himself up to the cross for the sake of the other in love (2:20). The Galatians have been generated to new creation life by faith in what Paul represents: Christ the Isaianic servant who was crucified. Now the Galatians need to reflect the character of Christ, the servant, in their communities. They are to become a community of servants who serve one another in love (*dia tēs agapēs douleuete allēlois*) (5:13). This vision is thoroughly Isaianic in its shape. In Isaiah, the servant generates the restoration community that is described as the community of servants (Isa 54:17; see ch. 4).

Just like Paul identified with the cross of Christ (*christō synestaurōmai*) (Gal 2:19), so also are the Galatians to construct their identity and life in community from the cross of Christ (*hoi de tou christou [iēsou] tēn sarka estaurōsan syn tois pathēmasin kai tais epithymiais*) (5:24). Christ's cross and resurrection has granted them life in the Spirit—the Galatians have received the Spirit by faith in Christ (3:1-5). Thus, Paul calls the Galatians to finish as they have begun. They have been divinely generated, and now they need to learn to live in ongoing dependence on divine sufficiency—"as you have life in the Spirit, so also live in line with the Spirit" (5:25). The exhortation to align with the Spirit is a call to live in line with the vision and reality of new creation that is antithetical to living according to the "flesh."[122] Identity and

---

place' within communities whose behavior instantiates its novelty. Galatians 5:13-6:10 seems designed both to describe and to encourage that social expression of the good news" (*Paul and the Gift*, 425). Also Vouga, *An die Galater*, 127.

122. For discussion on defining Paul's use of the term "flesh," see Barclay, *Obeying the Truth*, 178-215. Paul's personified way of talking about the desires of the flesh leads Schlier to describe it as a personal power (*an die Galater*, 249). Martyn transposes this

life that is patterned according to "Ishmael" belongs to the sphere of the flesh, and it can be expressed even in the righteous zeal, or in the boasting about status and human potential that doing the Law affords to both the Jew and the Judaizing Gentile (1:13–14; 2:15; 6:12–13; cf. Phil 3:3–6). This is not the purpose of the Law, but an expression of its weakness to deal with the condition of humanity whose claim even for righteousness and Law observance can be corrupted by sin (cf. Isa 58). Thus, flesh is a complex category that describes the sphere of existence that is under the corruption of sin, and does not align with the vision of the re-created humanity (5:19–21)—flesh is the condition of alienated humanity living in an old cosmos. Life in the Spirit is the realm of existence for the re-created humanity—the restoration people—that is antithetical to the flesh, but not in opposition with the intention of the Law (*kata tōn toioutōn ouk estin nomos*) (5:23). Yet it is beyond the reach, or regulatory sphere, of the Mosaic Law that cannot make alive—deliver the Spirit (*ei de pneumati agesthe, ouk este hypo nomon*) (5:18).[123]

As Christ delivers people from the condition of bondage/alienation (5:1), he also delivers the Law from its enslavement to the condition of sinful humanity. When the Jew and Gentile are generated to be the children of the promise of restoration, they are called to live in love (5:13), which is a fulfillment of what the Law envisaged (*ho gar pas nomos en heni logō peplērōtai, en tō; agapēseis ton plēsion sou hōs seauton*) (5:14). This fulfillment is now enabled by the Spirit (5:16, 22–23) and defined by Christ to be the way of life for the re-created humanity: "carry one another's burdens and in this way you will fulfill the law of Christ" (6:2).[124]

---

notion to the level of a cosmic battle: "[t]he flesh is rather a supra-human power, indeed an inimical, martial power seeking to establish a military base of operations in the Galatian churches, with the intention of destroying them as genuine communities . . ." (*Galatians*, 483; similarly de Boer, *Galatians*, 335–39). I find this misdirected (see also Barclay, *Paul and the Gift*, 427), and I take as my starting point Barclay's definition of "flesh" in terms of a sphere of existence: "[l]ike 'the present evil age' (1:4), 'the flesh' represents the environment of all human agency untransformed by the Spirit—including life under the Torah, which was incapable of 'creating life' because of the power of sin (3:21–22)" (426). I develop this by placing it within the framework of the restoration vision.

123. Cf. O'Donovan: "[t]his, I take Paul to say of the virtues, 'is the kind of thing that lies beyond the scope of the law'" ("Flesh and Spirit," 282).

124. For discussion on interpreting 5:14 and 6:2 see Barclay, *Obeying the Truth*, 125–42. I hold that the *nomos* in Gal 5:14 refers to the Mosaic Law, which he immediately cites (Lev 19:18) (cf. Barclay; pace de Boer, *Galatians*, 344–45, who thinks it refers to Scripture that contains Law and promises), and that Paul is making here the initial and limited point that the intention of the Law is fulfilled in living out the one commandment to love (cf. Rom 13:8, 10) (cf. Rohde, *an die Galater*, 229–30). Paul goes on to develop the thought that this intention of the Law is fulfilled in the way of life that is now defined by Christ and empowered by the Spirit. Barclay makes the important observation that Paul is in 5:14 and 6:2 deliberately choosing a term ([*ana*]*plēroō*; contra 5:3)

Synthesis

I first present a sequential reading of Gal 4:21—5:1 that outlines the movement of the argument and highlights key insights gained from my structural, hermeneutical, and intertextual analysis. I then synthesize the discussion from the above sections to configure Paul's theological vision and logic by the two contrastive generative lines.

Sequential Reading of Galatians 4:21—5:1

My structural analysis has demonstrated that Paul's thought in the central section of Gal 4:21—5:1 (vv. 24-28) is constructed in a chiastic fashion. The argument moves towards and out from the pivotal point that is about the two Jerusalems. This center exerts its influence on the allegorical construction of the passage, and guides the proper identification of the allegorical figures of the "slave woman" and the "free woman." The chiastic structure also guides in the identification of the two covenants in terms of the covenant from Sinai and the covenant of promise, which is confirmed by Paul's treatment of these themes similarly elsewhere in the letter (especially 3:15-18). With these key structural insights in view, I proceed to a sequential reading of 4:21—5:1.

Paul's question in Gal 4:21 already indicates the strategy of the argument: "tell me, you who desire to be under the Law, do you not listen to the law?" The compulsion to align with the covenant from Sinai is to be rejected, because the Law must be recalibrated in the new "intertextual" revelatory field that has been extended by the revelation of Christ (wider sense of *nomos*). Thus, in what follows, Paul reads the Abraham narrative together with Isaiah in line with the reality of the Christ-event to argue that coming under the Law is not the way to be included in the restored people of God, but that it is counterproductive for participating in the re-created humanity.

He first schematically summarizes the Genesis narrative about the births of Abraham's two sons from the "slave woman" and the "free woman" (4:22) with focus on the manner of their births—one is born according to flesh and the other by a promise (4:23). This presentation highlights the central themes that Paul further develops: slavery/freedom and flesh/promise. Paul then explains that he treats the story of the birth of Abraham's two sons on an "allegorical" level, in which the story has a broader horizon of

---

that makes the distinction that "Christians do not 'observe' the law" and yet "they 'fulfil' it through the one love-command and as it is redefined as the 'law of Christ'" that allows him simultaneously to "establish his point without wholly compromising his statements elsewhere . . . " (*Obeying the Truth*, 142; cf. de Boer, *Galatians*, 345).

meaning that speaks about two different covenants (4:24). These two covenants become the governing framework of the argument.

The first covenant is clearly identified as the covenant from Sinai, which now corresponds with the realities associated with Hagar (4:24). The connection between Hagar and Sinai is established initially on a geographical level—Hagar and Sinai meet in Arabia (4:25a). But, this surprising connection is designed to "startle," and lead into a quest for a deeper meaning. The primary link between Hagar and Sinai is the shared theme of slavery (4:24, 25b), and the deeper level of meaning in this connection is built on the scriptural matrix formed by the Abraham narrative and Isaiah. The potential for Hagar to represent Israel's life under the Law that leads to slavery draws partly from the narrative of Ishmael's birth. Genesis portrays Ishmael as an alternative construal of the identity of Israel that focuses on natural human potential that conforms to the requirements of physical descent and circumcision in the identity of God's people. It also suggests that the oppression of Hagar/Ishmael prefigures Israel's slavery in Egypt, and that the configuration of Israel according to the pattern of Ishmael results in exclusion from the inheritance. Hagar represents the covenant of the Law also in her status as the "slave woman" that corresponds with Paul's conception of the Law being "enslaved"—being constrained in its ability to produce right-relatedness by the condition of sinful humanity (3:21–22). But this is only part of the matrix that underlies Paul's logic.

The Isaianic vision of restoration that surfaces in the quotation of Isa 54:1 in Gal 4:27 makes its presence felt already in the correspondence that Paul makes with the Hagar-Sinai covenant and the "present Jerusalem," which Paul perceives also to be in slavery with her children (4:25b). The term "present Jerusalem" stems from the Isaianic matrix of the "tale of two cities" that is re-appropriated by Paul to refer to the condition of alienation/slavery outside of the inheritance of the restoration reality inaugurated in the sending of the Son and the giving of the Spirit. Already with the first covenantal line, Paul demonstrates how he argues against coming under the Law with a reading of the Genesis narrative together with Isaiah in light of the Christ-event.

Paul's hermeneutical strategy, logic, and the theological vision that drives the argument are opened more fully in the moves that he makes next. Paul aligns himself and the Galatian believers with the mother "Jerusalem above" that is free (4:26). The "Jerusalem above" is their mother, because they are identified as the children of the barren-made-fruitful woman of Isa 54:1 (4:27). Both the "Jerusalem above" and the children of the barren-made-fruitful woman connect Paul's vision with the Isaianic vision of the restored, regenerated people of God. The vision of the regenerated people in Isa 54:1 is patterned on the birth of Isaac from the barren Sarah. Hence, the Galatian believers are also designated children of promise according to the pattern of Isaac's birth (4:28). This pattern emphasizes divine generation as the essential feature in the identification of God's people. The promise refers both to the Abrahamic promise of blessing to the nations and its re-appropriation in the Isaianic vision as inclusion in the regenerated people that is defined theologically rather than ethnically.

The Isaianic influence on the line of promise is also perceived in the following characterization in the allegorical re-appropriation of Abraham's two sons who represent the tension that the Galatians' face. The Galatian believers are now represented by the "allegorical" Isaac who is described as having been generated by the Spirit (4:29)—an extension of the earlier category of promise (4:23). The Spirit is not an element in the Abraham narrative, but is an integral part of the Isaianic vision of the regeneration of the new creation people. Hence, Paul configures the gift of the Spirit, which the Galatians have received (3:2–5; 4:6), into the line of the promise with the help of the Isaianic vision of restoration.

The following exhortation to "cast out the slave woman and her child" (4:30) must also be read in light of the allegorical correspondences that have been established earlier. This exhortation draws the Galatians to a place of decision that is about constructing their identity and aligning their lives rightly in light of the outcome of the two contrastive generative lines—the inheritance. The slave woman and her child refer to Hagar-Ishmael, but only as they represent the covenant from Sinai. Paul's point is that the covenant from Sinai does not lead into the inheritance (4:30), and hence the compulsion to come under the Law must be rejected. It is only the generative line of the promise that leads to the inheritance. Hence, the Galatians are not to identify with the "slave woman" (4:31), who is Hagar, as she represents the covenant from Sinai that defines the "present Jerusalem" (4:24–25). They are to identify with the "free woman" (4:31), which is a reference to Sarah only indirectly, as she represents the pattern of the promise that generates the children of the allegorical "free woman"—the mother "Jerusalem above" who is free (4:26). This means that the inheritance is about inclusion in the restored people of God—the "Jerusalem above" community—and exclusion from the inheritance is a reference to being outside of the restoration reality in the "present Jerusalem." Accordingly, slavery and freedom are also defined in relation to the inheritance. Slavery is connected to alienation—being outside of the inheritance of restoration. Freedom is to be in the inheritance of inclusion in the restored people of God.

Finally, Paul concludes his argument with reference to Christ (5:1). Inclusion in and exclusion from the inheritance of restoration are ultimately determined in relation to Christ. Christ's role is configured in terms of the Isaianic servant who generates the children of the barren woman—the heirs of the "Jerusalem above." Hence, Paul concludes by urging the Galatians to stand firm in the reality of restoration—freedom—that Christ has delivered them into, and not to submit to the "yoke of slavery" (5:1) that coming under the Law would imply.

Configuration of the Theological Vision and Logic of Galatians

I now give a synthesized discussion to bring together insights gained in the above sections of this chapter to deepen the understanding of central themes in Galatians within the framework of the two covenants as two contrastive generative lines for constructing the identity of God's people. These two constructions/covenants/generative lines correspond also with Paul's letter framing categories of the "truth of the gospel" and the "distorted gospel" (see ch. 2).

The key for configuring the two generative lines is to work out from the pivotal point of the contrast between the "present Jerusalem" and the "Jerusalem above" in Gal 4:25-26. The "Jerusalem above" designates the inheritance of the restoration reality that is envisioned in Isaiah as the fulfillment of the Abrahamic promise of blessing that includes all the nations in the regenerated people of God. Since both the Abrahamic promise of blessing and the Isaianic vision of restoration have all of humanity in view and a cosmic scope (see chs. 3-4), Paul's vision about the "Jerusalem above" community is a vision of the re-creation of humanity and the restructuring of the cosmos. This vision defines Paul's gospel and drives his mission.

The "present Jerusalem" refers to a realm of existence outside of the regenerated community and the new creation reality. Thus, it is not about Judaism as such, or directly about a competing Gentile mission, although they can both potentially represent a configuration of the people and cosmos that has not (fully) embraced the impact of the gospel—the revelation of the Son and the inauguration of restoration. The "present Jerusalem" is about a configuration of the people of God according to the *nomos* of Moses (Sinai covenant), which has not been recalibrated by the *nomos* of Christ (4:21 and 6:2; see ch. 5).

The categories of slavery and freedom are configured in relation to the inheritance of the restoration reality. Freedom is found in inclusion in the inheritance. Slavery is in the realm of alienation outside of the inheritance of restoration. But these categories reach deeper. Freedom is also about deliverance from sin in the "present evil age" (1:4), and generation into the realm of "new creation" in the Spirit (5:16–25). Slavery, by contrast, is a condition bound by the power of sin—being enslaved to a life that is not in line with the *nomos* defined by Christ (4:21; 6:2), nor in line with the "canon" of "new creation" that shapes a new community (6:14–16). Thus, they become also categories for the social vision Paul has for the "new creation" people (2:4; 5:13). Freedom means to live in line with the full implications of the work of Christ and the giving of the Spirit that have inaugurated the restoration reality. Slavery denotes a social practice that upholds the divisions that are embedded in the construction of reality (cosmos) outside of "new creation" (3:28; 6:14–15).

The logic of inclusion in the new creation people of God is configured by the alienation-restoration paradigm in Isaiah (Isa 54:1 in Gal 4:27) and the corresponding pattern in the birth of Abraham's two sons (4:22). The alienation-restoration paradigm is ultimately mapped on to the Christ-event, and vice versa. Isaiah's theological interpretation of Israel's exile and the promise of restoration provides the matrix for configuring the present condition of Israel and the nations in relation to the Christ-event. Christ delivers into freedom (5:1)—he delivers humanity from the state of alienation into the life of the restored people of God. Israel's alienation—reflected in the category of the "present Jerusalem"—is expressed by her violation of the "law" (of Christ); her resistance towards the divine revelation in Christ. Israel's restoration is envisioned as an act of mercy—the offer of divine grace in the work of Christ as the Isaianic servant. Israel's restoration depends on her response to the offer of mercy and not on her right to be included by virtue of ancestry or existing covenant of circumcision (2:16; 6:16). The offer of mercy opens the door also for the alienated/"sinful" Gentiles (2:15–16). The configuration of Israel's identity with an emphasis on physical descent and the covenant of circumcision conforms to the realities associated with Ishmael, which does not lead to the inheritance of the Abrahamic promise, as interpreted by Isaiah in terms of inclusion in the restored people of God. This configuration compels the Gentiles, contrary to the "truth of the gospel," to align with Israel according to the flesh—according to the pattern of Ishmael—by the means of circumcision and adoption of the Law from Sinai. Inclusion is patterned on the birth of Isaac, which leads to dependence on the God of promise who has acted in Christ and the Spirit.

The generative line of the promise is primary for Paul. It is the realities associated with the promise that determine Paul's view of the covenant from Sinai. In this respect Paul works from solution to plight. The generative line of the promise is anchored in the work of Christ that Paul configures by the Isaianic servant. Christ deals with the root of alienation, sin (1:4; 3:13), and generates the children of the "free woman" who are the heirs of the restoration community. Connected with the work of Christ is the generative activity of the Spirit (4:29; cf. 4:4-7) that enables the life of the new people of God. Paul perceives a pattern in the divine activity in Christ and the Spirit that corresponds with the birth of Isaac, on the one hand, and the vision of restoration that is imaged by the barren-made-fruitful woman, on the other hand. Promise is the category that summarizes for Paul the divine generative activity. *God acts in the line of promise. He sends* the Son as the Christ who delivers from slavery. *He supplies* the Spirit that enables the life of the new people of God. The community of the "Jerusalem above" are a people *of God*. Divine generation into the restoration community determines for Paul also the inheritance of the Abrahamic promise of blessing. Those who have responded by faith (trust and dependence) to the act of divine promise in Christ have been generated by the Spirit to be the children of the "Jerusalem above," and are thus "children of promise." This is the "truth of the gospel" that Paul defends and re-proclaims in Galatians.

The other generative line is set in contrast to the line of promise. It is not evil, but it is limited in its ability to generate what God intends. It is fundamentally a false construction for what it means to be included in the people of God—"a distorted gospel"—and hence to be firmly rejected. This generative line originates from Sinai that represents the regulatory sphere of the Law, as much as it represents also the boundaries that circumcision sets in the flesh of the Sinai-covenant people. Thus, the generative means in this covenant is described by "flesh" that focuses on physical descent from Abraham and circumcision, but also on human potential in doing the Law (3:10-12) that is compromised by sin (3:22). This line is patterned in the birth of Ishmael. He is the product of flesh—an act of theologically reasoned human potential. Ishmael is Abraham's descendant, he is also circumcised, but yet outside of the inheritance. He does not count, because he is not generated by the promise. Ishmael leaves room for human boasting that upholds conformity with the expected ordering of the cosmos and dependence on human potential (6:13-14). He is not a "child of laughter"—Isaac—that unsettles the natural order and empties the sense of human potential in generating what God is after. Hence, he cannot be a "child of promise." The category of flesh reaches beyond physical descent and circumcision, and refers to an identity that is derived from human being and doing in relation to the Law and the conventional ordering of the cosmos. The limitation of this generative line is in its inability to lead into the life of the restoration community and to conform with the canon of "new creation."

The above charted theological vision about the re-creation of humanity and the logic of mercy in the generative line of the promise are the reason why Paul calls the Galatians to a place of decision; to embrace and align their identity as the new creation people of God (truth of the gospel), and to resist the desire/pressure to validate their inclusion in the people of God according to the Mosaic Law and expected ordering of cosmos and community (distorted gospel). This is why Paul is in labor pains (4:19). Paul's mission joins in the divine generative activity for the formation of a community that is shaped by the cross of Christ and empowered by the Spirit. The Galatians need to maintain their dependence on the God of promise by ongoing trust in the grace of Christ (2:16, 20–21; 5:2–4), and reliance on the empowering presence of the Spirit in the life of the re-created humanity (5:13—6:10).

7

Conclusions

It is time to close the circle with this book, and use the insights gained from the analysis in chs. 2–6 to return to the key questions articulated in my introduction. Following the division of the questions into the structural, hermeneutical, and theological categories, my discussion below moves from the structural to the hermeneutical, which then offers the unique perspective of this work to engage with the theological questions.

I began the argument of this book by analyzing the structure of the letter to the Galatians. This established the grounds for taking Gal 4:21—5:1 as the vantage point for configuring Paul's theological vision and logic in the whole letter. This vantage point has two major implications for the quest to configure the theology of Galatians. First, Gal 4:21—5:1 reveals Paul's *hermeneutical strategy* for redressing the application of the Law in the new situation brought about by the Christ-event and the giving of the Spirit. By attending to this, we locate Paul's theological matrix, capture his theological vision and logic, and discern the shape of Paul's retelling of Israel's story. Second, and partially following from the first, but also because the passage functions as the culmination point for the preceding argument as well as a bridge to what follows it, it is at this point in the letter that *important themes can be best defined*, e.g., what does righteousness refer to, what is the promise about, and what does the inheritance point to?

I argued in ch. 5 that Paul's hermeneutical strategy becomes visible by analyzing his allegorical practice in Gal 4:21—5:1. In contrast to Boyarin, I argued that Paul's allegorical mode is essentially intertextual, in which the interpretative field is extended to encompass the revelatory impact of the Christ-event. Hence, rather than discovering a Hellenistic matrix (as is the case with Philo) underlying Paul's theological vision and logic (as Boyarin argues), we find Paul grounding his understanding of the gospel by drawing from the resources of Israel's Scriptures as they are reconfigured by the Christ-event. But it is possible to be more precise about the form of the dialogical matrix of Scripture and the experience of Christ and the Spirit, and how it shapes Paul's theological vision and logic.

I have demonstrated in chs. 5–6 that an integral feature in Paul's intertextual practice is his reading of the Abraham narrative *together* with Isaiah. Together these texts shape Paul's theological vision to be about the divine generation of the restoration people that can be understood as the re-creation of humanity. The Abrahamic promise of blessing to all the nations has as its purpose the "spiritual renewal of humanity" that becomes apparent from the context from which the Abraham narrative emerges (see ch. 3). The promised blessing that extends to all the nations is envisioned ultimately in terms of their inclusion in the people of God. This is the foundational promise to which Paul anchors the gospel (Gal 3:8). But the initial promise receives a new dimension from its re-appropriation in the Isaianic promise of restoration that has Israel and all the nations in its scope. This interplay between the Abrahamic promise and the Isaianic vision of restoration is brought to the surface in the quotation of Isa 54:1 in Gal 4:27 that offers the logic for integrating the Galatian believers among the children of promise according to the pattern of Isaac (4:28). The alienation-restoration paradigm that underlies the imagery of the barren-made-fruitful woman (Isa 54:1) corresponds with the pattern in the birth of Isaac. Both highlight the necessity of divine generation for inclusion in the people of God. This does not apply only to the Gentiles (pace RNPP), since to be rightly related with God is to be included in the restoration people—the "Jerusalem above" community (4:26). For Paul, a natural or "supernatural" connection to Abraham is not the point (pace Thiessen), as it is rather participation in the "new creation" that is the determining "canon" for inclusion in the regenerated "Israel of God" (6:14–16). For this, both the Jew and Gentile are dependent on the divine performance of the promise in Christ and the Spirit. Responding in faith to the revelation of Christ is the only means by which the regenerative act of God transfers any human being into the inheritance of the restoration reality.

The above description of my configuration of Paul's theological vision that is about divine generation of the restoration people is encapsulated in Gal 4:21—5:1 by the concept of the *Jerusalem above*. Unlike many commentators, I argued in ch. 6 that this term is not a reference to a future heavenly city but rather derives its meaning from the Isaianic matrix of the "tale of two cities" that is expressed in Isa 54:1 with the figures of the two women, and introduced in the opening two chapters of the book of Isaiah. Thus, the *Jerusalem above* denotes in Paul's use in Galatians the inauguration of the restoration reality that is about the restored presence and rule of God among the community of the regenerated people of God comprised of both Jews and Gentiles.

From this vantage point, I also argued in ch. 6 that it is possible to detect the hermeneutical influence of the Isaianic vision of restoration in other strategic moments in the letter. In Gal 6:15, Paul highlights that the reality of *new creation* relativizes the value of circumcision and uncircumcision. Inheriting the *kingdom of God* (5:21) extends the vision towards a fuller future realization that is the source of motivation and cause for exhortation to align fully with life in the Spirit (5:16–25; 6:7–10). I argued that both of these concepts stem from the Isaianic vision of restoration, and have intimate links with Isa 54:1. Moreover, I demonstrated in ch. 6 how the influence of the Isaianic vision can also be detected in the way Paul envisions the Spirit as part of the fulfillment of the Abrahamic promise of blessing that creates the new inclusive "we" of the recipients of the Spirit in 3:14 (cf. Isa 44:1–5). This blurs the distinction between the Jewish "we" and Gentile "you" in the argument of the letter, while retaining Jewish "priority" in the story of Israel's restoration that includes the Gentiles. Similarly, the theological vision and logic in Gal 4:4–7 reflects the restoration matrix in Isa 63. Here, Paul presents his vision for the regeneration of the "sons" of God who consist of both the Jews and Gentiles that have received the Spirit of the Son, and have been made heirs of the restoration reality that is not predicated on a genealogical connection to Abraham but rather on the divine act of mercy that unites humanity as one family of the *Abba*, Father. Hence, Paul's reading of the Abraham narrative together with Isaiah gives his retelling of Israel's story its unique shape that is best captured by the notion of incongruent grace.

Incongruent grace is the defining feature in the shape of Paul's retelling of Israel's story that integrates the Gentiles into its scope. I agree with Barclay that Paul's own experience of being called by this grace (1:13–16) initially generated the conception of the Christ-gift as being incongruous with the recipients' worth. Yet, as Paul works out the implications of his revelatory experience of Christ, the role of the Scriptures of Israel can be perceived as more formative for the understanding of Paul's own mission and the "truth of the gospel" than Barclay has explored.

I have demonstrated in ch. 3 how the incongruence of divine "calling in grace" is ingrained in Israel's foundational story of the birth of Isaac. God chooses the childless Abraham with a sterile wife as the unfitting candidate to carry forward the promise of a "great nation" and blessing to all the nations (Gen 11:30; 12:1–3). The birth of Isaac from the barren womb of Sarah is an act of incongruence—a most unlikely and unnatural event that establishes the paradigm for the character of God's people (Gen 17–18). What is established with Isaac as being essential for the identity of God's people is further emphasized by setting it in contrast to Ishmael. Ishmael is portrayed in the narrative as an alternative construal of the "great nation" that issues out of theologically reasoned human potential and is focused on natural descent and conformity to the requirement of circumcision, and yet is outside of the inheritance (Gen 16–21; cf. Gal 4:22–31). Unlike the character of Ishmael, God's people are, like Isaac, "children of laughter." They have been stripped from any claim for natural fittingness, or possessing the potential to perform what God is after, and thus have become totally dependent on God (Gen 21–22). I argued in chapter 6 that this is part of the matrix that shapes Paul's vision and logic that works out the identity of the restoration people as *children of promise* according to the pattern of Isaac (Gal 4:28). Thus, Paul capitalizes on the foundational promise to Abraham that is by design subversive towards the categories of fittingness and worth. This is also true of the restoration promise.

I demonstrated in ch. 4, that the logic of mercy is central in the Isaianic vision of restoration. Israel's inclusion in restoration is not predicated on Abrahamic ancestry or success with the Law. Rather, her failure to follow the Law led her to the realm of exile, where she becomes in fact a non-people comparable to the other nations (Isa 1; 63:19; 65:1). The promise of her restoration is envisioned as an act of divine mercy that subverts human calculations of worth (Isa 54:7–10; 55:1). It is again an act of performing the unlikely, gracing the unworthy—the barren woman has more children than the one who is married (Isa 54:1). Since this is true for Israel in her state of alienation, it holds the promise of being true also for other non-peoples who are alienated from God. This is why Paul can incorporate the Gentiles as recipients of Israel's promises of restoration—the "Jerusalem above" is *our* mother (4:26).

The resurrection of Christ (Gal 1:1) and the gift of the Spirit (Gal 3:1–5; 5:25) signaled for Paul that the reality of restoration had begun. Thus, on the one hand, Paul maps the Christ-event onto the matrix of the Isaianic vision of restoration. But, on the other hand, the vision of restoration, and especially the alienation-restoration paradigm, is also mapped onto the Christ-event. Alienation is now the realm outside of the reality defined by the revelation of Christ, and it is denoted by the concept of the *present Jerusalem* (4:25). Inclusion in restoration—in the "Jerusalem above" community—is now defined by dependence on the divine performance of the promise in Christ (5:1) and the Spirit (4:29)—faith in Christ. Hence, it is not necessary to configure Paul's theological vision and logic, as Wright does, by an underlying sense of Israel's ongoing/extended exile. Rather, irrespective of whether or not there was a sense of an ongoing/extended exile, the sphere of alienation from God is re-conceptualized in Paul's new frame of reference—the Christ-event.

However, as Wright correctly emphasizes, Paul's conception of the role of Christ is not independent of the scriptural matrix. Rather, the direction from Scripture to Christ in Paul's dialogical hermeneutic is formative for Paul's Christology. Thus, both Martyn and Barclay overemphasize the discontinuity between Christ and the story of Israel, as they perceive a connection between the Abrahamic promise and the coming of Christ without any substantial development in the story in between (punctiliar emphasis). This misses, e.g., the theological potential that the Isaianic servant provides for Paul's conception of the work of Christ. I argued in chapter 6 that this notion is present in Gal 4:21—5:1 where Christ defines the covenant of promise. The freedom that Christ has delivered (5:1) is the restoration reality—the "Jerusalem above" that is free—and thus, just as the servant in Isa 53 generates the children of the barren woman in Isa 54:1, so also Christ is the one who generates the restored people of God. Paul's conception of Christ as the Isaianic servant became even more evident, as I followed how Paul's identification with Christ shapes his own sense of mission and defines his labor pains (4:19). Paul participates in the divine "labor" by the servant and the Spirit to generate the new creation people that lives as a community of servants (5:13) within the law defined by the servant—the "law of Christ" (6:2; cf. Isa 42:4 LXX).

The above results of my analysis of Paul's hermeneutic, his theological vision and logic, and the shape of his retelling of Israel's story give the unique perspective for my work to engage with the other theological questions raised in the introduction.

The starting point for my configuration of Paul's view about the *Law* begins from his hermeneutical move in Gal 4:21 that plays on two senses of *nomos* (narrow sense = the Mosaic Law/Torah; wider sense = the totality of revelation). In Gal 4:21—5:1, Paul extends the divine revelatory field to recalibrate the understanding of *nomos*. Furthermore, I argued in ch. 5 that Paul's interpretative framework (intertextual field) does not give the Mosaic Torah priority or an independent status, but subsumes it under the "law of Christ," thus placing the revelatory Christ-event at the center of gravity and reading the Torah in the context of the Prophets, especially Isaiah. I suspect that the disjunction between Paul's former zeal for the Law in accordance with the interpretative tradition of the fathers and his revelatory experience of Christ (1:13–16; Paul became an enemy of God with his zeal for the Law) generated this new hermeneutic. I argued in ch. 6 that results from this are perceived in Paul's own reconstituted identity, in which the new Christ-defined-law occasioned the radical break (death) to his old understanding and application of the Law and then a reorientation in his living for God (2:19). This is one of the ways in which Paul tells his own narrative as a paradigm for the Galatians to adopt (cf. 4:12).

Even with the sense of the radical break with his past and the Law as he knew it, Paul finds that the *nomos* is in fact very much more alive than he earlier experienced it. For Paul, the intention of the Law to produce righteousness—right-relatedness both to God and in community—is fulfilled by its "death and resurrection" with Christ. I demonstrated in chapter 6 how Paul conceives that the Law is fulfilled in the service of love (5:13–14) that is modelled in the act of the Son who gave himself for the sake of the other (1:4; 2:20). Furthermore, this kind of loving service is only possible by the power of the Spirit (5:17) that is received by faith in Christ (3:1–5). This sets the Law free from its own bondage, or impotence, due to the power of sin over humanity, as well as sets the people free from the Law as the "yoke of slavery." Before elaborating on Paul's connection between Law and slavery, I summarize the hermeneutical move that transforms Paul's conception of the Law:

1. The Law with a capital L—denoting the Mosaic Law—"dies" as it is subsumed under the law with a lower case l—denoting the totality of revelation now defined by the Christ-event.
2. But the Law comes through the "death," yet without the capital L, as its intention to produce right-relatedness is now fulfilled by the people who live according to the law of Christ in loving service by the power of the Spirit.

Thus, there is a sense in Paul, in which not only the people are rescued from the curse of the Law, but also the Law *itself* is rescued from the condition of slavery that it is implicated in. In ch. 6, I approached the connection between slavery and Law from the connection Paul sets up between Hagar, Sinai, and the "present Jerusalem" (4:24–25), which functions as a short-hand for the reality outside of the inheritance of the restoration reality. From this vantage point, I argued that, like the Hagar-Ishmael configuration led outside of the inheritance (4:30), and just as Israel's life under the Law resulted in exile, so also Paul perceives the Law as a condemning agent due to people's sin (3:10–13, curse/alienation). But like the status of Hagar, so also is the Law itself enslaved, i.e., it is implicated under the condition of sin, and thus incapable of offering the remedy—to make alive and produce righteousness (3:21–22). Again, Paul came to this realization after his own experience of being generated into the "new creation," which was not due to his Law-observant status but by the grace given to him in Christ. Now Paul operates within the "law of Christ" (6:2), and calls the Galatians to do the same with the confidence that the Law is not against such practice (5:23). Living within the "law of Christ" is exclusive of living under the Law of Moses, and yet is also its fulfillment. This is the paradox of the letter to the Galatians that can be best approached from the vantage point of Gal 4:21—5:1.

My work offers also some more nuance to the discussion about the meaning of *righteousness*. Together with Martyn, my work indicates that justification is about more than forgiveness of sins for the individual, as it includes the dimension of deliverance from enslavement. Yet, unlike Martyn, I do not configure the categories of slavery and freedom within the matrix of religion vs. the apocalyptic deliverance of God, but rather within the matrix of the alienation-restoration paradigm. In Paul's conceptual world, *slavery* is the condition outside of realized inheritance (4:1–3), and thus denotes the condition of alienation from the reality of restoration (4:24–31) that is marked by bondage to the power of sin (3:22). *Freedom* is the condition of being delivered from the "present evil age" (1:4) into the reality of restoration / new creation by Christ and the life-giving power of the Spirit (4:26—5:1, cf. 4:4–7).

However, even as my approach moves beyond Martyn's apocalyptic perspective, and also beyond the traditional Reformation construction of righteousness as the imputation of the benefits of Christ on the believer in a narrow judicial sense, it does not settle with the constructions of either the NPP/RNPP without modifications. As my structural analysis in chapter 2 has demonstrated, Paul develops the theme of righteousness/right-relatedness until it culminates in 4:21—5:1. Righteousness is not a self-explanatory concept—it needs to be filled with content. Hence, my rather open way of translating it as right-relatedness is designed to evoke the question: What does a right relationship with God consist of? Paul answers this question, as he moves along in the argument in Galatians. Thus, the NPP is correct in emphasizing that right-relatedness is essentially about "sonship" and inheritance that denote membership in God's people. But rather than being primarily about membership in the one worldwide Abrahamic family, I have argued in ch. 6 that the inheritance is ultimately about participation in the restoration reality—membership in the "Jerusalem above" community, and living as the new creation people of God. Yes, to be sure, this is also about the inheritance of the Abrahamic promise of blessing to all the nations, but *only* as it is mediated by the Isaianic promise of restoration. This has the impact of introducing the theologically significant "rupture" of incongruent grace in the form of the alienation-restoration paradigm into the covenantal trajectory envisioned by the RNPP or Wright.

In contrast to the RNPP emphasis, Paul does not remain in the position that he assumes (only to subvert it) in his extended speech to Peter, which regards only the Gentiles as sinners and the Jews as the rightly related covenant people (2:15). In Paul's reconfigured cosmos, all flesh—all human beings—depend on faith in Christ for right-relatedness (2:16). Both Jew and Gentile need to respond to the promissory act of God in Christ and the Spirit to be rightly related with God and (re)generated into the people of the "Jerusalem above." Thus, the Jewish people are also justified as the "Israel of God" only as they again respond in faith like Abraham to the divine promise, or better yet, as they are regenerated by God according to the pattern of Isaac to inherit the reality of restoration and new creation (see chapter 6). With regard to Wright's covenantal trajectory, I have already suggested above how it is modified by the notion of incongruent grace that provides the deeper logic for understanding why the Torah is not just outdated in its function to adjudicate membership in the people of God—to demarcate right-relatedness. Yet despite my modifications of Wright's configuration, I perceive that we are in essential agreement that justification is about participation in the reconstituted people of God.

Overall, I have demonstrated throughout this book that a reading of Galatians from the vantage point of Gal 4:21—5:1 has integrative power. In ch. 2, I followed how the development of the letter's important themes is brought together in 4:21—5:1. Accordingly, I presented at the end of ch. 6 a synthesis of my configuration of Paul's theological vision and logic in Galatians by a reading of 4:21—5:1 that demonstrated how the key themes are coordinated with the construction of the two-covenant structure.

Finally, as was the case with the review of the six different perspectives in the introduction, so I also now pose to my own work the focusing question of how my configuration of Paul's theological vision and logic explains Paul's resistance to Gentile circumcision. In my view, the answer to why Paul opposed the "distorted gospel" operates on three levels:

1. *Inadequate hermeneutic*—it does not accord the revelation of Christ enough weight to recalibrate the Law. Paul resists Gentile circumcision because it leads to life under the law as the Law from Sinai and not as the law of Christ. This is a failure to (fully) embrace the revelation of the Son and its implication on the reading of Israel's Scriptures (4:21). It resists the impact of the cross and resurrection of Jesus to restructure individual identity (2:19-21), and reshape cosmos and community according to the new creation reality (6:14-16) and the law of Christ (6:2).

2. *Limited vision*—it does not align with the reality of restoration / new creation that has already begun. Paul resists Gentile circumcision because it is against the vision of the re-created humanity that is to live

as the "Jerusalem above" community. Circumcision would give weight to distinctions that are made obsolete in the "new creation." Circumcision or uncircumcision do not carry weight in identifying the newly generated people of God, since generation to be the "Jerusalem above" people is not predicated on such categories.

3. *Misleading logic*—it configures the identity and life of the people of God according to the flesh that is antithetical to the incongruent grace of Christ and life in the Spirit. Paul's gospel emphasizes the sufficiency of divine generative activity that does not give regard to the recipients' worth or require complementation by "flesh." Paul resists Gentile circumcision also, because it would lead to life under the Law with the danger of observing the Law *in the flesh* by means of circumcision and *doing* the requirements of the Law to secure membership in the people of God. This is a "yoke" that does not produce what it prescribes (2:15–16; 3:10; cf. Acts 15:10), and it is reckoned limited due to its inability to make alive (3:21–22). If the Law has been impotent in leading Paul and other Jews into the reality of restoration, it cannot be the means for Gentile participation in "new creation" life either. God's people are the "children of laughter" (4:28), the unlikely people who emerge from the barrenness of their alienation as they depend on the divine performance of the promise that leads to the fulfillment of the law as the "law of Christ" in the power of the Spirit (5:13–25; 6:2). Coming under the Law is a "yoke of slavery" because it displaces dependence on the grace of Christ (5:2–4), and thus severs from the inheritance of the "Jerusalem above."

I now make some *evaluations* of the present work and give suggestions for *further research*. This book has demonstrated the validity of its claim that Gal 4:21—5:1 offers an unparalleled vantage point for configuring Paul's theological vision and logic in the letter to the Galatians. Yet it is by no means a complete reading nor the final word on the epistle. My contribution to the study of Galatians and Paul's theology comes from the analysis of Paul's dialogical hermeneutical practice that operates within the matrix formed by the experience of Christ and the Spirit, and the Scriptures of Israel. My approach incorporates an analysis of the theological potential of the two key intertexts of the Abraham narrative and Isaiah. I am not aware of any other work that has focused so extensively on both of these two major texts in Paul's theological matrix to harvest their joint potential for configuring Paul's theological vision and logic. My configuration is not totally new, as it continues the trend to read Paul within his Jewish matrix in conversation with Scripture. Yet it has been able to combine the strengths from both Wright's broad work on the scriptural matrix underlying Paul's narrative theology and Barclay's detailed construction of the deep logic of incongruent grace that shapes Paul's retelling of Israel's story in a unique way. The critical integration and modification of these two major perspectives in my own reading is one of the contributions of this work.

The limitations of this study are manifold, of which I mention here only a few. My focus on Gal 4:21—5:1 has led me to explore the major key in Paul's hermeneutic, but I have not been able to incorporate all the various texts of Scripture that are part of Paul's theological matrix in Galatians, and thus have not analyzed the larger contour of Paul's reading of Scripture. Paul's mind seems to be able to hold much more together than one modern book can focus on. It would be a worthwhile further research project to critically integrate the insights from this work and from others who have looked at different aspects of Paul's engagement with Scripture in Galatians (Eastman, Ciampa, Harmon, Watson, Wright, etc.), and produce a work under a modified title from Ciampa: *The Presence and Function on Scripture in Galatians*.

My research has focused exclusively on Galatians, and thus the results have not been placed on the larger canvas of the Pauline corpus to evaluate whether my configuration of Paul's theological vision and logic would either be confirmed or challenged by the material in his other letters. As Gal 4:21—5:1 quite naturally leads to a conversation with Rom 9-11, this would be a good place to start.[1] Furthermore, the expectation of Israel's future full restoration in Rom 11 has been the reason for Donaldson to reject the "eschatological pilgrimage" vision (premised on the scheme that, when Israel is restored, then the Gentiles are also included) as the driving conviction for Paul's Gentile mission.[2] Hence, it would be important to evaluate whether my reading of Paul's theological vision in Galatians can be reconciled with the apparent future expectation of Israel's full restoration in Romans.

I give now only some reflections for exploring the possibilities to integrate the different scheme in Rom 9-11 with my reading of Gal 4:21—5:1. Although both texts combine the theological potential from the paradigmatic birth of Isaac (Rom 9:6-9) and the vision of restoration in Isaiah (Rom 9:27-33; 10:14-21; 11:26-27) in their argument, I suspect that there is a different focus in these texts. In Gal 4:21—5:1, Paul's burden

---

1. See, e.g., Wolter, "Das Israelproblem." A more comprehensive analysis could look at the different ways Israel's story is integrated into Paul's arguments in Galatians and Romans (see, e.g., Longenecker, "Sharing in Their Spiritual Blessings?," and Hooker's response, "'Heirs of Abraham'").

2. Donaldson, *Paul and the Gentiles*, 187-97; Donaldson changed his position from what he proposed in 1986 in "'Curse of the Law.'"

is to highlight that the reality of restoration has been inaugurated, which necessitates a new position on the Mosaic Law and a new social practice. In Rom 9–11, Paul spells out what he only hinted at in Gal 6:16; he expects the *process* of restoration to move on to its fulfillment, in which all Israel—the "Israel of God"—would be included, as the promise of God in the restorative mercy offered in Christ finally finds the response of faith not only from the remnant but also from the rest. I suggest that Isa 66 (especially vv. 18–20) could provide us with a clue for how Paul both works from a sense of an inaugurated restoration and still expects an ongoing movement towards its full completion.

This dynamic movement seems to be present also in the flow of thought in Romans 15. Paul explains that Christ came to serve the "circumcised" to confirm the promises made to the fathers (15:8) that has resulted in the manifestation of divine mercy (15:9)—inauguration of the restoration reality—that has incorporated also the Gentiles into the joint worship of the God of Israel (15:6, 9). The catena of Scripture Paul cites (15:9–12), with the voice of Isaiah singled out (15:12), witnesses to this reality. Paul brackets his presentation with the notion of hope and encouragement of Scripture (15:4, 13), which speaks of his confidence that God will take to completion what he has promised.

A more complete inquiry into Paul's theological vision and logic could adopt a canonical reading of Paul that incorporates all the letters attributed to Paul in the Christian canon and also Luke's portrayal of Paul in the book of Acts to evaluate whether the central discoveries of this research find resonance or need modification. I suspect that both would be true in a fuller picture of Paul's theology and mission. Yet I am confident that the central claim of this book would remain valid. I maintain that the coherent core in Paul's theology is his conviction that the divine promise to Abraham, as understood by its re-appropriation in the vision of Isaiah, is the Creator God's commitment to humanity and the whole cosmos that blessing and restoration will have the final word over curse and alienation, and that the promise is designed to generate the "children of laughter"—a regenerated people of God from both Jews and Gentiles who depend on Christ and the Spirit in their life together as the re-created humanity.

Appendix

I BRIEFLY DEAL HERE with one major text-critical issue to establish the text of Gal 4:21—5:1. This has to do with the first line in 4:25 that stands in the NA28 thus: *to de hagar sina oros estin en tē arabia*. The text critical question concerns the three words at the beginning of the sentence (*de hagar sina*) where the manuscripts are heavily divided (see the apparatus in NA28). Carlson's recent work has helpfully reviewed and evaluated the different options based on external evidence, transcriptional probabilities, and intrinsic features of the text.[1] He suggests that out of the five possibilities, two text forms are best supported in the manuscript evidence: 1) *to de hagar sina oros* . . . and 2) *to gar sina oros* . . . with the latter held stronger by Carlson (most widely spread in early witnesses).[2] But since the external evidence and transcriptional probabilities are inconclusive in determining the original text form, the intrinsic features of the text become decisive.[3]

As Carlson evaluates the intrinsic features, he concludes that the whole note in 4:25a is "semantically superfluous" and structurally "sticks out like a sore thumb," and hence is most likely originally an early marginal note (possibly even Paul's own) that was later interpolated as part of the text.[4] The problem with this conclusion is that it follows from Carlson's

---

1. Carlson, "For Sinai," 80-101. Also Carlson, *Text of Galatians*, 163-69. See also earlier discussion in Burton, *Galatians*, 259-61.

2. Carlson, *Text of Galatians*, 163; Carlson, "For Sinai," 99. The second option is also taken by Lightfoot, *Galatians*, 192-93; and Wright, "Paul, Arabia and Elijah (Galatians 1.17)," 155n12. The difficulty of basing the decision on the manuscript evidence and transcriptional probabilities is reflected in the UBS rating C. The evidence that supports the first option is: A, B, D, 0278. 323. 365. 1175. 2464, sy^{hmg}, bo^{pt}; and the support for the second option is: ℵ, C, F, G, 1241. 1739, lat, (sa; Ambst).

3. Carlson, "For Sinai," 90-95.

4. Carlson, "For Sinai," 95-101. Cf. Burton: "The difficulty of interpretation, especially the absence of definite evidence of any usage that would account for the identification of Hagar and Sinai, either as names or places suggest the possibility of an interpolation at this point" (*Galatians*, 260).

own sense of it being semantically superfluous,[5] and his unconvincing structural analysis.[6] I agree that the precise meaning and role of the note in 4:25a is difficult, but I suspect that the sense of it being superfluous stems from the nature of the text that "abuses" normal use of language, and makes contradictory statements that invite an engagement with the "deeper meaning" of the scriptural matrix that Paul appeals to.[7] Hence, e.g., the geographical discrepancy of locating Sinai first in Arabia and then associating it with the "present Jerusalem" is not about an argument based on concrete locations,[8] but about a deeper level of meaning in the connection between Hagar and Law that is reflected in the "present Jerusalem." Also, in contrast to Carlson, my structural analysis in chapter 2 gives support for the note belonging intrinsically to the text, and hence I have not relegated it to the margins. Thus, 4:25a is in my evaluation part of the text that needs to be included in the analysis of the passage, and I discuss it in chapter 6 with regard to the two strongest text forms.

5. Carlson, "For Sinai," 95–96.
6. Carlson, "For Sinai," 96–97.
7. Davis argues that the center section (4:24–28) of 4:21—5:1 is full of allegorical devices that "abuse" normal use of language, and introduce contradictory statements that are aimed to "startle" ("Allegorically Speaking," 164–71). She concludes: "I suggest that the puzzling nature of these allegorical assertions leads the reader to the Hebrew Scriptures to find deeper aspects of understanding such key words and concepts as freedom, slavery, the Law, heritage, and the promised inheritance" (171).
8. See Carlson, "For Sinai," 88–89.

Bibliography

Ackroyd, Peter R. *Exile and Restoration: A Study of Hebrew Thought of the Sixth Century B.C.* The Old Testament Library. Philadelphia: Westminster, 1968.
Alexander, T. Desmond. "Further Observations on the Term 'Seed' in Genesis." *Tyndale Bulletin* 48 (1997) 363–67.
Alter, Robert, *The Art of Biblical Narrative*. New York: Basic Books, 1981.
———, ed. *Genesis: Translation and Commentary*. New York: Norton, 1996.
———. "Sodom as Nexus: The Web of Design in Biblical Narrative." In *The Book and the Text: The Bible and Literary Theory*, edited by Regina M. Schwartz, 146–60. Cambridge, MA: Basil Blackwell, 1990.
Aune, David Edward. *The New Testament in Its Literary Environment*. Philadelphia: Westminster John Knox, 1987.
Bachmann, Michael. *Anti-Judaism in Galatians?: Exegetical Studies on a Polemical Letter and on Paul's Theology*. Grand Rapids: Eerdmans, 2008.
Baer, David A. "'It's All about Us!' Nationalistic Exegesis in the Greek Isaiah (Chapters 1–12)." In *"As Those Who Are Taught": The Interpretation of Isaiah from the LXX to the SBL*, edited by Claire Mathews McGinnis and Patricia K. Tull, 29–48. SBLSymS 27. Atlanta: SBL, 2006.
Barclay, John M. G. *Jews in the Mediterranean Diaspora: From Alexander to Trajan (323 BCE–117 CE)*. Edinburgh: T. & T. Clark, 1996.
———. *Obeying the Truth: A Study of Paul's Ethics in Galatians*. Studies of the New Testament and Its World. Edinburgh: T. & T. Clark, 1988.
———. *Paul and the Gift*. Grand Rapids: Eerdmans, 2015.
———. "Paul's Story: Theology as Testimony." In *Narrative Dynamics in Paul: A Critical Assessment*, edited by Bruce W. Longenecker, 133–56. Louisville: Westminster John Knox, 2002.
Barr, James. *Old and New in Interpretation: A Study of the Two Testaments*. Currie lectures 1964. London: SCM, 1966.
Barrett, Charles Kingsley. "The Allegory of Abraham, Sarah, and Hagar in the Argument of Galatians." In *Rechtfertigung: Festschrift für Ernst Käsemann zum 70. Geburtstag*, edited by Johannes Friedrich et al., 1–16. Tübingen: Mohr Siebeck, 1976.
Beale, G. K. "Peace and Mercy Upon the Israel of God: The Old Testament Background of Galatians 6,16b." *Biblica* 80 (1999) 204–23.
Berek, Peter. "Interpretation, Allegory, and Allegoresis." *College English* 40 (1978) 117–32.

Berlin, Adele. *Poetics and Interpretation of Biblical Narrative*. Bible and Literature Series 9. Sheffield: Almond, 1983.
Betz, Hans Dieter. *Galatians: A Commentary on Paul's Letter to the Churches in Galatia*. Hermeneia. Philadelphia: Fortress, 1979.
Bird, Michael F., and Preston M. Sprinkle, eds. *The Faith of Jesus Christ: Exegetical, Biblical, and Theological Studies*. Peabody, MA: Baker Academic, 2010.
Blass, Friedrich, and Albert Debrunner. *A Greek Grammar of the New Testament and Other Early Christian Literature*. Translated and revised by Robert W. Funk. Chicago: University of Chicago Press, 1961.
Blenkinsopp, Joseph. *Creation, Un-Creation, Re-Creation: A Discursive Commentary on Genesis 1–11*. London: T. & T. Clark, 2011.
———. *Isaiah 1–39: A New Translation with Introduction and Commentary*. AB 19. New York: Doubleday, 2000.
———. *Isaiah 40–55: A New Translation with Introduction and Commentary*. AB 19A. New York: Doubleday, 2000.
———. *Isaiah 56–66: A New Translation with Introduction and Commentary*. AB 19B. New York: Doubleday, 2003.
———. *Opening the Sealed Book: Interpretations of the Book of Isaiah in Late Antiquity*. Grand Rapids: Eerdmans, 2006.
Bligh, John. *Galatians: A Discussion of St. Paul's Epistle*. Householder Commentaries 1. London: St Paul, 1969.
de Boer, Martinus C. *Galatians: A Commentary*. New Testament Library. Louisville: Westminster John Knox, 2011.
———. "Paul's Quotation of Isaiah 54.1 in Galatians 4.27." *NTS* 50 (2004) 370–89.
Borgen, Peder. "Philo of Alexandria as Exegete." In *A History of Biblical Interpretation*, Vol. 1: *The Ancient Period*, edited by Alan J Hauser and Duane Frederick Watson, 114–43. Grand Rapids: Eerdmans, 2003.
———. "Some Hebrew and Pagan Features in Philo's and Paul's Interpretation of Hagar and Ishmael." In *The New Testament and Hellenistic Judaism*, edited by Peder Borgen and Søren Giversen, 151–64. Aarhus: Aarhus University Press, 1995.
Boyarin, Daniel. *A Radical Jew: Paul and the Politics of Identity*. Contraversions 1. Berkeley: University of California Press, 1994.
———. "The Song of Songs: Lock or Key? Intertextuality, Allegory and Midrash." In *The Book and the Text: The Bible and Literary Theory*, edited by Regina M. Schwartz, 214–30. Cambridge, MA: Basil Blackwell, 1990.
Brawley, Robert L. "Contextuality, Intertextuality, and the Hendiadic Relationship of Promise and Law in Galatians." *ZNW* 93 (2002) 99–119.
Brisson, Luc. *How Philosophers Saved Myths: Allegorical Interpretation and Classical Mythology*. Chicago: University of Chicago Press, 2004.
Brooke, George J. "On Isaiah in Qumran." In *"As Those Who Are Taught": The Interpretation of Isaiah from the LXX to the SBL*, edited by Claire Mathews McGinnis and Patricia K. Tull, 69–85. SBLSymS 27. Atlanta: SBL, 2006.
Bruce, F. F. *The Epistle of Paul to the Galatians: A Commentary on the Greek Text*. NIGTC. Grand Rapids: Paternoster and Eerdmans, 1982.
Bruckner, James K. *Implied Law in the Abraham Narrative: A Literary and Theological Analysis*. JSOTSup 335. Sheffield: Sheffield Academic, 2001.
Brueggemann, Walter. *Isaiah*. Westminster Bible Companion. Louisville: Westminster John Knox, 1998.

Bruns, Gerald L. "The Hermeneutics of Midrash." In *The Book and the Text: The Bible and Literary Theory*, edited by Regina M. Schwartz, 189–213. Cambridge, MA: Basil Blackwell, 1990.

———. "Midrash and Allegory: The Beginnings of Scriptural Interpretation." In *The Literary Guide to the Bible*, edited by Robert Alter and Frank Kermode, 625–46. London: Fontana, 1989.

Burton, Ernest De Witt. *A Critical and Exegetical Commentary on the Epistle to the Galatians*. ICC. Edinburgh: T. & T. Clark, 1921.

Byrne, Brendan SJ. "Jerusalems Above and Below: A Critique of J. L. Martyn's Interpretation of the Hagar-Sarah Allegory in Gal 4.21–5.1." *NTS* 60 (2014) 215–31.

Callaway, Mary. *Sing, O Barren One: A Study in Comparative Midrash*. SBLDS 91. Atlanta: Scholars, 1986.

Carlson, Stephen C. "'For Sinai Is a Mountain in Arabia': A Note on the Text of Galatians 4,25." *ZNW* 105 (2014) 80–101.

———. *The Text of Galatians and Its History*. WUNT 2. 385. Tübingen: Mohr Siebeck, 2015.

Cassuto, Umberto. *A Commentary on the Book of Genesis*. Jerusalem: Magnes, the Hebrew University, 1964.

Charlesworth, James H., ed. *The Old Testament Pseudepigrapha: Volumes 1 and 2*. New Haven, CT: Yale University Press, 1983, 1985.

Chester, Stephen J. *Conversion at Corinth: Perspectives on Conversion in Paul's Theology and the Corinthian Church*. London: T. & T. Clark, 2005.

Childs, Brevard S. *The Church's Guide for Reading Paul: The Canonical Shaping of the Pauline Corpus*. Grand Rapids: Eerdmans, 2008.

———. *Introduction to the Old Testament as Scripture*. London: SCM, 1979.

———. *Isaiah: A Commentary*. Louisville: Westminster John Knox, 2001.

Ciampa, Roy E. *The Presence and Function of Scripture in Galatians 1 and 2*. WUNT 102. Tübingen: Mohr Siebeck, 1998.

Copeland, Rita, and Struck, Peter T. *The Cambridge Companion to Allegory*. Cambridge Companions to Literature. Cambridge: Cambridge University Press, 2010.

Cosgrove, Charles H. "The Law Has given Sarah No Children (Gal 4:21–30)." *Novum Testamentum* 29 (1987) 219–35.

Davies, W. D. *Paul and Rabbinic Judaism: Some Rabbinic Elements in Pauline Theology*. London: SPCK, 1948.

Davis, Anne. "Allegorically Speaking in Galatians 4:21–5:1." *BBR* 14 (2004) 161–74.

Dawson, John David. *Allegorical Readers and Cultural Revision in Ancient Alexandria*. Berkeley: University of California Press, 1992.

———. *Christian Figural Reading and the Fashioning of Identity*. Berkeley: University of California Press, 2002.

Di Mattei, Steven. "Paul's Allegory of the Two Covenants (Gal 4.21–31) in Light of First-Century Hellenistic Rhetoric and Jewish Hermeneutics." *NTS* 52 (2006) 102–22.

Dodd, C. H. *According to the Scriptures: The Sub-Structure of New Testament Theology*. London: Nisbet, 1952.

Donaldson, Terence L. "The 'Curse of the Law' and the Inclusion of the Gentiles: Galatians 3. 13–14." *NTS* 32 (1986) 94–112.

———. *Paul and the Gentiles: Remapping the Apostle's Convictional World*. Minneapolis: Fortress, 1997.

———. "Paul within Judaism: A Critical Evaluation from a 'New Perspective' Perspective." In *Paul Within Judaism: Restoring the First-Century Context to the Apostle*, edited by Mark D. Nanos and Magnus Zetterholm, 277–301. Minneapolis: Fortress, 2015.

Dumbrell, William J. *The End of the Beginning: Revelation 21–22 and the Old Testament*. Grand Rapids: Baker Book House, 1985.

Dunn, James D. G. *A Commentary on the Epistle to the Galatians*. Black's New Testament Commentaries. London: A. & C. Black, 1993.

———. *Jesus, Paul, and the Gospels*. Grand Rapids: Eerdmans, 2011.

———. "The New Perspective on Paul." *Bulletin John Rylands University Library. Manchester* 65 (1983) 95–122.

———. *The Theology of Paul's Letter to the Galatians*. New Testament Theology. Cambridge: Cambridge University Press, 1993.

Eastman, Susan Grove. "Israel and the Mercy of God: A Re-Reading of Galatians 6.16 and Romans 9–11." *NTS* 56 (2010) 367–95.

———. *Recovering Paul's Mother Tongue: Language and Theology in Galatians*. Grand Rapids: Eerdmans, 2007.

Eisenbaum, Pamela. *Paul Was Not a Christian: The Original Message of a Misunderstood Apostle*. New York: HarperOne, 2010.

Ekblad, Eugene Robert. *Isaiah's Servant Poems According to the Septuagint: An Exegetical and Theological Study*. Leuven: Peeters, 1999.

Emerson, Matthew Y. "Arbitrary Allegory, Typical Typology, or Intertextual Interpretation? Paul's Use of the Pentateuch in Galatians 4:21–31." *BTB* 43 (2013) 14–22.

Engberg-Pedersen, Troels. *Paul and the Stoics*. Edinburgh: T. & T. Clark, 2000.

Evans, Craig A. "Listening for Echoes of Interpreted Scripture." In *Paul and the Scriptures of Israel*, edited by Craig A. Evans and James A. Sanders, 47–51. JSNTSup 83. Sheffield: JSOT, 1993.

Fishbane, Michael A. *Biblical Interpretation in Ancient Israel*. Oxford: Clarendon, 1985.

Foster, Paul. "Echoes without Resonance: Critiquing Certain Aspects of Recent Scholarly Trends in the Study of the Jewish Scriptures in the New Testament." *JSNT* 38 (2015) 96–111.

Fowl, Stephen E. "Who Can Read Abraham's Story? Allegory and Interpretive Power in Galatians." *JSNT* 55 (1994) 77–95.

Fredriksen, Paula. "Judaism, the Circumcision of Gentiles, and Apocalyptic Hope: Another Look at Galatians 1 and 2." *JTS* 42 (1991) 532–64.

———. "Judaizing the Nations: The Ritual Demands of Paul's Gospel." *NTS* 56 (2010) 232–52.

Gaventa, Beverly Roberts. "The Maternity of Paul: An Exegetical Study of Galatians 4:19." In *The Conversation Continues: Studies in Paul & John, In Honor of J. Louis Martyn*, edited by Robert T. Fortna and Beverly Roberts Gaventa, 189–201. Nashville: Abingdon, 1990.

———. *Our Mother Saint Paul*. Louisville: Westminster John Knox, 2007.

Geljon, Albert C., and David T. Runia. *Philo of Alexandria, On Cultivation: Introduction, Translation and Commentary*. PACS 4. Leiden: Brill, 2013.

Gignilliat, Mark S. "Paul, Allegory, and the Plain Sense of Scripture: Galatians 4:21–31." *JTI* 2 (2008) 135–46.

———. "Singing Women and Promised Seed: Isaiah 54:1-3 as Christian Scripture." In *Searching the Scriptures: Studies in Context and Intertextuality*, edited by Craig A. Evans and Jeremiah J. Johnston, 3-15. LNTS 543. London: Bloomsbury T. & T. Clark, 2015.

Goldingay, John. *The Message of Isaiah 40-55: A Literary-Theological Commentary*. London: T. & T. Clark, 2005.

Greek New Testament. Nestle-Aland (NA), *Novum Testamentum Graece*. 28th ed. Stuttgart: Deutsche Bibelgesellschaft, 2012.

Grüneberg, Keith Nigel. *Abraham, Blessing and the Nations: A Philological and Exegetical Study of Genesis 12:3 in Its Narrative Context*. BZAW 332. Berlin: Walter de Gruyter, 2003.

Hansen, G. Walter. *Abraham in Galatians: Epistolary and Rhetorical Contexts*. JSNTSup 29. Sheffield: JSOT, 1989.

Harmon, Matthew S. *She Must and Shall Go Free: Paul's Isaianic Gospel in Galatians*. BZNW. Berlin: de Gruyter, 2010.

Hays, Richard B. *The Conversion of the Imagination: Paul as Interpreter of Israel's Scripture*. Grand Rapids: Eerdmans, 2005.

———. *Echoes of Scripture in the Letters of Paul*. New Haven, CT: Yale University Press, 1989.

———. *The Faith of Jesus Christ: The Narrative Substructure of Galatians 3:1-4:11*. 2nd ed. The Biblical Resource Series. Grand Rapids: Eerdmans, 2002.

Hebrew Bible. *Biblia Hebraica Stuttgartensia* (BHS). Stuttgart: Deutsche Bibelgesellschaft, 1967-1977.

Hengel, Martin. *The Septuagint as Christian Scripture: Its Prehistory and the Problem of Its Canon*. Translated by Mark E. Biddle. Old Testament Studies. Edinburgh: T. & T. Clark, 2002.

Heskett, Randall. *Messianism within the Scriptural Scroll of Isaiah*. The Library of Hebrew Bible/Old Testament Studies 456. New York: T. & T. Clark, 2007.

Hooker, Morna D. "'Heirs of Abraham': The Gentiles' Role in Israel's Story—A Response to Bruce W. Longenecker." In *Narrative Dynamics in Paul: A Critical Assessment*, edited by Bruce W. Longenecker, 85-96. Louisville: Westminster John Knox, 2002.

———. *Jesus and the Servant: The Influence of the Servant Concept of Deutero-Isaiah in the New Testament*. London: SPCK, 1959.

Horbury, William. "Land, Sanctuary and Worship." In *Early Christian Thought in Its Jewish Context*, edited by John M. G. Barclay and John Sweet, 207-24. Cambridge: Cambridge University Press, 1996.

———. *Messianism among Jews and Christians: Twelve Biblical and Historical Studies*. London: T. & T. Clark, 2003.

Horn, Friedrich Wilhelm, ed. *Paulus Handbuch*. Tübingen: Mohr Siebeck, 2013.

Huizenga, Leroy A. "The Old Testament in the New, Intertextuality and Allegory." *JSNT* 38 (2015) 17-35.

Jobes, Karen H. "Jerusalem, Our Mother: Metalepsis and Intertextuality in Galatians 4:21-31." *WTJ* 55 (1993) 299-320.

Johnson Hodge, Caroline. *If Sons, Then Heirs: A Study of Kinship and Ethnicity in the Letters of Paul*. New York: Oxford University Press, 2007.

Kahl, Brigitte. *Galatians Re-Imagined: Reading with the Eyes of the Vanquished*. Minneapolis: Fortress, 2010.

Kaminsky, Joel S. "Humor and the Theology of Hope: Isaac as a Humorous Figure." *Interpretation* 54 (2000) 363–75.

Kawashima, Robert S. "Literary Analysis." In *The Book of Genesis: Composition, Reception, and Interpretation*, edited by Craig A. Evans et al., 83–104. VTSup 152. Leiden: Brill, 2012.

Koch, Dietrich-Alex. *Die Schrift als Zeuge des Evangeliums: Untersuchungen zur Verwendung und zum Verständnis der Schrift bei Paulus*. BHT 69. Tübingen: Mohr Siebeck, 1986.

———. "The Quotations of Isaiah 8,14 and 28,16 in Romans 9,33 and 1Peter 2,6.8 as Test Case for Old Testament Quotations in the New Testament." *ZNW* 101 (2010) 223–40.

Koole, Jan Leunis. *Isaiah III, Vol. 1 / Isaiah 40–48*. Historical Commentary on the Old Testament. Kampen: Kok Pharos, 1997.

———. *Isaiah III, Vol. 2 / Isaiah 49–55*. Historical Commentary on the Old Testament. Leuven: Peeters, 1998.

———. *Isaiah III, Vol. 3 / Isaiah 56–66*. Historical Commentary on the Old Testament. Leuven: Peeters, 2001.

Laato, Antti. *"About Zion I Will Not Be Silent": The Book of Isaiah as an Ideological Unity*. Coniectanea Biblica 44. Stockholm: Almqvist & Wiksell International, 1998.

Lee, Chee-Chiew. *The Blessing of Abraham, the Spirit, and Justification in Galatians: Their Relationship and Significance for Understanding Paul's Theology*. Eugene, OR: Pickwick, 2013.

———. "גוים in Genesis 35:11 and the Abrahamic Promise of Blessings for the Nations." *JETS* 52 (2009) 467–82.

Levenson, Jon Douglas. *The Death and Resurrection of the Beloved Son: The Transformation of Child Sacrifice in Judaism and Christianity*. New Haven, CT: Yale University Press, 1993.

———. *Inheriting Abraham: The Legacy of the Patriarch in Judaism, Christianity, and Islam*. Library of Jewish Ideas. Princeton: Princeton University Press, 2012.

———. *Resurrection and the Restoration of Israel: The Ultimate Victory of the God of Life*. New Haven, CT: Yale University Press, 2006.

———. *Sinai and Zion: An Entry into the Jewish Bible*. New Voices in Biblical Studies. Minneapolis: Winston, 1985.

Lightfoot, Joseph Barber. *Saint Paul's Epistle to the Galatians: A Revised Text*. 10th ed. Epistles of St. Paul 2. London: Macmillan, 1890.

Lincoln, Andrew T. *Paradise Now and Not Yet: Studies in the Role of the Heavenly Dimension in Paul's Thought with Special Reference to His Eschatology*. SNTSMS 43. Cambridge: Cambridge University Press, 1981.

Longenecker, Bruce W. "Sharing in Their Spiritual Blessings?: The Stories of Israel in Galatians and Romans." In *Narrative Dynamics in Paul: A Critical Assessment*, edited by Bruce W. Longenecker, 58–84. Louisville: Westminster John Knox, 2002.

Longenecker, Richard N. *Biblical Exegesis in the Apostolic Period*. 2nd ed. Grand Rapids: Eerdmans, 1999.

———. *Galatians*. WBC 41. Dallas: Word Books, 1990.

Luther, Martin. *A Commentary on St. Paul's Epistle to the Galatians*. London: James Clarke, 1953.

Ma, Wonsuk. *Until the Spirit Comes: The Spirit of God in the Book of Isaiah*. JSOTSup 271. Sheffield: Sheffield Academic, 1999.

Mannermaa, Tuomo, and Stjerna, Kirsi Irmeli. *Christ Present In Faith: Luther's View Of Justification*. Minneapolis: Fortress, 2005.
Martyn, J. Louis. "Apocalyptic Antinomies in Paul's Letter to the Galatians." *NTS* 31 (1985) 410–24.
———. "The Apocalyptic Gospel in Galatians." *Interpretation* 54 (2000) 246–66.
———. *Galatians*. AB 33A. New York: Doubleday, 1997.
———. "A Tale of Two Churches." In *Theological Issues in the Letters of Paul*, 25–36. Studies of the New Testament and its World. Edinburgh: T. & T. Clark, 1997.
———. *Theological Issues in the Letters of Paul*. Studies of the New Testament and its World. Nashville: Abingdon, 1997.
McNamara, Martin. *Targum and New Testament: Collected Essays*. Tübingen: Mohr Siebeck, 2011.
Moberly, R. W. L. *The Bible, Theology, and Faith: A Study of Abraham and Jesus*. Cambridge Studies in Christian Doctrine 5. Cambridge: Cambridge University Press, 2000.
———. "The Earliest Commentary on the Akedah." *VT* 38 (1988) 302–23.
Moo, Douglas J. *Galatians*. Baker Exegetical Commentary on the New Testament. Grand Rapids: Baker Academic, 2013.
Morales, Rodrigo Jose. *The Spirit and the Restoration of Israel: New Exodus and New Creation Motifs in Galatians*. WUNT 2.282. Tübingen: Mohr Siebeck, 2010.
Mußner, Franz. *Der Galaterbrief*. 5th ed. HTKNT. Freiburg: Herder, 1988.
Nanos, Mark D. *The Irony of Galatians: Paul's Letter in First-Century Context*. Minneapolis: Fortress, 2002.
Nanos, Mark D., and Zetterholm, Magnus, eds. *Paul Within Judaism: Restoring the First-Century Context to the Apostle*. Minneapolis: Fortress, 2015.
Nickelsburg, George W. E. "Philo among Greeks, Jews and Christians." In *Philo und das Neue Testament: wechselseitige Wahrnehmungen ; I. Internationales Symposium zum Corpus Judaeo-Hellenisticum, 1.–4. Mai 2003, Eisenach/Jena*, edited by Roland Deines and Karl-Wilhelm Niebuhr, 53–72. WUNT 172. Tübingen: Mohr Siebeck, 2004.
Noort, Ed. "Abraham and the Nations." In *Abraham, the Nations, and the Hagarites: Jewish, Christian, and Islamic Perspectives on Kinship with Abraham*, edited by Martin Goodman et al., 3–31. Leiden: Brill, 2010.
———. "Created in the Image of the Son: Ishmael and Hagar." In *Abraham, the Nations, and the Hagarites: Jewish, Christian, and Islamic Perspectives on Kinship with Abraham*, edited by Martin Goodman et al., 33–44. Leiden: Brill, 2010.
Nordgaard Svendsen, Stefan. *Allegory Transformed: The Appropriation of Philonic Hermeneutics in the Letter to the Hebrews*. WUNT 2.269. Tübingen: Mohr Siebeck, 2009.
Novenson, Matthew V. "Paul's Former Occupation in *Ioudaismos*." In *Galatians and Christian Theology: Justification, the Gospel, and Ethics in Paul's Letter*, edited by Mark W. Elliott et al., 24–39. Grand Rapids: Baker Academic, 2014.
Oakes, Peter. *Galatians*. Paideia: Commentaries on the New Testament. Grand Rapids: Baker Academic, 2015.
O'Donovan, Oliver. "Flesh and Spirit." In *Galatians and Christian Theology: Justification, the Gospel, and Ethics in Paul's Letter*, edited by Mark W. Elliott et al., 271–84. Grand Rapids: Baker Academic, 2014.

Oepke, Albrecht. *Der Brief des Paulus an die Galater.* Edited by Joachim Rohde. 4th ed. THKNT. Berlin: Evangelische Verlagsanstalt, 1979.

Ottley, Richard Rusden, ed. *The Book of Isaiah According to the Septuagint.* Vol. 2. Cambridge: Cambridge University Press, 1906.

Philo. *The Works of Philo, Completed and Unabridged.* New Updated Edition. Translated by C. D. Yonge. Peabody, MA: Hendrickson, 1993.

Plumer, Eric Antone. *Augustine's Commentary on Galatians.* Oxford Early Christian Studies. Oxford: Oxford University Press, 2003.

Popović, Mladen. "Abraham and the Nations in the Dead Sea Scrolls: Exclusivism and Inclusivism in the Texts from Qumran and the Absence of a Reception History for Gen 12:3." In *Abraham, the Nations, and the Hagarites: Jewish, Christian, and Islamic Perspectives on Kinship with Abraham*, edited by Martin Goodman et al., 77–103. Leiden: Brill, 2010.

Porton, Gary G. "Rabbinic Midrash." In *A History of Biblical Interpretation.* Vol. 1: *The Ancient Period*, edited by Alan J Hauser and Duane Frederick Watson, 198–224. Grand Rapids: Eerdmans, 2003.

Punt, Jeremy. "Revealing Rereading. Part 1: Pauline Allegory in Galatians 4:21–5:1." *Neotestamentica* 40 (2006) 87–100.

———. "Revealing Rereading. Part 2: Paul and the Wives of the Father of Faith in Galatians 4:21–5:1." *Neotestamentica* 40 (2006) 101–18.

Rabens, Volker. "'Indicative and Imperative' as the Substructure of Paul's Theology-and-Ethics in Galatians?: A Discussion of Divine and Human Agency in Paul." In *Galatians and Christian Theology: Justification, the Gospel, and Ethics in Paul's Letter*, edited by Mark W. Elliott et al., 285–305. Grand Rapids: Baker Academic, 2014.

Räisänen, Heikki. "The 'Law' of Faith and the Spirit." In *Jesus, Paul and Torah: Collected Essays*, 69–94. London: Bloomsbury Academic, 2015.

———. "Paul's Word-Play on 'νόμος': a Linguistic Study." In *Jesus, Paul and Torah: Collected Essays*, 48–68. London: Bloomsbury Academic, 2015.

Riesner, Rainer. *Die Frühzeit des Apostels Paulus: Studien zur Chronologie, Missionsstrategie und Theologie.* WUNT 71. Tübingen: Mohr Siebeck, 1994.

———. "Pauline Chronology." In *Blackwell Companion to Paul*, edited by Stephen Westerholm, 9–29. Chichester: Wiley-Blackwell, 2011.

Riffaterre, Michael. "Compulsory Reader Response: The Intertextual Drive." In *Intertextuality: Theories and Practices*, edited by Michael Worton and Judith Still, 56–78. Manchester: Manchester University Press, 1990.

Rohde, Joachim. *Der Brief des Paulus an die Galater.* THKNT 9. Berlin: Evangelische Verlagsanstalt, 1989.

Sanders, E. P. *Paul and Palestinian Judaism: A Comparison of Patterns of Religion.* London: SCM, 1977.

Sandmel, Samuel. *Philo of Alexandria: An Introduction.* New York: Oxford University Press, 1979.

Sawyer, John F. A. "Daughter of Zion and Servant of the Lord in Isaiah: A Comparison." *JSOT* 44 (1989) 89–107.

———. *The Fifth Gospel: Isaiah in the History of Christianity.* Cambridge: Cambridge University Press, 1996.

Schlier, Heinrich. *Der Brief an die Galater*. 12th ed. Kritisch-Exegetischer Kommentar über das Neue Testament Begründet von Heinrich August Wilhelm Meyer 7. Göttingen: Vandenhoeck & Ruprecht, 1962.

Schliesser, Benjamin. "'Christ-Faith' as an Eschatological Event (Galatians 3.23-26): A 'Third View' on Πίστις Χριστοῦ." *JSNT* 38 (2016) 277-300.

Schultz, Richard L. "Nationalism and Universalism in Isaiah." In *Interpreting Isaiah: Issues and Approaches*, edited by David G. Firth and H. G. M. Williamson, 122-44. Downers Grove, IL: IVP Academic, 2009.

Scott, James M. "'For as Many as Are of Works of the Law Are under a Curse' (Galatians 3.10)." In *Paul and the Scriptures of Israel*, edited by Craig A. Evans and James A. Sanders, 187-221. JSNTSup 83. Sheffield: JSOT, 1993.

———. *Paul and the Nations: The Old Testament and Jewish Background of Paul's Mission to the Nations with Special Reference to the Destination of Galatians*. WUNT 84. Tübingen: Mohr Siebeck, 1995.

Seeligmann, Isaac Leo. *The Septuagint Version of Isaiah: A Discussion of Its Problems*. Mededelingen en verhandelingen van het Vooraziatisch-Egyptisch Genootschap "Ex Oriente Lux" 9. Leiden: Brill, 1948.

Seitz, Christopher R. *Zion's Final Destiny: The Development of the Book of Isaiah: A Reassessment of Isaiah 36-39*. Minneapolis: Fortress, 1991.

Sellin, Gerhard. *Allegorie-Metapher-Mythos-Schrift: Beiträge zur Religiösen Sprache im Neuen Testament und in seiner Umwelt*. NTOA 90. Göttingen: Vandenhoeck & Ruprecht, 2011.

———. "Hagar und Sara: Religionsgeschichtliche Hintergründe der Schriftallegorese Gal 4, 21-31." In *Das Urchristentum in seiner literarischen Geschichte: Festschrift für Jürgen Becker zum 65. Geburtstag*, edited by Ulrich Mell and Ulrich B. Müller, 59-84. BZNW 100. Berlin: de Gruyter, 1999.

Septuagint (LXX). *Editio altera (Rahlfs)*. 2nd rev. ed. Edited by Alfred Rahlfs and Robert Hahnart. Göttingen: Vandenhoeck & Ruprecht, 2007.

———. *Vetus Testamentum Graecum Auctoritate Academiae Scientiarum Göttingensis editum*. Göttingen: Vandenhoeck & Ruprecht, 1931-. Genesis, edited by John William Wevers, 1974. Isaiah, edited by Joseph Ziegler, 1983.

Shum, Shiu-Lun. *Paul's Use of Isaiah in Romans*. WUNT 2.156. Tübingen: Mohr Siebeck, 2002.

Standhartinger, Angela. "Zur Freiheit ... Befreit?" *EvT* 62 (2002) 288-303.

Stanley, Christopher D. *Arguing with Scripture: The Rhetoric of Quotations in the Letters of Paul*. New York: T. & T. Clark International, 2004.

———. *Paul and the Language of Scripture: Citation Technique in the Pauline Epistles and Contemporary Literature*. SNTSMS 74. Cambridge: Cambridge University Press, 1992.

Starling, David Ian. *Not My People: Gentiles As Exiles in Pauline Hermeneutics*. Berlin: de Gruyter, 2011.

Stendahl, Krister. "The Apostle Paul and the Introspective Conscience of the West." In *Paul Among Jews and Gentiles and Other Essays*, 78-96. Philadelphia: Fortress, 1976.

———. "Paul Among Jews and Gentiles." In *Paul Among Jews and Gentiles and Other Essays*, 1-77. Philadelphia: Fortress, 1976.

Sterling, Gregory E. "The Place of Philo of Alexandria in the Study of Christian Origins." In *Philo und das Neue Testament: wechselseitige Wahrnehmungen: I.*

Internationales Symposium zum Corpus Judaeo-Hellenisticum, 1.-4. Mai 2003, Eisenach/Jena, edited by Roland Deines and Karl-Wilhelm Niebuhr, 21–52. WUNT 172. Tübingen: Mohr Siebeck, 2004.

Syrén, Roger. *The Forsaken First-Born: A Study of a Recurrent Motif in the Patriarchal Narratives.* JSOTSup 133. Sheffield: JSOT, 1993.

Thiessen, Matthew. *Contesting Conversion: Genealogy, Circumcision, and Identity in Ancient Judaism and Christianity.* New York: Oxford University Press, 2011.

———. *Paul and the Gentile Problem.* New York: Oxford University Press, 2016.

———. "The Text of Genesis 17:14." *JBL* 128 (2009) 625–42.

Thraede, Klaus. *Grundzuge griechisch-römischer Brieftopik.* München: C. H. Beck, 1970.

Thurén, Lauri, *Derhetorizing Paul: A Dynamic Perspective on Pauline Theology and the Law.* WUNT 124. Tübingen: Mohr Siebeck, 2000.

Trible, Phyllis. "Ominous Beginnings for a Promise of Blessing." In *Hagar, Sarah, and Their Children: Jewish, Christian, and Muslim Perspectives*, edited by Phyllis Trible and Letty M. Russell, 33–69. Louisville: Westminster John Knox, 2006.

Uhlig, Torsten. "Too Hard to Understand? The Motif of Hardening in Isaiah." In *Interpreting Isaiah: Issues and Approaches*, edited by David G. Firth and H. G. M. Williamson, 62–83. Downers Grove, IL: IVP Academic, 2009.

Von Rad, Gerhard. *Genesis: A Commentary.* The Old Testament Library. London: SCM, 1961.

Vouga, François. *An die Galater.* HNT 10. Tübingen: Mohr Siebeck, 1998.

Wagner, J. Ross. *Heralds of the Good News: Isaiah and Paul "in Concert" in the Letter to the Romans.* NovTSup 101. Leiden: Brill, 2002.

———. "Isaiah in Romans and Galatians." In *Isaiah in the New Testament*, edited by Steve Moyise and M. J. J. Menken, 117–32. London: T. & T. Clark, 2005.

———. "Moses and Isaiah in Concert: Paul's Reading of Isaiah and Deuteronomy in the Letter to the Romans." In *"As Those Who Are Taught": The Interpretation of Isaiah from the LXX to the SBL*, edited by Claire Mathews McGinnis and Patricia K. Tull, 87–105. SBLSymS 27. Atlanta: SBL, 2006.

Wallace, Daniel B. *Greek Grammar beyond the Basics: An Exegetical Syntax of the New Testament.* Grand Rapids: Zondervan, 1996.

Walters, James C. "Paul, Adoption, and Inheritance." In *Paul in the Greco-Roman World: A Handbook*, edited by J. Paul Sampley, 42–76. Harrisburg: Trinity Press International, 2003.

Wan, Sze-kar. "Charismatic Exegesis: Philo and Paul Compared." *SPhilo* 6 (1994) 54–82.

Watson, Francis. "Is There a Story in These Texts?" In *Narrative Dynamics in Paul: A Critical Assessment*, edited by Bruce W. Longenecker, 231–39. Louisville: Westminster John Knox, 2002.

———. "Mistranslation and the Death of Christ: Isaiah 53 LXX and Its Pauline Reception." In *Translating the New Testament: Text, Translation, Theology*, edited by Stanley E. Porter and Mark J. Boda, 215–50. McMaster New Testament Studies. Grand Rapids: Eerdmans, 2009.

———. *Paul and the Hermeneutics of Faith.* 2nd ed. London: Bloomsbury T. & T. Clark, 2016.

Wengert, Timothy. "Martin Luther on Gal 3:6–14: Justification by Curses and Blessings." In *Galatians and Christian Theology: Justification, the Gospel, and Ethics in Paul's Letter*, edited by Mark W. Elliott et al., 91–116. Grand Rapids: Baker Academic, 2014.

Wenham, Gordon J. *Genesis 1–15*. WBC 1. Waco: Word Books, 1987.
———. *Genesis 16–50*. WBC 2. Dallas: Word Books, 1994.
Westermann, Claus. *Genesis: A Commentary*. Vol. 2. London: SPCK, 1984.
———. *Isaiah 40–66: A Commentary*. The Old Testament Library. London: SCM, 1969.
Wevers, John William. *Notes on the Greek Text of Genesis*. Septuagint and Cognate Studies Series 35. Atlanta: Scholars, 1993.
White, Joel R. "N. T. Wright's Narrative Approach." In *God and the Faithfulness of Paul: A Critical Examination of the Pauline Theology of N. T. Wright*, edited by Christoph Heilig et al., 181–204. WUNT 2.413. Tübingen: Mohr Siebeck, 2016.
Whitman, Jon. *Allegory: The Dynamics of an Ancient and Medieval Technique*. Oxford: Clarendon, 1987.
———, ed. *Interpretation and Allegory: Antiquity to the Modern Period*. Brill's Studies in Intellectual History 101. Leiden: Brill, 2000.
Wilk, Florian. *Die Bedeutung des Jesajabuches für Paulus*. FRLANT 179. Göttingen: Vandenhoeck & Ruprecht, 1998.
Williams, Ronald J. *Williams' Hebrew Syntax*. 3rd ed. Toronto: University of Toronto Press, 2007.
Williams, Sam K. "The Hearing of Faith: ΑΚΟΗ ΠΙΣΤΕΩΣ in Galatians 3." *NTS* 35 (1989) 82–93.
Williamson, H. G. M. "Recent Issues in the Study of Isaiah." In *Interpreting Isaiah: Issues and Approaches*, edited by David G. Firth and H. G. M. Williamson, 21–39. Downers Grove, IL: IVP Academic, 2009.
———. *Variations on a Theme: King, Messiah and Servant in the Book of Isaiah*. Didsbury Lectures 1997. Carlisle: Paternoster, 1998.
Williamson, Paul R. *Abraham, Israel and the Nations: The Patriarchal Promise and Its Covenantal Development in Genesis*. JSOTSup 315. Sheffield: Sheffield Academic, 2000.
Willitts, Joel. "Isa 54,1 In Gal 4,24b–27: Reading Genesis in Light of Isaiah." *ZNW* 96 (2005) 188–210.
Wilson, Todd A. *The Curse of the Law and the Crisis in Galatia: Reassessing the Purpose of Galatians*. WUNT 2.225. Tübingen: Mohr Siebeck, 2007.
Wischmeyer, Oda. "Wie kommt Abraham in den Galaterbrief? Überlegungen zu Gal 3,6–29." In *Umstrittener Galaterbrief: Studien zur Situierung und Theologie des Paulus-Schreiben*, edited by Michael Bachmann and Bernd Kollmann, 119–63. BThSt 106. Neukirchen-Vluyn: Neukirchener, 2010.
Wolter, Michael. "Das Israelproblem nach Gal 4,21–31 und Röm 9–11." *ZTK* 107 (2010) 1–30.
———. "Die Unfruchtbare Frau und ihre Kinder: zur Rezeptionsgeschichte von Jes 54,1." In *Paulus—Werk Und Wirkung: Festschrift für Andreas Lindemann zum 70. Geburtstag*, edited by Paul Gerhard Klumbies and David S. du Toit, 103–27. Tübingen: Mohr Siebeck, 2013.
Wright, N. T. "The Challenge of Dialogue: A Partial and Preliminary Response." In *God and the Faithfulness of Paul: A Critical Examination of the Pauline Theology of N. T. Wright*, edited by Christoph Heilig et al., 711–68. WUNT 2.413. Tübingen: Mohr Siebeck, 2016.
———. *Christian Origins and the Question of God*. [Vol. 4]: *Paul and the Faithfulness of God*. Minneapolis: Fortress, 2013.

———. *The Climax of the Covenant: Christ and the Law in Pauline Theology.* Minneapolis: Fortress, 1992.

———. "Gospel and Theology in Galatians (1994)." In *Pauline Perspectives: Essays on Paul, 1978–2013*, 79–92. London: SPCK, 2013.

———. "Israel's Scriptures in Paul's Narrative Theology (2012)." In *Pauline Perspectives: Essays on Paul, 1978–2013*, 547–53. London: SPCK, 2013.

———. "The Letter to the Galatians: Exegesis and Theology (2000)." In *Pauline Perspectives: Essays on Paul, 1978–2013*, 191–215. London: SPCK, 2013.

———. "Paul, Arabia and Elijah (Galatians 1.17)." In *Pauline Perspectives: Essays on Paul, 1978–2013*, 152–59. London: SPCK, 2013.

———. *Paul and His Recent Interpreters: Some Contemporary Debates.* London: SPCK, 2015.

Young, Frances. "Allegory and the Ethics of Reading." In *The Open Text: New Directions for Biblical Studies?*, edited by Francis Watson, 103–20. London: SCM, 1993.

Zetterholm, Magnus. *Approaches to Paul: A Student's Guide to Recent Scholarship.* Minneapolis: Fortress, 2009.

Zimmermann, Ruben. "The 'Implicit Ethics' of New Testament Writings: A Draft on a New Methodology in Analysing New Testament Ethics." *Neotestamentica* 43 (2009) 399–423.

www.ingramcontent.com/pod-product-compliance
Lightning Source LLC
Chambersburg PA
CBHW030823230426
43667CB00008B/1345